Table of Contents

National Legal and Policy Center (NLPC) Mission Statement	iii
NLPC Highlights 1993-2023	iv
NLPC Gift Annuity	vi
Remembering NLPC Through a Bequest	vii
About Peter Flaherty, NLPC Chairman	viii
Directory Key	1
Congressional Staff	1
Emailing Congress	1
Senate and House Office Buildings	2
Useful Telephone Numbers	3
Useful Legislative and Media Websites	3
Party Information	3
The White House	4
The Cabinet	5
Selected Agencies	11
The Supreme Court	13
2024 Congressional Calendar	14
State Order Index	15
The Senate	
Leadership, Officers, Offices	29
Re-election Years	30
Senator Bios	31
Senate Committees and Subcommittees	51
The House of Representatives	
Leadership, Officers, Offices	63
Representative Bios	64
Vacancies	137
House Committees and Subcommittees	139
2024 Election Schedule	158
State Maps, Stats, and Governors	159
Governor Re-election Years	189
Engaging with Congress	190

National Legal and Policy Council, Fall Church, Virginia 22046
© 2024 by Peter Flaherty
All rights reserved.
Printed in the United States of America

ISBN 979-8-218-37366-5

No part of this book may be reproduced or used in any manner without the prior written permission of the publisher, except for the use of brief quotations in a book review.

To purchase additional copies of this directory, write to National Legal and Policy Council, 107 Park Washington Court, Falls Church, Virginia 22046, or visit www.nlpc.org, or send an email to directory@nlpc.org.

Information in this directory corrected to February 11, 2024

Our Mission

NLPC promotes ethics in public life through research, education and legal action.

NLPC's lasting vision is a single standard of ethics. The "moral relativism" of the Left has created a double standard where anything is excused as long as the politics of the perpetrator are "correct." We seek to undermine this double standard and expose the selective indignation and hypocrisy of the Left.

We also recognize that the bigger the government, the more opportunities for corruption; and the more intervention in the economy, the more reason for special interests to seek influence. We believe that the best way to promote ethics is to reduce the size of government.

The liberals' solution is more laws or "better guidelines," even as existing ones are ignored. We don't believe the problem is with laws, but with men and women. We believe the missing ingredients are character, morality and common sense.

NLPC Highlights 1993-2023

2023 - NLPC Chairman Peter Flaherty had his microphone cut and was arrested at the Berkshire Hathaway shareholders' meeting for raising Bill Gates' links to Jeffrey Epstein and Warren Buffett's close identification with Gates.

2022 - Charmaine Bogue, a high official of the Department of Veterans Affairs, resigned after NLPC exposed conflicts of interest.

2022 - NLPC exposed organizational and financial irregularities in Black Lives Matter, detailed in Complaints filed with the IRS and state charitable regulators.

2021 - Through a front-page *New York Post* story, NLPC exposed that Hunter Biden's art dealer received an inordinate amount of disaster relief "loans" after Biden became president.

2021 - Following NLPC's exposé that Black Lives Matter cofounder Patrisse Cullors owned four homes, she was forced to resign from the group.

2020 - NLPC exposed that the University of Pennsylvania, home of the Biden Center for Diplomacy and Global Engagement, received $67 million in donations from China, including $22 million that were anonymous, which the University failed to disclose. The issue erupted again in 2023 when classified documents were "discovered" at the Biden Center.

2019 - In a Complaint to the Internal Revenue Service, NLPC detailed how a nonprofit headed by Maya Rockeymoore Cummings, wife of Rep. Elijah Cummings (D-MD), served as a conduit for private benefits of the Cummings. Mrs. Cummings lost the election to replace her husband following his death.

2018 - NLPC initiated a constitutional challenge to Special Counsel Robert Mueller. Rejected by the U.S. Court of Appeals for the District of Columbia, the suit nonetheless raised questions about Mueller's actions and legitimacy.

2016 - The FBI seized a laptop belonging to Anthony Weiner and Huma Abedin after a *Daily Mail* story about Weiner texting a minor. The girl and her father had been put in touch with the *Daily Mail* by NLPC.

2016 - NLPC exposed five instances of "pay to play" involving the State Department and the Clinton Foundation, including one that was the basis for a front-page *Washington Post* story.

2013-2016 - Through dozens of stories in the *New York Post, New York Times* and *New York Daily News*, NLPC exposed New York corruption, resulting in the prosecution of three state senators, including two former state Senate presidents, and several other politicians.

2015 - In New York, ex-Senate Majority Leader Dean Skelos and ex-Assembly Speaker Sheldon Silver were convicted on corruption charges. The prosecutions resulted from the disbanding of the "Moreland Commission," established in response to NLPC-generated headlines.

2015 - Senator Robert Menendez (D-NJ) was indicted as a result of info exposed through a front-page *New York Times* story provided by NLPC on an exclusive basis.

NLPC Highlights 1993-2023

2014 - In response to NLPC's request, General Motors recalled 1.3 million vehicles with a power steering defect.

2010 - Rep. Charles Rangel (D-NY) was censured by the entire House of Representatives. NLPC exposed his failure to report or disclose rental income from his beach house in the Dominican Republic, which led to a more far-reaching scrutiny of his finances.

2010 - Rangel resigned as Chairman of the House Ways and Means Committee after he was admonished by the House Ethics Committee for leading a Caribbean junket in violation of House rules. The Committee's action was based on NLPC's photographs and audio recordings made by Peter Flaherty, an uninvited observer on the trip.

2009 - Al Sharpton was fined $285,000 by the Federal Election Commission as a result of an NLPC Complaint for running an "off the books" presidential campaign.

2007 - Senator Lisa Murkowski (R-AK) sold back land to a developer a day after NLPC alleged in a Complaint to the Senate Ethics Committee that the original sale was a "sweetheart" deal.

2006-2010 - NLPC exposed cozy financial dealings between Rep. Alan Mollohan (D-WV) and recipients of his earmarks. Mollohan resigned as Chairman of the Ethics Committee. In May 2010, Mollohan lost re-election in the Democratic primary.

2005 - The New York Stock Exchange ended its support for Jesse Jackson's groups after NLPC protests.

2004 - Two PACs associated with Rep. Nancy Pelosi (D-CA) were fined $21,000 as a result of an NLPC Complaint to the FEC.

2004 - As a result of NLPC Complaints filed with the Federal Election Commission (FEC), Al Sharpton was fined $5,500 and forced to return $100,000 in presidential campaign matching funds.

2003 - NLPC exposed the Boeing Tanker Deal Scandal, eventually sending two Boeing executives to jail, and saving taxpayers at least $4 billion.

1999 - NLPC broke a scandal involving the taxpayer-funded Legal Services Corporation (LSC), which was grossly inflating the number of cases it claimed to handle.

1996 - NLPC exposed then-FDA Commissioner David Kessler for overbilling on his expense reimbursements. Kessler resigned soon after. In his 2001 book, Kessler said NLPC "brought me as close to despair as I have ever been."

1993 - NLPC successfully sued Hillary Rodham Clinton's secret health care task force to open its meetings and records. In their 2003 books, both Hillary and Sidney Blumenthal acknowledged NLPC's role in sinking her plan.

Gift Annuity

How it works:
You transfer cash or securities to NLPC.

NLPC pays you, or up to two annuitants you name, fixed income for life, guaranteed.

The principal passes to NLPC when the contract ends.

Benefits:
You receive an immediate income tax deduction for a portion of your gift.

Your annuity payments are treated as part ordinary income, part capital gains income, and part tax-free income.

You can have the satisfaction of making a significant gift that benefits you now and NLPC later.

To receive a confidential proposal:
Please tear out this entire page and return to NLPC, 107 Park Washington Court, Falls Church, VA 22046.

Name _____

Address _____

City _____ **State** _____ **ZIP** _____

Birthdate(s) of proposed annuitant(s):
1) _____ 2) _____

Value of gift _____

Type of gift *(circle one)*:   Cash   Securities

If securities, donor basis _____ date acquired _____

Payment preference *(circle one)*:
Monthly   Quarterly   Semi-Annually   Annually

Remembering NLPC Through a Bequest

Our great Republic will only survive if our leaders commit themselves to high standards of ethical behavior. NLPC is a permanent watchdog in Washington.

Your bequest or other planned gift to NLPC will help ensure that successive generations will enjoy the freedoms guaranteed by our Constitution.

You don't have to be wealthy to make a bequest. Indeed, many people who modestly support groups like NLPC over the years make bequests.
Many NLPC supporters have assets that are not liquid, such as a home. They give modestly, but can increase their support through a bequest once they pass away.

To put NLPC in your will, the following language may be used:

"I give, devise, and bequeath to the National Legal and Policy Center, a D.C. nonprofit corporation (Taxpayer ID #52- 1750188), the sum of _____ dollars (or _____ % of my estate) to be used for the general purposes of promoting ethics in public life."

You don't have to make a will to make a bequest to NLPC. Most financial accounts,
retirement accounts and life insurance policies allow you to designate NLPC as a beneficiary.

If you need more information, or are interested in a planned giving program that would provide immediate tax benefits, please call NLPC Chairman Peter Flaherty at 703-237-1970.

Peter Flaherty, Chairman

Peter Flaherty is Chairman and Chief Executive Officer of the National Legal and Policy Center (NLPC), which he co-founded with Ken Boehm in 1991.

He is a longtime anti-corruption activist who has successfully pursued some of the most powerful members of Congress.

In 2008, he was an uninvited observer on a Congressional junket to the Caribbean, led by Rep. Charles Rangel (D-NY). Flaherty's photographs and audio recordings showing corporate sponsorship of the event were the basis for House Ethics Committee action against Rangel. As a result, Rangel resigned his Chairmanship of the House Ways and Means Committee. The evidence was also the basis, in part, for Rangel's Censure by the entire House in 2010.

In his 1994 book *Worth It All,* former House Speaker Jim Wright (D-TX) described and lamented Flaherty's actions that helped force Wright's resignation.

Flaherty has also confronted the CEOs of some of America's largest corporations on what he believes to be the widespread corruption of the corporate mission.

At the 2023 Berkshire Hathaway shareholders' meeting, his microphone was cut and he was arrested for citing the reputational risk to the company of Bill Gates' links to Jeffrey Epstein, and Warren Buffett's close identification with Gates. Video of his arrest went viral, with millions of views. (The charge of criminal trespass was dropped.)

Flaherty has spoken at the annual meetings of public companies like Amazon, Walmart, Meta (Facebook), Goldman Sachs, Boeing, Alphabet (Google), PepsiCo, GE, Colgate-Palmolive, Pfizer, Procter & Gamble, United Airlines and Citigroup in support of NLPC-sponsored shareholder proposals.

Flaherty has been interviewed on more than 1,000 radio and television programs. He is the author of opinion articles that have appeared in *USA Today, Washington Post, Los Angeles Times, Baltimore Sun, Detroit News, Atlanta Constitution, Philadelphia Daily News, San Francisco Chronicle, Human Events, Policy Review, Daily Caller* and *The Hill.*

He is the co-author of a 1996 book titled *The First Lady: A Comprehensive View of Hillary Rodham Clinton.* He provided instant analysis on MSNBC to Hillary's 1998 NBC Today Show interview in which she alleged a "massive right-wing conspiracy."

Directory Key

United States Senate

Senator Photo	**Senator Name, State**	Rank	Term	Last Election% (win margin) Building-Room Number	Phone Number	Fax Number Website	**X** (formerly Twitter) @Handle **Bio**—Resides; Birthplace, Birthdate; Degree, Institution, Year; Military Service; Former Occupation; Political Experience; Marital Status, Spouse Name; Religious Affiliation **Committees**—Assigned Committees **District Offices**—City, Phone Number
Member Party	

United States House of Representatives

Representative Photo	**Representative Name, State**	District	Term	Last Election% (win margin) Room Number Building	Phone Number	Fax Number Website	**X** (formerly Twitter) @Handle **Bio**—Resides; Birthplace, Birthdate; Degree, Institution, Year; Military Service; Former Occupation; Political Experience; Marital Status, Spouse Name; Religious Affiliation **Committees**—Assigned Committees **District Offices**—City, Phone Number
Member Party	

Congressional Staff

Congressional staff play a key role on Capitol Hill. Your interaction with an office will likely be with them. Each office is free to organize however it sees fit, but most are roughly set up the same way: a **Chief of Staff (or Administrative Assistant)** is in charge of the office and reports directly to the Member; a **Legislative Director (or Senior Legislative Assistant or Policy Director)** handles legislative issues; a **Press Secretary(or Communications Director)** communicates with the media; and a **Scheduler (or Appointment Secretary)** maintains the Member's schedule.

Additionally, offices often have several Legislative Assistants who are assigned to cover a number of policy areas, such as agriculture, defense, or immigration. Other staffers you may encounter include caseworkers and legislative correspondents.

E-mailing Congress

This directory does not contain e-mail addresses because no Member of Congress has a public e-mail address anymore. Instead, you need to go to the Members' official website, which is contained in the directory, and find the webform, generally located on a "contact" page, or something similarly named. *Keep in mind, Members will usually only assist their own constituents.*

State Maps, Stats, and Governors

On population stats, the "Trend" refers to the percentage change from the U.S. Census Bureau's 2020 apportionment population that was used to determine congressional representation and the 2022 American Community Survey 1-year Estimate.

NatAm/AN = American Indian and Alaska Native | NH/PI = Native Hawaiian and Other Pacific Islander

Governor Photo	**Governor Name**	Next Election	Term	Last Election% (win margin) Capitol Address Phone Number	Fax Number	Website	**X** (formerly Twitter) @Handle **Bio**—Resides; Birthplace, Birthdate; Degree, Institution, Year; Military Service; Former Occupation; Political Experience; Marital Status, Spouse Name; Religious Affiliation
Party	

Senate and House Office Buildings

U.S. Senate

Dirksen Senate Office Building (SD)
Entrances
First Street & Constitution Avenue
First Street & C Street

Opened 1958 • 750,520 square feet

Hart Senate Office Building (SH)
Entrances
Constitution Avenue
Second Street, NE

Opened 1982 • 1,271,030 square feet

Russell Senate Office Building (SR)
Entrances
First Street & Constitution Avenue
First Street & C Street
Delaware Avenue, NE

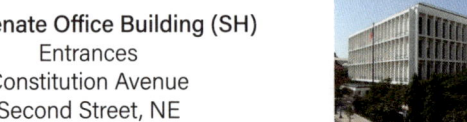
Opened 1909 • 698,921 square feet

Senate addresses are Washington, DC 20510
Doors are open Monday—Friday, 7:30 a.m. to 8:00 p.m. When in session, doors close at 6:30 p.m.

U.S. House

Cannon House Office Building (CHOB)
3-digit room numbers
Entrances
First Street, SE
New Jersey Avenue, SE

Opened 1908 • 826,465 square feet

Longworth House Office Building (LHOB)
4-digit room numbers beginning with 1
Entrances
Independence Avenue
South Capitol Street

Opened 1933 • 702,608 square feet

Rayburn House Office Building (RHOB)
4-digit room numbers beginning with 2
Entrances
Independence Avenue
South Capitol Street

Opened 1965 • 2,395,914 square feet

House addresses are Washington, DC 20515
Doors are open Monday—Friday, 7:30 a.m. to 7:00 p.m. When in session, doors close at 5:00 p.m.

Other Buildings
S: Capitol, Senate side | H: Capitol, House side | SVC: Capitol Visitor Center, Senate side | HVC: Capitol Visitor Center, House side | FHOB: Ford House Office Building | OHOB: O'Neill House Office Building

Photos courtesy of the Architect of the Capitol

Useful Telephone Numbers

Architect of the Capitol	202-228-1793
Capitol Switchboard (House)	202-225-3121
Capitol Switchboard (Senate)	202-224-3121
Capitol Visitor Center	202-226-8000
Congressional Accessibility Services	202-224-4048
Congressional Budget Office	202-226-2600
Congressional Record Index	202-512-0275
Congressional Research Service (CRS)	202-707-5700
Library of Congress	202-707-5000

Useful Legislative Websites

Current House activity	live.house.gov
Senate floor proceedings	www.senate.gov/legislative/floor_activity_pail.htm
Legislative information	www.congress.gov

Useful Media Websites

ABC News	abcnews.go.com
Axios	www.axios.com
CBS News	www.cbsnews.com
Citizen Free Press	citizenfreepress.com
CNN	www.cnn.com
C-SPAN	www.c-span.org
Daily Caller	dailycaller.com
Daily Signal, The	www.dailysignal.com
Fox News	www.foxnews.com
LA Times	www.latimes.com
NBC News	www.nbcnews.com
New York Times	www.nytimes.com
Newsmax	www.newsmax.com
NTD	www.ntd.com
NY Post	nypost.com
One America News	www.oann.com
Politico	www.politico.com
Real America's Voice	americasvoice.news
RealClearPolitics	www.realclearpolitics.com
Roll Call	rollcall.com
The Hill	thehill.com
Wall Street Journal	www.wsj.com
Washington Examiner	www.washingtonexaminer.com
Washington Free Beacon	freebeacon.com
Washington Post	www.washingtonpost.com
Washington Times	www.washingtontimes.com

Party Information

Democratic National Committee	democrats.org	202-863-8000
Democratic Congressional Campaign Committee	dccc.org	202-863-1500
Democratic Senatorial Campaign Committee	dscc.org	202-224-2447
Democratic Governors Association	democraticgovernors.org	202-772-5600
Republican National Committee	gop.com	202-863-8500
National Republican Congressional Committee	www.nrcc.org	202-479-7000
National Republican Senatorial Committee	www.nrsc.org	202-675-6000
Republican Governors Association	www.rga.org	202-662-4140

The White House

1600 Pennsylvania Avenue, NW | Washington, DC 20500 | www.whitehouse.gov

President Joe Biden | 202-456-1414
*Chief of Staff—Jeff Zients

Bio—Wilmington, DE; Scranton, PA, 11/20/1942; JD, Syracuse Univ., 1968; lawyer, public official; New Castle Co. council, 1970-72; US Senate, 1973-2009; Vice President, 2009-17; President, 2021-present; m. Jill; Catholic

Vice President Kamala Harris | 202-456-1414
Chief of Staff—Lorraine Voles | Press Secretary—Kirsten Allen

Bio—San Francisco, CA; Oakland, CA, 10/20/1964; JD, Univ. of CA, Hastings Col. of the Law, 1989; lawyer, public official; San Francisco district attorney, 2004-11; CA attorney general, 2011-16; US Senate, 2017-21; Vice President, 2021-present; m. Douglas Emhoff; Baptist

First Lady Jill Biden | 202-456-7064
Press Secretary—Vanessa Valdivia

Bio—Wilmington, DE; Hammonton, NJ, 6/3/1951; EdD, Univ. of DE, 2007; teacher; m. Joe

Executive Offices of the President

Cabinet Secretary—Evan M. Ryan
*Central Intelligence Agency—William Burns
Communications Director—Ben LaBolt
*Council of Economic Advisers—Jared Bernstein
Counsel—Ed Siskel
Counselor to the President—Steven J. Ricchetti
Digital Strategy—Christian L. Tom
Domestic Climate Policy—Ali Zaidi
Domestic Policy Council—Neera Tanden
*Environmental Protection Agency—Michael Regan
Gender Policy Council—Jennifer Klein
Intergovernmental Affairs—Tom Perez
Legislative Affairs—Shuwanza Goff
Management and Administration—Dave Noble
National Cyber Director—Harry Coker, Jr.
National Drug Control Policy—Rahul Gupta
National Economic Council—Lael Brainard
*National Intelligence Director—Avril Haines
National Space Council—Chirag Parikh
*Office of Management & Budget—Shalanda Young
Presidential Advance—Connolly J. Keigher
Presidential Personnel—Gautam Raghavan
Press Secretary—Karine Jean-Pierre
Public Engagement—Stephen Benjamin
Scheduling and Advance—Ryan Montoya
*Science and Technology Policy—Arati Prabhakar
Senior Advisor to the President—Mike Donilon
*Small Business Administration—Isabel Guzman
US Ambassador to the UN—Linda Thomas-Greenfield
*US Trade Representative—Katherine Tai

*Cabinet rank

The Cabinet

DEPARTMENT OF AGRICULTURE | 202-720-3631 | www.usda.gov
Jamie L. Whitten Building | 1400 Independence Avenue, SW | Washington, DC 20250

Secretary Tom Vilsack
Bio—Pittsburgh, PA, 12/30/1950; JD, Albany Law School, 1975; lawyer; IA senate, 1993-99; IA governor, 1999-2007; Agriculture secretary, 2009-17, 2021-present; m. Christie; Catholic
Director of Communications—Cathy Cochran, 202-720-4623

Agricultural Research Service | 202-720-3656 | www.ars.usda.gov
1400 Independence Ave., SW | Rm. 302-A | Washington, DC 20250

Animal & Plant Health Inspection Service | 202-720-2511 | www.aphis.usda.gov
1400 Independence Ave., SW | Rm. 312-E | Washington, DC 20250

Farm Service Agency | 202-720-3467 | www.fsa.usda.gov
1400 Independence Ave., SW | Rm. 3086-S | Washington, DC 20250

Food, Nutrition, & Consumer Services | 703-305-2060 | www.fns.usda.gov
1320 Braddock Place | Alexandria, VA 22314

Food Safety & Inspection Service | 202-720-7025 | www.fsis.usda.gov
1400 Independence Ave., SW | Rm. 331-E | Washington, DC 20250

Foreign Agricultural Service | 202-720-3935 | fas.usda.gov
1400 Independence Ave., SW | Room 5071 | Washington, DC 20250

Forest Service | 800-832-1355 | www.fs.usda.gov
1400 Independence Ave., SW | Washington, DC 20250

National Agricultural Statistics Service | 800-727-9540 | www.nass.usda.gov
1400 Independence Ave., SW | Washington, DC 20250

Natural Resources Conservation Service | 202-720-4525 | www.nrcs.usda.gov
1400 Independence Ave., SW, Rm. 5105-A | Washington, DC 20250

DEPARTMENT OF COMMERCE | 202-482-2000 | www.doc.gov
Herbert C. Hoover Building | 1401 Constitution Avenue, NW | Washington, DC 20230

Secretary Gina Raimondo
Bio—Smithfield, RI, 5/17/1971; DPhil, New College (UK), 2002; financial executive, public official; RI treasurer, 2011-15; RI governor, 2015-21; Commerce secretary, 2021-present; m. Andy Moffit
Sr. Advisor, Public Affairs—Caitlin Legacki, 202-482-4436

Census, Bureau of the | 301-763-4636 | www.census.gov
4600 Silver Hill Rd. | Suitland, MD 20746

Economic Analysis, Bureau of | 301-278-9004 | www.bea.gov
4600 Silver Hill Rd. | Suitland, MD 20746

National Institute of Standards & Technology | 301-975-2000 | www.nist.gov
100 Bureau Dr. | Gaithersburg, MD 20899

National Oceanic & Atmospheric Administration | 202-482-6090 | www.noaa.gov
1401 Constitution Ave., NW | Washington, DC 20230

National Telecommunications & Information Administration | 202-482-2000 | www.ntia.doc.gov
1401 Constitution Ave., NW | Washington, DC 20230

The Cabinet

Patent & Trademark Office | 800-786-9199 | www.uspto.gov
600 Dulany St. | Arlington, VA 22313

National Weather Service | 301-427-9855 | www.weather.gov
1325 East-West Hwy. | Silver Spring, MD 20910

DEPARTMENT OF DEFENSE | 703-545-6700 | www.defense.gov
The Pentagon | Washington, DC 20301

Secretary Lloyd Austin
Bio—Mobile, AL, 8/8/1953; MBM, Webster Univ.; USA, 1975-2016; military officer; Defense secretary, 2021-present; m. Charlene; Catholic
Assistant to the Secretary for Public Affairs—Chris Meagher, 703-697-5131

Defense Advanced Research Projects Agency | 703-526-6630 | www.darpa.mil
675 North Randolph St. | Arlington, VA 22203

U.S. Army Corps of Engineers | 202-761-0011 | www.usace.army.mil
441 G St., NW | Washington, DC 20314

Joint Chiefs of Staff | 703-545-6700 | www.jcs.mil
9999 Joint Staff Pentagon | Washington, D.C. 20318

National Security Agency | 301-688-6311 | www.nsa.gov
9800 Savage Rd. | Ft. Meade, MD 20755

DEPARTMENT OF EDUCATION | 202-401-3000 | www.ed.gov
400 Maryland Avenue, SW | Washington, DC 20202

Secretary Miguel Cardona
Bio—Meriden; Meriden, CT, 7/11/1975; EdD, Univ. of CT, 2011; educator; m. Marissa; Catholic
Acting Assistant Secretary, Office of Communications and Outreach— Shin Inouye (acting), 202-401-2000

Federal Student Aid, Office of | 319-337-5665 | studentaid.gov
830 First St., NE | Washington, DC 20202

Institute of Education Sciences | 202-245-6940 | ies.ed.gov
550 12th St., SW | Washington, DC 20004

DEPARTMENT OF ENERGY | 202-586-5000 | www.energy.gov
James Forrestal Building | 1000 Independence Avenue, SW | Washington, DC 20585

Secretary Jennifer Granholm
Bio—Vancouver, Canada, 2/5/1959; JD, Harvard Univ., 1987; lawyer, public official; MI attorney general, 1998-2002; MI governor, 2003-11; Energy secretary, 2021-present; m. Daniel Mulhern
Director, Office of Public Affairs—David Mayorga, 202-586-1760

Federal Energy Regulatory Commission | 202-502-6088 | www.ferc.gov
888 First St., NE | Washington, DC 20426

The Cabinet

DEPARTMENT OF HEALTH AND HUMAN SERVICES | 202-690-7000 | www.hhs.gov
200 Independence Avenue, SW | Washington, DC 20201

Secretary Xavier Becerra
Bio—Sacramento, CA, 1/26/1958; JD, Stanford Univ., 1984; lawyer; CA assembly, 1990-92; US House, 1993-2017; CA attorney general, 2017-21; HHS secretary, 2021-present; m. Carolina Reyes; Catholic
Assistant Secretary for Public Affairs—Sarah Lovenheim, 202-260-7441

Centers for Disease Control & Prevention | 404-639-3311 | www.cdc.gov
1600 Clifton Rd. | Atlanta, GA 30333

Centers for Medicare and Medicaid Services | 410-786-3000 | www.cms.gov
7500 Security Blvd. | Baltimore, MD 21244

Food & Drug Administration | 888-463-6332 | www.fda.gov
10903 New Hampshire Ave. | Silver Spring, MD 20993

Health Resources & Services Administration | 877-464-4772 | www.hrsa.gov
5600 Fishers Lane | Rockville, MD 20857

Indian Health Service | 301-443-1083 | www.ihs.gov
5600 Fishers Lane | Rockville, MD 20857

National Institutes of Health | 301-496-4000 | www.nih.gov
9000 Rockville Pike | Bethesda, MD 20892

Substance Abuse & Mental Health Services Administration | 877-726-4727 | samhsa.gov
5600 Fishers Lane | Rockville, MD 20857

Surgeon General, Office of the | 202-401-8073 | www.surgeongeneral.gov
200 Independence Ave., SW | Washington, DC 20201

DEPARTMENT OF HOMELAND SECURITY | 202-282-8000 | www.dhs.gov
2707 Martin Luther King Jr. Avenue, SE | Washington, DC 20528

Secretary Alejandro Mayorkas
Bio—Havana, Cuba, 11/24/1959; JD, Loyola Marymount Univ., 1985; lawyer, law enforcement official; Homeland Security secretary, 2021-present; m. Tanya
Assistant Secretary, Office of Public Affairs—Marsha Espinosa, 202-282-8010

Customs & Border Protection, Bureau of | 877-227-5511 | www.cbp.gov
1300 Pennsylvania Ave., NW | Washington, DC 20229

Federal Emergency Management Agency | 202-646-2500 | www.fema.gov
500 C St., SW | Washington, DC 20472

Secret Service | 202-406-5708 | www.secretservice.gov
245 Murray Dr., SW | Bldg. T-5 | Washington, DC 20223

Transportation Security Administration | 866-289-9673 | www.tsa.gov
6595 Springfield Center Dr. | Springfield, VA 20598

U.S. Citizenship & Immigration Services | 800-375-5283 | www.uscis.gov
5900 Capital Gateway Dr. | Camp Springs, MD 20588

The Cabinet

U.S. Coast Guard | 202-372-4400 | www.uscg.mil
2703 Martin Luther King Jr. Ave., SE | Washington, DC 20593

U.S. Immigration & Customs Enforcement | 202-344-2001 | www.ice.gov
500 12th St., SW | Washington, DC 20536

DEPARTMENT OF HOUSING AND URBAN DEVELOPMENT | 202-708-1112 | www.hud.gov
Robert C. Weaver Federal Building | 451 7th Street, SW | Washington, DC 20410

Secretary Marcia Fudge

Bio—Cleveland, OH, 10/29/1952; JD, Cleveland Marshall Col. of Law, 1983; lawyer, public official; Warrensville Heights, OH mayor, 2000-08; US House, 2008-21; HUD secretary, 2021-present; single; Baptist

Assistant Secretary for Public Affairs—Beth Lynk, 202-708-0980

DEPARTMENT OF THE INTERIOR | 202-208-3100 | www.doi.gov
Interior Building, 1849 C Street, NW | Washington, DC 20240

Secretary Deb Haaland

Bio—Winslow, AZ, 12/2/1960; JD Univ. of NM, 2006; businesswoman; US House, 2019-21; Interior secretary, 2021-present; m. Skip Sayre; Catholic

Dir., Office of Communications—Melissa Schwartz

Fish & Wildlife Service | 800-344-9453 | www.fws.gov
1849 C St., NW | Washington, DC 20240

Land Management, Bureau of | 202-208-3801 | www.blm.gov
1849 C St., NW | Washington, DC 20240

National Park Service | 202-208-6843 | www.nps.gov
1849 C St., NW | Washington, DC 20240-0001

U.S. Geological Survey | 888-392-8545 | www.usgs.gov
12201 Sunrise Valley Dr. | Reston, VA 20192

DEPARTMENT OF JUSTICE | 202-514-2000 | www.usdoj.gov
Robert F. Kennedy DOJ Building | 950 Pennsylvania Avenue, NW | Washington, DC 20530

Attorney General Merrick Garland

Bio—Bethesda; Chicago, IL, 11/13/1952; JD, Harvard Univ., 1977; lawyer, judge, public official; Attorney General, 2021-present; m. Lynn

Dir., Office of Public Affairs—Xochitl Hinojosa, 202-514-2007

Alcohol, Tobacco, Firearms & Explosives, Bureau of | 202-648-8410 | www.atf.gov
99 New York Ave., NE | Washington, DC 20226

Drug Enforcement Administration | 202-307-1000 | www.dea.gov
8701 Morrissette Dr. | Springfield, VA 22152

Federal Bureau of Investigation | 202-324-3000 | www.fbi.gov
935 Pennsylvania Ave | NW, Washington, DC 20535

The Cabinet

Federal Bureau of Prisons | 202-307-3198 | www.bop.gov
320 First St., NW | Washington, DC 20534

Foreign Claims Settlement Commission | 202-616-6975 | www.justice.gov/fcsc
441 G St., NW | Washington, DC 20579

Immigration Review, Executive Office for | 703-305-0289 | www.justice.gov/eoir
5107 Leesburg Pike | Falls Church, VA 22041

Organized Crime Drug Enforcement Task Forces, Executive Office for | 202-514-2000 | www.justice.gov/ocdetf
441 G St., NW, | Washington, DC 20530

U.S. Marshals Service | 202-307-9100 | www.usmarshals.gov
1215 S. Clark St. | Arlington, VA 22202

U.S. Parole Commission | 202-346-7000 | www.justice.gov/uspc
90 K St., NE, 3rd Fl. | Washington, DC 20530

DEPARTMENT OF LABOR | 202-693-6000 | www.dol.gov
Frances Perkins Building | 200 Constitution Avenue, NW | Washington, DC 20210

Acting Secretary Julie Su
Bio—Madison, WI 2/19/1969; JD, Harvard Univ.; lawyer, public official; CA labor commissioner, 2011-18; Acting Labor secretary, 2023-present

Assistant Secretary, Office of Public Affairs— Julie McClain Downey, 202-693-4676

Labor Statistics, Bureau of | 202-691-5200 | www.bls.gov
Postal Square Building | 2 Massachusetts Ave. | NE, Ste. 4040, Washington, DC 20212

Mine Safety & Health Administration | 202-693-9400 | msha.gov
201 12th St. South | Arlington, VA 22202

Occupational Safety & Health Administration | 800-321-6742 | www.osha.gov
200 Constitution Ave., NW | Washington, DC 20210

DEPARTMENT OF STATE | 202-647-4000 | www.state.gov
2201 C Street, NW | Washington, DC 20520

Secretary Antony J. Blinken
Bio—Yonkers, NY, 4/16/1962; JD, Columbia Univ., 1988; lawyer, public official; secretary of State, 2021-present; m. Evan Ryan; Jewish

Under Secretary for Public Diplomacy and Public Affairs—Elizabeth M. Allen

DEPARTMENT OF TRANSPORTATION | 202-366-4000 | www.dot.gov
1200 New Jersey Avenue, SE | Washington, DC 20590

Secretary Pete Buttigieg
Bio—South Bend, IN, 1/19/1982; BA, Oxford Univ., 2007; USAR, 2009-17; consultant, public official; South Bend mayor, 2012-20; Transportation secretary, 2021-present; m. Chasten Glezman

Director of Public Affairs—Ben Halle, 202-366-4000

The Cabinet

Federal Aviation Administration | 866-835-5322 | www.faa.gov
800 Independence Ave., SW | Washington, DC 20591

Federal Highway Administration | 202-366-4000 | www.fhwa.dot.gov
1200 New Jersey Ave., SE | Washington, DC 20590

Federal Railroad Administration | 202-366-4000 | www.fra.dot.gov
1200 New Jersey Ave., SE | Washington, DC 20590

Federal Transit Administration | 202-366-4043 | www.fta.dot.gov
1200 New Jersey Ave., SE | Washington, DC 20590

Maritime Administration | 202-366-4000 | www.maritime.dot.gov
1200 New Jersey Ave., SE | Washington, DC 20590

National Highway Traffic Safety Administration | 888-327-4236 | www.nhtsa.gov
1200 New Jersey Ave., SE | Washington, DC 20590

Pipeline & Hazardous Materials Safety Administration | 202-366-4433 | www.phmsa.dot.gov
1200 New Jersey Ave., SE | Washington, DC 20590

DEPARTMENT OF THE TREASURY | 202-622-2000 | www.ustreas.gov
1500 Pennsylvania Avenue, NW | Washington, DC 20220

Secretary Janet Yellen

Bio—Brooklyn, NY, 8/13/1946; PhD, Yale Univ., 1971; professor, economist; Federal Reserve board of governors; Treasury secretary, 2021-present; m. George

Assistant Secretary for Public Affairs—Lily Adams, 202-622-2910

Comptroller of the Currency | 202-649-6800 | www.occ.treas.gov
400 7th St., SW | Washington, DC 20219

Engraving & Printing, Bureau of | 202-874-3188 | www.bep.gov
14th & C Sts., SW | Washington, DC 20228

Financial Crimes Enforcement Network | 703-905-3591 | www.fincen.gov
2070 Chain Bridge Rd. | Vienna, VA 22182

Internal Revenue Service | 800-829-1040 | www.irs.gov
1111 Constitution Ave., NW | Washington, DC 20224

U.S. Mint | 202-354-7200 | www.usmint.gov
801 9th St., NW | Washington, DC 20220

DEPARTMENT OF VETERANS AFFAIRS | 202-461-4800 | www.va.gov
810 Vermont Avenue, NW | Washington, DC 20420

Secretary Denis McDonough

Bio—Stillwater, MN, 12/2/1969; MSFS, Georgetown Univ., 1996; congressional staffer, policy advisor; Veterans Affairs secretary, 2021-present; m. Kari

Assistant Secretary for Public and Intergovernmental Affairs—
   Vacant, 202-461-7500

Selected Agencies

Advisory Council on Historic Preservation | 202-517-0200 | www.achp.gov
401 F St., NW | Ste. 308 | Washington, DC 20001

American Battle Monuments Commission | 703-584-1501 | www.abmc.gov
2300 Clarendon Blvd. | Ste. 500 | Arlington, VA 22201

AmeriCorps | 202-606-5000 | americorps.gov
250 E St., SW | Washington, DC 20525

Central Intelligence Agency | 703-482-0623 | www.cia.gov
Office of Public Affairs | Washington, DC 20505

Committee For Purchase From People Who Are Blind Or Severely Disabled | 703-603-2100
    www.abilityone.gov
355 E St. SW, Ste. 325 | Washington, DC 20024

Commodity Futures Trading Commission | 202-418-5000 | cftc.gov
Three Lafayette Centre, 1155 21st St., NW | Washington, DC 20581

Consumer Product Safety Commission | 301-504-7923 | www.cpsc.gov
4330 East-West Hwy. | Bethesda, MD 20814

Defense Nuclear Facilities Safety Board | 202-694-7000 | www.dnfsb.gov
625 Indiana Ave., NW | Ste. 700 | Washington, DC 20004

Environmental Protection Agency | 202-564-4700 | www.epa.gov
1200 Pennsylvania Ave., NW | Washington, DC 20460

Equal Employment Opportunity Commission | 202-663-4900 | www.eeoc.gov
131 M St., NE | Washington, DC 20507

Export-Import Bank of the United States | 202-565-3946 | www.exim.gov
811 Vermont Ave., NW | Washington, DC 20571

Farm Credit Administration | 703-883-4056 | www.fca.gov
1501 Farm Credit Dr. | McLean, VA 22102

Federal Communications Commission | 202-418-0200 | www.fcc.gov
45 L St. NE | Washington, DC 20554

Federal Deposit Insurance Corporation | 866-217-3342 | www.fdic.gov
550 17th St., NW | Washington, DC 20429

Federal Election Commission | 202-694-1000 | www.fec.gov
1050 First St., NE | Washington, DC 20463

Federal Housing Finance Agency | 202-649-3800 | www.fhfa.gov
400 7th St., NW | Washington, DC 20024

Federal Labor Relations Authority | 771-444-5801 | www.flra.gov
1400 K St., NW | Washington, DC 20424-0001

Federal Maritime Commission | 202-523-5725 | www.fmc.gov
800 N. Capitol St., NW | Washington, DC 20573

Federal Mediation & Conciliation Service | 202-606-8100 | www.fmcs.gov
250 E St., SW | Washington, DC 20427

Federal Reserve System | 202-452-3000 | federalreserve.gov
20th St. & Constitution Ave., NW | Washington, DC 20551

Federal Retirement Thrift Investment Board | 202-942-1600 | www.frtib.gov
77 K St., NE | Washington, DC 20002

Federal Trade Commission | 202-326-2222 | www.ftc.gov
600 Pennsylvania Ave., NW | Washington, DC 20580

General Services Administration | 844-472-4111 | www.gsa.gov
1800 F St. | Washington, DC 20405

Government Accountability Office | 202-512-3000 | www.gao.gov
441 G St., NW | Washington, DC 20548

Government Printing Office | 202-512-1800 | www.gpo.gov
732 N. Capitol St., NW | Washington, DC 20401

Legal Services Corporation | 202-295-1500 | www.lsc.gov
3333 K St., NW | 3rd Fl. | Washington, DC 20007-3522

Selected Agencies

National Aeronautics & Space Administration | 202-358-0000 | www.nasa.gov
300 E St., SW | Washington, DC 20546

National Archives & Records Administration | 866-272-6272 | archives.gov
700 Pennsylvania Ave., NW | Washington, DC 20408-0001

National Endowment for the Arts | 202-682-5400 | arts.gov
400 7th St., SW | Washington, DC 20506

National Endowment for the Humanities | 202-606-8400 | www.neh.gov
400 7th St., SW | Washington, DC 20506

National Science Foundation | 703-292-5111 | www.nsf.gov
2415 Eisenhower Ave. | Alexandria, VA 22314

Organization of American States | 202-370-5000 | www.oas.org/en
17th St. & Constitution Ave., NW | Washington, DC 20006

Pan American Health Organization | 202-974-3000 | www.paho.org/en
525 23rd St., NW | Washington, DC 20037

Pension Benefit Guaranty Corporation | 800-400-7242 | www.pbgc.gov
445 12th St. SW | Washington, DC 20024

Personnel Management, Office of | 202-606-1800 | www.opm.gov
1900 E. St, NW | Washington, DC 20415

Securities & Exchange Commission | 202-551-6000 | www.sec.gov
100 F St., NE | Washington, DC 20549

Small Business Administration | 800-827-5722 | www.sba.gov
409 3rd St., SW | Washington, DC 20416

Smithsonian Institution | 202-633-1000 | www.si.edu
1000 Jefferson Dr., SW | Washington, DC 20560

Social Security Administration | 800-772-1213 | www.ssa.gov
6401 Security Blvd. | Baltimore, MD 21235

U.S. Agency for International Development | 202-712-4300 | www.usaid.gov
1300 Pennsylvania Ave., NW | Washington, DC 20523

U.S. Commission of Fine Arts | 202-504-2200 | cfa.gov
401 F St., NW | Ste. 312 | Washington, DC 20001-2728

U.S. Commission on Civil Rights | 202-376-7700 | www.usccr.gov
1331 Pennsylvania Ave., NW | Ste. 1150 | Washington, DC 20425

U.S. Election Assistance Commission | 866-747-1471 | eac.gov
633 3rd St. NW | Ste. 200 | Washington, DC 20001

U.S. Holocaust Memorial Council | 202-488-0400 | www.ushmm.org
100 Raoul Wallenberg Place, SW | Washington, DC 20024

U.S. International Development Finance Corporation | 202-336-8400 | www.dfc.gov
1100 New York Ave., NW | Washington, DC 20527

U.S. International Trade Commission | 202-205-2000 | usitc.gov
500 E St., SW | Washington, DC 20436

U.S. Merit Systems Protection Board | 202-653-7200 | www.mspb.gov
1615 M St., NW | Washington, DC 20419

U.S. Postal Service | 202-268-2000 | www.usps.gov
475 L'Enfant Plaza, SW | Washington, DC 20260

U.S. Railroad Retirement Board | 312-751-4300 | www.rrb.gov
844 North Rush St. | Chicago, IL 60611

U.S. Sentencing Commission | 202-502-4500 | www.ussc.gov
One Columbus Circle, NE | Ste. 2-500, South Lobby | Washington, DC 20002

U.S. Small Business Administration | 800-827-5722 | sba.gov
409 Third St., SW | Washington, DC 20416

U.S. Trade & Development Agency | 703-875-4357 | www.ustda.gov
1101 Wilson Blvd. | Ste. 1100 | Arlington, VA 22209

The Supreme Court

Supreme Court of the United States
1 First Street, NE | Washington, DC 20543 | 202-479-3000 | www.supremecourt.gov

Seated, from left—Sotomayor; Thomas; Roberts; Alito; Kagan
Standing, from left—Coney Barrett; Gorsuch; Kavanaugh; Jackson

CHIEF JUSTICE

John G. Roberts, Jr.
Bio—Buffalo, NY, 1/27/1955; JD, Harvard Univ., 1979; law clerk, lawyer, judge; US Court of Appeals, DC Circuit; m. Jane; Catholic
Nominated as Chief Justice by President George W. Bush; sworn in 9/29/2005

ASSOCIATE JUSTICES

Clarence Thomas
Bio—Pinpoint, GA, 6/23/1948; JD, Yale Univ., 1974; lawyer, public official, judge; US Court of Appeals, DC Circuit; m. Virginia; Catholic
Nominated by President George H.W. Bush; sworn in 10/23/1991

Samuel A. Alito, Jr.
Bio—Trenton, NJ, 4/1/1950; JD, Yale Univ., 1975; law clerk, public official, judge; US Court of Appeals, Third Circuit; m. Martha-Ann; Catholic
Nominated by President George W. Bush; sworn in 1/31/2006

Sonia Sotomayor
Bio—Bronx, NY, 6/25/1954; JD, Yale Univ., 1979; lawyer; US Court of Appeals, Second Circuit; single; Catholic
Nominated by President Barack Obama; sworn in 8/8/2009

Elena Kagan
Bio—New York, NY, 4/28/1960; JD, Harvard Univ., 1986; law clerk, lawyer, professor; single; Jewish
Nominated by President Barack Obama; sworn in 8/7/2010

Neil M. Gorsuch
Bio—Denver, CO, 8/29/1967; DPhil, Oxford Univ., 2004; law clerk, lawyer; US Court of Appeals, Tenth Circuit; m. Louise; Episcopal
Nominated by President Donald J. Trump; sworn in 4/10/2017

Brett M. Kavanaugh
Bio—Washington, DC, 2/12/1965; JD, Yale Univ., 1990; law clerk, lawyer, judge; US Court of Appeals, DC Circuit; m. Ashley; Catholic
Nominated by President Donald J. Trump; sworn in 10/6/2018

Amy Coney Barrett
Bio—New Orleans, LA, 1/28/1972; JD, Univ. of Notre Dame, 1997; law clerk, lawyer, law professor; US Court of Appeals, Seventh Circuit; m. Jesse; Catholic
Nominated by President Donald J. Trump; sworn in 10/27/2020

Ketanji Brown Jackson
Bio—Washington, DC, 9/14/1970; JD, Harvard Univ., 1996; law clerk, lawyer; US Court of Appeals, DC Circuit; m. Patrick; Protestant
Nominated by President Joe Biden; sworn in 6/30/2022

2024 Congressional Calendar

1/8/24 Senate convenes | 1/9/24 House convenes

Jan. 15 | No session | Senate
Jan. 22-26 | District Work Week | House
Jan. 29 | No session | Senate
Feb. 2 | District Work Day | House
Feb. 5 | No session | Senate
Feb. 8-12 | District Work Day | House
Feb. 12-23 | State Work Period | Senate
Feb. 19-27 | District Work Week | House
Mar. 4 | No session | Senate
Mar. 4 | District Work Day | House
Mar. 14-18 | District Work Day | House
Mar. 15-18 | State Work Period | Senate
Mar. 25-Apr. 5 | State Work Period | Senate
Mar. 25-Apr. 8 | District Work Week | House
Apr. 19-26 | District Work Week | House
Apr. 22-26 | State Work Period | Senate
May 3 | District Work Day | House
May 3-6 | No session | Senate
May 10-13 | District Work Day | House
May 13 | No session | Senate
May 20 | District Work Day | House
May 27-31 | District Work Week | Senate
May 27-31 | District Work Week | House
June 7-10 | District Work Day | House
June 10 | No session | Senate
June 17-24 | District Work Week | House
June 19 | No session | Senate
June 24-July 5 | State Work Period | Senate
July 1-5 | District Work Week | House
July 12-19 | District Work Week | House
July 15-22 | State Work Period | Senate
July 26 | District Work Day | House
Aug. 2-Sept. 6 | District Work Week | House
Aug. 5-Sept. 6 | State Work Period | Senate
Sept. 13-16 | District Work Day | House
Sept. 30-Nov. 11 | District Work Week | Senate
Sept. 30-Nov. 11 | District Work Week | House
Nov. 22-Dec. 2 | District Work Week | House
Nov. 25-29 | State Work Period | Senate
Dec. 13 | District Work Day | House
Dec. 20 | Target Adjournment | Senate
Dec. 20-31 | District Work Week | House
Dec. 23-31 | State Work Period | Senate

2024 Important Dates

Jan. 15 | Martin Luther King Jr. Day
Feb. 11 | Super Bowl
Feb. 12 | Lincoln's Birthday
Feb. 13 | Shrove Tuesday/Mardi Gras
Feb. 14 | Ash Wednesday
Feb. 14 | Valentine's Day
Feb. 19 | Presidents' Day
Feb. 22 | Washington's Birthday
Feb. 29 | Leap Day
Mar. 10 | Daylight Saving Time begins
Mar. 11 | First Day of Ramadan
Mar. 17 | St. Patrick's Day
Mar. 19 | Spring begins
Mar. 24 | Palm Sunday
Mar. 28 | Opening day of Baseball
Mar. 29 | Good Friday
Mar. 31 | Easter Sunday
Apr. 10 | Eid al-Fitr
Apr. 15 | Tax Day
Apr. 23 | First Day of Passover
Apr. 30 | Last Day of Passover
May 2 | National Day of Prayer
May 5 | Orthodox Easter
May 18 | Armed Forces Day
May 27 | Memorial Day
June 14 | Flag Day
June 19 | Juneteenth
June 20 | Summer begins
July 4 | Independence Day
Sept. 2 | Labor Day
Sept. 22 | Fall begins
Oct. 3 | Rosh Hashana
Oct. 12 | Yom Kippur
Oct. 14 | Columbus Day
Oct. 31 | Halloween
Nov. 3 | Daylight Saving Time ends
Nov. 5 | Election Day
Nov. 11 | Veterans Day
Nov. 28 | Thanksgiving Day
Dec. 21 | Winter begins
Dec. 25 | Christmas Day
Dec. 26 | First Day of Hanukkah
Dec. 31 | New Year's Eve

State Order Index

	Seniority in Party	Office	Phone (202)	Page

ALABAMA
Senate
- Sr. - Tommy Tuberville (R) .... 43 .... SR-455 .... 224-4124 48
- Jr. - Katie Britt (R) .... 48 .... SH-502 .... 224-5744 32

House
- 1 - Jerry Carl (R) .... 139 .... 1330 .... 225-4931 73
- 2 - Barry Moore (R) .... 163 .... 1504 .... 225-2901 110
- 3 - Mike Rogers (R) .... 15 .... 2469 .... 225-3261 120
- 4 - Robert Aderholt (R) .... 5 .... 266 .... 225-4876 64
- 5 - Dale W. Strong (R) .... 216 .... 1337 .... 225-4801 128
- 6 - Gary Palmer (R) .... 75 .... 170 .... 225-4921 115
- 7 - Terri Sewell (D) .... 63 .... 1035 .... 225-2665 124

ALASKA
Senate
- Sr. - Lisa Murkowski (R) .... 6 .... SH-522 .... 224-6665 43
- Jr. - Dan Sullivan (R) .... 30 .... SH-302 .... 224-3004 48

House
- AL - Mary Sattler Peltola (D) .... 175 .... 153 .... 225-5765 116

ARIZONA
Senate
- Sr. - Kyrsten Sinema (I) .... SH-317 .... 224-4521 47
- Jr. - Mark Kelly (D) .... 40 .... SH-516 .... 224-2235 40

House
- 1 - David Schweikert (R) .... 46 .... 460 .... 225-2190 123
- 2 - Eli Crane (R) .... 188 .... 1229 .... 225-3361 78
- 3 - Ruben Gallego (D) .... 99 .... 1114 .... 225-4065 87
- 4 - Greg Stanton (D) .... 153 .... 207 .... 225-9888 127
- 5 - Andy Biggs (R) .... 88 .... 252 .... 225-2635 68
- 6 - Juan Ciscomani (R) .... 186 .... 1429 .... 225-2542 75
- 7 - Raúl M. Grijalva (D) .... 35 .... 1203 .... 225-2435 91
- 8 - Debbie Lesko (R) .... 103 .... 1214 .... 225-4576 103
- 9 - Paul A. Gosar (R) .... 41 .... 2057 .... 225-2315 90

ARKANSAS
Senate
- Sr. - John Boozman (R) .... 13 .... SD-555 .... 224-4843 32
- Jr. - Tom Cotton (R) .... 25 .... SR-326 .... 224-2353 35

House
- 1 - Rick Crawford (R) .... 37 .... 2422 .... 225-4076 78
- 2 - French Hill (R) .... 70 .... 1533 .... 225-2506 93
- 3 - Steve Womack (R) .... 49 .... 2412 .... 225-4301 136
- 4 - Bruce Westerman (R) .... 78 .... 202 .... 225-3772 134

CALIFORNIA
Senate
- Sr. - Alex Padilla (D) .... 43 .... SH-331 .... 224-3553 44
- Jr. - Laphonza Butler (D) .... 48 .... SH-112 .... 224-3841 33

House
- 1 - Doug LaMalfa (R) .... 55 .... 408 .... 225-3076 101
- 2 - Jared Huffman (D) .... 76 .... 2445 .... 225-5161 95
- 3 - Kevin Kiley (R) .... 201 .... 1032 .... 225-2523 99
- 4 - Mike Thompson (D) .... 30 .... 268 .... 225-3311 129
- 5 - Tom McClintock (R) .... 32 .... 2256 .... 225-2511 107
- 6 - Ami Bera (D) .... 70 .... 172 .... 225-5716 67
- 7 - Doris Matsui (D) .... 45 .... 2311 .... 225-7163 106

Notes

U.S. Congress Directory | 15

State Order Index

	Seniority in Party	Office	Phone (202)	Page
8 - John Garamendi (D)	59	2004	225-1880	87
9 - Josh Harder (D)	135	209	225-4540	92
10 - Mark DeSaulnier (D)	97	503	225-2095	81
11 - Nancy Pelosi (D)	3	1236	225-4965	116
12 - Barbara Lee (D)	26	2470	225-2661	102
13 - John Duarte (R)	191	1535	225-1947	82
14 - Eric Swalwell (D)	85	174	225-5065	128
15 - Kevin Mullin (D)	200	1404	225-3531	112
16 - Anna G. Eshoo (D)	11	272	225-8104	83
17 - Ro Khanna (D)	114	306	225-2631	99
18 - Zoe Lofgren (D)	17	1401	225-3072	104
19 - Jimmy Panetta (D)	116	304	225-2861	115
20 - Vacant		2468	225-2915	137
21 - Jim Costa (D)	40	2081	225-3341	77
22 - David G. Valadao (R)	83	2465	225-4695	132
23 - Jay Obernolte (R)	166	1029	225-5861	114
24 - Salud Carbajal (D)	108	2331	225-3601	72
25 - Raul Ruiz (D)	84	2342	225-5330	121
26 - Julia Brownley (D)	71	2262	225-5811	70
27 - Mike Garcia (R)	132	144	225-1956	88
28 - Judy Chu (D)	58	2423	225-5464	75
29 - Tony Cárdenas (D)	72	2181	225-6131	72
30 - Adam Schiff (D)	33	2309	225-4176	123
31 - Grace F. Napolitano (D)	28	1610	225-5256	112
32 - Brad Sherman (D)	23	2365	225-5911	124
33 - Pete Aguilar (D)	94	108	225-3201	64
34 - Jimmy Gomez (D)	119	506	225-6235	89
35 - Norma J. Torres (D)	102	2227	225-6161	131
36 - Ted W. Lieu (D)	100	2454	225-3976	104
37 - Sydney Kamlager-Dove (D)	193	1419	225-7084	98
38 - Linda T. Sanchez (D)	37	2428	225-6676	122
39 - Mark Takano (D)	86	2078	225-2305	129
40 - Young Kim (R)	155	1306	225-4111	100
41 - Ken Calvert (R)	3	2205	225-1986	72
42 - Robert Garcia (D)	186	1305	225-7924	88
43 - Maxine Waters (D)	7	2221	225-2201	134
44 - Nanette Diaz Barragán (D)	106	2312	225-8220	67
45 - Michelle Steel (R)	172	1127	225-2415	127
46 - Lou Correa (D)	109	2301	225-2965	77
47 - Katie Porter (D)	147	1233	225-5611	118
48 - Darrell Issa (R)	17	2108	225-5672	95
49 - Mike Levin (D)	140	2352	225-3906	104
50 - Scott Peters (D)	82	1201	225-0508	117
51 - Sara Jacobs (D)	163	1314	225-2040	96
52 - Juan Vargas (D)	87	2334	225-8045	132

COLORADO
Senate

Sr. - Michael Bennet (D)	19	SR-261	224-5852	31
Jr. - John Hickenlooper (D)	42	SR-374	224-5941	38

House

1 - Diana DeGette (D)	20	2111	225-4431	80
2 - Joe Neguse (D)	142	2400	225-2161	113
3 - Lauren Boebert (R)	137	1713	225-4761	69
4 - Ken Buck (R)	65	2455	225-4676	70
5 - Doug Lamborn (R)	25	2371	225-4422	101
6 - Jason Crow (D)	127	1323	225-7882	78

State Order Index

	Seniority in Party	Office	Phone (202)	Page
7 - Brittany Pettersen (D)	202	1230	225-2645	117
8 - Yadira Caraveo (D)	179	1024	225-5625	72

CONNECTICUT
Senate
Sr. - Richard Blumenthal (D)	23	SH-706	224-2823	31
Jr. - Chris Murphy (D)	26	SH-136	224-4041	43

House
1 - John B. Larson (D)	27	1501	225-2265	102
2 - Joe Courtney (D)	49	2449	225-2076	77
3 - Rosa DeLauro (D)	6	2413	225-3661	80
4 - Jim Himes (D)	54	2137	225-5541	93
5 - Jahana Hayes (D)	136	2458	225-4476	93

DELAWARE
Senate
Sr. - Tom Carper (D)	6	SH-513	224-2441	34
Jr. - Chris Coons (D)	22	SR-218	224-5042	34

House
AL - Lisa Blunt Rochester (D)	107	1724	225-4165	69

FLORIDA
Senate
Sr. - Marco Rubio (R)	15	SR-284	224-3041	45
Jr. - Rick Scott (R)	39	SH-110	224-5274	46

House
1 - Matt Gaetz (R)	92	2021	225-4136	87
2 - Neal Dunn (R)	89	466	225-5235	82
3 - Kat Cammack (R)	138	2421	225-5744	72
4 - Aaron Bean (R)	182	1239	225-0123	67
5 - John Rutherford (R)	98	1711	225-2501	121
6 - Mike Waltz (R)	129	244	225-2706	133
7 - Cory Mills (R)	210	1237	225-4035	110
8 - Bill Posey (R)	33	2150	225-3671	118
9 - Darren Soto (D)	118	2353	225-9889	126
10 - Maxwell Alejandro Frost (D)	185	1224	225-2176	86
11 - Daniel Webster (R)	48	2184	225-1002	134
12 - Gus M. Bilirakis (R)	22	2306	225-5755	68
13 - Anna Paulina Luna (R)	206	1017	225-5961	105
14 - Kathy Castor (D)	46	2052	225-3376	74
15 - Laurel Lee (R)	205	1118	225-5626	103
16 - Vern Buchanan (R)	23	2110	225-5015	70
17 - Greg Steube (R)	126	2457	225-5792	128
18 - Scott Franklin (R)	146	249	225-1252	86
19 - Byron Donalds (R)	141	1719	225-2536	82
20 - Sheila Cherfilus-McCormick (D)	174	242	225-1313	75
21 - Brian Mast (R)	97	2182	225-3026	106
22 - Lois Frankel (D)	75	2305	225-9890	86
23 - Jared Moskowitz (D)	199	1130	225-3001	111
24 - Frederica S. Wilson (D)	64	2080	225-4506	135
25 - Debbie Wasserman Schultz (D)	44	270	225-7931	133
26 - Mario Diaz-Balart (R)	14	374	225-4211	81
27 - María Elvira Salazar (R)	170	2162	225-3931	121
28 - Carlos A. Gimenez (R)	148	448	225-2778	88

Notes

State Order Index

	Seniority in Party	Office	Phone (202)	Page

GEORGIA
Senate
- Sr. - Jon Ossoff (D) .... 44 .... SH-303 .... 224-3521 43
- Jr. - Raphael Warnock (D) .... 45 .... SR-416 ...... 224-3643 49

House
- 1 - Earl L. "Buddy" Carter (R) .... 66 .... 2432 .... 225-5831 73
- 2 - Sanford D. Bishop, Jr. (D) .... 9 .... 2407 .... 225-3631 68
- 3 - Drew Ferguson (R) .... 90 .... 2239 .... 225-5901 84
- 4 - Henry C. "Hank" Johnson, Jr. (D) .... 50 .... 2240 .... 225-1605 97
- 5 - Nikema Williams (D) .... 170 .... 1406 .... 225-3801 135
- 6 - Rich McCormick (R) .... 208 .... 1213 .... 225-4272 108
- 7 - Lucy McBath (D) .... 141 .... 2246 .... 225-4501 107
- 8 - Austin Scott (R) .... 47 .... 2185 .... 225-6531 123
- 9 - Andrew Clyde (R) .... 140 .... 445 .... 225-9893 76
- 10 - Mike Collins (R) .... 187 .... 1223 .... 225-4101 77
- 11 - Barry Loudermilk (R) .... 71 .... 2133 .... 225-2931 104
- 12 - Rick W. Allen (R) .... 62 .... 462 .... 225-2823 64
- 13 - David Scott (D) .... 38 .... 468 .... 225-2939 124
- 14 - Marjorie Taylor Greene (R) .... 151 .... 403 .... 225-5211 91

HAWAII
Senate
- Sr. - Brian Schatz (D) .... 24 .... SH-722 .... 224-3934 46
- Jr. - Mazie K. Hirono (D) .... 27 .... SH-109 .... 224-6361 39

House
- 1 - Ed Case (D) .... 93 .... 2210 .... 225-2726 74
- 2 - Jill Tokuda (D) .... 209 .... 1005 .... 225-4906 130

IDAHO
Senate
- Sr. - Mike Crapo (R) .... 4 .... SD-239 .... 224-6142 35
- Jr. - Jim Risch (R) .... 11 .... SR-483 .... 224-2752 45

House
- 1 - Russ Fulcher (R) .... 112 .... 1514 .... 225-6611 87
- 2 - Mike Simpson (R) .... 7 .... 2084 .... 225-5531 125

ILLINOIS
Senate
- Sr. - Dick Durbin (D) .... 3 .... SH-711 .... 224-2152 36
- Jr. - Tammy Duckworth (D) .... 35 .... SH-524 .... 224-2854 36

House
- 1 - Jonathan L. Jackson (D) .... 192 .... 1641 .... 225-4372 96
- 2 - Robin Kelly (D) .... 89 .... 2329 .... 225-0773 99
- 3 - Delia C. Ramirez (D) .... 203 .... 1523 .... 225-5701 119
- 4 - Jesús G. "Chuy" García (D) .... 132 .... 1519 .... 225-8203 88
- 5 - Mike Quigley (D) .... 57 .... 2083 .... 225-4061 118
- 6 - Sean Casten (D) .... 125 .... 2440 .... 225-4561 74
- 7 - Danny K. Davis (D) .... 19 .... 2159 .... 225-5006 79
- 8 - Raja Krishnamoorthi (D) .... 115 .... 2367 .... 225-3711 100
- 9 - Jan Schakowsky (D) .... 29 .... 2408 .... 225-2111 122
- 10 - Brad Schneider (D) .... 105 .... 300 .... 225-4835 123
- 11 - Bill Foster (D) .... 60 .... 2366 .... 225-3515 85
- 12 - Mike Bost (R) .... 64 .... 352 .... 225-5661 69
- 13 - Nikki Budzinski (D) .... 178 .... 1009 .... 225-2371 71
- 14 - Lauren Underwood (D) .... 158 .... 1410 .... 225-2976 131
- 15 - Mary Miller (R) .... 161 .... 1740 .... 225-5271 109

Notes

State Order Index

	Seniority in Party	Office	Phone (202)	Page
16 - Darin LaHood (R)	80	1424	225-6201	101
17 - Eric Sorensen (D)	206	1205	225-5905	126

INDIANA
Senate
Sr. - Todd Young (R)	31	SD-185	224-5623	50
Jr. - Mike Braun (R)	37	SR-404	224-4814	32

House
1 - Frank J. Mrvan (D)	166	1607	225-2461	112
2 - Rudy Yakym III (R)	179	349	225-3915	136
3 - Jim Banks (R)	86	2418	225-4436	66
4 - Jim Baird (R)	108	2303	225-5037	66
5 - Victoria Spartz (R)	171	1609	225-2276	126
6 - Greg Pence (R)	120	404	225-3021	116
7 - André D. Carson (D)	52	2135	225-4011	73
8 - Larry Bucshon (R)	36	2313	225-4636	71
9 - Erin Houchin (R)	196	1632	225-5315	94

IOWA
Senate
Sr. - Chuck Grassley (R)	1	SH-135	224-3744	37
Jr. - Joni Ernst (R)	29	SR-260	224-3254	36

House
1 - Mariannette Miller-Meeks (R)	162	1034	225-6576	110
2 - Ashley Hinson (R)	153	1717	225-2911	93
3 - Zach Nunn (R)	213	1232	225-5476	114
4 - Randy Feenstra (R)	143	1440	225-4426	84

KANSAS
Senate
Sr. - Jerry Moran (R)	12	SD-521	224-6521	42
Jr. - Roger Marshall (R)	41	SR-479A	224-4774	42

House
1 - Tracey Mann (R)	159	344	225-2715	106
2 - Jake LaTurner (R)	156	2441	225-6601	102
3 - Sharice Davids (D)	128	2435	225-2865	79
4 - Ron Estes (R)	100	2234	225-6216	83

KENTUCKY
Senate
Sr. - Mitch McConnell (R)	2	SR-317	224-2541	42
Jr. - Rand Paul (R)	17	SR-295	224-4343	44

House
1 - James Comer (R)	82	2410	225-3115	77
2 - Brett Guthrie (R)	30	2434	225-3501	92
3 - Morgan McGarvey (D)	197	1527	225-5401	108
4 - Thomas Massie (R)	51	2453	225-3465	106
5 - Hal Rogers (R)	1	2406	225-4601	119
6 - Andy Barr (R)	52	2430	225-4706	66

LOUISIANA
Senate
Sr. - Bill Cassidy (R)	23	SD-455	224-5824	34
Jr. - John Kennedy (R)	32	SR-437	224-4623	40

House
1 - Steve Scalise (R)	29	2049	225-3015	122
2 - Troy A. Carter, Sr. (D)	171	442	225-6636	73

Notes

State Order Index

	Seniority in Party	Office	Phone (202)	Page
3 - Clay Higgins (R)	94	572	225-2031	93
4 - Mike Johnson (R)	95	568	225-2777	97
5 - Julia Letlow (R)	174	142	225-8490	103
6 - Garret Graves (R)	68	2402	225-3901	90

MAINE
Senate

Sr. - Susan Collins (R)	3	SD-413	224-2523	34
Jr. - Angus King (I)		SH-133	224-5344	40

House

1 - Chellie Pingree (D)	55	2354	225-6116	117
2 - Jared Golden (D)	134	1710	225-6306	88

MARYLAND
Senate

Sr. - Ben Cardin (D)	10	SH-509	224-4524	33
Jr. - Chris Van Hollen (D)	34	SH-730	224-4654	49

House

1 - Andy Harris (R)	43	1536	225-5311	92
2 - C.A. Dutch Ruppersberger (D)	36	2206	225-3061	121
3 - John Sarbanes (D)	51	2370	225-4016	122
4 - Glenn Ivey (D)	190	1529	225-8699	95
5 - Steny Hoyer (D)	1	1705	225-4131	94
6 - David Trone (D)	157	2404	225-2721	131
7 - Kweisi Mfume (D)	61	2263	225-4741	109
8 - Jamie Raskin (D)	117	2242	225-5341	119

MASSACHUSETTS
Senate

Sr. - Elizabeth Warren (D)	30	SH-309	224-4543	49
Jr. - Edward J. Markey (D)	31	SD-255	224-2742	41

House

1 - Richard Neal (D)	5	372	225-5601	113
2 - Jim McGovern (D)	21	370	225-6101	108
3 - Lori Trahan (D)	156	2439	225-3411	131
4 - Jake Auchincloss (D)	160	1524	225-5931	65
5 - Katherine Clark (D)	90	2368	225-2836	75
6 - Seth Moulton (D)	101	1126	225-8020	111
7 - Ayanna Pressley (D)	148	402	225-5111	118
8 - Stephen F. Lynch (D)	34	2109	225-8273	105
9 - William R. Keating (D)	62	2351	225-3111	98

MICHIGAN
Senate

Sr. - Debbie Stabenow (D)	7	SH-731	224-4822	47
Jr. - Gary Peters (D)	33	SD-B40A	224-6221	44

House

1 - Jack Bergman (R)	87	566	225-4735	67
2 - John Moolenaar (R)	72	246	225-3561	110
3 - Hillary J. Scholten (D)	205	1317	225-3831	123
4 - Bill Huizenga (R)	44	2232	225-4401	95
5 - Tim Walberg (R)	35	2266	225-6276	133
6 - Debbie Dingell (D)	98	102	225-4071	81
7 - Elissa Slotkin (D)	151	2245	225-4872	125
8 - Dan Kildee (D)	78	200	225-3611	99
9 - Lisa McClain (R)	160	444	225-2106	107
10 - John James (R)	198	1319	225-4961	96

State Order Index

	Seniority in Party	Office	Phone (202)	Page
11 - Haley Stevens (D)	154	2411	225-8171	128
12 - Rashida Tlaib (D)	155	2438	225-5126	130
13 - Shri Thanedar (D)	208	1039	225-5802	129

MINNESOTA
Senate
Sr. - Amy Klobuchar (D)	13	SD-425	224-3244	40
Jr. - Tina Smith (D)	38	SH-720	224-5641	47

House
1 - Brad Finstad (R)	178	1605	225-2472	84
2 - Angie Craig (D)	126	2442	225-2271	78
3 - Dean Phillips (D)	146	2452	225-2871	117
4 - Betty McCollum (D)	32	2426	225-6631	107
5 - Ilhan Omar (D)	144	1730	225-4755	115
6 - Tom Emmer (R)	67	464	225-2331	83
7 - Michelle Fischbach (R)	144	1004	225-2165	84
8 - Pete Stauber (R)	124	145	225-6211	127

MISSISSIPPI
Senate
Sr. - Roger F. Wicker (R)	10	SR-425	224-6253	50
Jr. - Cindy Hyde-Smith (R)	33	SH-702	224-5054	39

House
1 - Trent Kelly (R)	79	2243	225-4306	99
2 - Bennie G. Thompson (D)	14	2466	225-5876	129
3 - Michael Guest (R)	115	450	225-5031	92
4 - Mike Ezell (R)	193	443	225-5772	84

MISSOURI
Senate
Sr. - Josh Hawley (R)	38	SR-115	224-6154	38
Jr. - Eric Schmitt (R)	47	SR-387	224-5721	46

House
1 - Cori Bush (D)	162	2463	225-2406	71
2 - Ann Wagner (R)	57	2350	225-1621	133
3 - Blaine Luetkemeyer (R)	31	2230	225-2956	104
4 - Mark Alford (R)	181	1516	225-2876	64
5 - Emanuel Cleaver (D)	39	2217	225-4535	75
6 - Sam Graves (R)	9	1135	225-7041	90
7 - Eric Burlison (R)	184	1108	225-6536	71
8 - Jason Smith (R)	61	1011	225-4404	126

MONTANA
Senate
Sr. - Jon Tester (D)	15	SH-311	224-2644	48
Jr. - Steve Daines (R)	26	SH-320	224-2651	36

House
1 - Ryan Zinke (R)	180	512	225-5628	136
2 - Matt Rosendale (R)	169	1023	225-3211	120

NEBRASKA
Senate
Sr. - Deb Fischer (R)	21	SR-448	224-6551	37
Jr. - Pete Ricketts (R)	49	SR-139	224-4224	44

House
1 - Mike Flood (R)	177	343	225-4806	85
2 - Don Bacon (R)	85	2104	225-4155	66
3 - Adrian Smith (R)	26	502	225-6435	125

Notes

State Order Index

	Seniority in Party	Office	Phone (202)	Page

NEVADA
Senate
Sr. - Catherine Cortez Masto (D).....37...............SH-520...........224-3542....................35
Jr. - Jacky Rosen (D)........................... 39..............SH-713........ 224-6244..................45

House
1 - Dina Titus (D)...................................68................2464............225-5965...............130
2 - Mark Amodei (R) ....50...............104..........225-6155..................65
3 - Susie Lee (D).....................................139................365...........225-3252.................103
4 - Steven Horsford (D)................123 ....406.............225-9894..................94

NEW HAMPSHIRE
Senate
Sr. - Jeanne Shaheen (D)................16..............SH-506..........224-2841.................47
Jr. - Maggie Hassan (D) ....36............SH-324.........224-3324....................38

House
1 - Chris Pappas (D) ....145................452..............225-5456................115
2 - Annie Kuster (D) .... 80...............2201............225-5206................100

NEW JERSEY
Senate
Sr. - Bob Menendez (D)......................9...............SH-528.........224-4744....................42
Jr. - Cory A. Booker (D).......................32.............SH-717......... 224-3224....................32

House
1 - Donald Norcross (D)................. 92 ....2427 ....225-6501 113
2 - Jeff Van Drew (R)........................128................2447............225-6572..................132
3 - Andy Kim (D) ....138 .... 2444 ....225-4765.................100
4 - Chris Smith (R).................................2................2373............225-3765...............125
5 - Josh Gottheimer (D).................112.................203.............225-4465....................90
6 - Frank Pallone, Jr. (D).....................4................2107.............225-4671................115
7 - Tom Kean, Jr. (R).........................199 ....251.............225-5361...................98
8 - Rob Menendez (D)..................198 .... 1007 ....225-7919 108
9 - Bill Pascrell, Jr. (D).......................22 .... 2409 ....225-5751 116
10 - Donald M. Payne, Jr. (D)........67 .... 106 .... 225-3436................ 116
11 - Mikie Sherrill (D) ....150 ....1427 ....225-5034................125
12 - Bonnie Watson
    Coleman (D) ....103 ....168 ....225-5801..................134

NEW MEXICO
Senate
Sr. - Martin Heinrich (D)..................28............SH-709..........224-5521....................38
Jr. - Ben Ray Luján (D)......................41..............SR-498.........224-6621...................41

House
1 - Melanie Stansbury (D)............. 172 ....1421 ....225-6316 127
2 - Gabe Vasquez (D).......................210..............1517........ 225-2365..................132
3 - Teresa Leger
    Fernandez (D)...............................164............... 1510 ....225-6190 103

NEW YORK
Senate
Sr. - Chuck Schumer (D)...................5..............SH-322.........224-6542....................46
Jr. - Kirsten Gillibrand (D).............. 20............SR-478......... 224-4451....................37

House
1 - Nick LaLota (R)..............................202..........................1530.............225-3826................101
2 - Andrew Garbarino (R).............. 147............2344...........225-7896...................87
3 - Vacant..1117...........225-3335..................137
4 - Anthony D'Esposito (R)......... 189...............1508............225-5516....................81
5 - Gregory W. Meeks (D).............. 25...............2310............225-3461.................108
6 - Grace Meng (D) ....81................2209 ....225-2601.................109

State Order Index

	Seniority in Party	Office	Phone (202)	Page
7 - Nydia M. Velázquez (D)	13	2302	225-2361	133
8 - Hakeem Jeffries (D)	77	2433	225-5936	97
9 - Yvette Clarke (D)	47	2058	225-6231	75
10 - Dan Goldman (D)	188	245	225-7944	89
11 - Nicole Malliotakis (R)	158	351	225-3371	105
12 - Jerrold Nadler (D)	8	2132	225-5635	112
13 - Adriano Espaillat (D)	110	2332	225-4365	83
14 - Alexandria Ocasio-Cortez (D)	143	250	225-3965	114
15 - Ritchie Torres (D)	169	1414	225-4361	131
16 - Jamaal Bowman (D)	161	345	225-2464	69
17 - Mike Lawler (R)	204	1013	225-6506	102
18 - Pat Ryan (D)	176	1030	225-5614	121
19 - Marc Molinaro (R)	211	1207	225-5441	110
20 - Paul Tonko (D)	56	2369	225-5076	130
21 - Elise Stefanik (R)	77	2211	225-4611	127
22 - Brandon Williams (R)	218	1022	225-3701	135
23 - Nick Langworthy (R)	203	1630	225-3161	101
24 - Claudia Tenney (R)	134	2349	225-3665	129
25 - Joe Morelle (D)	120	570	225-3615	111
26 - Vacant		2269	225-3306	137

NORTH CAROLINA

Senate

Sr. - Thom Tillis (R)	28	SD-113	224-6342	48
Jr. - Ted Budd (R)	45	SR-304	224-3154	33

House

1 - Don Davis (D)	182	1123	225-3101	79
2 - Deborah Ross (D)	167	1221	225-3032	120
3 - Greg Murphy (R)	131	407	225-3415	112
4 - Valerie Foushee (D)	184	1716	225-1784	86
5 - Virginia Foxx (R)	18	2462	225-2071	86
6 - Kathy Manning (D)	165	307	225-3065	106
7 - David Rouzer (R)	76	2333	225-2731	120
8 - Dan Bishop (R)	130	2459	225-1976	68
9 - Richard Hudson (R)	53	2112	225-3715	94
10 - Patrick McHenry (R)	20	2134	225-2576	108
11 - Chuck Edwards (R)	192	1505	225-6401	82
12 - Alma S. Adams (D)	91	2436	225-1510	64
13 - Wiley Nickel (D)	201	1133	225-4531	113
14 - Jeff Jackson (D)	191	1318	225-5634	95

NORTH DAKOTA

Senate

Sr. - John Hoeven (R)	14	SR-338	224-2551	39
Jr. - Kevin Cramer (R)	35	SH-313	224-2043	35

House

AL - Kelly Armstrong (R)	107	2235	225-2611	65

OHIO

Senate

Sr. - Sherrod Brown (D)	11	SH-503	224-2315	32
Jr. - J.D. Vance (R)	46	SR-288	224-3353	49

House

1 - Greg Landsman (D)	194	1432	225-2216	101
2 - Brad Wenstrup (R)	59	2335	225-3164	134
3 - Joyce Beatty (D)	69	2079	225-4324	67
4 - Jim Jordan (R)	24	2056	225-2676	97

Notes

State Order Index

	Seniority in Party	Office	Phone (202)	Page
5 - Bob Latta (R)	27	2467	225-6405	102
6 - Vacant		2082	225-5705	137
7 - Max Miller (R)	209	143	225-3876	109
8 - Warren Davidson (R)	81	2113	225-6205	79
9 - Marcy Kaptur (D)	2	2186	225-4146	98
10 - Mike Turner (R)	16	2183	225-6465	131
11 - Shontel Brown (D)	173	449	225-7032	70
12 - Troy Balderson (R)	105	2429	225-5355	66
13 - Emilia Strong Sykes (D)	207	1217	225-6265	128
14 - Dave Joyce (R)	54	2065	225-5731	97
15 - Mike Carey (R)	176	1433	225-2015	72

OKLAHOMA
Senate

Sr. - James Lankford (R)	24	SH-316	224-5754	40
Jr. - Markwayne Mullin (R)	44	SH-330	224-4721	43

House

1 - Kevin Hern (R)	106	1019	225-2211	93
2 - Josh Brecheen (R)	183	1208	225-2701	70
3 - Frank Lucas (R)	4	2405	225-5565	104
4 - Tom Cole (R)	13	2207	225-6165	76
5 - Stephanie Bice (R)	136	2437	225-2132	68

OREGON
Senate

Sr. - Ron Wyden (D)	2	SD-221	224-5244	50
Jr. - Jeff Merkley (D)	18	SH-531	224-3753	42

House

1 - Suzanne Bonamici (D)	65	2231	225-0855	69
2 - Cliff Bentz (R)	135	409	225-6730	67
3 - Earl Blumenauer (D)	18	1111	225-4811	69
4 - Val Hoyle (D)	189	1620	225-6416	94
5 - Lori Chavez-DeRemer (R)	185	1722	225-5711	74
6 - Andrea Salinas (D)	204	109	225-5643	122

PENNSYLVANIA
Senate

Sr. - Bob Casey (D)	12	SR-393	224-6324	34
Jr. - John Fetterman (D)	47	SR-142	224-4254	37

House

1 - Brian Fitzpatrick (R)	91	271	225-4276	85
2 - Brendan F. Boyle (D)	96	1502	225-6111	70
3 - Dwight Evans (D)	104	1105	225-4001	83
4 - Madeleine Dean (D)	129	150	225-4731	80
5 - Mary Gay Scanlon (D)	121	1227	225-2011	122
6 - Chrissy Houlahan (D)	137	1727	225-4315	94
7 - Susan Wild (D)	122	1027	225-6411	135
8 - Matt Cartwright (D)	73	2102	225-5546	73
9 - Dan Meuser (R)	118	350	225-6511	109
10 - Scott Perry (R)	56	2160	225-5836	117
11 - Lloyd Smucker (R)	99	302	225-2411	126
12 - Summer Lee (D)	195	243	225-2135	103
13 - John Joyce (R)	117	152	225-2431	98
14 - Guy Reschenthaler (R)	121	342	225-2065	119
15 - Glenn "GT" Thompson (R)	34	400	225-5121	129
16 - Mike Kelly (R)	45	1707	225-5406	98
17 - Chris Deluzio (D)	183	1222	225-2301	80

Notes

State Order Index

	Seniority in Party	Office	Phone (202)	Page

RHODE ISLAND
Senate
Sr. - Jack Reed (D) ..... 4 ..... SH-728 ..... 224-4642 44
Jr. - Sheldon Whitehouse (D) ..... 14 ..... SH-530 ..... 224-2921 50

House
1 - Gabe Amo (D) ..... 212 ..... 2233 ..... 225-4911 65
2 - Seth Magaziner (D) ..... 196 ..... 1218 ..... 225-2735 105

SOUTH CAROLINA
Senate
Sr. - Lindsey Graham (R) ..... 7 ..... SR-211 ..... 224-5972 37
Jr. - Tim Scott (R) ..... 19 ..... SH-104 ..... 224-6121 47

House
1 - Nancy Mace (R) ..... 157 ..... 1728 ..... 225-3176 105
2 - Joe Wilson (R) ..... 10 ..... 1436 ..... 225-2452 136
3 - Jeff Duncan (R) ..... 39 ..... 2229 ..... 225-5301 82
4 - William Timmons (R) ..... 127 ..... 267 ..... 225-6030 130
5 - Ralph Norman (R) ..... 101 ..... 569 ..... 225-5501 114
6 - James E. Clyburn (D) ..... 10 ..... 274 ..... 225-3315 76
7 - Russell Fry (R) ..... 194 ..... 1626 ..... 225-9895 86

SOUTH DAKOTA
Senate
Sr. - John Thune (R) ..... 8 ..... SD-511 ..... 224-2321 48
Jr. - Mike Rounds (R) ..... 27 ..... SH-716 ..... 224-5842 45

House
AL - Dusty Johnson (R) ..... 116 ..... 1714 ..... 225-2801 97

TENNESSEE
Senate
Sr. - Marsha Blackburn (R) ..... 34 ..... SD-357 ..... 224-3344 31
Jr. - Bill Hagerty (R) ..... 42 ..... SR-251 ..... 224-4944 38

House
1 - Diana Harshbarger (R) ..... 152 ..... 167 ..... 225-6356 92
2 - Tim Burchett (R) ..... 109 ..... 1122 ..... 225-5435 71
3 - Chuck Fleischmann (R) ..... 40 ..... 2187 ..... 225-3271 85
4 - Scott DesJarlais (R) ..... 38 ..... 2304 ..... 225-6831 81
5 - Andy Ogles (R) ..... 214 ..... 151 ..... 225-4311 114
6 - John Rose (R) ..... 122 ..... 2238 ..... 225-4231 120
7 - Mark Green (R) ..... 114 ..... 2446 ..... 225-2811 91
8 - David Kustoff (R) ..... 96 ..... 560 ..... 225-4714 100
9 - Steve Cohen (D) ..... 48 ..... 2268 ..... 225-3265 76

TEXAS
Senate
Sr. - John Cornyn (R) ..... 5 ..... SH-517 ..... 224-2934 35
Jr. - Ted Cruz (R) ..... 20 ..... SR-167 ..... 224-5922 36

House
1 - Nathaniel Moran (R) ..... 212 ..... 1541 ..... 225-3035 111
2 - Dan Crenshaw (R) ..... 111 ..... 248 ..... 225-6565 78
3 - Keith Self (R) ..... 215 ..... 1113 ..... 225-4201 124
4 - Pat Fallon (R) ..... 142 ..... 2416 ..... 225-6673 84
5 - Lance Gooden (R) ..... 113 ..... 2431 ..... 225-3484 90
6 - Jake Ellzey (R) ..... 175 ..... 1721 ..... 225-2002 82
7 - Lizzie Fletcher (D) ..... 131 ..... 346 ..... 225-2571 85
8 - Morgan Luttrell (R) ..... 207 ..... 1320 ..... 225-4901 105
9 - Al Green (D) ..... 42 ..... 2347 ..... 225-7508 91
10 - Michael McCaul (R) ..... 19 ..... 2300 ..... 225-2401 107

State Order Index

	Seniority in Party	Office	Phone (202)	Page
11 - August Pfluger (R)	168	1124	225-3605	117
12 - Kay Granger (R)	6	2308	225-5071	90
13 - Ronny Jackson (R)	154	446	225-3706	96
14 - Randy Weber (R)	58	107	225-2831	134
15 - Monica De La Cruz (R)	190	1415	225-9901	80
16 - Veronica Escobar (D)	130	2448	225-4831	83
17 - Pete Sessions (R)	8	2204	225-6105	124
18 - Sheila Jackson Lee (D)	16	2314	225-3816	96
19 - Jodey Arrington (R)	84	1107	225-4005	65
20 - Joaquin Castro (D)	74	2241	225-3236	74
21 - Chip Roy (R)	123	103	225-4236	120
22 - Troy Nehls (R)	165	1104	225-5951	113
23 - Tony Gonzales (R)	149	2244	225-4511	89
24 - Beth Van Duyne (R)	173	1725	225-6605	132
25 - Roger Williams (R)	60	2336	225-9896	135
26 - Michael C. Burgess (R)	11	2161	225-7772	71
27 - Michael Cloud (R)	104	171	225-7742	76
28 - Henry Cuellar (D)	41	2372	225-1640	79
29 - Sylvia Garcia (D)	133	2419	225-1688	88
30 - Jasmine Crockett (D)	181	1616	225-8885	78
31 - John Carter (R)	12	2208	225-3864	73
32 - Colin Allred (D)	124	348	225-2231	64
33 - Marc Veasey (D)	88	2348	225-9897	133
34 - Vicente Gonzalez (D)	111	154	225-2531	89
35 - Greg Casar (D)	180	1339	225-5645	74
36 - Brian Babin (R)	63	2236	225-1555	65
37 - Lloyd Doggett (D)	15	2307	225-4865	81
38 - Wesley Hunt (R)	197	1520	225-5646	95

UTAH
Senate

Sr. - Mike Lee (R)	18	SR-363	224-5444	41
Jr. - Mitt Romney (R)	36	SR-354	224-5251	45

House

1 - Blake Moore (R)	164	1131	225-0453	111
2 - Celeste Maloy (R)	219	166	225-9730	106
3 - John Curtis (R)	102	2323	225-7751	79
4 - Burgess Owens (R)	167	309	225-3011	115

VERMONT
Senate

Sr. - Bernie Sanders (I)		SD-332	224-5141	46
Jr. - Peter Welch (D)	46	SR-124	224-4242	50

House

AL - Becca Balint (D)	177	1408	225-4115	66

VIRGINIA
Senate

Sr. - Mark R. Warner (D)	17	SH-703	224-2023	49
Jr. - Tim Kaine (D)	29	SR-231	224-4024	39

House

1 - Rob Wittman (R)	28	2055	225-4261	136
2 - Jen Kiggans (R)	200	1037	225-4215	99
3 - Bobby Scott (D)	12	2328	225-8351	124
4 - Jennifer McClellan (D)	211	2417	225-6365	107
5 - Bob Good (R)	150	461	225-4711	89
6 - Ben Cline (R)	110	2443	225-5431	76
7 - Abigail Spanberger (D)	152	562	225-2815	126

Notes

NLPC | 26

State Order Index

	Seniority in Party	Office	Phone (202)	Page
8 - Don Beyer (D)	95	1119	225-4376	68
9 - Morgan Griffith (R)	42	2202	225-3861	91
10 - Jennifer Wexton (D)	159	1210	225-5136	135
11 - Gerry Connolly (D)	53	2265	225-1492	77

WASHINGTON
Senate

Sr. - Patty Murray (D)	1	SR-154	224-2621	43
Jr. - Maria Cantwell (D)	8	SH-511	224-3441	33

House

1 - Suzan DelBene (D)	66	2330	225-6311	80
2 - Rick Larsen (D)	31	2163	225-2605	102
3 - Marie Gluesenkamp Perez (D)	187	1431	225-3536	116
4 - Dan Newhouse (R)	74	504	225-5816	113
5 - Cathy McMorris Rodgers (R)	21	2188	225-2006	119
6 - Derek Kilmer (D)	79	1226	225-5916	100
7 - Pramila Jayapal (D)	113	2346	225-3106	96
8 - Kim Schrier (D)	149	1110	225-7761	123
9 - Adam Smith (D)	24	2264	225-8901	125
10 - Marilyn Strickland (D)	168	1708	225-9740	128

WEST VIRGINIA
Senate

Sr. - Joe Manchin (D)	21	SH-306	224-3954	41
Jr. - Shelley Moore Capito (R)	22	SR-170	224-6472	33

House

1 - Carol Miller (R)	119	465	225-3452	109
2 - Alex X. Mooney (R)	73	2228	225-2711	110

WISCONSIN
Senate

Sr. - Ron Johnson (R)	16	SH-328	224-5323	39
Jr. - Tammy Baldwin (D)	25	SH-141	224-5653	31

House

1 - Bryan Steil (R)	125	1526	225-3031	127
2 - Mark Pocan (D)	83	1026	225-2906	118
3 - Derrick Van Orden (R)	217	1513	225-5506	132
4 - Gwen Moore (D)	43	2252	225-4572	111
5 - Scott Fitzgerald (R)	145	1507	225-5101	85
6 - Glenn Grothman (R)	69	1511	225-2476	91
7 - Tom Tiffany (R)	133	451	225-3365	130
8 - Mike Gallagher (R)	93	1211	225-5665	87

WYOMING
Senate

Sr. - John Barrasso (R)	9	SD-307	224-6441	31
Jr. - Cynthia Lummis (R)	40	SR-127A	224-3424	41

House

AL - Harriet Hageman (R)	195	1531	225-2311	92

Notes

State Order Index

	Seniority in Party	Office	Phone (202)	Page

AMERICAN SAMOA
Aumua Amata Coleman
  Radewagen (R) .... 2001 .... 225-8577 119

DISTRICT OF COLUMBIA
Eleanor Holmes Norton (D) .... 2136 .... 225-8050 114

GUAM
James Moylan (R) .... 1628 .... 225-1188 112

NORTHERN MARIANA ISLANDS
Gregorio Kilili Camacho
  Sablan (D) .... 2267 .... 225-2646 121

PUERTO RICO
Jenniffer González-Colón (R) .... 2338 .... 225-2615 89

VIRGIN ISLANDS
Stacey E. Plaskett (D) .... 2059 .... 225-1790 118

Notes

Party Breakdown

SENATE
  Democrats 48 | Republicans 49 | Independents 3

HOUSE
  Republicans 219 | Democrats 212 | Vacancies 4

Notes

Senate Leadership

PRESIDENT
Kamala Harris, Vice President | S-212 Capitol | 224-2424 | Director of Legislative Affairs—Andy Flick

PRESIDENT PRO TEMPORE
Patty Murray (D-WA) | S-125 Capitol | 224-9400

MAJORITY LEADER & DEMOCRATIC CONFERENCE CHAIR
Chuck Schumer (D-NY) | S-221 Capitol | 224-2158 | Chief of Staff—Mike Lynch

MAJORITY WHIP
Dick Durbin (D-IL) | S-321 Capitol | 224-9447 | Chief of Staff—Pat Souders

DEMOCRATIC POLICY & COMMUNICATIONS COMMITTEE CHAIR
Debbie Stabenow (D-MI) | SH-419 | 224-3232

MINORITY LEADER
Mitch McConnell (R-KY) | S-230 Capitol | 224-3135 | Chief of Staff—Sharon Soderstrom

MINORITY WHIP
John Thune (R-SD) | S-208 Capitol | 224-2708 | Chief of Staff—Geoffrey Antell

REPUBLICAN POLICY COMMITTEE CHAIR
Joni Ernst (R-IA) | SR-347 | 224-2946

REPUBLICAN CONFERENCE CHAIR
John Barrasso (R-WY) | SH-405 | 224-2764 | Staff Dir.—Arjun Mody

Senate Officers

SECRETARY OF THE SENATE
Sonceria Ann Berry | S-312 Capitol | 224-3622

SERGEANT AT ARMS
Karen Gibson | S-151 Capitol | 224-2341

PARLIAMENTARIAN
Elizabeth MacDonough | S-133 Capital | 224-6128

CHAPLAIN
Dr. Barry Black | S-332 Capitol | 224-2510

SENATE HISTORIAN
Vacant | SH-201 | 224-6900

MAJORITY SECRETARY
Gary Myrick | S-309 Capitol | 224-3735

MINORITY SECRETARY
Robert M. Duncan | S-337 Capitol | 224-3835

Senate Offices

Document Room | SH-B04 | 224-7701
Majority Cloakroom | S-225 Capitol | 224-4691
Minority Cloakroom | S-226 Capitol | 224-6191

Press Gallery | S-316 Capitol | 224-0241
Switchboard | 224-3121

Area code for all numbers in 202

Senate Re-election Years

CLASS I UP FOR RE-ELECTION IN 2024

Democrats (20)
Baldwin, Tammy (WI) | Brown, Sherrod (OH) | Butler, Laphonza (CA)* | Cantwell, Maria (WA) | Cardin, Ben (MD)* | Carper, Tom (DE)* | Casey, Bob (PA) | Gillibrand, Kirsten (NY) | Heinrich, Martin (NM) | Hirono, Mazie K. (HI) | Kaine, Tim (VA) | Klobuchar, Amy (MN) | Manchin, Joe (WV)* | Menendez, Bob (NJ) | Murphy, Chris (CT) | Rosen, Jacky (NV) | Stabenow, Debbie (MI)* | Tester, Jon (MT) | Warren, Elizabeth (MA) | Whitehouse, Sheldon (RI)

Independents (3)
King, Angus (ME) | Sanders, Bernie (VT) | Sinema, Kyrsten (AZ)

Republicans (10)
Barrasso, John (WY) | Blackburn, Marsha (TN) | Braun, Mike (IN)* | Cramer, Kevin (ND) | Cruz, Ted (TX) | Fischer, Deb (NE) | Hawley, Josh (MO) | Romney, Mitt (UT)* | Scott, Rick (FL) | Wicker, Roger F. (MS)

CLASS II UP FOR RE-ELECTION IN 2026

Democrats (13)
Booker, Cory A. (NJ) | Coons, Chris (DE) | Durbin, Dick (IL) | Hickenlooper, John (CO) | Luján, Ben Ray (NM) | Markey, Edward J. (MA) | Merkley, Jeff (OR) | Ossoff, Jon (GA) | Peters, Gary (MI) | Reed, Jack (RI) | Shaheen, Jeanne (NH) | Smith, Tina (MN) | Warner, Mark R. (VA)

Republicans (20)
Capito, Shelley Moore (WV) | Cassidy, Bill (LA) | Collins, Susan (ME) | Cornyn, John (TX) | Cotton, Tom (AR) | Daines, Steve (MT) | Ernst, Joni (IA) | Graham, Lindsey (SC) | Hagerty, Bill (TN) | Hyde-Smith, Cindy (MS) | Lummis, Cynthia (WY) | Marshall, Roger (KS) | McConnell, Mitch (KY) | Mullin, Markwayne (OK) | Ricketts, Pete (NE)# | Risch, Jim (ID) | Rounds, Mike (SD) | Sullivan, Dan (AK) | Tillis, Thom (NC) | Tuberville, Tommy (AL)

CLASS III UP FOR RE-ELECTION IN 2028

Democrats (15)
Bennet, Michael (CO) | Blumenthal, Richard (CT) | Cortez Masto, Catherine (NV) | Duckworth, Tammy (IL) | Fetterman, John (PA) | Hassan, Maggie (NH) | Kelly, Mark (AZ) | Murray, Patty (WA) | Padilla, Alex (CA) | Schatz, Brian (HI) | Schumer, Chuck (NY) | Van Hollen, Chris (MD) | Warnock, Raphael (GA) | Welch, Peter (VT) | Wyden, Ron (OR)

Republicans (19)
Boozman, John (AR) | Britt, Katie (AL) | Budd, Ted (NC) | Crapo, Mike (ID) | Grassley, Chuck (IA) | Hoeven, John (ND) | Johnson, Ron (WI) | Kennedy, John (LA) | Lankford, James (OK) | Lee, Mike (UT) | Moran, Jerry (KS) | Murkowski, Lisa (AK) | Paul, Rand (KY) | Rubio, Marco (FL) | Schmitt, Eric (MO) | Scott, Tim (SC) | Thune, John (SD) | Vance, J.D. (OH) | Young, Todd (IN)

* = retiring/not seeking re-election
 # = 2024 special election to fill unexpired term

United States Senate

Tammy Baldwin, WI | Junior | 2nd Term | 55% (+11)
SH-141 | 202-224-5653
baldwin.senate.gov | X @senatorbaldwin
Bio—Madison; Madison, WI, 2/11/1962; JD, Univ. of Wisconsin, 1989; lawyer; Dane Co. supervisors, 1986-94; WI Assembly, 1993-99; US House, 1999-2013; US Senate, 2013-present; single; not stated
Committees—Appropriations; Commerce, Science, & Transportation; Health, Education, Labor, & Pensions
District Offices—La Crosse, 608-796-0045; Milwaukee, 414-297-4451; Green Bay, 920-498-2668; Ladysmith, 715-832-8424; Madison, 608-264-5338; Eau Claire, 715-832-8424

Democrat

John Barrasso, WY | Senior | 3rd Term | 66% (+37)
SD-307 | 202-224-6441 | Fax: 224-1724
barrasso.senate.gov | X @senjohnbarrasso
Bio—Casper; Reading, PA, 7/21/1952; MD, Georgetown Univ., 1978; orthopedic surgeon; WY Senate, 2002-07; US Senate, 2007-present; wid.; Presbyterian
Committees—Energy & Natural Resources (Rnk. Mem.); Finance; Foreign Relations
District Offices—Casper, 307-261-6413; Cheyenne, 307-772-2451; Riverton, 307-856-6642; Rock Springs, 307-362-5012; Sheridan, 307-672-6456

Republican

Michael Bennet, CO | Senior | 4th Term | 55% (+15)
SR-261 | 202-224-5852 | Fax: 228-5097
bennet.senate.gov | X @senatorbennet
Bio—Denver; New Delhi, India, 11/28/1964; JD, Yale Univ., 1993; lawyer, financial executive, education administrator; US Senate, 2009-present; m. Susan Daggett; not stated
Committees—Agriculture, Nutrition, & Forestry; Finance; Rules & Administration; Intelligence
District Offices—Denver, 303-455-7600; Colorado Springs, 719-328-1100; Grand Junction, 970-241-6631; Fort Collins, 970-224-2200; Durango, 970-259-1710; Pueblo, 719-542-7550; Alamosa, 719-587-0096

Democrat

Marsha Blackburn, TN | Senior | 1st Term | 54% (+11)
SD-357 | 202-224-3344 | Fax: 228-0566
blackburn.senate.gov | X @marshablackburn
Bio—Brentwood; Laurel, MS, 6/6/1952; BS, Mississippi St. Univ., 1973; business owner; TN Senate, 1998-2002; US House, 2003-19; US Senate, 2019-present; m. Chuck; Presbyterian
Committees—Commerce, Science, & Transportation; Finance; Judiciary; Veterans' Affairs
District Offices—Memphis, 901-527-9199; Jackson, 731-660-3971; Nashville, 629-800-6600; Chattanooga, 423-541-2939; Knoxville, 865-540-3781; Johnson City, 423-753-4009

Republican

Richard Blumenthal, CT | Senior | 3rd Term | 55% (+13)
SH-706 | 202-224-2823 | Fax: 224-9673
blumenthal.senate.gov | X @senblumenthal
Bio—Greenwich; Brooklyn, NY, 2/13/1946; JD, Yale Univ., 1973; USMCR, 1970-76; White House aide, lawyer; CT House, 1984-87; CT Senate, 1987-90; CT attorney general, 1991-2010; US Senate, 2011-present; m. Cynthia; Jewish
Committees—Armed Services; Homeland Security & Governmental Affairs; Judiciary; Veterans' Affairs; Aging
District Offices—Hartford, 860-258-6940; Bridgeport, 203-330-0598

Democrat

United States Senate

Cory A. Booker, NJ | Junior | 3rd Term | 57% (+16)
SH-717 | 202-224-3224 | Fax: 224-8378
booker.senate.gov | X @senbooker
Bio—Newark; Washington, DC, 4/27/1969; JD, Yale Univ., 1997; lawyer; Newark city council 1998-2002; Newark mayor, 2006-13; US Senate, 2013-present; single; Baptist
Committees—Agriculture, Nutrition, & Forestry; Foreign Relations; Judiciary; Small Business & Entrepreneurship
District Offices—Newark, 973-639-8700; Camden, 856-338-8922

Democrat

John Boozman, AR | Senior | 3rd Term | 65% (+35)
SD-555 | 202-224-4843
boozman.senate.gov | X @johnboozman
Bio—Rogers; Shreveport, LA, 12/10/1950; OD, Southern Col. of Optometry, 1977; optometrist, business owner, rancher; US House, 2001-2011; US Senate, 2011-present; m. Cathy; Southern Baptist
Committees—Agriculture, Nutrition, & Forestry (Rnk. Mem.); Appropriations; Environment & Public Works; Veterans' Affairs
District Offices—Little Rock, 501-372-7153; Fort Smith, 479-573-0189; Lowell, 479-725-0400; Mountain Home, 870-424-0129; Jonesboro, 870-268-6925; Stuttgart, 870-672-6941; El Dorado, 870-863-4641

Republican

Mike Braun, IN | Junior | 1st Term | 50% (+6)
SR-404 | 202-224-4814
braun.senate.gov | X @senatorbraun
Bio—Jasper; Jasper, IN, 3/24/1954; MBA, Harvard Univ., 1978; business owner; IN House, 2014-17; US Senate, 2019-present; m. Maureen; Catholic
Committees—Agriculture, Nutrition, & Forestry; Budget; Health, Education, Labor, & Pensions; Aging (Rnk. Mem.)
District Offices—Indianapolis, 317-822-8240; Hammond, 219-937-9650

Republican

Katie Britt, AL | Junior | 1st Term | 66% (+36)
SH-502 | 202-224-5744
britt.senate.gov | X @senkatiebritt
Bio—Montgomery; Enterprise, AL, 2/2/1982; JD, Univ. of Alabama, 2013; lawyer, congressional staffer; US Senate, 2023-present; m. Wesley; Methodist
Committees—Appropriations; Banking, Housing, & Urban Affairs; Rules & Administration
District Offices—Birmingham, 205-731-1384; Huntsville, 256-772-0460; Montgomery, 334-223-7303; Mobile, 251-694-4164

Republican

Sherrod Brown, OH | Senior | 3rd Term | 53% (+7)
SH-503 | 202-224-2315 | Fax: 228-6321
brown.senate.gov | X @sensherrodbrown
Bio—Cleveland; Mansfield, OH, 11/9/1952; MA, Ohio St. Univ., 1981; educator, public official; OH House, 1975-82; OH secretary of state, 1983-91; US House, 1993-2007; US Senate, 2007-present; m. Connie Schultz; Lutheran
Committees—Agriculture, Nutrition, & Forestry; Banking, Housing, & Urban Affairs (Chair); Finance; Veterans' Affairs
District Offices—Cincinnati, 513-684-1021; Cleveland, 216-522-7272; Columbus, 614-469-2083; Lorain, 440-242-4100

Democrat

United States Senate

Ted Budd, NC | Junior | 1st Term | 50% (+3)
SR-304 | 202-224-3154
budd.senate.gov | X @sentedbuddnc
Bio—Advance; Davie County, NC, 10/21/1971; MBA, Wake Forest Univ., 2007; business owner; US House, 2017-23; US Senate, 2023-present; m. Amy Kate; Christian
Committees—Armed Services; Commerce, Science, & Transportation; Health, Education, Labor, & Pensions; Small Business & Entrepreneurship
District Offices—Advance, 336-941-4470; Asheville, 828-333-4130; Wilmington, 910-218-7600

Republican

Laphonza Butler, CA | Junior | 1st Term | Appt.
SH-112 | 202-224-3841
butler.senate.gov | X @senlaphonza
Bio—Los Angeles; Magnolia, MS, 5/11/1979; BA, Jackson St. Univ., 2001; union organizer, campaign strategist; US Senate, 2023-present; m. Neneki Lee; not stated
Committees—Banking, Housing, & Urban Affairs; Homeland Security & Governmental Affairs; Judiciary; Rules & Administration
District Offices—San Francisco, 415-393-0707; Los Angeles, 310-914-7300; San Diego, 619-231-9712; Fresno, 559-485-7430

Democrat

Maria Cantwell, WA | Junior | 4th Term | 58% (+17)
SH-511 | 202-224-3441 | Fax: 228-0514
cantwell.senate.gov | X @senatorcantwell
Bio—Edmonds; Indianapolis, IN, 10/13/1958; BA, Miami Univ., 1980; public relations consultant; WA House, 1987-93; US House, 1993-95; US Senate, 2001-present; single; Catholic
Committees—Commerce, Science, & Transportation (Chair); Energy & Natural Resources; Finance; Small Business & Entrepreneurship; Indian Affairs; Joint Taxation
District Offices—Seattle, 206-220-6400; Spokane, 509-353-2507; Tacoma, 253-572-2281; Everett, 425-303-0114; Vancouver, 360-696-7838; Richland, 509-946-8106

Democrat

Shelley Moore Capito, WV | Junior | 2nd Term | 70% (+43)
SR-170 | 202-224-6472
capito.senate.gov | X @sencapito
Bio—Charleston; Glendale, WV, 11/26/1953; MEd, Univ. of Virginia, 1976; college counselor; WV House, 1997-2001; US House, 2001-15; US Senate, 2015-present; m. Charles; Presbyterian
Committees—Appropriations; Commerce, Science, & Transportation; Environment & Public Works (Rnk. Mem.); Rules & Administration
District Offices—Charleston, 304-347-5372; Martinsburg, 304-262-9285; Morgantown, 304-292-2310

Republican

Ben Cardin, MD | Senior | 3rd Term | 64% (+35)
SH-509 | 202-224-4524
cardin.senate.gov | X @senatorcardin
Bio—Baltimore; Baltimore, MD, 10/5/1943; JD, Univ. of Maryland, 1967; lawyer; MD House, 1967-87; US House, 1987-2007; US Senate, 2007-present; m. Myrna; Jewish
Committees—Environment & Public Works; Finance; Foreign Relations (Chair); Small Business & Entrepreneurship
District Offices—Baltimore, 410-962-4436; Bowie, 301-860-0414; Easton, 301-860-0414; Cumberland, 301-777-2957; Rockville, 301-762-2974

Democrat

Notes

United States Senate

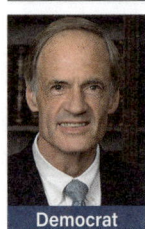

Tom Carper, DE | Senior | 4th Term | 59% (+22)
SH-513 | 202-224-2441 | Fax: 228-2190
carper.senate.gov | X @senatorcarper
Bio—Wilmington; Beckley, WV, 1/23/1947; MBA, Univ. of Delaware, 1975; USN, 1968-73; USNR, 1973-91; public official; DE treasurer, 1976-83; US House, 1983-93; DE governor, 1993-2001; US Senate, 2001-present; m. Martha; Presbyterian
Committees—Environment & Public Works (Chair); Finance; Homeland Security & Governmental Affairs
District Offices—Wilmington, 302-573-6291; Dover, 302-674-3308; Georgetown, 302-856-7690

Democrat

Bob Casey, PA | Senior | 3rd Term | 55% (+13)
SR-393 | 202-224-6324 | Fax: 228-0604
casey.senate.gov | X @senbobcasey
Bio—Scranton; Scranton, PA, 4/13/1960; JD, Catholic Univ. of America, 1988; lawyer; PA auditor general, 1997-2005; PA treasurer, 2005-06; US Senate, 2007-present; m. Terese; Catholic
Committees—Finance; Health, Education, Labor, & Pensions; Intelligence; Aging (Chair)
District Offices—Allentown, 610-782-9470; Erie, 814-240-5213; Harrisburg, 717-231-7540; Philadelphia, 215-405-9660; Pittsburgh, 412-803-7370; Scranton, 570-941-0930; State College, 814-357-0314

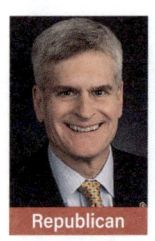

Democrat

Bill Cassidy, LA | Senior | 2nd Term | 59% (+40)
SD-455 | 202-224-5824
cassidy.senate.gov | X @senbillcassidy
Bio—Baton Rouge; Highland Park, IL, 9/28/1957; MD, Louisiana St. Univ., 1983; physician; LA Senate, 2006-08; US House, 2009-15; US Senate, 2015-present; m. Laura; Christian
Committees—Energy & Natural Resources; Finance; Health, Education, Labor, & Pensions (Rnk. Mem.); Veterans' Affairs
District Offices—Alexandria, 318-448-7176; Baton Rouge, 225-929-7711; Lafayette, 337-261-1400; Metairie, 504-838-0130; Lake Charles, 337-602-7253; Monroe, 318-324-2111; Shreveport, 318-798-3215

Republican

Susan Collins, ME | Senior | 5th Term | 50% (+9)
SD-413 | 202-224-2523
collins.senate.gov | X @senatorcollins
Bio—Bangor; Caribou, ME, 12/7/1952; BA, St. Lawrence Univ., 1975; congressional staffer; US Senate, 1997-present; m. Thomas Daffron; Catholic
Committees—Appropriations (Rnk. Mem.); Health, Education, Labor, & Pensions; Intelligence
District Offices—Augusta, 207-622-8414; Bangor, 207-945-0417; Biddeford, 207-283-1101; Caribou, 207-493-7873; Lewiston, 207-784-6969; Portland, 207-618-5560

Republican

Chris Coons, DE | Junior | 3rd Term | 59% (+22)
SR-218 | 202-224-5042
coons.senate.gov | X @chriscoons
Bio—Wilmington; Greenwich, CT, 9/9/1963; JD, Yale Univ., 1992; lawyer; New Castle Co. council, 2001-05; New Castle Co. executive, 2005-10; US Senate, 2010-present; m. Annie; Presbyterian
Committees—Appropriations; Foreign Relations; Judiciary; Small Business & Entrepreneurship; Ethics (Chair)
District Offices—Wilmington, 302-573-6345; Dover, 302-736-5601

Democrat

Notes

United States Senate

John Cornyn, TX | Senior | 4th Term | 53% (+10)
SH-517 | 202-224-2934
cornyn.senate.gov
Bio—Austin; Houston, TX, 2/2/1952; LLM, Univ. of Virginia, 1995; attorney; TX Supreme Court, 1990-97; TX attorney general, 1999-2002; US Senate, 2002-present; m. Sandy; Christian
Committees—Finance; Judiciary; Intelligence
District Offices—Houston, 713-572-3337; Harlingen, 956-423-0162; Lubbock, 806-472-7533; Dallas, 972-239-1310; San Antonio, 210-224-7485; Tyler, 903-593-0902; Austin, 512-469-6034

Republican

Catherine Cortez Masto, NV | Senior | 2nd Term | 48% (+.8)
SH-520 | 202-224-3542
cortezmasto.senate.gov | X @sencortezmasto
Bio—Las Vegas; Las Vegas, NV, 3/29/1964; JD, Gonzaga Univ., 1990; lawyer, federal prosecutor; NV attorney general, 2007-15; US Senate, 2017-present; m. Paul; Catholic
Committees—Banking, Housing, & Urban Affairs; Energy & Natural Resources; Finance; Indian Affairs
District Offices—Las Vegas, 702-388-5020; Reno, 775-686-5750

Democrat

Tom Cotton, AR | Junior | 2nd Term | 66% (+33)
SR-326 | 202-224-2353
cotton.senate.gov | X @sentomcotton
Bio—Little Rock; Dardanelle, AR, 5/13/1977; JD, Harvard Univ., 2002; USA, 2004-09; lawyer, management consultant, farmer; US House, 2013-15; US Senate, 2015-present; m. Anna; Methodist
Committees—Armed Services; Judiciary; Intelligence; Joint Economic
District Offices—Rogers, 479-751-0879; Jonesboro, 870-933-6223; Little Rock, 501-223-9081; El Dorado, 870-864-8582

Republican

Kevin Cramer, ND | Junior | 1st Term | 55% (+11)
SH-313 | 202-224-2043
cramer.senate.gov | X @senkevincramer
Bio—Bismarck; Rolla, ND, 1/21/1961; MA, Univ. of Mary, 2003; public official; ND public service commissioner, 2003-12; US House, 2013-19; US Senate, 2019-present; m. Kris; Protestant
Committees—Armed Services; Banking, Housing, & Urban Affairs; Environment & Public Works; Veterans' Affairs
District Offices—Fargo, 701-232-5094; Minot, 701-837-6141; Bismarck, 701-204-0500; Grand Forks, 701-402-4540; Williston, 701-441-7230

Republican

Mike Crapo, ID | Senior | 5th Term | 60% (+32)
SD-239 | 202-224-6142 | Fax: 228-1375
crapo.senate.gov | X @mikecrapo
Bio—Idaho Falls; Idaho Falls, ID, 5/20/1951; JD, Harvard Univ., 1977; lawyer; ID Senate, 1985-92; US House, 1993-99; US Senate, 1999-present; m. Susan; Mormon
Committees—Banking, Housing, & Urban Affairs; Budget; Finance (Rnk. Mem.); Joint Taxation
District Offices—Boise, 208-334-1776; Idaho Falls, 208-522-9779; Pocatello, 208-236-6775; Coeur d' Alene, 208-664-5490; Lewiston, 208-743-1492; Twin Falls, 208-734-2515

Republican

United States Senate

Ted Cruz, TX | Junior | 2nd Term | 50% (+3)
SR-167 | 202-224-5922
cruz.senate.gov | X @sentedcruz
Bio—Houston; Calgary, Canada, 12/22/1970; JD, Harvard Univ., 1995; lawyer; US Senate, 2013-present; m. Heidi; Southern Baptist
Committees—Commerce, Science, & Transportation (Rnk. Mem.); Foreign Relations; Judiciary; Rules & Administration
District Offices—Austin, 512-916-5834; Dallas, 214-599-8749; Houston, 713-718-3057; San Antonio, 210-340-2885; Tyler, 903-593-5130; McAllen, 956-686-7339

Republican

Steve Daines, MT | Junior | 2nd Term | 55% (+10)
SH-320 | 202-224-2651 | Fax: 228-1236
daines.senate.gov
Bio—Bozeman; Van Nuys, CA, 8/20/1962; BS, Montana St. Univ., 1984; businessman; US House, 2013-15; US Senate, 2015-present; m. Cindy; Presbyterian
Committees—Banking, Housing, & Urban Affairs; Energy & Natural Resources; Finance; Indian Affairs
District Offices—Bozeman, 406-587-3446; Great Falls, 406-453-0148; Helena, 406-443-3189; Billings, 406-245-6822; Missoula, 406-549-8198; Kalispell, 406-257-3765; Sidney, 406-482-9010

Republican

Tammy Duckworth, IL | Junior | 2nd Term | 56% (+15)
SH-524 | 202-224-2854
duckworth.senate.gov | X @senduckworth
Bio—Hoffman Estates; Bangkok, Thailand, 3/12/1968; MA, George Washington University, 1992; USAR, 1992-96; ILARNG, 1996-2014; public official; US House, 2013-17; US Senate, 2017-present; m. Bryan Bowlsbey; not stated
Committees—Armed Services; Commerce, Science, & Transportation; Foreign Relations; Small Business & Entrepreneurship
District Offices—Chicago, 312-886-3506; Springfield, 217-528-6124; Carbondale, 618-677-7000; Rock Island, 309-606-7060; Belleville, 618-722-7070

Democrat

Dick Durbin, IL | Senior | 5th Term | 54% (+16)
SH-711 | 202-224-2152
durbin.senate.gov | X @senatordurbin
Bio—Springfield; East St. Louis, IL, 11/21/1944; JD, Georgetown Univ., 1969; lawyer; US House, 1983-97; US Senate, 1997-present; m. Loretta; Catholic
Committees—Agriculture, Nutrition, & Forestry; Appropriations; Judiciary (Chair); Majority Whip
District Offices—Chicago, 312-353-4952; Springfield, 217-492-4062; Carbondale, 618-351-1122; Rock Island, 309-786-5173

Democrat

Joni Ernst, IA | Junior | 2nd Term | 50% (+6)
SR-260 | 202-224-3254 | Fax: 224-9369
ernst.senate.gov | X @senjoniernst
Bio—Red Oak; Red Oak, IA, 7/1/1970; MPA, Columbia Col., 1995; USAR, 1993-2001; IAARNG, 2001-present; military officer, public official; IA Senate 2011-14; US Senate, 2015-present; div.; Lutheran
Committees—Agriculture, Nutrition, & Forestry; Armed Services; Small Business & Entrepreneurship (Rnk. Mem.)
District Offices—Cedar Rapids, 319-365-4504; Council Bluffs, 712-352-1167; Davenport, 563-322-0677; Des Moines, 515-284-4574; Sioux City, 712-252-1550

Republican

Notes

United States Senate

John Fetterman, PA | Junior | 1st Term | 51% (+5)
SR-142 | 202-224-4254
fetterman.senate.gov | X @senfettermanpa
Bio—Braddock; Reading, PA, 8/15/1969; MPP, Harvard Univ., 1999; social worker, non-profit executive; Braddock mayor, 2006-19; PA lt. governor, 2019-23; US Senate, 2023-present; m. Gisele; not stated
Committees—Agriculture, Nutrition, & Forestry; Banking, Housing, & Urban Affairs; Environment & Public Works; Aging; Joint Economic
District Offices—Philadelphia, 215-241-1090; Pittsburgh, 412-803-3501; Wilkes-Barre, 570-820-4088; Harrisburg, 717-782-3951; Erie, 814-453-3010

Democrat

Deb Fischer, NE | Senior | 2nd Term | 57% (+19)
SR-448 | 202-224-6551 | Fax: 228-1325
fischer.senate.gov | X @senatorfischer
Bio—Lincoln; Lincoln, NE, 3/1/1951; BS, Univ. of Nebraska, 1988; rancher; NE Legislature, 2005-12; US Senate, 2013-present; m. Bruce; Presbyterian
Committees—Agriculture, Nutrition, & Forestry; Appropriations; Armed Services; Commerce, Science, & Transportation; Rules & Administration (Rnk. Mem.); Ethics; Joint Library; Joint Printing
District Offices—Kearney, 308-234-2361; Lincoln, 402-441-4600; Omaha, 402-391-3411; Scottsbluff, 308-630-2329

Republican

Kirsten Gillibrand, NY | Junior | 3rd Term | 67% (+32)
SR-478 | 202-224-4451 | Fax: 228-4977
gillibrand.senate.gov | X @gillibrandny
Bio—Albany; Albany, NY, 12/9/1966; JD, Univ. of California, Los Angeles, 1991; lawyer; US House, 2007-09; US Senate, 2009-present; m. Jonathan; Catholic
Committees—Agriculture, Nutrition, & Forestry; Armed Services; Intelligence; Aging
District Offices—Albany, 518-431-0120; Buffalo, 716-854-9725; Melville, 631-249-2825; Yonkers, 845-875-4585; Lowville, 315-376-6118; New York, 212-688-6262; Rochester, 585-263-6250; Syracuse, 315-448-0470

Democrat

Lindsey Graham, SC | Senior | 4th Term | 54% (+10)
SR-211 | 202-224-5972 | Fax: 224-3808
lgraham.senate.gov
Bio—Seneca; Central, SC, 7/9/1955; JD, Univ. of South Carolina, 1981; USAF, 1982-88; SCANG, 1989-95; USAFR, 1995-present; lawyer; SC House 1992-94; US House, 1995-2003; US Senate, 2003-present; single; Baptist
Committees—Appropriations; Budget; Environment & Public Works; Judiciary (Rnk. Mem.)
District Offices—Greenville, 864-250-1417; Columbia, 803-933-0112; Florence, 843-669-1505; Charleston, 843-849-3887; Rock Hill, 803-366-2828; Pendleton, 864-646-4090

Republican

Chuck Grassley, IA | Senior | 8th Term | 55% (+12)
SH-135 | 202-224-3744 | Fax: 224-6020
grassley.senate.gov | X @chuckgrassley
Bio—New Hartford; New Hartford, IA, 9/17/1933; MA, Univ. of Northern Iowa, 1956; farmer, university instructor; IA House, 1959-74; US House, 1975-81; US Senate, 1981-present; m. Barbara; Baptist
Committees—Agriculture, Nutrition, & Forestry; Budget (Rnk. Mem.); Finance; Judiciary; Joint Taxation
District Offices—Sioux City, 712-233-1860; Cedar Rapids, 319-363-6832; Council Bluffs, 712-322-7103; Davenport, 563-322-4331; Des Moines, 515-288-1145; Waterloo, 319-232-6657

Republican

United States Senate

Bill Hagerty, TN | Junior | 1st Term | 62% (+27)
SR-251 | 202-224-4944
hagerty.senate.gov | X @senatorhagerty
Bio—Nashville; Gallatin, TN, 8/14/1959; JD, Vanderbilt Univ., 1984; White House staffer, finance executive; US ambassador to Japan, 2017-19; US Senate, 2021-present; m. Chrissy; Episcopalian
Committees—Appropriations; Banking, Housing, & Urban Affairs; Foreign Relations; Rules & Administration; Joint Printing
District Offices—Memphis, 901-544-4224; Jackson, 731-234-9358; Nashville, 615-736-5129; Cookeville, 931-400-7080; Chattanooga, 423-752-5337; Knoxville, 865-545-4253; Blountville, 423-325-6240

Republican

Maggie Hassan, NH | Junior | 2nd Term | 53% (+9)
SH-324 | 202-224-3324
hassan.senate.gov | X @senatorhassan
Bio—Newfields; Boston, MA, 2/27/1958; JD, Northeastern Univ., 1985; attorney; NH Senate, 2004-10; NH governor, 2013-16; US Senate, 2017-present; m. Tom; Congregationalist
Committees—Finance; Health, Education, Labor, & Pensions; Homeland Security & Governmental Affairs; Veterans' Affairs; Joint Economic
District Offices—Manchester, 603-622-2204; Portsmouth, 603-433-4445; Berlin, 603-752-6190; Concord, 603-622-2204

Democrat

Josh Hawley, MO | Senior | 1st Term | 51% (+6)
SR-115 | 202-224-6154 | Fax: 228-0526
hawley.senate.gov | X @senhawleypress
Bio—Ozark; Springdale, AR, 12/31/1979; JD, Yale Univ., 2006; lawyer, law professor; MO attorney general, 2017-18; US Senate, 2019-present; m. Erin; Protestant
Committees—Energy & Natural Resources; Homeland Security & Governmental Affairs; Judiciary; Small Business & Entrepreneurship
District Offices—Cape Girardeau, 573-334-5995; Columbia, 573-554-1919; Kansas City, 816-960-4694; Springfield, 417-869-4433; St. Louis, 314-354-7060

Republican

Martin Heinrich, NM | Senior | 2nd Term | 54% (+24)
SH-709 | 202-224-5521 | Fax: 228-2841
heinrich.senate.gov | X @martinheinrich
Bio—Albuquerque; Fallon, NV, 10/17/1971; BS, Univ. of Missouri, 1995; engineer, business owner; Albuquerque city council, 2003-07; US House, 2009-13; US Senate, 2013-present; m. Julie; Lutheran
Committees—Appropriations; Energy & Natural Resources; Intelligence; Joint Economic (Chair)
District Offices—Albuquerque, 505-346-6601; Las Cruces, 575-523-6561; Santa Fe, 505-988-6647; Farmington, 505-325-5030; Roswell, 575-622-7113

Democrat

John Hickenlooper, CO | Junior | 1st Term | 53% (+9)
SR-374 | 202-224-5941
hickenlooper.senate.gov | X @senatorhick
Bio—Denver; Narbeth, PA, 2/7/1952; MS, Wesleyan Univ., 1980; geologist, restaurant owner; Denver mayor, 2003-11; CO governor, 2011-19; US Senate, 2021-present; m. Robin Pringle; Quaker
Committees—Commerce, Science, & Transportation; Energy & Natural Resources; Health, Education, Labor, & Pensions; Small Business & Entrepreneurship
District Offices—Denver, 303-244-1628; Colorado Springs, 719-632-6706; Greeley, 970-352-5546; Fort Collins, 970-484-3502; Glenwood Springs, 970-989-7075; Grand Junction, 970-822-4530; Durango, 970-880-7236

Democrat

Notes

United States Senate

Mazie K. Hirono, HI | Junior | 2nd Term | 69% (+41)
SH-109 | 202-224-6361 | Fax: 224-2126
hirono.senate.gov | X @maziehirono
Bio—Honolulu; Fukushima, Japan, 11/3/1947; JD, Georgetown Univ., 1978; lawyer; HI House, 1981-94; HI lt. governor, 1994-2002; US House, 2007-13; US Senate, 2013-present; m. Leighton Kim Oshima; Buddhist
Committees—Armed Services; Energy & Natural Resources; Judiciary; Small Business & Entrepreneurship; Veterans' Affairs
District Offices—Honolulu, 808-522-8970

Democrat

John Hoeven, ND | Senior | 3rd Term | 56% (+31)
SR-338 | 202-224-2551
hoeven.senate.gov | X @senjohnhoeven
Bio—Bismarck; Bismarck, ND, 3/13/1957; MBA, Northwestern Univ., 1981; bank executive; ND governor, 2000-10; US Senate, 2011-present; m. Mikey; Catholic
Committees—Agriculture, Nutrition, & Forestry; Appropriations; Energy & Natural Resources; Indian Affairs
District Offices—Bismarck, 701-250-4618; Fargo, 701-239-5389; Grand Forks, 701-746-8972; Minot, 701-838-1361; Watford City, 701-609-2727

Republican

Cindy Hyde-Smith, MS | Junior | 2nd Term | 54% (+10)
SH-702 | 202-224-5054 | Fax: 224-5321
hydesmith.senate.gov | X @senhydesmith
Bio—Brookhaven; Brookhaven, MS, 5/10/1959; BA, Univ. of Southern Mississippi, 1981; cattle farmer; MS Senate 2000-12; MS agriculture & commerce commissioner, 2012-18; US Senate, 2018-present; m. Mike; Baptist
Committees—Agriculture, Nutrition, & Forestry; Appropriations; Energy & Natural Resources; Rules & Administration; Joint Library
District Offices—Jackson, 601-965-4459; Gulfport, 228-867-9710; Oxford, 662-236-1018; Brookhaven, 601-748-8024

Republican

Ron Johnson, WI | Senior | 3rd Term | 50% (+1)
SH-328 | 202-224-5323 | Fax: 228-6965
ronjohnson.senate.gov | X @senronjohnson
Bio—Oshkosh; Mankato, MN, 4/8/1955; BS, Univ. of Minnesota, 1977; plastics manufacturer, accountant; US Senate, 2011-present; m. Jane; Lutheran
Committees—Budget; Finance; Homeland Security & Governmental Affairs
District Offices—Milwaukee, 414-276-7282; Madison, 608-240-9629; Oshkosh, 920-230-7250

Republican

Tim Kaine, VA | Junior | 2nd Term | 57% (+16)
SR-231 | 202-224-4024 | Fax: 228-6363
kaine.senate.gov
Bio—Richmond; St. Paul, MN, 2/26/1958; JD, Harvard Univ., 1983; lawyer; Richmond city council, 1994-98; Richmond mayor, 1998-2001; VA lt. governor, 2002-06; VA governor, 2006-10; US Senate, 2013-present; m. Anne; Catholic
Committees—Armed Services; Budget; Foreign Relations; Health, Education, Labor, & Pensions
District Offices—Richmond, 804-771-2221; Roanoke, 540-682-5693; Virginia Beach, 757-518-1674; Manassas, 703-361-3192; Abingdon, 276-525-4790; Fredericksburg, 540-369-7667

Democrat

Notes

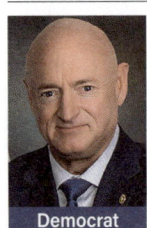

United States Senate

Mark Kelly, AZ | Junior | 2nd Term | 51% (+5)
SH-516 | 202-224-2235
kelly.senate.gov | X @senmarkkelly
Bio—Tucson; Orange, NJ, 2/21/1964; MS, U.S. Naval Postgraduate School, 1994; USN, 1987-2012; astronaut, business owner; US Senate, 2020-present; m. Gabby Giffords; Catholic
Committees—Armed Services; Environment & Public Works; Intelligence; Aging; Joint Economic
District Offices—Phoenix, 602-671-7901; Tucson, 520-475-5177

Democrat

John Kennedy, LA | Junior | 2nd Term | 61% (+44)
SR-437 | 202-224-4623
kennedy.senate.gov | X @senjohnkennedy
Bio—Madisonville; Centreville, MS, 11/21/1951; BCL, Oxford Univ., 1979; lawyer; LA treasurer, 1999-2016; US Senate, 2016-present; m. Becky; Methodist
Committees—Appropriations; Banking, Housing, & Urban Affairs; Budget; Judiciary; Small Business & Entrepreneurship
District Offices—Alexandria, 318-445-2892; Baton Rouge, 225-926-8033; Houma, 985-851-0956; Lafayette, 337-269-5980; Lake Charles, 337-573-6800; Mandeville, 985-809-8153; Monroe, 318-361-1489; New Orleans, 504-581-6190; Shreveport, 318-670-5192

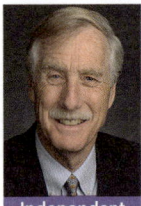

Republican

Angus King, ME | Junior | 2nd Term | 53% (+19)
SH-133 | 202-224-5344
king.senate.gov | X @senangusking
Bio—Brunswick; Alexandria, VA, 3/31/1944; JD, Univ. of Virginia, 1969; lawyer, television host, business owner; ME governor, 1995-2003; US Senate, 2013-present; m. Mary Herman; Episcopalian
Committees—Armed Services; Energy & Natural Resources; Veterans' Affairs; Intelligence
District Offices—Augusta, 207-622-8292; Bangor, 207-945-8000; Biddeford, 207-352-5216; Portland, 207-245-1565; Presque Isle, 207-764-5124

Independent

Amy Klobuchar, MN | Senior | 3rd Term | 60% (+24)
SD-425 | 202-224-3244 | Fax: 228-2186
klobuchar.senate.gov | X @senamyklobuchar
Bio—Minneapolis; Plymouth, MN, 5/25/1960; JD, Univ. of Chicago, 1985; lawyer; Hennepin Co. attorney, 1999-2006; US Senate, 2007-present; m. John Bessler; Congregationalist
Committees—Agriculture, Nutrition, & Forestry; Commerce, Science, & Transportation; Judiciary; Rules & Administration (Chair); Joint Economic; Joint Library (Chair); Joint Printing
District Offices—Minneapolis, 612-727-5220; Rochester, 507-288-5321; Moorhead, 218-287-2219; Virginia, 218-741-9690

Democrat

James Lankford, OK | Senior | 3rd Term | 64% (+32)
SH-316 | 202-224-5754
lankford.senate.gov | X @senatorlankford
Bio—Oklahoma City; Dallas, TX, 3/4/1968; MDiv, Southwestern Theological Baptist Seminary, 1994; youth camp director; US House, 2011-15; US Senate, 2015-present; m. Cindy; Baptist
Committees—Finance; Homeland Security & Governmental Affairs; Ethics (Vice Chair); Intelligence
District Offices—Oklahoma City, 405-231-4941; Tulsa, 918-581-7651

Republican

United States Senate

Mike Lee, UT | Senior | 3rd Term | 53% (+10)
SR-363 | 202-224-5444
lee.senate.gov | X @senmikelee
Bio—Alpine; Mesa, AZ, 6/4/1971; JD, Brigham Young Univ., 1997; lawyer; US Senate, 2010-present; m. Sharon; Mormon
Committees—Budget; Energy & Natural Resources; Judiciary; Joint Economic
District Offices—Ogden, 801-392-9633; Salt Lake City, 801-524-5933; St. George, 435-628-5514; Vernal, 435-503-9335

Republican

Ben Ray Luján, NM | Junior | 1st Term | 51% (+6)
SR-498 | 202-224-6621 | Fax: 224-3370
lujan.senate.gov | X @senatorlujan
Bio—Nambe; Santa Fe, NM, 6/7/1972; BBA, New Mexico Highlands Univ., 2007; public official; US House, 2009-21; US Senate, 2021-present; single; Catholic
Committees—Agriculture, Nutrition, & Forestry; Budget; Commerce, Science, & Transportation; Health, Education, Labor, & Pensions; Indian Affairs
District Offices—Albuquerque, 505-337-7023; Las Cruces, 575-288-4644; Las Vegas, 505-398-9465; Portales, 575-252-6188; Santa Fe, 505-230-7040

Democrat

Cynthia Lummis, WY | Junior | 1st Term | 71% (+45)
SR-127A | 202-224-3424
lummis.senate.gov | X @senlummis
Bio—Cheyenne; Cheyenne, WY, 9/10/1954; JD, Univ. of Wyoming, 1985; rancher, lawyer; WY House, 1979-83, 1985-93; WY Senate, 1993-95; WY treasurer, 1999-2007; US House, 2009-17; US Senate, 2021-present; wid.; Lutheran
Committees—Banking, Housing, & Urban Affairs; Commerce, Science, & Transportation; Environment & Public Works
District Offices—Casper, 307-261-6572; Cheyenne, 307-772-2477; Cody, 307-527-9444; Jackson, 307-886-6050; Afton, 307-248-1736; Sundance, 307-283-3461

Republican

Joe Manchin, WV | Senior | 3rd Term | 49% (+3)
SH-306 | 202-224-3954 | Fax: 228-0002
manchin.senate.gov | X @senjoemanchin
Bio—Fairmont; Farmington, WV, 8/24/1947; BA, West Virginia Univ., 1970; businessman; WV House, 1982-86; WV Senate, 1986-96; WV secretary of state, 2001-05; WV governor, 2005-10; US Senate, 2010-present; m. Gayle; Catholic
Committees—Appropriations; Armed Services; Energy & Natural Resources (Chair); Veterans' Affairs
District Offices—Charleston, 304-342-5855; Martinsburg, 304-264-4626; Fairmont, 304-368-0567

Democrat

Edward J. Markey, MA | Junior | 3rd Term | 64% (+32)
SD-255 | 202-224-2742
markey.senate.gov | X @senmarkey
Bio—Malden; Malden, MA, 7/11/1946; JD, Boston Col., 1972; USAR, 1968-73; lawyer; MA House, 1973-76; US House, 1976-2013; US Senate, 2013-present; m. Susan Blumenthal; Catholic
Committees—Commerce, Science, & Transportation; Environment & Public Works; Health, Education, Labor, & Pensions; Small Business & Entrepreneurship
District Offices—Boston, 617-565-8519; Springfield, 413-785-4610

Democrat

United States Senate

Roger Marshall, KS | Junior | 1st Term | 53% (+11)
SR-479A | 202-224-4774
marshall.senate.gov | X @rogermarshallmd
Bio—Great Bend; El Dorado, KS, 8/9/1960; MD, Univ. of Kansas, 1987; USAR, 1984-91; physician; US House, 2017-21; US Senate, 2021-present; m. Laina; Christian
Committees—Agriculture, Nutrition, & Forestry; Budget; Health, Education, Labor, & Pensions; Homeland Security & Governmental Affairs
District Offices—Garden City, 620-765-7800; Overland Park, 913-879-7070; Pittsburg, 620-404-7016; Salina, 785-829-9000; Topeka, 785-414-7501; Wichita, 316-803-6120; Kansas City, 913-549-1570

Republican

Mitch McConnell, KY | Senior | 7th Term | 57% (+20)
SR-317 | 202-224-2541 | Fax: 224-2499
mcconnell.senate.gov | X @mcconnellpress
Bio—Louisville; Tuscumbia, AL, 2/20/1942; JD, Univ. of Kentucky, 1967; lawyer; Jefferson Co. judge-executive, 1978-85; US Senate, 1985-present; m. Elaine Chao; Baptist
Committees—Agriculture, Nutrition, & Forestry; Appropriations; Rules & Administration; Intelligence (Ex Officio); Minority Leader
District Offices—Louisville, 502-582-6304; Lexington, 859-224-8286; Fort Wright, 859-578-0188; London, 606-864-2026; Bowling Green, 270-781-1673; Paducah, 270-442-4554

Republican

Bob Menendez, NJ | Senior | 4th Term | 54% (+11)
SH-528 | 202-224-4744 | Fax: 228-2197
menendez.senate.gov | X @senatormenendez
Bio—Englewood Cliffs; New York, NY, 1/1/1954; JD, Rutgers Univ., 1979; lawyer, public official; Union City mayor, 1986-92; NJ Assembly, 1987-91; NJ Senate, 1991-93; US House, 1993-2006; US Senate, 2006-present; m. Nadine; Catholic
Committees—Banking, Housing, & Urban Affairs; Finance; Foreign Relations
District Offices—Jersey City, 973-645-3030; Barrington, 856-757-5353

Democrat

Jeff Merkley, OR | Junior | 3rd Term | 56% (+18)
SH-531 | 202-224-3753 | Fax: 228-3997
merkley.senate.gov | X @senjeffmerkley
Bio—Portland; Myrtle Creek, OR, 10/24/1956; MPA, Princeton Univ., 1982; nonprofit executive; OR House, 1999-2008; US Senate, 2009-present; m. Mary; Lutheran
Committees—Appropriations; Budget; Environment & Public Works; Foreign Relations; Rules & Administration; Joint Printing
District Offices—Baker City, 541-278-1129; Bend, 541-318-1298; Eugene, 541-465-6750; Medford, 541-608-9102; Portland, 503-326-3386; Salem, 503-362-8102

Democrat

Jerry Moran, KS | Senior | 3rd Term | 60% (+23)
SD-521 | 202-224-6521 | Fax: 228-6998
moran.senate.gov | X @jerrymoran
Bio—Manhattan; Great Bend, KS, 5/29/1954; JD, Kansas Univ., 1981; lawyer, bank officer, college instructor; KS Senate, 1989-97; US House, 1997-2011; US Senate, 2011-present; m. Robba; Christian
Committees—Appropriations; Commerce, Science, & Transportation; Veterans' Affairs (Rnk. Mem.); Intelligence
District Offices—Hays, 785-628-6401; Manhattan, 785-539-8973; Pittsburg, 620-232-2286; Wichita, 316-269-9257; Olathe, 913-393-0711; Garden City, 620-260-3025

Republican

Notes

United States Senate

Markwayne Mullin, OK | Junior | 1st Term | 61% (+27)
SH-330 | 202-224-4721
mullin.senate.gov | X @senmullin
Bio—Westville; Tulsa, OK, 7/26/1977; AAS, Oklahoma St. Univ. Institute of Technology, 2010; business owner, plumber, rancher; US House, 2013-23; US Senate, 2023-present; m. Christie; Pentecostal
Committees—Armed Services; Environment & Public Works; Health, Education, Labor, & Pensions; Indian Affairs
District Offices—Oklahoma City, 405-246-0025; Tulsa, 918-921-8520

Republican

Lisa Murkowski, AK | Senior | 5th Term | 43% (+.8)
SH-522 | 202-224-6665 | Fax: 224-5301
murkowski.senate.gov | X @lisamurkowski
Bio—Girdwood; Ketchikan, AK, 5/22/1957; JD, Willamette Col. of Law, 1985; lawyer; AK House, 1999-2002; US Senate, 2002-present; m. Verne Martell; Catholic
Committees—Appropriations; Energy & Natural Resources; Health, Education, Labor, & Pensions; Indian Affairs (Vice Chair)
District Offices—Anchorage, 907-271-3735; Fairbanks, 907-456-0233; Juneau, 907-586-7277; Wasilla, 907-376-7665; Soldotna, 907-262-4220; Ketchikan, 907-225-6880

Republican

Chris Murphy, CT | Junior | 2nd Term | 56% (+17)
SH-136 | 202-224-4041
murphy.senate.gov
Bio—Hartford; White Plains, NY, 8/3/1973; JD, Univ. of Connecticut, 2002; lawyer; CT House, 1999-2003; CT Senate, 2003-06; US House, 2007-13; US Senate, 2013-present; m. Cathy Holahan; Protestant
Committees—Appropriations; Foreign Relations; Health, Education, Labor, & Pensions
District Offices—Hartford, 860-549-8463

Democrat

Patty Murray, WA | Senior | 6th Term | 57% (+15)
SR-154 | 202-224-2621
murray.senate.gov | X @pattymurray
Bio—Bothell; Seattle, WA, 10/11/1950; BA, Washington St. Univ., 1972; education activist; WA Senate, 1988-92; US Senate, 1993-present; m. Rob; Catholic
Committees—Appropriations (Chair); Budget; Health, Education, Labor, & Pensions; Veterans' Affairs; President Pro Tempore
District Offices—Everett, 425-259-6515; Seattle, 206-553-5545; Spokane, 509-624-9515; Tacoma, 253-572-3636; Vancouver, 360-696-7797; Richland, 509-453-7462

Democrat

Jon Ossoff, GA | Senior | 1st Term | 49% (+1)
SH-303 | 202-224-3521 | Fax: 224-2575
ossoff.senate.gov | X @senossoff
Bio—Atlanta; Atlanta, GA, 2/16/1987; MS, London School of Economics, 2013; congressional staffer, journalist; US Senate, 2021-present; m. Alisha Kramer; Jewish
Committees—Homeland Security & Governmental Affairs; Judiciary; Rules & Administration; Intelligence; Joint Library
District Offices—Atlanta, 470-786-7800; Augusta, 706-261-5031; Savannah, 912-200-9402; Columbus, 706-780-7053

Democrat

Notes

United States Senate

Alex Padilla, CA | Senior | 2nd Term | 61% (+22)
SH-331 | 202-224-3553 | Fax: 224-2200
padilla.senate.gov | X @senalexpadilla
Bio—Los Angeles; Panorama City, CA, 3/22/1973; BS, Massachusetts Institute of Technology, 1994; mechanical engineer, congressional aide; Los Angeles city council, 1999-2006; CA Senate, 2006-14; CA secretary of state, 2015-21; US Senate, 2021-present; m. Angela; Catholic
Committees—Budget; Energy & Natural Resources; Environment & Public Works; Judiciary; Rules & Administration; Joint Printing
District Offices—Fresno, 559-497-5109; San Francisco, 415-981-9369; Sacramento, 916-448-2787; Los Angeles, 310-231-4494; San Diego, 619-239-3884

Democrat

Rand Paul, KY | Junior | 3rd Term | 61% (+24)
SR-295 | 202-224-4343
paul.senate.gov | X @randpaul
Bio—Bowling Green; Pittsburgh, PA, 1/7/1963; MD, Duke Univ., 1988; ophthalmologist; US Senate, 2011-present; m. Kelley; Presbyterian
Committees—Foreign Relations; Health, Education, Labor, & Pensions; Homeland Security & Governmental Affairs (Rnk. Mem.); Small Business & Entrepreneurship
District Offices—Bowling Green, 270-782-8303

Republican

Gary Peters, MI | Junior | 2nd Term | 49% (+1.7)
SD-B40A | 202-224-6221
peters.senate.gov | X @sengarypeters
Bio—Bloomfield Hills; Pontiac, MI, 12/1/1958; MA, Wayne St. Univ., 2020; USNR, 1993-2000, 2001-05; financial executive, professor; Rochester Hills city council, 1991-93; MI Senate, 1995-2002; US House, 2009-15; US Senate, 2015-present; m. Colleen; Episcopalian
Committees—Appropriations; Armed Services; Commerce, Science, & Transportation; Homeland Security & Governmental Affairs (Chair)
District Offices—Detroit, 313-226-6020; Flint, 989-754-0112; Grand Rapids, 616-233-9150; Lansing, 517-377-1508; Marquette, 906-226-4554; Pontiac, 248-608-8040; Traverse City, 231-947-7773

Democrat

Jack Reed, RI | Senior | 5th Term | 66% (+33)
SH-728 | 202-224-4642 | Fax: 224-4680
reed.senate.gov | X @senjackreed
Bio—Jamestown; Providence, RI, 11/12/1949; JD, Harvard Univ., 1982; USA, 1971-79; USAR, 1979-91; professor, lawyer; RI Senate, 1985-90; US House, 1991-97; US Senate, 1997-present; m. Julia; Catholic
Committees—Appropriations; Armed Services (Chair); Banking, Housing, & Urban Affairs; Intelligence (Ex Officio)
District Offices—Cranston, 401-943-3100; Providence, 401-528-5200

Democrat

Pete Ricketts, NE | Junior | 1st Term | Appt.
SR-139 | 202-224-4224
ricketts.senate.gov | X @senatorricketts
Bio—Omaha; Nebraska City, NE, 8/19/1964; MBA, Univ. of Chicago, 1991; business executive; NE governor, 2015-23; US Senate, 2023-present; m. Susanne; Catholic
Committees—Environment & Public Works; Foreign Relations; Aging
District Offices—Scottsbluff, 308-632-6032; Omaha, 402-550-8040; Kearney, 308-233-3677; Lincoln, 402-476-1400

Republican

United States Senate

Jim Risch, ID | Junior | 3rd Term | 62% (+29)
SR-483 | 202-224-2752 | Fax: 224-2573
risch.senate.gov | X @senatorrisch
Bio—Boise; Milwaukee, WI, 5/3/1943; JD, Univ. of Idaho, 1968; lawyer, public official; ID Senate, 1974-89, 1995-2003; ID lt. governor, 2003-06, 2007-09; ID governor, 2006; US Senate, 2009-present; m. Vicki; Catholic
Committees—Energy & Natural Resources; Foreign Relations (Rnk. Mem.); Small Business & Entrepreneurship; Ethics; Intelligence
District Offices—Boise, 208-342-7985; Coeur d'Alene, 208-667-6130; Idaho Falls, 208-523-5541; Lewiston, 208-743-0792; Pocatello, 208-236-6817; Twin Falls, 208-734-6780

Republican

Mitt Romney, UT | Junior | 1st Term | 62% (+32)
SR-354 | 202-224-5251 | Fax: 228-0836
romney.senate.gov | X @senatorromney
Bio—Holladay; Detroit, MI, 3/12/1947; MBA, Harvard Univ., 1975; business executive; MA governor, 2003-07; US Senate, 2019-present; m. Ann; Mormon
Committees—Budget; Foreign Relations; Health, Education, Labor, & Pensions; Homeland Security & Governmental Affairs
District Offices—Ogden, 385-264-7885; Salt Lake City, 801-524-4380; Spanish Fork, 801-515-7230; St. George, 435-522-7100

Republican

Jacky Rosen, NV | Junior | 1st Term | 50% (+5)
SH-713 | 202-224-6244
rosen.senate.gov | X @senjackyrosen
Bio—Henderson; Chicago, IL, 8/2/1957; BA, Univ. of Minnesota, 1979; software developer, business owner; US House, 2017-19; US Senate, 2019-present; m. Larry; Jewish
Committees—Armed Services; Commerce, Science, & Transportation; Homeland Security & Governmental Affairs; Small Business & Entrepreneurship
District Offices—Las Vegas, 702-388-0205; Reno, 775-337-0110

Democrat

Mike Rounds, SD | Junior | 2nd Term | 65% (+31)
SH-716 | 202-224-5842 | Fax: 224-7482
rounds.senate.gov | X @senatorrounds
Bio—Fort Pierre; Huron, SD, 10/24/1954; BS, South Dakota St. Univ., 1977; insurance and real estate executive; SD Senate, 1991-2000; SD governor, 2003-11; US Senate, 2015-present; wid.; Catholic
Committees—Armed Services; Banking, Housing, & Urban Affairs; Veterans' Affairs; Indian Affairs; Intelligence
District Offices—Pierre, 605-224-1450; Rapid City, 605-343-5035; Sioux Falls, 605-336-0486; Aberdeen, 605-225-0366

Republican

Marco Rubio, FL | Senior | 3rd Term | 57% (+16)
SR-284 | 202-224-3041
rubio.senate.gov | X @senrubiopress
Bio—West Miami; Miami, FL, 5/28/1971; JD, Univ. of Miami, 1996; lawyer; West Miami city commission, 1998-2000; FL House, 2000-08; US Senate, 2011-present; m. Jeanette; Catholic
Committees—Appropriations; Foreign Relations; Small Business & Entrepreneurship; Intelligence (Vice Chair); Aging
District Offices—Fort Myers, 239-318-6464; Jacksonville, 904-354-4300; Miami, 305-596-4224; Orlando, 407-254-2573; Pensacola, 850-433-2603; Tallahassee, 850-599-9100; Tampa, 813-947-6288; Palm Beach, 561-775-3360

Republican

Notes

United States Senate

Bernie Sanders, VT | Senior | 3rd Term | 66% (+39)
SD-332 | 202-224-5141 | Fax: 228-0776
sanders.senate.gov | X @sensanders
Bio—Burlington; Brooklyn, NY, 9/8/1941; BS, Univ. of Chicago, 1964; carpenter, journalist; Burlington mayor, 1981-89; US House, 1991-2007; US Senate, 2007-present; m. Jane; Jewish
Committees—Budget; Energy & Natural Resources; Environment & Public Works; Health, Education, Labor, & Pensions (Chair); Veterans' Affairs
District Offices—Burlington, 802-862-0697

Independent

Brian Schatz, HI | Senior | 3rd Term | 69% (+44)
SH-722 | 202-224-3934
schatz.senate.gov | X @senbrianschatz
Bio—Honolulu; Ann Arbor, MI, 10/20/1972; BA, Pomona Col., 1994; teacher, nonprofit executive; HI House, 1998-2006; HI lt. governor, 2010-12; US Senate, 2012-present; m. Linda; Jewish
Committees—Appropriations; Commerce, Science, & Transportation; Foreign Relations; Indian Affairs (Chair); Ethics
District Offices—Honolulu, 808-523-2061

Democrat

Eric Schmitt, MO | Junior | 1st Term | 55% (+13)
SR-387 | 202-224-5721
schmitt.senate.gov | X @senericschmitt
Bio—Glendale; Bridgeton, MO, 6/20/1975; JD, Saint Louis Univ., 2000; lawyer; Glendale alderman, 2005-08; MO Senate, 2009-17; MO treasurer, 2017-19; MO attorney general, 2019-23; US Senate, 2023-present; m. Jaime; Catholic
Committees—Armed Services; Commerce, Science, & Transportation; Joint Economic
District Offices—Columbia, 573-514-8680; Springfield, 417-290-5000; St. Louis, 314-230-7263

Republican

Chuck Schumer, NY | Senior | 5th Term | 55% (+14)
SH-322 | 202-224-6542 | Fax: 228-3027
schumer.senate.gov | X @senschumer
Bio—Brooklyn; Brooklyn, NY, 11/23/1950; JD, Harvard Univ., 1974; lawyer; NY Assembly, 1975-80; US House, 1981-99, US Senate, 1999-present; m. Iris Weinshall; Jewish
Committees—Rules & Administration; Intelligence (Ex Officio); Majority Leader
District Offices—Albany, 518-431-4070; Binghamton, 607-772-6792; Buffalo, 716-846-4111; Melville, 631-753-0978; New York, 212-486-4430; Peekskill, 914-734-1532; Rochester, 585-263-5866; Syracuse, 315-423-5471

Democrat

Rick Scott, FL | Junior | 1st Term | 50% (+.1)
SH-110 | 202-224-5274
rickscott.senate.gov | X @senrickscott
Bio—Naples; Bloomington, IL, 12/1/1952; JD, Southern Methodist Univ., 1978; USN, 1971-74; lawyer, venture capitalist; FL governor, 2011-18; US Senate, 2019-present; m. Ann; Christian
Committees—Armed Services; Budget; Homeland Security & Governmental Affairs; Aging
District Offices—Tallahassee, 850-942-8415; Tampa, 813-225-7040; Naples, 239-231-7890; Orlando, 407-872-7161; West Palm Beach, 561-514-0189; Kissimmee, 407-586-7879; Pensacola, 850-760-5151; Miami, 786-501-7141; Jacksonville, 904-479-7227

Republican

United States Senate

Tim Scott, SC | Junior | 3rd Term | 62% (+26)
SH-104 | 202-224-6121 | Fax: 228-5143
scott.senate.gov | X @senatortimscott
Bio—North Charleston; North Charleston, SC, 9/19/1965; BS, Charleston Southern Univ., 1988; entrepreneur; Charleston Co. council, 1995-2008; SC House, 2009-10; US House, 2011-13; US Senate, 2013-present; eng.; Christian
Committees—Banking, Housing, & Urban Affairs (Rnk. Mem.); Finance; Foreign Relations; Small Business & Entrepreneurship; Aging
District Offices—Columbia, 803-771-6112; Greenville, 864-233-5366; North Charleston, 843-727-4525

Republican

Jeanne Shaheen, NH | Senior | 3rd Term | 56% (+16)
SH-506 | 202-224-2841
shaheen.senate.gov | X @senatorshaheen
Bio—Madbury; St. Charles, MO, 1/28/1947; MSS, Univ. of Mississippi, 1973; public official; NH Senate, 1990-96; NH governor, 1997-2003; US Senate, 2009-present; m. Bill; Protestant
Committees—Appropriations; Armed Services; Foreign Relations; Small Business & Entrepreneurship (Chair); Ethics
District Offices—Berlin, 603-752-6300; Claremont, 603-542-4872; Dover, 603-750-3004; Keene, 603-358-6604; Manchester, 603-647-7500; Nashua, 603-883-0196

Democrat

Kyrsten Sinema, AZ | Senior | 1st Term | 49% (+2)
SH-317 | 202-224-4521 | Fax: 224-4521
sinema.senate.gov | X @senatorsinema
Bio—Phoenix; Tucson, AZ, 7/12/1976; PhD, Arizona St. Univ., 2012; social worker, lawyer, professor; AZ House, 2004-10; AZ Senate, 2010-12; US House, 2013-19; US Senate, 2019-present; single; unaffiliated
Committees—Appropriations; Commerce, Science, & Transportation; Homeland Security & Governmental Affairs; Veterans' Affairs
District Offices—Phoenix, 602-598-7327; Tucson, 520-639-7080

Independent

Tina Smith, MN | Junior | 2nd Term | 48% (+5)
SH-720 | 202-224-5641
smith.senate.gov | X @sentinasmith
Bio—Minneapolis; Albuquerque, NM, 3/4/1958; MBA, Dartmouth Col., 1984; marketing executive, gubernatorial aide; MN lt. governor, 2015-18; US Senate, 2018-present; m. Archie; Presbyterian
Committees—Agriculture, Nutrition, & Forestry; Banking, Housing, & Urban Affairs; Health, Education, Labor, & Pensions; Indian Affairs
District Offices—Saint Paul, 651-221-1016; Rochester, 507-218-2003; Moorhead, 218-284-8721; Duluth, 218-722-2390

Democrat

Debbie Stabenow, MI | Senior | 4th Term | 52% (+7)
SH-731 | 202-224-4822
stabenow.senate.gov | X @senstabenow
Bio—Lansing; Gladwin, MI, 4/29/1950; MSW, Michigan St. Univ., 1975; social worker, leadership training consultant; Ingham Co. commissioner, 1975-78; MI House, 1979-90; MI Senate, 1991-94; US House, 1997-2001; US Senate, 2001-present; div.; Methodist
Committees—Agriculture, Nutrition, & Forestry (Chair); Budget; Environment & Public Works; Finance; Joint Taxation
District Offices—East Lansing, 517-203-1760; Detroit, 313-961-4330; Grand Rapids, 616-975-0052; Flint, 810-720-4172; Marquette, 906-228-8756; Traverse City, 231-929-1031

Democrat

United States Senate

Dan Sullivan, AK | Junior | 2nd Term | 53% (+13)
SH-302 | 202-224-3004 | Fax: 224-6501
sullivan.senate.gov | X @sendansullivan
Bio—Anchorage; Fairview Park, OH, 11/13/1964; MFS/JD, Georgetown Univ., 1993; USMC, 1993-97; USMCR, 1997-present; lawyer, White House aide; AK attorney general, 2009-10; US Senate, 2015-present; m. Julie; Catholic
Committees—Armed Services; Commerce, Science, & Transportation; Environment & Public Works; Veterans' Affairs
District Offices—Anchorage, 907-271-5915; Fairbanks, 907-456-0261; Juneau, 907-586-7277; Wasilla, 907-357-9956; Soldotna, 907-262-4040; Ketchikan, 907-225-6880

Republican

Jon Tester, MT | Senior | 3rd Term | 50% (+4)
SH-311 | 202-224-2644 | Fax: 224-8594
tester.senate.gov | X @senatortester
Bio—Big Sandy; Havre, MT, 8/21/1956; BS, Univ. of Great Falls, 1978; teacher; MT Senate, 1999-2006; US Senate, 2007-present; m. Sharla; Protestant
Committees—Appropriations; Banking, Housing, & Urban Affairs; Commerce, Science, & Transportation; Veterans' Affairs (Chair); Indian Affairs
District Offices—Billings, 406-252-0550; Bozeman, 406-586-4450; Butte, 406-723-3277; Great Falls, 406-452-9585; Helena, 406-449-5401; Kalispell, 406-257-3360; Missoula, 406-728-3003

Democrat

John Thune, SD | Senior | 4th Term | 69% (+43)
SD-511 | 202-224-2321 | Fax: 228-5429
thune.senate.gov | X @senjohnthune
Bio—Sioux Falls; Pierre, SD, 1/7/1961; MBA, Univ. of South Dakota, 1984; public official; US House, 1997-2003; US Senate, 2005-present; m. Kimberley; Protestant
Committees—Agriculture, Nutrition, & Forestry; Commerce, Science, & Transportation; Finance; Minority Whip
District Offices—Aberdeen, 605-225-8823; Rapid City, 605-348-7551; Sioux Falls, 605-334-9596

Republican

Thom Tillis, NC | Senior | 2nd Term | 48% (+1.7)
SD-113 | 202-224-6342 | Fax: 228-2563
tillis.senate.gov | X @senthomtillis
Bio—Huntersville; Jacksonville, FL, 8/30/1960; BA, Univ. of Maryland Univ. Col., 1997; management consultant; Cornelius board of commissioners, 2003-05; NC House, 2007-14; US Senate, 2015-present; m. Susan; Catholic
Committees—Banking, Housing, & Urban Affairs; Finance; Judiciary; Veterans' Affairs
District Offices—Raleigh, 919-856-4630; Charlotte, 704-509-9087; Greenville, 252-329-0371; Hendersonville, 828-693-8750; Greensboro, 336-885-0685

Republican

Tommy Tuberville, AL | Senior | 1st Term | 60% (+20)
SR-455 | 202-224-4124
tuberville.senate.gov | X @senatortuberville
Bio—Auburn; Camden, AR, 9/18/1954; BS, Southern Arkansas Univ., 1976; college football coach, sports broadcaster; US Senate, 2021-present; m. Suzanne; Christian
Committees—Agriculture, Nutrition, & Forestry; Armed Services; Health, Education, Labor, & Pensions; Veterans' Affairs
District Offices—Mobile, 251-308-7233; Huntsville, 256-692-7500; Birmingham, 205-760-7307; Montgomery, 334-523-7424; Dothan, 334-547-7441

Republican

Notes

United States Senate

Chris Van Hollen, MD | Junior | 2nd Term | 65% (+32)
SH-730 | 202-224-4654 | Fax: 228-0629
vanhollen.senate.gov | X @chrisvanhollen
Bio—Kensington; Karachi, Pakistan, 1/10/1959; JD, Georgetown Univ., 1990; lawyer; MD House, 1990-94; MD Senate, 1994-2002; US House, 2003-17; US Senate, 2017-present; m. Katherine; Episcopalian
Committees—Appropriations; Banking, Housing, & Urban Affairs; Budget; Foreign Relations
District Offices—Baltimore, 667-212-4610; Rockville, 301-545-1500; Hagerstown, 301-797-2826; Annapolis, 410-263-1325; Largo, 301-322-6560; Cambridge, 410-221-2074

Democrat

J.D. Vance, OH | Junior | 1st Term | 53% (+6)
SR-288 | 202-224-3353
vance.senate.gov | X @senvancepress
Bio—Cincinnati; Middletown, OH, 8/2/1984; JD, Yale Univ., 2013; USMC, 2003-07; lawyer, venture capitalist, writer; US Senate, 2023-present; m. Usha; Catholic
Committees—Banking, Housing, & Urban Affairs; Commerce, Science, & Transportation; Aging; Joint Economic
District Offices—Columbus, 614-369-4925; Cleveland, 216-539-7877; Toledo, 567-304-3777; Middletown, 513-318-1100

Republican

Mark R. Warner, VA | Senior | 3rd Term | 55% (+12)
SH-703 | 202-224-2023
warner.senate.gov | X @markwarner
Bio—Alexandria; Indianapolis, IN, 12/15/1954; JD, Harvard Univ., 1980; congressional staffer, entrepreneur; VA governor, 2002-06; US Senate, 2009-present; m. Lisa Collis; Presbyterian
Committees—Banking, Housing, & Urban Affairs; Budget; Finance; Rules & Administration; Intelligence (Chair); Joint Library
District Offices—Abingdon, 276-628-8158; Norfolk, 757-441-3079; Richmond, 804-775-2314; Vienna, 703-442-0670; Roanoke, 540-857-2676

Democrat

Raphael Warnock, GA | Junior | 2nd Term | 51% (+3)
SR-416 | 202-224-3643
warnock.senate.gov | X @senatorwarnock
Bio—Atlanta; Savannah, GA, 7/23/1969; PhD, Union Theological Seminary; pastor; US Senate, 2021-present; div.; Baptist
Committees—Agriculture, Nutrition, & Forestry; Banking, Housing, & Urban Affairs; Commerce, Science, & Transportation; Aging
District Offices—Atlanta, 770-694-7828

Democrat

Elizabeth Warren, MA | Senior | 2nd Term | 59% (+24)
SH-309 | 202-224-4543
warren.senate.gov | X @senwarren
Bio—Cambridge; Oklahoma City, OK, 6/22/1949; JD, Rutgers Univ., 1976; teacher, lawyer, professor; US Senate, 2013-present; m. Bruce Mann; Methodist
Committees—Armed Services; Banking, Housing, & Urban Affairs; Finance; Aging
District Offices—Boston, 617-565-3170; Springfield, 413-788-2690

Democrat

Notes

United States Senate

Peter Welch, VT | Junior | 1st Term | 67% (+40)
SR-124 | 202-224-4242 | Fax: 651-1674
welch.senate.gov | X @senpeterwelch
Bio—Norwich; Springfield, MA, 5/2/1947; JD, Univ. of California, Berkeley, 1973; lawyer; VT Senate, 1981-89, 2002-07; US House, 2007-23; US Senate, 2023-present; m. Margaret; Catholic
Committees—Agriculture, Nutrition, & Forestry; Commerce, Science, & Transportation; Judiciary; Rules & Administration; Joint Economic
District Offices—Burlington, 802-863-2525

Democrat

Sheldon Whitehouse, RI | Junior | 3rd Term | 61% (+23)
SH-530 | 202-224-2921 | Fax: 228-6362
whitehouse.senate.gov | X @senwhitehouse
Bio—Newport; Manhattan, NY, 10/20/1955; JD, Univ. of Virginia, 1982; lawyer; RI attorney general, 1999-2003; US Senate, 2007-present; m. Sandra; Episcopalian
Committees—Budget (Chair); Environment & Public Works; Finance; Judiciary
District Offices—Providence, 401-453-5294

Democrat

Roger F. Wicker, MS | Senior | 3rd Term | 58% (+19)
SR-425 | 202-224-6253
wicker.senate.gov | X @senwicker
Bio—Tupelo; Pontotoc, MS, 7/5/1951; JD, Univ. of Mississippi, 1975; USAF, 1976-80; USAFR, 1980-2003; lawyer, congressional staffer; MS Senate, 1988-94; US House, 1995-2007; US Senate, 2007-present; m. Gayle; Baptist
Committees—Armed Services (Rnk. Mem.); Commerce, Science, & Transportation; Environment & Public Works; Rules & Administration; Intelligence (Ex Officio)
District Offices—Gulfport, 228-871-7017; Hernando, 662-429-1002; Jackson, 601-965-4644; Tupelo, 662-844-5010

Republican

Ron Wyden, OR | Senior | 6th Term | 55% (+15)
SD-221 | 202-224-5244 | Fax: 228-2717
wyden.senate.gov | X @ronwyden
Bio—Portland; Wichita, KS, 5/3/1949; JD, Univ. of Oregon, 1974; public official, lawyer; US House, 1981-96; US Senate, 1996-present; m. Nancy; Jewish
Committees—Budget; Energy & Natural Resources; Finance (Chair); Intelligence; Joint Taxation (Chair)
District Offices—Portland, 503-326-7525; Salem, 503-589-4555; Eugene, 541-431-0229; Bend, 541-330-9142; La Grande, 541-962-7691; Medford, 541-858-5122

Democrat

Todd Young, IN | Senior | 2nd Term | 58% (+21)
SD-185 | 202-224-5623
young.senate.gov | X @sentoddyoung
Bio—Bargersville; Lancaster, PA, 8/24/1972; JD, Indiana Univ., 2006; USN, 1990-91; USMC, 1995-2000; consultant, lawyer; US House, 2011-17; US Senate, 2017-present; m. Jenny; Protestant
Committees—Commerce, Science, & Transportation; Finance; Foreign Relations; Small Business & Entrepreneurship
District Offices—Indianapolis, 317-226-6700; Fort Wayne, 317-226-6700; New Albany, 812-542-4820; Valparaiso, 219-747-7780

Republican

Notes

Senate Standing Committees

AGRICULTURE, NUTRITION, AND FORESTRY
SR-328A | 202-224-2035 | agriculture.senate.gov

DEMOCRATS (12)
Debbie Stabenow, MI, Chair | Sherrod Brown, OH | Amy Klobuchar, MN | Michael Bennet, CO | Kirsten Gillibrand, NY | Tina Smith, MN | Dick Durbin, IL | Cory A. Booker, NJ | Ben Ray Luján, NM | Raphael Warnock, GA | Peter Welch, VT | John Fetterman, PA

REPUBLICANS (11)
John Boozman, AR, Rnk. Mem. | Mitch McConnell, KY | John Hoeven, ND | Joni Ernst, IA | Cindy Hyde-Smith, MS | Roger Marshall, KS | Tommy Tuberville, AL | Mike Braun, IN | Chuck Grassley, IA | John Thune, SD | Deb Fischer, NE

Dem. Staff Dir.—Eyang Garrison | Rep. Staff Dir.—Fitzhugh Elder

SUBCOMMITTEES
The chair and ranking member are ex officio members of all subcommittees.

Commodities, Risk Management, and Trade
Dem—Smith, Chair | Gillibrand | Durbin | Booker | Warnock | Fetterman
Rep—Hyde-Smith, Rnk. Mem. | McConnell | Ernst | Tuberville | Grassley

Conservation, Climate, Forestry, and Natural Resources
Dem—Bennet, Chair | Klobuchar | Smith | Luján | Warnock | Welch
Rep—Marshall, Rnk. Mem. | McConnell | Hoeven | Hyde-Smith | Thune

Food and Nutrition, Specialty Crops, Organics, and Research
Dem—Fetterman, Chair | Brown | Klobuchar | Gillibrand | Booker | Warnock
Rep—Braun, Rnk. Mem. | McConnell | Ernst | Marshall | Tuberville

Livestock, Dairy, Poultry, Local Food Systems, and Food Safety and Security
Dem—Gillibrand, Chair | Brown | Durbin | Booker | Luján | Welch
Rep—Hoeven, Rnk. Mem. | Hyde-Smith | Marshall | Thune | Fischer

Rural Development and Energy
Dem—Welch, Chair | Klobuchar | Bennet | Smith | Durbin | Luján
Rep—Tuberville, Rnk. Mem. | Ernst | Braun | Grassley | Fischer

APPROPRIATIONS
S-128 Capitol | 202-224-7363 | appropriations.senate.gov

DEMOCRATS (15)
Patty Murray, WA, Chair | Dick Durbin, IL | Jack Reed, RI | Jon Tester, MT | Jeanne Shaheen, NH | Jeff Merkley, OR | Chris Coons, DE | Brian Schatz, HI | Tammy Baldwin, WI | Chris Murphy, CT | Joe Manchin, WV | Chris Van Hollen, MD | Martin Heinrich, NM | Gary Peters, MI | Kyrsten Sinema, AZ

REPUBLICANS (14)
Susan Collins, ME, Rnk. Mem. | Mitch McConnell, KY | Lisa Murkowski, AK | Lindsey Graham, SC | Jerry Moran, KS | John Hoeven, ND | John Boozman, AR | Shelley Moore Capito, WV | John Kennedy, LA | Cindy Hyde-Smith, MS | Bill Hagerty, TN | Katie Britt, AL | Marco Rubio, FL | Deb Fischer, NE

Dem. Staff Dir.—Evan Schatz | Rep. Staff Dir.—Betsy McDonnell

SUBCOMMITTEES
The chair and ranking member are ex officio members of subcommittees on which they do not serve as regular members.

Agriculture, Rural Development, Food and Drug Administration, and Related Agencies
Dem—Heinrich, Chair | Tester | Merkley | Baldwin | Manchin | Peters | Sinema
Rep—Hoeven, Rnk. Mem. | McConnell | Collins | Moran | Hyde-Smith | Fischer

Senate Standing Committees

SUBCOMMITTEES (Appropriations)

Commerce, Justice, Science, and Related Agencies
Dem—Shaheen, Chair | Reed | Coons | Schatz | Manchin | Van Hollen | Merkley | Peters | Heinrich
Rep—Moran, Rnk. Mem. | Murkowski | Collins | Capito | Kennedy | Hagerty | Britt | Fischer

Defense
Dem—Tester, Chair | Durbin | Murray | Reed | Schatz | Baldwin | Shaheen | Murphy | Coons
Rep—Collins, Rnk. Mem. | McConnell | Murkowski | Graham | Moran | Hoeven | Boozman | Capito

Energy and Water Development
Dem—Murray, Interim Chair | Tester | Durbin | Shaheen | Merkley | Coons | Baldwin | Heinrich | Sinema
Rep—Kennedy, Rnk. Mem. | McConnell | Murkowski | Graham | Hoeven | Hyde-Smith | Hagerty | Britt

Financial Services and General Government
Dem—Van Hollen, Chair | Durbin | Coons | Manchin | Heinrich
Rep—Hagerty, Rnk. Mem. | Boozman | Kennedy | Rubio

Homeland Security
Dem—Murphy, Chair | Murray | Tester | Shaheen | Baldwin | Peters
Rep—Britt, Rnk. Mem. | Murkowski | Capito | Kennedy | Hyde-Smith

Interior, Environment, and Related Agencies
Dem—Merkley, Chair | Reed | Tester | Van Hollen | Heinrich | Peters | Sinema
Rep—Murkowski, Rnk. Mem. | McConnell | Capito | Hoeven | Fischer | Britt

Labor, Health and Human Services, and Education, and Related Agencies
Dem—Baldwin, Chair | Murray | Durbin | Reed | Shaheen | Merkley | Schatz | Murphy | Manchin
Rep—Capito, Rnk. Mem. | Graham | Moran | Kennedy | Hyde-Smith | Boozman | Britt | Rubio

Legislative Branch
Dem—Reed, Chair | Murphy | Van Hollen
Rep—Fischer, Rnk. Mem. | Rubio

Military Construction, Veterans Affairs, and Related Agencies
Dem—Murray, Chair | Reed | Tester | Schatz | Baldwin | Heinrich | Manchin | Peters | Sinema
Rep—Boozman, Rnk. Mem. | McConnell | Murkowski | Hoeven | Collins | Rubio | Hagerty | Fischer

State, Foreign Operations, and Related Programs
Dem—Coons, Chair | Durbin | Shaheen | Merkley | Murphy | Van Hollen | Schatz
Rep—Graham, Rnk. Mem. | McConnell | Boozman | Moran | Rubio | Hagerty

Transportation, Housing and Urban Development, and Related Agencies
Dem—Schatz, Chair | Murray | Durbin | Reed | Coons | Murphy | Manchin | Van Hollen | Sinema
Rep—Hyde-Smith, Rnk. Mem. | Collins | Boozman | Capito | Graham | Hoeven | Kennedy | Moran

ARMED SERVICES

SR-228 | 202-224-3871 | armed-services.senate.gov

DEMOCRATS (13)
Jack Reed, RI, Chair | Jeanne Shaheen, NH | Kirsten Gillibrand, NY | Richard Blumenthal, CT | Mazie K. Hirono, HI | Tim Kaine, VA | Angus King, ME | Elizabeth Warren, MA | Gary Peters, MI | Joe Manchin, WV | Tammy Duckworth, IL | Jacky Rosen, NV | Mark Kelly, AZ

REPUBLICANS (12)
Roger F. Wicker, MS, Rnk. Mem. | Deb Fischer, NE | Tom Cotton, AR | Mike Rounds, SD | Joni Ernst, IA | Dan Sullivan, AK | Kevin Cramer, ND | Rick Scott, FL | Tommy Tuberville, AL | Markwayne Mullin, OK | Ted Budd, NC | Eric Schmitt, MO

Dem. Staff Dir.—Elizabeth King | Rep. Staff Dir.—John Keast

Senate Standing Committees

SUBCOMMITTEES (Armed Services)
The chair and ranking member are ex officio members of all subcommittees.

Airland
Dem—Kelly, Chair | Blumenthal | King | Peters | Manchin | Duckworth
Rep—Cotton, Rnk. Mem. | Fischer | Ernst | Scott | Mullin

Cybersecurity
Dem—Manchin, Chair | Gillibrand | Peters | Duckworth | Rosen
Rep—Rounds, Rnk. Mem. | Ernst | Budd | Schmitt

Emerging Threats and Capabilities
Dem—Gillibrand, Chair | Shaheen | Warren | Peters | Rosen | Kelly
Rep—Ernst, Rnk. Mem. | Cotton | Mullin | Budd | Schmitt

Personnel
Dem—Warren, Chair | Blumenthal | Hirono | Kaine | Duckworth
Rep—Scott, Rnk. Mem. | Rounds | Sullivan | Budd

Readiness and Management Support
Dem—Hirono, Chair | Shaheen | Blumenthal | Kaine | Duckworth | Kelly
Rep—Sullivan, Rnk. Mem. | Fischer | Cramer | Tuberville | Mullin

Seapower
Dem—Kaine, Chair | Shaheen | Blumenthal | Hirono | King | Peters
Rep—Cramer, Rnk. Mem. | Sullivan | Scott | Tuberville | Schmitt

Strategic Forces
Dem—King, Chair | Gillibrand | Warren | Manchin | Rosen | Kelly
Rep—Fischer, Rnk. Mem. | Cotton | Rounds | Cramer | Tuberville

BANKING, HOUSING, AND URBAN AFFAIRS
SD-534 | 202-224-7391 | Fax: 224-5137 | banking.senate.gov

DEMOCRATS (12)
Sherrod Brown, OH, Chair | Jack Reed, RI | Bob Menendez, NJ | Jon Tester, MT | Mark R. Warner, VA | Elizabeth Warren, MA | Chris Van Hollen, MD | Catherine Cortez Masto, NV | Tina Smith, MN | Raphael Warnock, GA | John Fetterman, PA | Laphonza Butler, CA

REPUBLICANS (11)
Tim Scott, SC, Rnk. Mem. | Mike Crapo, ID | Mike Rounds, SD | Thom Tillis, NC | John Kennedy, LA | Bill Hagerty, TN | Cynthia Lummis, WY | J.D. Vance, OH | Katie Britt, AL | Kevin Cramer, ND | Steve Daines, MT

Dem. Staff Dir.—Laura Swanson | Rep. Staff Dir.—Lila Nieves-Lee

SUBCOMMITTEES
The chair and ranking member are ex officio members of all subcommittees.

Economic Policy
Dem—Warren, Chair | Reed | Menendez | Van Hollen | Smith | Fetterman
Rep—Kennedy, Rnk. Mem. | Rounds | Tillis | Lummis | Daines

Financial Institutions and Consumer Protection
Dem—Warnock, Chair | Warner | Warren | Van Hollen | Cortez Masto | Smith | Fetterman
Rep—Tillis, Rnk. Mem. | Crapo | Lummis | Vance | Britt | Cramer

Housing, Transportation, and Community Development
Dem—Smith, Chair | Reed | Menendez | Tester | Cortez Masto | Warnock | Fetterman | Butler
Rep—Lummis, Rnk. Mem. | Crapo | Rounds | Kennedy | Hagerty | Vance | Britt

National Security and International Trade and Finance
Dem—Warner, Chair | Tester | Van Hollen | Cortez Masto | Butler
Rep—Hagerty, Rnk. Mem. | Britt | Cramer | Daines

Senate Standing Committees

SUBCOMMITTEES (Banking)

Securities, Insurance, and Investment
Dem—Menendez, Chair | Reed | Tester | Warner | Warren | Warnock | Butler
Rep—Rounds, Rnk. Mem. | Crapo | Tillis | Kennedy | Hagerty | Vance

BUDGET

SD-624 | 202-224-0642 | Fax: 224-4835 | budget.senate.gov

DEMOCRATS (11)
Sheldon Whitehouse, RI, Chair | Patty Murray, WA | Ron Wyden, OR | Debbie Stabenow, MI | Bernie Sanders, VT | Mark R. Warner, VA | Jeff Merkley, OR | Tim Kaine, VA | Chris Van Hollen, MD | Ben Ray Luján, NM | Alex Padilla, CA

REPUBLICANS (10)
Chuck Grassley, IA, Rnk. Mem. | Mike Crapo, ID | Lindsey Graham, SC | Ron Johnson, WI | Mitt Romney, UT | Roger Marshall, KS | Mike Braun, IN | John Kennedy, LA | Rick Scott, FL | Mike Lee, UT

Dem. Staff Dir.—Dan Dudis | Rep. Staff Dir.—Kolan Davis

NO SUBCOMMITTEES

COMMERCE, SCIENCE, AND TRANSPORTATION

SR-254 | 202-224-0411 | commerce.senate.gov

DEMOCRATS (14)
Maria Cantwell, WA, Chair | Amy Klobuchar, MN | Brian Schatz, HI | Edward J. Markey, MA | Gary Peters, MI | Tammy Baldwin, WI | Tammy Duckworth, IL | Jon Tester, MT | Kyrsten Sinema, AZ | Jacky Rosen, NV | Ben Ray Luján, NM | John Hickenlooper, CO | Raphael Warnock, GA | Peter Welch, VT

REPUBLICANS (13)
Ted Cruz, TX, Rnk. Mem. | John Thune, SD | Roger F. Wicker, MS | Deb Fischer, NE | Jerry Moran, KS | Dan Sullivan, AK | Marsha Blackburn, TN | Todd Young, IN | Ted Budd, NC | Eric Schmitt, MO | J.D. Vance, OH | Shelley Moore Capito, WV | Cynthia Lummis, WY

Dem. Staff Dir.—Lila Helms | Rep. Staff Dir.—Brad Grantz

SUBCOMMITTEES
The chair and ranking member are ex officio members of all subcommittees.

Aviation Safety, Operations, and Innovation
Dem—Duckworth, Chair | Tester | Sinema | Rosen | Hickenlooper | Warnock
Rep—Moran, Rnk. Mem. | Thune | Wicker | Sullivan | Young

Communications, Media, and Broadband
Dem—Luján, Chair | Klobuchar | Schatz | Markey | Peters | Baldwin | Duckworth | Tester | Sinema | Rosen | Hickenlooper | Warnock | Welch
Rep—Thune, Rnk. Mem. | Wicker | Fischer | Moran | Sullivan | Blackburn | Young | Budd | Schmitt | Vance | Capito | Lummis

Consumer Protection, Product Safety, and Data Security
Dem—Hickenlooper, Chair | Klobuchar | Schatz | Markey | Baldwin | Duckworth | Luján | Welch
Rep—Blackburn, Rnk. Mem. | Fischer | Moran | Sullivan | Young | Budd | Lummis

Oceans, Fisheries, Climate Change, and Manufacturing
Dem—Baldwin, Chair | Schatz | Markey | Luján | Warnock | Welch
Rep—Sullivan, Rnk. Mem. | Wicker | Moran | Blackburn | Vance

Senate Standing Committees

SUBCOMMITTEES (Commerce)

Space and Science
Dem—Sinema, Chair | Markey | Peters | Luján | Hickenlooper
Rep—Schmitt, Rnk. Mem. | Fischer | Vance | Lummis

Surface Transportation, Maritime, Freight, and Ports
Dem—Peters, Chair | Klobuchar | Schatz | Markey | Baldwin | Duckworth | Warnock | Welch
Rep—Young, Rnk. Mem. | Thune | Wicker | Fischer | Schmitt | Capito | Budd

Tourism, Trade, and Export Promotion
Dem—Rosen, Chair | Klobuchar | Duckworth | Sinema | Hickenlooper
Rep—Budd, Rnk. Mem. | Thune | Blackburn | Capito

ENERGY AND NATURAL RESOURCES
SD-304 | 202-224-4971 | Fax: 224-6163 | energy.senate.gov

DEMOCRATS (10)
Joe Manchin, WV, Chair | Ron Wyden, OR | Maria Cantwell, WA | Bernie Sanders, VT | Martin Heinrich, NM | Mazie K. Hirono, HI | Angus King, ME | Catherine Cortez Masto, NV | John Hickenlooper, CO | Alex Padilla, CA

REPUBLICANS (9)
John Barrasso, WY, Rnk. Mem. | Jim Risch, ID | Mike Lee, UT | Steve Daines, MT | Lisa Murkowski, AK | John Hoeven, ND | Bill Cassidy, LA | Cindy Hyde-Smith, MS | Josh Hawley, MO

Dem. Staff Dir.—Renae Black | Rep. Staff Dir.—Richard Russell

SUBCOMMITTEES
The chair and ranking member are ex officio members of all subcommittees.

Energy
Dem—Sanders, Chair | Wyden | Heinrich | Hirono | King | Cortez Masto | Hickenlooper
Rep—Hawley, Rnk. Mem. | Risch | Murkowski | Hoeven | Cassidy | Hyde-Smith

National Parks
Dem—King, Chair | Sanders | Heinrich | Hirono | Padilla
Rep—Daines, Rnk. Mem. | Lee | Murkowski | Hyde-Smith

Public Lands, Forests, and Mining
Dem—Cortez Masto, Chair | Wyden | Heinrich | Hirono | King | Hickenlooper | Padilla
Rep—Lee, Rnk. Mem. | Risch | Daines | Murkowski | Cassidy | Hawley

Water and Power
Dem—Wyden, Chair | Sanders | Cortez Masto | Hickenlooper | Padilla
Rep—Risch, Rnk. Mem. | Lee | Hoeven | Cassidy

Senate Standing Committees

ENVIRONMENT AND PUBLIC WORKS
SD-410 | 202-224-8832 | epw.senate.gov

DEMOCRATS (10)
Tom Carper, DE, Chair | Ben Cardin, MD | Bernie Sanders, VT | Sheldon Whitehouse, RI | Jeff Merkley, OR | Edward J. Markey, MA | Debbie Stabenow, MI | Mark Kelly, AZ | Alex Padilla, CA | John Fetterman, PA

REPUBLICANS (9)
Shelley Moore Capito, WV, Rnk. Mem. | Kevin Cramer, ND | Cynthia Lummis, WY | Markwayne Mullin, OK | Pete Ricketts, NE | John Boozman, AR | Roger F. Wicker, MS | Dan Sullivan, AK | Lindsey Graham, SC

Dem. Staff Dir.—Courtney Taylor | Rep. Staff Dir.—Adam Tomlinson

SUBCOMMITTEES
The chair and ranking member are ex officio members of all subcommittees.

Chemical Safety, Waste Management, Environmental Justice, and Regulatory Oversight
Dem—Merkley, Chair | Sanders | Whitehouse | Markey | Fetterman
Rep—Mullin, Rnk. Mem. | Boozman | Wicker | Sullivan

Clean Air, Climate, and Nuclear Safety
Dem—Markey, Chair | Cardin | Sanders | Whitehouse | Merkley | Stabenow | Kelly | Padilla
Rep—Ricketts, Rnk. Mem. | Cramer | Lummis | Mullin | Wicker | Sullivan | Graham

Fisheries, Water, and Wildlife
Dem—Padilla, Chair | Cardin | Whitehouse | Markey | Stabenow | Kelly
Rep—Lummis, Rnk. Mem. | Cramer | Ricketts | Boozman | Sullivan

Transportation and Infrastructure
Dem—Kelly, Chair | Cardin | Sanders | Merkley | Markey | Stabenow | Padilla | Fetterman
Rep—Cramer, Rnk. Mem. | Lummis | Mullin | Ricketts | Boozman | Wicker | Graham

FINANCE
SD-219 | 202-224-4515 | Fax: 228-0554 | finance.senate.gov

DEMOCRATS (14)
Ron Wyden, OR, Chair | Debbie Stabenow, MI | Maria Cantwell, WA | Bob Menendez, NJ | Tom Carper, DE | Ben Cardin, MD | Sherrod Brown, OH | Michael Bennet, CO | Bob Casey, PA | Mark R. Warner, VA | Sheldon Whitehouse, RI | Maggie Hassan, NH | Catherine Cortez Masto, NV | Elizabeth Warren, MA

REPUBLICANS (13)
Mike Crapo, ID, Rnk. Mem. | Chuck Grassley, IA | John Cornyn, TX | John Thune, SD | Tim Scott, SC | Bill Cassidy, LA | James Lankford, OK | Steve Daines, MT | Todd Young, IN | John Barrasso, WY | Ron Johnson, WI | Thom Tillis, NC | Marsha Blackburn, TN

Dem. Staff Dir.—Joshua Sheinkman | Rep. Staff Dir.—Gregg Richard

SUBCOMMITTEES
The chair and ranking member are ex officio members of subcommittees on which they do not serve as regular members.

Energy, Natural Resources, and Infrastructure
Dem—Stabenow, Chair | Wyden | Carper | Bennet | Whitehouse | Cortez Masto
Rep—Lankford, Rnk. Mem. | Cornyn | Scott | Daines | Barrasso

Fiscal Responsibility and Economic Growth
Dem—Hassan, Chair | Wyden
Rep—Grassley, Rnk. Mem.

Senate Standing Committees

SUBCOMMITTEES (Finance)

Health Care
Dem—Cardin, Chair | Wyden | Stabenow | Menendez | Carper | Casey | Warner | Whitehouse | Hassan | Cortez Masto | Warren
Rep—Daines, Rnk. Mem. | Grassley | Thune | Scott | Cassidy | Lankford | Young | Barrasso | Johnson | Blackburn

International Trade, Customs, and Global Competitiveness
Dem—Carper, Chair | Wyden | Stabenow | Menendez | Cardin | Brown | Bennet | Casey | Warner | Cortez Masto
Rep—Cornyn, Rnk. Mem. | Thune | Scott | Cassidy | Daines | Young | Barrasso | Johnson | Tillis

Social Security, Pensions, and Family Policy
Dem—Brown, Chair | Wyden | Casey | Hassan | Warren
Rep—Tillis, Rnk. Mem. | Cassidy | Young | Blackburn

Taxation and IRS Oversight
Dem—Bennet, Chair | Wyden | Menendez | Cardin | Warner | Whitehouse | Warren
Rep—Thune, Rnk. Mem. | Grassley | Cornyn | Lankford | Johnson | Blackburn

FOREIGN RELATIONS
SD-423 | 202-224-4651 | foreign.senate.gov

DEMOCRATS (11)
Ben Cardin, MD, Chair | Bob Menendez, NJ | Jeanne Shaheen, NH | Chris Coons, DE | Chris Murphy, CT | Tim Kaine, VA | Jeff Merkley, OR | Cory A. Booker, NJ | Brian Schatz, HI | Chris Van Hollen, MD | Tammy Duckworth, IL

REPUBLICANS (10)
Jim Risch, ID, Rnk. Mem. | Marco Rubio, FL | Mitt Romney, UT | Pete Ricketts, NE | Rand Paul, KY | Todd Young, IN | John Barrasso, WY | Ted Cruz, TX | Bill Hagerty, TN | Tim Scott, SC

Dem. Staff Dir.—Damian Murphy | Rep. Staff Dir.—Chris Socha

SUBCOMMITTEES
The chair and ranking member are ex officio members of subcommittees on which they do not serve as regular members.

Africa and Global Health Policy
Dem—Booker, Chair | Coons | Merkley | Schatz | Van Hollen
Rep—Scott, Rnk. Mem. | Young | Paul | Barrasso

East Asia, the Pacific, and International Cybersecurity Policy
Dem—Van Hollen, Chair | Merkley | Schatz | Duckworth | Coons
Rep—Romney, Rnk. Mem. | Scott | Hagerty | Ricketts

Europe and Regional Security Cooperation
Dem—Shaheen, Chair | Murphy | Van Hollen | Duckworth | Cardin
Rep—Ricketts, Rnk. Mem. | Paul | Barrasso | Rubio

Multilateral International Development, Multilateral Institutions, and International Economic, Energy, and Environmental Policy
Dem—Duckworth, Chair | Coons | Schatz | Shaheen | Kaine
Rep—Barrasso, Rnk. Mem. | Romney | Hagerty | Paul

Near East, South Asia, Central Asia, and Counterterrorism
Dem—Murphy, Chair | Cardin | Shaheen | Kaine | Booker
Rep—Young, Rnk. Mem. | Romney | Cruz | Rubio

Senate Standing Committees

SUBCOMMITTEES (Foreign Relations)

State Department and USAID Management, International Operations, and Bilateral International Development
Dem—Cardin, Chair | Kaine | Booker | Coons | Murphy
Rep—Hagerty, Rnk. Mem. | Ricketts | Cruz | Paul

Western Hemisphere, Transnational Crime, Civilian Security, Democracy, Human Rights, and Global Women's Issues
Dem—Kaine, Chair | Merkley | Cardin | Shaheen | Murphy
Rep—Rubio, Rnk. Mem. | Cruz | Young | Scott

HEALTH, EDUCATION, LABOR, AND PENSIONS
SR-428 | 202-224-5375 | help.senate.gov

DEMOCRATS (11)
Bernie Sanders, VT, Chair | Patty Murray, WA | Bob Casey, PA | Tammy Baldwin, WI | Chris Murphy, CT | Tim Kaine, VA | Maggie Hassan, NH | Tina Smith, MN | Ben Ray Luján, NM | John Hickenlooper, CO | Edward J. Markey, MA

REPUBLICANS (10)
Bill Cassidy, LA, Rnk. Mem. | Rand Paul, KY | Susan Collins, ME | Lisa Murkowski, AK | Mike Braun, IN | Roger Marshall, KS | Mitt Romney, UT | Tommy Tuberville, AL | Markwayne Mullin, OK | Ted Budd, NC

Dem. Staff Dir.—Warren Gunnels | Rep. Staff Dir.—Amanda Lincoln

SUBCOMMITTEES
The chair and ranking member are ex officio members of all subcommittees.

Children and Families
Dem—Casey, Chair | Murray | Murphy | Kaine | Hassan | Smith
Rep—Tuberville, Rnk. Mem. | Paul | Murkowski | Romney | Mullin

Employment and Workplace Safety
Dem—Hickenlooper, Chair | Casey | Baldwin | Kaine | Luján | Markey
Rep—Braun, Rnk. Mem. | Marshall | Romney | Tuberville | Budd

Primary Health and Retirement Security
Dem—Markey, Chair | Murray | Baldwin | Murphy | Hassan | Smith | Luján | Hickenlooper
Rep—Marshall, Rnk. Mem. | Paul | Collins | Murkowski | Braun | Mullin | Budd

HOMELAND SECURITY AND GOVERNMENTAL AFFAIRS
SD-340 | 202-224-2627 | hsgac.senate.gov

DEMOCRATS (8)
Gary Peters, MI, Chair | Tom Carper, DE | Maggie Hassan, NH | Kyrsten Sinema, AZ | Jacky Rosen, NV | Jon Ossoff, GA | Richard Blumenthal, CT | Laphonza Butler, CA

REPUBLICANS (7)
Rand Paul, KY, Rnk. Mem. | Ron Johnson, WI | James Lankford, OK | Mitt Romney, UT | Rick Scott, FL | Josh Hawley, MO | Roger Marshall, KS

Dem. Staff Dir.—David Weinberg | Rep. Staff Dir.—William Henderson

SUBCOMMITTEES
The chair and ranking member are ex officio members of all subcommittees.

Emerging Threats and Spending Oversight
Dem—Hassan, Chair | Sinema | Rosen | Ossoff
Rep—Romney, Rnk. Mem. | Lankford | Scott

Senate Standing Committees

SUBCOMMITTEES (Homeland Security)

Government Operations and Border Management
Dem—Sinema, Chair | Carper | Blumenthal | Butler
Rep—Lankford, Rnk. Mem. | Johnson | Romney

Permanent Subcommittee on Investigations
Dem—Blumenthal, Chair | Carper | Hassan | Ossoff | Butler
Rep—Johnson, Rnk. Mem. | Scott | Hawley | Marshall

JUDICIARY
SD-224 | 202-224-7703 | judiciary.senate.gov

DEMOCRATS (11)
Dick Durbin, IL, Chair | Sheldon Whitehouse, RI | Amy Klobuchar, MN | Chris Coons, DE | Richard Blumenthal, CT | Mazie K. Hirono, HI | Cory A. Booker, NJ | Alex Padilla, CA | Jon Ossoff, GA | Peter Welch, VT | Laphonza Butler, CA

REPUBLICANS (10)
Lindsey Graham, SC, Rnk. Mem. | Chuck Grassley, IA | John Cornyn, TX | Mike Lee, UT | Ted Cruz, TX | Josh Hawley, MO | Tom Cotton, AR | John Kennedy, LA | Thom Tillis, NC | Marsha Blackburn, TN

Dem. Staff Dir.—Joe Zogby | Rep. Staff Dir.—Katherine Nikas

SUBCOMMITTEES
The chair and ranking member are ex officio members of all subcommittees.

Competition Policy, Antitrust, and Consumer Rights
Dem—Klobuchar, Chair | Whitehouse | Coons | Blumenthal | Hirono | Booker | Welch
Rep—Lee, Rnk. Mem. | Grassley | Hawley | Cotton | Tillis | Blackburn

Constitution
Dem—Butler, Chair | Blumenthal | Booker | Ossoff
Rep—Cruz, Rnk. Mem. | Cornyn | Lee

Criminal Justice and Counterterrorism
Dem—Booker, Chair | Whitehouse | Klobuchar | Coons | Padilla | Ossoff | Butler
Rep—Cotton, Rnk. Mem. | Grassley | Cornyn | Lee | Cruz | Kennedy

Federal Courts, Oversight, Agency Action, and Federal Rights
Dem—Whitehouse, Chair | Blumenthal | Hirono | Booker | Padilla | Welch | Butler
Rep—Kennedy, Rnk. Mem. | Grassley | Lee | Cruz | Tillis | Hawley

Human Rights and the Law
Dem—Ossoff, Chair | Blumenthal | Welch | Butler
Rep—Blackburn, Rnk. Mem. | Kennedy | Hawley

Immigration, Citizenship, and Border Safety
Dem—Padilla, Chair | Whitehouse | Klobuchar | Coons | Hirono | Booker | Welch
Rep—Cornyn, Rnk. Mem. | Grassley | Cruz | Cotton | Tillis | Blackburn

Intellectual Property
Dem—Coons, Chair | Hirono | Padilla | Ossoff | Welch
Rep—Tillis, Rnk. Mem. | Cornyn | Cotton | Blackburn

Privacy, Technology, and the Law
Dem—Blumenthal, Chair | Klobuchar | Coons | Hirono | Padilla | Ossoff
Rep—Hawley, Rnk. Mem. | Kennedy | Blackburn | Lee | Cornyn

Senate Standing Committees

RULES AND ADMINISTRATION
SR-305 | 202-224-6352 | rules.senate.gov

DEMOCRATS (9)
Amy Klobuchar, MN, Chair | Chuck Schumer, NY | Mark R. Warner, VA | Jeff Merkley, OR | Alex Padilla, CA | Jon Ossoff, GA | Michael Bennet, CO | Peter Welch, VT | Laphonza Butler, CA

REPUBLICANS (8)
Deb Fischer, NE, Rnk. Mem. | Mitch McConnell, KY | Ted Cruz, TX | Shelley Moore Capito, WV | Roger F. Wicker, MS | Cindy Hyde-Smith, MS | Bill Hagerty, TN | Katie Britt, AL

Dem. Staff Dir.—Elizabeth Farrar | Rep. Staff Dir.—Jackie Barber

NO SUBCOMMITTEES

SMALL BUSINESS AND ENTREPRENEURSHIP
SR-428A | 202-224-5175 | Fax: 224-5619 | sbc.senate.gov

DEMOCRATS (10)
Jeanne Shaheen, NH, Chair | Maria Cantwell, WA | Ben Cardin, MD | Edward J. Markey, MA | Cory A. Booker, NJ | Chris Coons, DE | Mazie K. Hirono, HI | Tammy Duckworth, IL | Jacky Rosen, NV | John Hickenlooper, CO

REPUBLICANS (9)
Joni Ernst, IA, Rnk. Mem. | Marco Rubio, FL | Jim Risch, ID | Rand Paul, KY | Tim Scott, SC | Todd Young, IN | John Kennedy, LA | Josh Hawley, MO | Ted Budd, NC

Dem. Staff Dir.—Sean Moore | Rep. Staff Dir.—Meredith West

NO SUBCOMMITTEES

VETERANS' AFFAIRS
SR-412 | 202-224-9126 | veterans.senate.gov

DEMOCRATS (10)
Jon Tester, MT, Chair | Patty Murray, WA | Bernie Sanders, VT | Sherrod Brown, OH | Richard Blumenthal, CT | Mazie K. Hirono, HI | Joe Manchin, WV | Kyrsten Sinema, AZ | Maggie Hassan, NH | Angus King, ME

REPUBLICANS (9)
Jerry Moran, KS, Rnk. Mem. | John Boozman, AR | Bill Cassidy, LA | Mike Rounds, SD | Thom Tillis, NC | Dan Sullivan, AK | Marsha Blackburn, TN | Kevin Cramer, ND | Tommy Tuberville, AL

Dem. Staff Dir.—Tony McClain | Rep. Staff Dir.—David Shearman

NO SUBCOMMITTEES

Senate Other Committee

INDIAN AFFAIRS
SH-838 | 202-224-2251 | Fax: 228-2589 | indian.senate.gov

DEMOCRATS (6)
Brian Schatz, HI, Chair | Maria Cantwell, WA | Jon Tester, MT | Catherine Cortez Masto, NV | Tina Smith, MN | Ben Ray Luján, NM

REPUBLICANS (5)
Lisa Murkowski, AK, Vice Chair | John Hoeven, ND | Steve Daines, MT | Markwayne Mullin, OK | Mike Rounds, SD

Dem. Staff Dir.—Jennifer Romero Monaco | Rep. Staff Dir.—Amber Ebarb

NO SUBCOMMITTEES

Senate Select Committees

ETHICS
SH-220 | 202-224-2981 | Fax: 224-7416 | ethics.senate.gov

DEMOCRATS (3)
Chris Coons, DE, Chair | Brian Schatz, HI | Jeanne Shaheen, NH

REPUBLICANS (3)
James Lankford, OK, Vice Chair | Jim Risch, ID | Deb Fischer, NE

Staff Dir.—Shannon Hamilton Kopplin

NO SUBCOMMITTEES

INTELLIGENCE
SH-211 | 202-224-1700 | Fax: 224-1772 | intelligence.senate.gov

DEMOCRATS (11)
Mark R. Warner, VA, Chair | Ron Wyden, OR | Martin Heinrich, NM | Angus King, ME | Michael Bennet, CO | Bob Casey, PA | Kirsten Gillibrand, NY | Jon Ossoff, GA | Mark Kelly, AZ | Chuck Schumer, NY, Ex Officio | Jack Reed, RI, Ex Officio

REPUBLICANS (10)
Marco Rubio, FL, Vice Chair | Jim Risch, ID | Susan Collins, ME | Tom Cotton, AR | John Cornyn, TX | Jerry Moran, KS | James Lankford, OK | Mike Rounds, SD | Mitch McConnell, KY, Ex Officio | Roger F. Wicker, MS, Ex Officio

Dem. Staff Dir.—William Wu | Rep. Staff Dir.—Brian W. Walsh

NO SUBCOMMITTEES

Senate Special Committee

AGING

SD-G16 | 202-224-5364 | aging.senate.gov

DEMOCRATS (7)
Bob Casey, PA, Chair | Kirsten Gillibrand, NY | Richard Blumenthal, CT | Elizabeth Warren, MA | Mark Kelly, AZ | Raphael Warnock, GA | John Fetterman, PA

REPUBLICANS (6)
Mike Braun, IN, Rnk. Mem. | Tim Scott, SC | Marco Rubio, FL | Rick Scott, FL | J.D. Vance, OH | Pete Ricketts, NE

Dem. Staff Dir.—Lizzy Letter | Rep. Staff Dir.—Matt Sommer

NO SUBCOMMITTEES

House of Representatives Leadership

SPEAKER
Mike Johnson (R-4th LA) | H-232 Capitol | 225-4000 | Chief of Staff—Hayden Haynes

MAJORITY LEADER
Steve Scalise (R-1st LA) | H-329 Capitol | 225-0197 | Chief of Staff—Brett Horton

MAJORITY WHIP
Tom Emmer (R-6th MN) | H-107 Capitol | 225-2210 | Chief of Staff—Robert Boland

REPUBLICAN POLICY COMMITTEE CHAIR
Gary Palmer (R-6th AL) | 170 CHOB | 225-4921 | Chief of Staff—William Smith

REPUBLICAN CONFERENCE CHAIR
Elise Stefanik (R-21st NY) | 2211 RHOB | 225-4611 | Chief of Staff—Patrick Stewart Hester

MINORITY LEADER
Hakeem Jeffries (D-8th NY) | H-204 Capitol | 225-4700 | Chief of Staff—Tasia Jackson

MINORITY WHIP
Katherine Clark (D-5th MA) | H-148 Capitol | 225-2020 | Chief of Staff—Brooke Scannell

ASSISTANT DEMOCRATIC LEADER
James Clyburn (D-6th SC) | 274 CHOB | 226-3210 | Chief of Staff—Yelberton Watkins

DEMOCRATIC CAUCUS CHAIR
Pete Aguilar (D-33rd CA) | 1420 LHOB | 225-1400 | Exec. Dir.—Sonali Desai

House of Representatives Officers

CLERK OF THE HOUSE
Kevin F. McCumber (Acting) | H-154 Capitol | 225-7000

CHIEF ADMINISTRATIVE OFFICER
Catherine Szpindor | H-B28 Capitol | 225-5555

SERGEANT AT ARMS
William McFarland | H-124 Capitol | 225-2456

PARLIAMENTARIAN
Jason Smith | H-209 Capitol | 225-7373

INSPECTOR GENERAL
Joseph C. Picolla | 386 FHOB | 226-1250

CHAPLAIN
Dr. Margaret Grun Kibben | HB25, Capitol | 225-2509

HOUSE HISTORIAN
Matt Wasniewski | LJ-Attic | 226-5525

House of Representatives Offices

Legislative Resource Center | B81 CHOB | 226-5200

Republican Cloakroom | H-223 Capitol | 225-7350

Democratic Cloakroom | H-222 Capitol | 225-7330

Floor Information | 225-7400

Daily Press Gallery | H-315 Capitol | 225-3945

Periodical Press Gallery | H-304 Capitol | 225-2941

Radio and Television Gallery | H-320 Capitol | 225-5214

Switchboard | 225-3121

Area code for all numbers in 202

United States House of Representatives — Notes

Alma S. Adams, NC | 12th District | 6th Term | 62% (+25)
2436 RHOB | 202-225-1510 | Fax: 225-1512
adams.house.gov | X @repadams
Bio—Charlotte; High Point, NC, 5/27/1946; PhD, Ohio St. Univ., 1981; artist, educator; Greensboro city council, 1987-94; NC House, 1994-2014; US House, 2014-present; div.; Baptist
Committees—Agriculture; Education & the Workforce
District Offices—Charlotte, 704-344-9950

Democrat

Robert Aderholt, AL | 4th District | 14th Term | 84% (+70)
266 CHOB | 202-225-4876 | Fax: 225-5587
aderholt.house.gov | X @robertaderholt
Bio—Haleyville; Haleyville, AL, 7/22/1965; JD, Samford Univ., 1990; lawyer; Haleyville municipal judge, 1992-95; US House, 1997-present; m. Caroline; Congregationalist
Committees—Appropriations
District Offices—Jasper, 205-221-2310; Cullman, 256-734-6043; Gadsden, 256-546-0201; Tuscumbia, 256-381-3450

Republican

Pete Aguilar, CA | 33rd District | 5th Term | 57% (+15)
108 CHOB | 202-225-3201
aguilar.house.gov | X @reppeteaguilar
Bio—Redlands; Fontana, CA, 6/19/1979; BS, Univ. of Redlands, 2001; business owner, credit union executive; Redlands city council, 2006-14; Redlands mayor, 2010-14; US House, 2015-present; m. Alisha; Catholic
Committees—Appropriations
District Offices—San Bernardino, 909-890-4445

Democrat

Mark Alford, MO | 4th District | 1st Term | 71% (+45)
1516 LHOB | 202-225-2876
alford.house.gov | X @repmarkalford
Bio—Lake Winnebago; Baytown, TX, 10/4/1963; attended Univ. of Texas; television news anchor, realtor, business owner; US House, 2023-present; m. Leslie; Protestant
Committees—Agriculture; Armed Services; Small Business
District Offices—Raymore, 816-441-6318; Columbia, 573-540-6600; Lebanon, 417-532-5582

Republican

Rick W. Allen, GA | 12th District | 5th Term | 59% (+19)
462 CHOB | 202-225-2823 | Fax: 225-3377
allen.house.gov | X @reprickallen
Bio—Augusta; Augusta, GA, 11/7/1951; BS, Auburn Univ., 1973; business owner; US House, 2015-present; m. Robin; Methodist
Committees—Education & the Workforce; Energy & Commerce
District Offices—Augusta, 706-228-1980; Dublin, 478-291-6324; Statesboro, 912-243-9452

Republican

Colin Allred, TX | 32nd District | 3rd Term | 65% (+31)
348 CHOB | 202-225-2231
allred.house.gov | X @repcolinallred
Bio—Dallas; Dallas, TX, 4/15/1983; JD, Univ. of California, Berkeley, 2014; professional athlete, lawyer; US House, 2019-present; m. Alexandra; Methodist
Committees—Foreign Affairs; Transportation & Infrastructure
District Offices—Richardson, 972-972-7949

Democrat

United States House of Representatives

Notes

Gabe Amo, RI | 1st District | 1st Term | 64% (+30)
2233 RHOB | 202-225-4911 | Fax: 225-3290
amo.house.gov | X @repgabeamo
Bio—Providence; Pawtucket, RI, 12/11/1987; MSc, Oxford Univ., 2010; government official; US House, 2023-present; single; Catholic
Committees—Foreign Affairs; Science, Space, & Technology
District Offices—Pawtucket, 401-729-5600

Democrat

Mark Amodei, NV | 2nd District | 7th Term | 59% (+22)
104 CHOB | 202-225-6155 | Fax: 225-5679
amodei.house.gov | X @markamodeinv2
Bio—Carson City; Carson City, NV, 6/12/1958; JD, Univ. of the Pacific, 1983; USA, 1984-87; lawyer; NV Assembly, 1997; NV Senate, 1999-2011; US House, 2011-present; div.; Protestant
Committees—Appropriations; Joint Library
District Offices—Elko, 775-777-7705; Reno, 775-686-5760

Republican

Kelly Armstrong, ND | At Large | 3rd Term | 62% (+25)
2235 RHOB | 202-225-2611 | Fax: 226-3410
armstrong.house.gov | X @reparmstrongnd
Bio—Bismarck; Dickinson, ND, 10/8/1976; JD, Univ. of North Dakota, 2003; lawyer, business executive; ND Senate, 2013-18; US House, 2019-present; m. Kjersti; Lutheran
Committees—Energy & Commerce; Judiciary
District Offices—Bismarck, 701-354-6700; Fargo, 701-353-6665

Republican

Jodey Arrington, TX | 19th District | 4th Term | 80% (+61)
1107 LHOB | 202-225-4005 | Fax: 225-9615
arrington.house.gov | X @reparrington
Bio—Lubbock; Plainview, TX, 3/9/1972; MA, Texas Tech Univ., 1997; business executive; US House, 2017-present; m. Anne; Presbyterian
Committees—Budget (Chair); Ways and Means; Joint Economic
District Offices—Lubbock, 806-763-1611; Abilene, 325-675-9779

Republican

Jake Auchincloss, MA | 4th District | 2nd Term | Unc.
1524 LHOB | 202-225-5931 | Fax: 225-0182
auchincloss.house.gov | X @repauchincloss
Bio—Newton; Boston, MA, 1/29/1988; MBA, Massachusetts Institute of Technology, 2016; USMC, 2010-15; USMCR; business professional; Newton city council, 2016-20; US House, 2021-present; m. Michelle; Jewish
Committees—Transportation & Infrastructure; Select CCP
District Offices—Newton, 617-332-3333; Attleboro, 508-431-1110

Democrat

Brian Babin, TX | 36th District | 5th Term | 69% (+39)
2236 RHOB | 202-225-1555 | Fax: 226-0396
babin.house.gov | X @repbrianbabin
Bio—Woodville; Port Arthur, TX, 3/23/1948; DDS, Univ. of Texas, 1976; USAF, 1975-79; TXARNG, 1969-75; dentist; Woodville alderman, 1981-82, 1984-89; Woodville mayor, 1982-84; US House, 2015-present; m. Roxanne; Baptist
Committees—Science, Space, & Technology; Transportation & Infrastructure
District Offices—Deer Park, 832-780-0966; Lumberton, 409-883-8075; Woodville, 409-331-8066; Dayton, 832-780-0966

Republican

United States House of Representatives   Notes

Don Bacon, NE | 2nd District | 4th Term | 51% (+3)
2104 RHOB | 202-225-4155
bacon.house.gov | X @repdonbacon
Bio—Papillion; Chicago Heights, IL, 8/16/1963; MA, National War Col., 2004; USAF, 1985-2014; professor, congressional staffer; US House, 2017-present; m. Angie; Christian
Committees—Agriculture; Armed Services
District Offices—Omaha, 402-938-0300; Wahoo, 402-607-0077

Republican

Jim Baird, IN | 4th District | 3rd Term | 68% (+36)
2303 RHOB | 202-225-5037 | Fax: 226-0544
baird.house.gov | X @repjimbaird
Bio—Greencastle; Fountain County, IN, 6/4/1945; PhD, Univ. of Kentucky, 1975; USA, 1969-72; farmer, small business owner; Putnam Co. commissioner, 2006-10; IN Assembly, 2010-18; US House, 2019-present; m. Danise; Methodist
Committees—Agriculture; Foreign Affairs; Science, Space, & Technology
District Offices—Danville, 317-563-5567

Republican

Troy Balderson, OH | 12th District | 4th Term | 69% (+39)
2429 RHOB | 202-225-5355
balderson.house.gov | X @repbalderson
Bio—Zanesville; Zanesville, OH, 1/16/1962; attended Ohio St. Univ., 1982-83; farmer, automobile dealer; OH House, 2009-11; OH Senate, 2011-18; US House, 2018-present; div.; Christian
Committees—Energy & Commerce
District Offices—Pickerington, 614-523-2555

Republican

Becca Balint, VT | At Large | 1st Term | 60% (+34)
1408 LHOB | 202-225-4115 | Fax: 200-5791
balint.house.gov | X @repbeccab
Bio—Brattleboro; Heidelberg, Germany, 5/4/1968; MA, Univ. of Massachusetts, 2000; teacher, editorial columnist; VT Senate, 2015-23; US House, 2023-present; m. Elizabeth Wohl; Jewish
Committees—Budget; Judiciary
District Offices—Burlington, 802-652-2450; Brattleboro, 802-652-2450

Democrat

Jim Banks, IN | 3rd District | 4th Term | 65% (+35)
2418 RHOB | 202-225-4436
banks.house.gov | X @repjimbanks
Bio—Columbia City; Columbia City, IN, 7/16/1979; MBA, Grace Col. and Seminary, 2013; USNR, 2012-present; real estate broker; Whitley Co. council, 2008-10; IN Senate, 2010-16; US House, 2017-present; m. Amanda; Presbyterian
Committees—Armed Services; Education & the Workforce; Select CCP
District Offices—Fort Wayne, 260-702-4750

Republican

Andy Barr, KY | 6th District | 6th Term | 62% (+29)
2430 RHOB | 202-225-4706
barr.house.gov | X @repandybarr
Bio—Lexington; Lexington, KY, 7/24/1973; JD, Univ. of Kentucky, 2001; lawyer; US House, 2013-present; m. Davis; Episcopalian
Committees—Financial Services; Foreign Affairs; Select CCP
District Offices—Lexington, 859-219-1366

Republican

United States House of Representatives

Nanette Diaz Barragán, CA | 44th District | 4th Term | 72% (+44)
2312 RHOB | 202-225-8220
barragan.house.gov | X @repbarragan
Bio—Los Angeles; Los Angeles, CA, 9/15/1976; JD, Univ. of Southern California, Los Angeles, 2005; lawyer; Hermosa Beach, city council, 2013-15; US House, 2017-present; single; Catholic
Committees—Energy & Commerce
District Offices—Long Beach, 310-831-1799; South Gate, 310-831-1799; Carson, 310-831-1799; San Pedro, 310-831-1799

Democrat

Aaron Bean, FL | 4th District | 1st Term | 60% (+21)
1239 LHOB | 202-225-0123
bean.house.gov | X @repaaronbean
Bio—Fernandina Beach; Fernandina Beach, FL, 1/25/1967; BS, Jacksonville Univ., 1989; auctioneer, business owner, bank president; Fernandina Beach city commissioner, 1996-99; Fernandina Beach mayor, 1997-99; FL House, 2000-08; FL Senate, 2012-22; US House, 2023-present; m. Abby; Protestant
Committees—Education & the Workforce; Small Business; Transportation & Infrastructure
District Offices—Jacksonville, 904-319-9433; Fernandina Beach, 904-557-9550; Green Cove Springs, 904-319-9433

Republican

Joyce Beatty, OH | 3rd District | 6th Term | 70% (+41)
2079 RHOB | 202-225-4324 | Fax: 225-1984
beatty.house.gov | X @repbeatty
Bio—Columbus; Dayton, OH, 3/12/1950; MS, Wright State Univ., 1974; professor, businesswoman; OH House, 1999-2008, US House, 2013-present; wid.; Baptist
Committees—Financial Services
District Offices—Columbus, 614-220-0003

Democrat

Cliff Bentz, OR | 2nd District | 2nd Term | 67% (+35)
409 CHOB | 202-225-6730 | Fax: 225-5774
bentz.house.gov | X @repbentz
Bio—Ontario; Salem, OR, 1/12/1952; JD, Lewis and Clark Col., 1977; rancher, farmer, lawyer; OR House, 2008-18; OR Senate, 2018-20; US House, 2021-present; m. Lindsay; Catholic
Committees—Judiciary; Natural Resources
District Offices—Medford, 541-776-4646; Ontario, 541-709-2040

Republican

Ami Bera, CA | 6th District | 6th Term | 55% (+12)
172 CHOB | 202-225-5716 | Fax: 226-1298
bera.house.gov | X @repbera
Bio—Elk Grove; Los Angeles, CA, 3/2/1965; MD, Univ. of California, 1991; physician, professor; US House, 2013-present; m. Janine; Unitarian
Committees—Foreign Affairs; Intelligence
District Offices—Sacramento, 916-635-0505

Democrat

Jack Bergman, MI | 1st District | 4th Term | 59% (+23)
566 CHOB | 202-225-4735
bergman.house.gov | X @repjackbergman
Bio—Watersmeet; Shakopee, MN, 2/2/1947; MBA, Univ. of West Florida, 1975; USMC, 1969-2009; pilot, business owner; US House, 2017-present; m. Cindy; Lutheran
Committees—Armed Services; Budget; Veterans' Affairs
District Offices—Traverse City, 231-944-7633; Gwinn, 906-273-2227; Manistique, 906-286-4191

Republican

Notes

U.S. Congress Directory | 67

United States House of Representatives

Don Beyer, VA | 8th District | 5th Term | 73% (+49)
1119 LHOB | 202-225-4376 | Fax: 225-0017
beyer.house.gov | X @repdonbeyer
Bio—Alexandria; Trieste, Italy, 6/20/1950; BA, Williams Col., 1972; automobile dealer; VA lt. governor, 1990-98; US ambassador to Switzerland and Liechtenstein, 2009-13; US House, 2015-present; m. Megan; Episcopalian
Committees—Ways and Means; Joint Economic
District Offices—Arlington, 703-658-5403
Democrat

Stephanie Bice, OK | 5th District | 2nd Term | 59% (+22)
2437 RHOB | 202-225-2132
bice.house.gov | X @repbice
Bio—Oklahoma City; Oklahoma City, OK, 11/11/1973; BA, Oklahoma St. Univ., 1995; marketing executive; OK Senate, 2014-20; US House, 2021-present; m. Geoffrey; Catholic
Committees—Appropriations; House Administration; Science, Space, & Technology
District Offices—Oklahoma City, 405-300-6890
Republican

Andy Biggs, AZ | 5th District | 4th Term | 56% (+19)
252 CHOB | 202-225-2635
biggs.house.gov | X @repandybiggsaz
Bio—Gilbert; Tucson, AZ, 11/7/1958; MA, Arizona St. Univ., 1999; lawyer; AZ House, 2003-11; AZ Senate, 2011-16; US House, 2017-present; m. Cindy; Mormon
Committees—Judiciary; Oversight & Accountability
District Offices—Mesa, 480-699-8239
Republican

Gus M. Bilirakis, FL | 12th District | 9th Term | 70% (+41)
2306 RHOB | 202-225-5755
bilirakis.house.gov | X @repgusbilirakis
Bio—Palm Harbor; Gainesville, FL, 2/8/1963; JD, Stetson Univ., 1989; lawyer, professor; FL House, 1998-2006; US House, 2007-present; m. Eva; Greek Orthodox
Committees—Energy & Commerce
District Offices—Brooksville, 352-691-1231; New Port Richey, 727-232-2921; Inverness, 352-654-1004
Republican

Dan Bishop, NC | 8th District | 3rd Term | 69% (+40)
2459 RHOB | 202-225-1976
danbishop.house.gov | X @repdanbishop
Bio—Charlotte; Charlotte, NC, 7/1/1964; JD, Univ. of North Carolina, 1990; lawyer; Mecklenburg Co. commission, 2004-08; NC House, 2015-17; NC Senate, 2017-19; US House, 2019-present; m. Jo; Methodist
Committees—Homeland Security; Judiciary
District Offices—Monroe, 704-218-5300
Republican

Sanford D. Bishop, Jr., GA | 2nd District | 16th Term | 54% (+10)
2407 RHOB | 202-225-3631 | Fax: 225-2203
bishop.house.gov | X @sanfordbishop
Bio—Albany; Mobile, AL, 2/4/1947; JD, Emory Univ., 1971; USA, 1969-71; lawyer; GA House, 1977-91; GA Senate, 1991-93; US House, 1993-present; m. Vivian; Baptist
Committees—Agriculture; Appropriations
District Offices—Albany, 229-439-8067; Columbus, 706-320-9477; Macon, 478-803-2631
Democrat

United States House of Representatives

Earl Blumenauer, OR | 3rd District | 15th Term | 69% (+44)
1111 LHOB | 202-225-4811 | Fax: 225-8941
blumenauer.house.gov
Bio—Portland; Portland, OR, 8/16/1948; JD, Lewis and Clark Law School, 1976; education administrator, public official; OR House, 1973-78; Multnomah Co. commission, 1978-85; Portland city commission, 1986-96; US House, 1996-present; m. Margaret Kirkpatrick; not stated
Committees—Budget; Ways and Means
District Offices—Portland, 503-231-2300

Democrat

Lisa Blunt Rochester, DE | At Large | 4th Term | 55% (+13)
1724 LHOB | 202-225-4165
bluntrochester.house.gov | X @replbr
Bio—Wilmington; Philadelphia, PA, 2/10/1962; MA, Univ. of Delaware, 2003; public official; DE labor secy., 1998-2001; US House, 2017-present; single; Protestant
Committees—Energy & Commerce
District Offices—Wilmington, 302-830-2330; Georgetown, 302-858-4773

Democrat

Lauren Boebert, CO | 3rd District | 2nd Term | 50% (+.2)
1713 LHOB | 202-225-4761
boebert.house.gov | X @repb
Bio—Silt; Altamonte Springs, FL, 12/19/1986; GED, 2020; restaurateur, business owner; US House, 2021-present; div.; Christian
Committees—Natural Resources; Oversight & Accountability
District Offices—Durango, 970-317-6130; Pueblo, 719-696-6970; Grand Junction, 970-208-0460

Republican

Suzanne Bonamici, OR | 1st District | 7th Term | 67% (+36)
2231 RHOB | 202-225-0855 | Fax: 225-9497
bonamici.house.gov | X @repbonamici
Bio—Beaverton; Detroit, MI, 10/14/1954; JD, Univ. of Oregon, 1983; lawyer; OR House, 2007-08; OR Senate, 2008-11; US House, 2012-present; m. Michael; not stated
Committees—Education & the Workforce; Science, Space, & Technology
District Offices—Beaverton, 503-469-6010

Democrat

Mike Bost, IL | 12th District | 5th Term | 75% (+50)
352 CHOB | 202-225-5661 | Fax: 448-4233
bost.house.gov | X @repbost
Bio—Murphysboro; Murphysboro, IL, 12/30/1960; Certified Firefighter II Academy, University of Illinois, 1993; USMC, 1979-82; firefighter, business owner; Jackson Co. board, 1984-88; IL House, 1995-2014; US House, 2015-present; m. Tracy; Baptist
Committees—Agriculture; Transportation & Infrastructure; Veterans' Affairs (Chair)
District Offices—Mascoutah, 618-622-0766; Murphysboro, 618-457-5787; Effingham, 217-240-3170

Republican

Jamaal Bowman, NY | 16th District | 2nd Term | 64% (+28)
345 CHOB | 202-225-2464 | Fax: 225-5513
bowman.house.gov | X @repbowman
Bio—Yonkers; Manhattan, NY, 4/1/1976; EdD, Manhattanville Col., 2019; teacher, principal; US House, 2021-present; m. Melissa Oppenheimer; not stated
Committees—Education & the Workforce; Science, Space, & Technology
District Offices—Mt. Vernon, 914-371-9220; White Plains, 914-323-5550

Democrat

United States House of Representatives

Brendan F. Boyle, PA | 2nd District | 5th Term | 75% (+51)
1502 LHOB | 202-225-6111 | Fax: 226-0611
boyle.house.gov | X @congboyle
Bio—Philadelphia; Philadelphia, PA, 2/6/1977; MPP, Harvard Univ., 2005; radio broadcaster, management consultant; PA House, 2008-14; US House, 2015-present; m. Jennifer; Catholic
Committees—Budget (Rnk. Mem.)
District Offices—Philadelphia, 267-335-5643; Philadelphia, 215-335-3355; Philadelphia, 215-982-1156

Democrat

Josh Brecheen, OK | 2nd District | 1st Term | 72% (+49)
1208 LHOB | 202-225-2701
brecheen.house.gov | X @repbrecheen
Bio—Coalgate; Ada, OK, 6/19/1979; BS, Oklahoma St. Univ., 2002; rancher; small business owner; OK Senate, 2010-18; US House, 2023-present; m. Kacie; Protestant
Committees—Budget; Homeland Security
District Offices—Claremore, 918-283-6262

Republican

Shontel Brown, OH | 11th District | 2nd Term | 77% (+56)
449 CHOB | 202-225-7032
shontelbrown.house.gov | X @repshontelbrown
Bio—Warrensville Heights; Cleveland, OH, 6/24/1975; AS, Cuyahoga Comm. Col.; business owner; Warrensville Heights city council, 2012-15; Cuyahoga Co. council, 2015-21; US House, 2021-present; single; Baptist
Committees—Agriculture; Oversight & Accountability; Select CCP
District Offices—Cleveland, 216-535-1100; Beachwood, 216-522-4900

Democrat

Julia Brownley, CA | 26th District | 6th Term | 54% (+9)
2262 RHOB | 202-225-5811 | Fax: 225-1100
juliabrownley.house.gov | X @repbrownley
Bio—Westlake Village; Aiken, SC, 8/28/1952; MBA, American Univ., 1979; marketing executive; CA Assembly, 2006-12; US House, 2013-present; single; Episcopalian
Committees—Transportation & Infrastructure; Veterans' Affairs
District Offices—Thousand Oaks, 805-379-1779; Oxnard, 805-379-1779

Democrat

Vern Buchanan, FL | 16th District | 9th Term | 62% (+24)
2110 RHOB | 202-225-5015 | Fax: 226-0828
buchanan.house.gov | X @vernbuchanan
Bio—Sarasota; Detroit, MI, 5/8/1951; MBA, Univ. of Detroit, 1986; MIANG, 1970-76; businessman; US House, 2007-present; m. Sandy; Baptist
Committees—Ways and Means; Joint Taxation
District Offices—Brandon, 813-657-1013; Bradenton, 941-951-6643; Longboat Key, 941-951-6643

Republican

Ken Buck, CO | 4th District | 5th Term | 60% (+24)
2455 RHOB | 202-225-4676
buck.house.gov | X @repkenbuck
Bio—Windsor; Ossining, NY, 2/16/1959; JD, Univ. of Wyoming, 1985; business executive, lawyer; US House, 2015-present; div.; Christian
Committees—Foreign Affairs; Judiciary
District Offices—Castle Rock, 720-639-9165; Windsor, 970-702-2136

Republican

NLPC | 70

United States House of Representatives

Larry Bucshon, IN | 8th District | 7th Term | 65% (+34)
2313 RHOB | 202-225-4636 | Fax: 225-3284
bucshon.house.gov | X @replarrybucshon
Bio—Evansville; Taylorville, IL, 5/31/1962; MD, Univ. of Illinois, 1988; USNR, 1989-98; physician; US House, 2011-present; m. Kathryn; Lutheran
Committees—Energy & Commerce
District Offices—Evansville, 812-465-6484; Terre Haute, 812-232-0523

Republican

Nikki Budzinski, IL | 13th District | 1st Term | 56% (+13)
1009 LHOB | 202-225-2371
budzinski.house.gov | X @repnikkib
Bio—Springfield; Peoria, IL, 3/11/1977; BA, Univ. of Illinois, 1999; union activist; US House, 2023-present; single; not stated
Committees—Agriculture; Veterans' Affairs
District Offices—Springfield, 217-814-2880; Belleville, 618-212-7333; Champaign, 217-305-6991; Decatur, 217-859-5313

Democrat

Tim Burchett, TN | 2nd District | 3rd Term | 67% (+36)
1122 LHOB | 202-225-5435
burchett.house.gov | X @reptimburchett
Bio—Knoxville; Knoxville, TN, 8/25/1964; BS, Univ. of Tennessee, 1988; business owner; TN House, 1994-98; TN Senate, 1998-2010; Knox Co. mayor, 2010-18; US House, 2019-present; m. Kelly; Presbyterian
Committees—Foreign Affairs; Oversight & Accountability; Transportation & Infrastructure
District Offices—Knoxville, 865-523-3772; Maryville, 865-984-5464

Republican

Michael C. Burgess, TX | 26th District | 11th Term | 69% (+39)
2161 RHOB | 202-225-7772 | Fax: 225-2919
burgess.house.gov | X @michaelcburgess
Bio—Pilot Point; Rochester, MN, 12/23/1950; MD, University of Texas, 1977; physician; US House, 2003-present; m. Laura; Episcopalian
Committees—Budget; Energy & Commerce; Rules
District Offices—Lake Dallas, 940-497-5031

Republican

Eric Burlison, MO | 7th District | 1st Term | 70% (+44)
1108 LHOB | 202-225-6536
burlison.house.gov | X @repericburlison
Bio—Ozark; Springfield, MO, 10/2/1976; MBA, Missouri St. Univ., 2002; financial analyst, tax consultant, software engineer; MO House, 2009-17; MO Senate, 2019-23; US House, 2023-present; m. Angie; Protestant
Committees—Education & the Workforce; Oversight & Accountability; Transportation & Infrastructure
District Offices—Springfield, 417-889-1800; Joplin, 417-781-1041

Republican

Cori Bush, MO | 1st District | 2nd Term | 72% (+49)
2463 RHOB | 202-225-2406 | Fax: 226-3717
bush.house.gov | X @repcori
Bio—St. Louis; St. Louis, MO, 7/21/1976; RN, Lutheran School of Nursing, 2008; teacher, nurse, pastor; US House, 2021-present; m. Cortney Merritts; Christian
Committees—Judiciary; Oversight & Accountability
District Offices—St. Louis, 314-955-9980

Democrat

United States House of Representatives

Ken Calvert, CA | 41st District | 16th Term | 52% (+5)
2205 RHOB | 202-225-1986 | Fax: 225-2004
calvert.house.gov | X @kencalvert
Bio—Corona; Corona, CA, 6/8/1953; BA, San Diego St. Univ., 1975; business owner; US House, 1993-present; div.; Episcopalian
Committees—Appropriations
District Offices—Palm Desert, 760-620-0041; Corona, 951-277-0042
Republican

Kat Cammack, FL | 3rd District | 2nd Term | 62% (+26)
2421 RHOB | 202-225-5744
cammack.house.gov | X @repkatcammack
Bio—Gainesville; Denver, CO, 2/16/1988; MS, Naval War Col., 2018; small business owner, congressional staff; US House, 2021-present; m. Matt; Protestant
Committees—Agriculture; Energy & Commerce
District Offices—Ocala, 352-421-9052; Gainesville, 352-505-0838
Republican

Yadira Caraveo, CO | 8th District | 1st Term | 48% (+.7)
1024 LHOB | 202-225-5625 | Fax: 200-5726
caraveo.house.gov | X @repcaraveomd
Bio—Thornton; Denver, CO, 12/23/1980; MD, Univ. of Colorado, 2009; pediatrician, union executive; CO House, 2019-22; US House, 2023-present; single; Catholic
Committees—Agriculture; Science, Space, & Technology
District Offices—Northglenn, 303-723-6560; Greeley, 970-324-2567
Democrat

Salud Carbajal, CA | 24th District | 4th Term | 60% (+21)
2331 RHOB | 202-225-3601
carbajal.house.gov | X @repcarbajal
Bio—Santa Barbara; Moroleon, Mexico, 11/18/1964; MA, Fielding Graduate Univ., 1994; USMCR, 1984-92; public official; Santa Barbara Co. supervisor, 2004-16; US House, 2017-present; m. Gina; Catholic
Committees—Agriculture; Armed Services; Transportation & Infrastructure
District Offices—Santa Barbara, 805-730-1710; Ventura, 805-730-1710; San Luis Obispo, 805-546-8348
Democrat

Tony Cárdenas, CA | 29th District | 6th Term | 58% (+17)
2181 RHOB | 202-225-6131 | Fax: 225-0819
cardenas.house.gov | X @repcardenas
Bio—Pacoima; San Fernando, CA, 3/31/1963; BA, Univ. of California, Santa Barbara, 1986; realtor, insurance agent; CA Assembly, 1996-2002; Los Angeles city council, 2003-13; US House, 2013-present; m. Norma; Christian
Committees—Energy & Commerce
District Offices—Panorama City, 818-221-3718
Democrat

Mike Carey, OH | 15th District | 2nd Term | 56% (+14)
1433 LHOB | 202-225-2015
carey.house.gov | X @mikecarey
Bio—Columbus; Sabina, OH, 3/13/1971; BA, Ohio St. Univ., 1993; USAR, 1989-99; political staffer, business executive; US House, 2021-present; m. Meghan; Catholic
Committees—House Administration; Ways and Means; Joint Library
District Offices—Columbus, 614-927-6902
Republican

United States House of Representatives

Notes

Jerry Carl, AL | 1st District | 2nd Term | 83% (+68)
1330 LHOB | 202-225-4931 | Fax: 225-0562
carl.house.gov | X @repjerrycarl
Bio—Mobile; Mobile, AL, 6/17/1958; attended Lake City Comm. Col.; business owner, entrepreneur; Mobile Co. commissioner, 2012-20; US House, 2021-present; m. Tina; Baptist
Committees—Appropriations; Natural Resources
District Offices—Mobile, 251-283-6280; Summerdale, 251-677-6630

Republican

André D. Carson, IN | 7th District | 9th Term | 66% (+36)
2135 RHOB | 202-225-4011 | Fax: 225-5633
carson.house.gov | X @repandrecarson
Bio—Indianapolis; Indianapolis, IN, 10/16/1974; MS, Indiana Wesleyan Univ., 2005; marketing executive, government official; Indianapolis/Marion city-county council, 2007-08; US House, 2008-present; single; Muslim
Committees—Transportation & Infrastructure; Intelligence; Select CCP
District Offices—Indianapolis, 317-283-6516

Democrat

Earl L. "Buddy" Carter, GA | 1st District | 5th Term | 59% (+18)
2432 RHOB | 202-225-5831 | Fax: 226-2269
buddycarter.house.gov | X @repbuddycarter
Bio—Pooler; Port Wentworth, GA, 9/6/1957; BS, Univ. of Georgia, 1980; pharmacist, business owner; Pooler city council, 1994-95; Pooler mayor, 1996-2004; GA House, 2005-09; GA Senate, 2009-14; US House, 2015-present; m. Amy; Methodist
Committees—Budget; Energy & Commerce
District Offices—Brunswick, 912-265-9010; Savannah, 912-352-0101

Republican

John Carter, TX | 31st District | 11th Term | Unc.
2208 RHOB | 202-225-3864
carter.house.gov | X @judgecarter
Bio—Round Rock; Houston, TX, 11/6/1941; JD, Univ. of Texas, 1969; lawyer, judge; US House, 2003-present; m. Erika; Lutheran
Committees—Appropriations
District Offices—Belton, 254-933-1392; Georgetown, 512-591-9061

Republican

Troy A. Carter, Sr., LA | 2nd District | 2nd Term | 77% (+54)
442 CHOB | 202-225-6636
troycarter.house.gov | X @reptroycarter
Bio—New Orleans; New Orleans, LA, 10/26/1963; BA, Xavier Univ., 1986; entrepreneur, business consultant; LA House, 1992-94; New Orleans city council, 1994-2002; LA Senate, 2016-21; US House, 2021-present; m. Ana; Baptist
Committees—Homeland Security; Transportation & Infrastructure
District Offices—New Orleans, 504-381-3970; New Orleans, 504-288-3777

Democrat

Matt Cartwright, PA | 8th District | 6th Term | 51% (+2)
2102 RHOB | 202-225-5546 | Fax: 226-0996
cartwright.house.gov | X @repcartwright
Bio—Moosic; Erie, PA, 5/1/1961; JD, Univ. of Pennsylvania, 1986; lawyer; US House, 2013-present; m. Marion; Catholic
Committees—Appropriations
District Offices—Scranton, 570-341-1050; Wilkes-Barre, 570-371-0317; Hazleton, 570-751-0050; Tannersville, 570-355-1818; Hawley, 570-576-8005

Democrat

U.S. Congress Directory | 73

United States House of Representatives

Greg Casar, TX | 35th District | 1st Term | 72% (+45)
1339 LHOB | 202-225-5645
casar.house.gov | X @repcasar
Bio—Austin; Houston, TX, 5/4/1989; BA, Univ. of Virginia, 2011; nonprofit executive; Austin city council, 2015-2022; US House, 2023-present; single; Catholic
Committees—Agriculture; Oversight & Accountability
District Offices—Austin, 512-691-1200; San Antonio, 210-580-7000

Democrat

Ed Case, HI | 1st District | 6th Term | 70% (+46)
2210 RHOB | 202-225-2726
case.house.gov | X @repedcase
Bio—Kane'ohe; Hilo, HI, 9/27/1952; JD, Univ. of California, 1981; lawyer, business executive, congressional staffer; HI House, 1994-2002; US House, 2002-07, 2019-present; m. Audrey; Episcopalian
Committees—Appropriations; Natural Resources
District Offices—Honolulu, 808-650-6688

Democrat

Sean Casten, IL | 6th District | 3rd Term | 54% (+9)
2440 RHOB | 202-225-4561
casten.house.gov | X @repcasten
Bio—Downers Grove; Dublin, Ireland, 11/23/1971; MEM, Dartmouth Col., 1998; businessman, scientist, consultant; US House, 2019-present; m. Kara; not stated
Committees—Financial Services; Science, Space, & Technology
District Offices—Glen Ellyn, 630-520-9450

Democrat

Kathy Castor, FL | 14th District | 9th Term | 56% (+14)
2052 RHOB | 202-225-3376 | Fax: 225-5652
castor.house.gov | X @usrepkcastor
Bio—Tampa; Miami, FL, 8/20/1966; JD, Florida St. Univ., 1991; lawyer; Hillsborough Co. commissioners, 2002-06; US House, 2007-present; m. Bill Lewis; Presbyterian
Committees—Energy & Commerce; Select CCP
District Offices—Tampa, 813-871-2817; St. Petersburg, 727-369-0201

Democrat

Joaquin Castro, TX | 20th District | 6th Term | 68% (+37)
2241 RHOB | 202-225-3236 | Fax: 225-1915
castro.house.gov | X @joaquincastrotx
Bio—San Antonio; San Antonio, TX, 9/16/1974; JD, Harvard Univ., 2000; lawyer; TX House, 2002-12; US House, 2013-present; m. Anna Flores; Catholic
Committees—Foreign Affairs; Intelligence
District Offices—San Antonio, 210-348-8216

Democrat

Lori Chavez-DeRemer, OR | 5th District | 1st Term | 50% (+2)
1722 LHOB | 202-225-5711
chavez-deremer.house.gov | X @replcd
Bio—Happy Valley; Santa Clara County, CA, 4/7/1968; BS, California St. Univ.; substitute teacher, business owner; Happy Valley city council, 2005-10; Happy Valley mayor, 2011-18; US House, 2023-present; m. Shawn DeRemer; Catholic
Committees—Agriculture; Education & the Workforce; Transportation & Infrastructure
District Offices—Oregon City, 503-387-8651; Redmond, 541-604-3141

Republican

United States House of Representatives | Notes

Sheila Cherfilus-McCormick, FL | 20th District | 2nd Term | 72% (+45)
242 CHOB | 202-225-1313
cherfilus-mccormick.house.gov | X @congresswomansc
Bio—Miramar; Brooklyn, NY, 1/25/1979; JD, St. Thomas Univ. School of Law, 2010; health care executive; US House, 2022-present; m. Corlie; Protestant
Committees—Foreign Affairs; Veterans' Affairs
District Offices—Tamarac, 954-733-2800; West Palm Beach, 561-461-6767

Democrat

Judy Chu, CA | 28th District | 8th Term | 66% (+32)
2423 RHOB | 202-225-5464 | Fax: 225-5467
chu.house.gov | X @repjudychu
Bio—Monterey Park; Los Angeles, CA, 7/7/1953; PhD, California School of Professional Psychology, 1979; professor; Monterey Park city council, 1988-2001; CA Assembly, 2001-06; CA Board of Equalization, 2006-09; US House, 2009-present; m. Michael Eng; Unitarian
Committees—Small Business; Ways and Means
District Offices—Claremont, 909-625-5394; Pasadena, 626-304-0110

Democrat

Juan Ciscomani, AZ | 6th District | 1st Term | 50% (+1.5)
1429 LHOB | 202-225-2542
ciscomani.house.gov | X @repciscomani
Bio—Tucson; Hermosillo, Mexico, 8/31/1982; BA, Univ. of Arizona, 2005; university development specialist, non-profit executive, gubernatorial aide; US House, 2023-present; m. Laura; Christian
Committees—Appropriations; Veterans' Affairs
District Offices—Tucson, 520-881-3588; Sierra Vista, 520-459-3115

Republican

Katherine Clark, MA | 5th District | 6th Term | 71% (+47)
2368 RHOB | 202-225-2836
katherineclark.house.gov | X @repkclark
Bio—Revere; New Haven, CT, 7/17/1963; MPA, Harvard Univ., 1997; lawyer; MA House, 2008-10; MA Senate, 2010-13; US House, 2013-present; m. Rodney Dowell; Protestant
Committees—Minority Whip
District Offices—Malden, 617-354-0292

Democrat

Yvette Clarke, NY | 9th District | 9th Term | 82% (+66)
2058 RHOB | 202-225-6231 | Fax: 226-0112
clarke.house.gov | X @repyvetteclarke
Bio—Brooklyn; Brooklyn, NY, 11/21/1964; attended Oberlin Col., 1982-86; childcare specialist, business development director; New York city council, 2002-07; US House, 2007-present; single; Protestant
Committees—Energy & Commerce; Homeland Security
District Offices—Brooklyn, 718-287-1142

Democrat

Emanuel Cleaver, MO | 5th District | 10th Term | 61% (+25)
2217 RHOB | 202-225-4535 | Fax: 225-4403
cleaver.house.gov | X @repcleaver
Bio—Kansas City; Waxahachie, TX, 10/26/1944; MDiv, St. Paul School of Theology, 1974; pastor, radio show host; Kansas City city council, 1979-91; Kansas City mayor, 1991-99; US House, 2005-present; m. Dianne; Methodist
Committees—Financial Services
District Offices—Independence, 816-833-4545; Kansas City, 816-842-4545

Democrat

United States House of Representatives — Notes

Ben Cline, VA | 6th District | 3rd Term | 64% (+29)
2443 RHOB | 202-225-5431 | Fax: 857-2675
cline.house.gov | X @repbencline
Bio—Botetourt; Stillwater, OK, 2/29/1972; JD, Univ. of Richmond, 2007; congressional staffer, marketing consultant, lawyer; VA House, 2002-18; US House, 2019-present; m. Elizabeth; Catholic
Committees—Appropriations; Budget; Judiciary
District Offices—Winchester, 540-546-0876; Staunton, 540-885-3861; Harrisonburg, 540-432-2391; Roanoke, 540-857-2672
Republican

Michael Cloud, TX | 27th District | 4th Term | 64% (+29)
171 CHOB | 202-225-7742
cloud.house.gov | X @repcloudtx
Bio—Victoria; Baton Rouge, LA, 5/13/1975; BS, Oral Roberts Univ., 1997; business owner; US House, 2018-present; m. Rosel; Protestant
Committees—Appropriations; Oversight & Accountability
District Offices—Corpus Christi, 361-884-2222; Victoria, 361-894-6446
Republican

James E. Clyburn, SC | 6th District | 16th Term | 62% (+24)
274 CHOB | 202-225-3315 | Fax: 225-2313
clyburn.house.gov | X @repjamesclyburn
Bio—Columbia; Sumter, SC, 7/21/1940; BA, South Carolina St. Univ., 1961; teacher, newspaper publisher; US House, 1993-present; m. Emily; African Methodist Episcopal
Committees—none
District Offices—Columbia, 803-799-1100; Kingstree, 843-355-1211; Santee, 803-854-4700; Sumter, 803-883-5020
Democrat

Andrew Clyde, GA | 9th District | 2nd Term | 72% (+45)
445 CHOB | 202-225-9893 | Fax: 226-1224
clyde.house.gov | X @rep_clyde
Bio—Athens; Walkerton, Canada, 11/22/1963; MBA, Univ. of Georgia, 1999; USN, 1985-96; USNR, 1996-2013; business owner; US House, 2021-present; m. Jennifer; Christian
Committees—Appropriations
District Offices—Gainesville, 470-768-6520
Republican

Steve Cohen, TN | 9th District | 9th Term | 70% (+44)
2268 RHOB | 202-225-3265 | Fax: 225-5663
cohen.house.gov | X @repcohen
Bio—Memphis; Memphis, TN, 5/24/1949; JD, Univ. of Memphis, 1973; lawyer; Shelby Co. commissioner, 1978-80; TN Senate, 1982-2006; US House, 2007-present; single; Jewish
Committees—Judiciary; Transportation & Infrastructure
District Offices—Memphis, 901-544-4131
Democrat

Tom Cole, OK | 4th District | 11th Term | 66% (+34)
2207 RHOB | 202-225-6165 | Fax: 225-3512
cole.house.gov | X @tomcoleok04
Bio—Moore; Shreveport, LA, 4/28/1949; PhD, Univ. of Oklahoma, 1984; consultant, public official; OK Senate, 1988-91; OK secretary of state, 1995-99; US House, 2003-present; m. Ellen; Methodist
Committees—Appropriations; Rules (Chair)
District Offices—Lawton, 580-357-2131; Norman, 405-329-6500; Ada, 580-436-5375
Republican

United States House of Representatives

Notes

Mike Collins, GA | 10th District | 1st Term | 64% (+29)
1223 LHOB | 202-225-4101
collins.house.gov | X @repmikecollins
Bio—Jackson; Jackson, GA, 7/2/1967; BBA, Georgia St. Univ., 1990; business owner, trucking company executive; US House, 2023-present; m. Leigh Ann; Methodist
Committees—Natural Resources; Science, Space, & Technology; Transportation & Infrastructure
District Offices—Monroe , 770-207-1776

Republican

James Comer, KY | 1st District | 5th Term | 74% (+50)
2410 RHOB | 202-225-3115
comer.house.gov | X @repjamescomer
Bio—Tompkinsville; Carthage, TN, 8/19/1972; BS, Western Kentucky Univ., 1993; businessman, farmer; KY House, 2001-12; KY agriculture commissioner, 2012-15; US House, 2016-present; m. Tamara Jo; Baptist
Committees—Education & the Workforce; Oversight & Accountability (Chair)
District Offices—Madisonville, 270-487-9509; Paducah, 270-408-1865; Tompkinsville, 270-487-9509

Republican

Gerry Connolly, VA | 11th District | 8th Term | 66% (+34)
2265 RHOB | 202-225-1492
connolly.house.gov
Bio—Fairfax; Boston, MA, 3/30/1950; MPA, Harvard Univ., 1979; business executive; Fairfax Co. supervisors, 1995-2008; US House, 2009-present; m. Cathy; Catholic
Committees—Foreign Affairs; Oversight & Accountability
District Offices—Fairfax, 703-256-3071

Democrat

Lou Correa, CA | 46th District | 4th Term | 61% (+24)
2301 RHOB | 202-225-2965
correa.house.gov | X @reploucorrea
Bio—Santa Ana; Los Angeles, CA, 1/24/1958; MBA, Univ. of California, Los Angeles, 1985; investment banker, real estate broker; CA Assembly, 1998-2004; Orange Co. supervisors, 2005-06; CA Senate, 2006-14; US House, 2017-present; m. Esther; Catholic
Committees—Homeland Security; Judiciary
District Offices—Santa Ana, 714-559-6190

Democrat

Jim Costa, CA | 21st District | 10th Term | 54% (+8)
2081 RHOB | 202-225-3341 | Fax: 225-9308
costa.house.gov | X @repjimcosta
Bio—Fresno; Fresno, CA, 4/13/1952; BA, California St. Univ., Fresno, 1974; public official; CA Assembly, 1978-94; CA Senate, 1994-2002; US House, 2005-present; single; Catholic
Committees—Agriculture; Foreign Affairs
District Offices—Fresno, 559-495-1620

Democrat

Joe Courtney, CT | 2nd District | 9th Term | 58% (+18)
2449 RHOB | 202-225-2076 | Fax: 225-4977
courtney.house.gov | X @repjoecourtney
Bio—Vernon; West Hartford, CT, 4/6/1953; JD, Univ. of Connecticut, 1978; lawyer; CT House, 1987-94; US House, 2007-present; m. Audrey; Catholic
Committees—Armed Services; Education & the Workforce
District Offices—Norwich, 860-886-0139; Enfield, 860-741-6011

Democrat

United States House of Representatives

Angie Craig, MN | 2nd District | 3rd Term | 50% (+5)
2442 RHOB | 202-225-2271
craig.house.gov | X @repangiecraig
Bio—Prior Lake; West Helena, AR, 2/14/1972; BA, Univ. of Memphis, 1994; journalist, healthcare executive; US House, 2019-present; m. Cheryl Greene; Lutheran
Committees—Agriculture; Energy & Commerce
District Offices—Burnsville, 651-846-2120

Democrat

Eli Crane, AZ | 2nd District | 1st Term | 53% (+8)
1229 LHOB | 202-225-3361
crane.house.gov | X @repelicrane
Bio—Oro Valley; Tucson, AZ, 1/3/1980; attended Univ. of Arizona, 2000-2001; USN, 2001-14; writer, business owner; US House, 2023-present; m. Jen; Christian
Committees—Homeland Security; Small Business; Veterans' Affairs
District Offices—Prescott, 928-286-5338; Maricopa, 928-286-5338

Republican

Rick Crawford, AR | 1st District | 7th Term | 73% (+48)
2422 RHOB | 202-225-4076
crawford.house.gov | X @reprickcrawford
Bio—Jonesboro; Homestead AFB, FL, 1/22/1966; BS, Arkansas St. Univ., 1996; USA, 1985-89; journalist, business owner; US House, 2011-present; m. Stacy; Baptist
Committees—Agriculture; Science, Space, & Technology; Transportation & Infrastructure; Intelligence
District Offices—Jonesboro, 870-203-0540; Cabot, 501-843-3043; Mountain Home, 870-424-2075; Dumas, 870-377-5571

Republican

Dan Crenshaw, TX | 2nd District | 3rd Term | 65% (+32)
248 CHOB | 202-225-6565
crenshaw.house.gov | X @repdancrenshaw
Bio—Humble; Aberdeen, Scotland, 3/14/1984; MPA, Harvard Univ., 2017; USN, 2006-16; military officer; US House, 2019-present; m. Tara; Methodist
Committees—Energy & Commerce; Intelligence
District Offices—Kingwood, 713-860-1330; The Woodlands, 281-640-7720

Republican

Jasmine Crockett, TX | 30th District | 1st Term | 74% (+53)
1616 LHOB | 202-225-8885
crockett.house.gov | X @repjasmine
Bio—Dallas; St. Louis, MO, 3/29/1981; JD, Univ. of Houston, 2006; lawyer; TX House, 2021-23; US House, 2023-present; single; Baptist
Committees—Agriculture; Oversight & Accountability
District Offices—Dallas, 214-922-8885

Democrat

Jason Crow, CO | 6th District | 3rd Term | 60% (+23)
1323 LHOB | 202-225-7882
crow.house.gov | X @repjasoncrow
Bio—Aurora; Madison, WI, 3/15/1979; JD, Univ. of Denver, 2009; USA, 2002-06; USARNG; professor, lawyer; US House, 2019-present; m. Deserai; Christian
Committees—Foreign Affairs; Intelligence
District Offices—Aurora, 720-748-7514

Democrat

Notes

United States House of Representatives

Henry Cuellar, TX | 28th District | 10th Term | 56% (+13)
2372 RHOB | 202-225-1640 | Fax: 225-1641
cuellar.house.gov | X @repcuellar
Bio—Laredo; Laredo, TX, 9/19/1955; PhD, Univ. of Texas, 1998; lawyer; TX House, 1987-2001; TX secretary of state, 2001; US House, 2005-present; m. Imelda; Catholic
Committees—Appropriations
District Offices—Laredo, 956-725-0639; Rio Grande City, 956-487-5603; San Antonio, 210-271-2851

Democrat

John Curtis, UT | 3rd District | 4th Term | 64% (+35)
2323 RHOB | 202-225-7751
curtis.house.gov | X @repjohncurtis
Bio—Provo; Ogden, UT, 5/10/1960; BS, Brigham Young Univ., 1985; business executive; Provo mayor, 2009-17; US House, 2017-present; m. Sue; Mormon
Committees—Energy & Commerce; Natural Resources
District Offices—Provo, 801-922-5400

Republican

Sharice Davids, KS | 3rd District | 3rd Term | 54% (+12)
2435 RHOB | 202-225-2865
davids.house.gov | X @repdavids
Bio—Roeland Park; Frankfurt, Germany, 5/22/1980; JD, Cornell Univ., 2010; lawyer, business owner, professional athlete; US House, 2019-present; single; not stated
Committees—Agriculture; Small Business; Transportation & Infrastructure
District Offices—Overland Park, 913-621-0832

Democrat

Warren Davidson, OH | 8th District | 5th Term | 64% (+29)
2113 RHOB | 202-225-6205
davidson.house.gov | X @warrendavidson
Bio—Troy; Sidney, OH, 3/1/1970; MBA, Univ. of Notre Dame, 2005; USA; business owner; US House, 2016-present; m. Lisa; Christian
Committees—Financial Services; Foreign Affairs
District Offices—West Chester, 937-339-1524; Cincinnati, 513-779-5400

Republican

Danny K. Davis, IL | 7th District | 14th Term | Unc.
2159 RHOB | 202-225-5006 | Fax: 225-5641
davis.house.gov | X @repdannydavis
Bio—Chicago; Parkdale, AR, 9/6/1941; PhD, Union Institute, 1977; postal clerk, teacher, professor; Chicago city council, 1979-90; Cook Co. commissioner, 1990-96; US House, 1997-present; m. Vera; Baptist
Committees—Ways and Means
District Offices—Chicago, 773-533-7520

Democrat

Don Davis, NC | 1st District | 1st Term | 52% (+5)
1123 LHOB | 202-225-3101
dondavis.house.gov | X @repdondavis
Bio—Snow Hill; Snow Hill, NC, 8/29/1971; EdD, East Carolina Univ., 2007; USAF, 1994-2001; professor, minister; Snow Hill mayor, 2001-08; NC Senate, 2009-11, 2013-22; US House, 2023-present; m. Yuvonka; Presbyterian
Committees—Agriculture; Armed Services
District Offices—Greenville, 252-999-7600

Democrat

Notes

United States House of Representatives

Monica De La Cruz, TX | 15th District | 1st Term | 53% (+8)
1415 LHOB | 202-225-9901
delacruz.house.gov | X @repmonicadlc
Bio—McAllen; Brownsville, TX, 11/11/1974; BBA, Univ. of Texas, San Antonio, 1997; business owner, insurance agent; US House, 2023-present; div.; Episcopalian
Committees—Agriculture; Financial Services
District Offices—McAllen, 956-800-6069; Seguin, 830-463-0800

Republican

Madeleine Dean, PA | 4th District | 3rd Term | 61% (+23)
150 CHOB | 202-225-4731
dean.house.gov | X @repdean
Bio—Bala Cynwyd; Philadelphia, PA, 6/6/1959; JD, Widener Univ. Delaware Law School, 1984; lawyer, columnist; PA House, 2012-18; US House, 2019-present; m. PJ; Catholic
Committees—Foreign Affairs; Judiciary
District Offices—Glenside, 215-884-4300; Pottstown, 610-382-1250

Democrat

Diana DeGette, CO | 1st District | 14th Term | 80% (+63)
2111 RHOB | 202-225-4431 | Fax: 225-5657
degette.house.gov | X @repdianadegette
Bio—Denver; Tachikawa, Japan, 7/29/1957; JD, New York Univ., 1982; lawyer; CO House, 1992-96; US House, 1997-present; m. Lino Lipinsky; Presbyterian
Committees—Energy & Commerce
District Offices—Denver, 303-844-4988

Democrat

Rosa DeLauro, CT | 3rd District | 17th Term | 56% (+16)
2413 RHOB | 202-225-3661 | Fax: 225-4890
delauro.house.gov | X @rosadelauro
Bio—New Haven; New Haven, CT, 3/2/1943; MA, Columbia Univ., 1966; public official, congressional staffer; US House, 1991-present; m. Stanley Greenberg; Catholic
Committees—Appropriations (Rnk. Mem.)
District Offices—New Haven, 203-562-3718

Democrat

Suzan DelBene, WA | 1st District | 7th Term | 63% (+27)
2330 RHOB | 202-225-6311 | Fax: 226-1606
delbene.house.gov | X @repdelbene
Bio—Medina; Selma, AL, 2/17/1962; MBA, Univ. of Washington, 1990; business executive; US House, 2012-present; m. Kurt; Episcopalian
Committees—Ways and Means
District Offices—Kirkland, 425-485-0085

Democrat

Chris Deluzio, PA | 17th District | 1st Term | 53% (+7)
1222 LHOB | 202-225-2301
deluzio.house.gov | X @repdeluzio
Bio—Aspinwall; Pittsburgh, PA, 7/13/1984; JD, Georgetown Univ., 2013; USN, 2006-12; lawyer; US House, 2023-present; m. Zoe; Catholic
Committees—Armed Services; Veterans' Affairs
District Offices—Monaca, 724-206-4860; Pittsburgh, 412-344-5583; Carnegie, 412-344-5583

Democrat

United States House of Representatives

Mark DeSaulnier, CA | 10th District | 5th Term | 78% (+58)
503 CHOB | 202-225-2095 | Fax: 225-5609
desaulnier.house.gov | X @repdesaulnier
Bio—Concord; Lowell, MA, 3/31/1952; BA, Col. of the Holy Cross, 1974; small business owner; Concord city council, 1991-1994; Contra Costa Co. supervisors, 1994-2006; CA Assembly, 2006-08; CA Senate, 2008-14; US House, 2015-present; single; Catholic
Committees—Education & the Workforce; Ethics; Transportation & Infrastructure
District Offices—Antioch, 925-754-0716; Walnut Creek, 925-933-2660

Democrat

Scott DesJarlais, TN | 4th District | 7th Term | 70% (+45)
2304 RHOB | 202-225-6831 | Fax: 226-5172
desjarlais.house.gov | X @desjarlaistn04
Bio—Sherwood; Des Moines, IA, 2/21/1964; MD, Univ. of South Dakota, 1991; physician; US House, 2011-present; m. Amy; Episcopalian
Committees—Agriculture; Armed Services
District Offices—Murfreesboro, 615-896-1986; Winchester, 931-962-3180

Republican

Anthony D'Esposito, NY | 4th District | 1st Term | 51% (+4)
1508 LHOB | 202-225-5516
desposito.house.gov | X @repdesposito
Bio—Island Park; Island Park, NY, 2/22/1982; BA, Hofstra Univ., 2004; police detective, fire fighter; Hempstead council, 2016-23; US House, 2023-present; single; Catholic
Committees—Homeland Security; House Administration; Transportation & Infrastructure
District Offices—Garden City, 516-739-3008

Republican

Mario Diaz-Balart, FL | 26th District | 11th Term | 70% (+42)
374 CHOB | 202-225-4211 | Fax: 225-8576
mariodiazbalart.house.gov | X @mariodb
Bio—Miami; Fort Lauderdale, FL, 9/25/1961; attended the Univ. of South Florida; marketing executive; FL House, 1988-92, 2000-02; FL Senate, 1992-2000; US House, 2003-present; m. Tia; Catholic
Committees—Appropriations
District Offices—Doral, 305-470-8555; Naples, 239-348-1620

Republican

Debbie Dingell, MI | 6th District | 5th Term | 65% (+32)
102 CHOB | 202-225-4071
debbiedingell.house.gov | X @repdebdingell
Bio—Ann Arbor; Detroit, MI, 11/23/1953; MS, Georgetown Univ., 1996; business executive, non-profit executive; US House, 2015-present; wid.; Catholic
Committees—Energy & Commerce; Natural Resources
District Offices—Ann Arbor, 734-481-1100; Woodhaven, 313-278-2936

Democrat

Lloyd Doggett, TX | 37th District | 15th Term | 76% (+56)
2307 RHOB | 202-225-4865
doggett.house.gov | X @replloyddoggett
Bio—Austin; Austin, TX, 10/6/1946; JD, Univ. of Texas, 1970; public official; TX Senate, 1973-85; TX Supreme Court, 1989-94; US House, 1995-present; m. Libby; Methodist
Committees—Budget; Ways and Means; Joint Taxation
District Offices—Austin, 512-916-5921

Democrat

U.S. Congress Directory | 81

United States House of Representatives

Byron Donalds, FL | 19th District | 2nd Term | 68% (+36)
1719 LHOB | 202-225-2536
donalds.house.gov | X @repdonaldspress
Bio—Naples; Brooklyn, NY, 10/28/1978; BA, Florida St. Univ., 2002; financial advisor; FL House, 2016-20; US House, 2021-present; m. Erika; Christian
Committees—Financial Services; Oversight & Accountability
District Offices—Naples, 239-252-6225; Cape Coral, 239-599-6033
Republican

John Duarte, CA | 13th District | 1st Term | 50% (+.4)
1535 LHOB | 202-225-1947
duarte.house.gov | X @repduarteca13
Bio—Modesto; Modesto, CA, 9/9/1966; MBA., Univ. of the Pacific, 1997; farmer, business owner; US House, 2023-present; m. Alexandra; Episcopalian
Committees—Agriculture; Natural Resources; Transportation & Infrastructure
District Offices—Turlock, 209-226-6880
Republican

Jeff Duncan, SC | 3rd District | 7th Term | Unc.
2229 RHOB | 202-225-5301 | Fax: 225-3216
jeffduncan.house.gov | X @repjeffduncan
Bio—Laurens; Greenville, SC, 1/7/1966; BA, Clemson Univ., 1988; banker, real estate broker; SC House, 2003-10; US House, 2011-present; m. Melody; Southern Baptist
Committees—Energy & Commerce
District Offices—Anderson, 864-224-7401; Clinton, 864-681-1028
Republican

Neal Dunn, FL | 2nd District | 4th Term | 59% (+20)
466 CHOB | 202-225-5235
dunn.house.gov | X @drnealdunnfl2
Bio—Panama City; Boston, MA, 2/16/1953; MD, George Washington Univ., 1979; USA, 1989-2010; urologist, banker; US House, 2017-present; m. Leah; Catholic
Committees—Energy & Commerce; Select CCP
District Offices—Panama City, 850-785-0812; Tallahassee, 850-891-8610
Republican

Chuck Edwards, NC | 11th District | 1st Term | 53% (+9)
1505 LHOB | 202-225-6401
edwards.house.gov | X @repchuckedwards
Bio—Flat Rock; Waynesville, NC, 9/13/1960; attended Blue Ridge Comm. Col., 1979-1983; business owner, entrepreneur; NC Senate, 2016-22; US House, 2023-present; m. Teresa; Christian
Committees—Appropriations
District Offices—Hendersonville, 828-435-7310
Republican

Jake Ellzey, TX | 6th District | 2nd Term | Unc.
1721 LHOB | 202-225-2002
ellzey.house.gov | X @repellzey
Bio—Midlothian; Potter County, TX, 1/24/1970; BS, U.S. Naval Academy, 1992; USN, 1992-2012; business executive, commercial pilot; TX House, 2021; US House, 2021-present; m. Shelby; Christian
Committees—Appropriations; Small Business
District Offices—Waxahachie, 469-550-7150; Corsicana, 903-602-7860
Republican

United States House of Representatives

Tom Emmer, MN | 6th District | 5th Term | 61% (+24)
464 CHOB | 202-225-2331 | Fax: 225-6475
emmer.house.gov | X @reptomemmer
Bio—Delano; South Bend, IN, 3/3/1961; JD, Mitchell Col. of Law, 1988; radio host, lawyer; Independence city council, 1995-2002; Delano city council, 2003-04; MN House, 2004-10; US House, 2015-present; m. Jacquie; Catholic
Committees—Financial Services; Majority Whip
District Offices—Otsego, 763-241-6848; Chaska, 952-262-2999

Republican

Veronica Escobar, TX | 16th District | 3rd Term | 63% (+27)
2448 RHOB | 202-225-4831
escobar.house.gov | X @repescobar
Bio—El Paso; El Paso, TX, 9/15/1969; MA, New York Univ., 1993; college professor, nonprofit executive; El Paso Co. commissioner, 2006-10; El Paso Co. judge, 2011-17; US House, 2019-present; m. Michael; Catholic
Committees—Armed Services; Ethics; Judiciary
District Offices—El Paso, 915-541-1400

Democrat

Anna G. Eshoo, CA | 16th District | 16th Term | 57% (+16)
272 CHOB | 202-225-8104 | Fax: 225-8890
eshoo.house.gov | X @repannaeshoo
Bio—Atherton; New Britain, CT, 12/13/1942; AA, Canada Col., 1975; public official; San Mateo Co. supervisors, 1983-92; US House, 1993-present; single; Catholic
Committees—Energy & Commerce
District Offices—Palo Alto, 650-323-2984

Democrat

Adriano Espaillat, NY | 13th District | 4th Term | Unc.
2332 RHOB | 202-225-4365 | Fax: 226-9731
espaillat.house.gov | X @repespaillat
Bio—New York; Santiago, Dominican Republic, 9/27/1954; BA, Queens Col., 1979; public official, advocate; NY Assembly, 1996-2010; NY Senate, 2010-16; US House, 2017-present; m. Martha; Catholic
Committees—Appropriations; Budget
District Offices—New York, 212-663-3900; New York, 212-497-5959; Bronx, 646-740-3632

Democrat

Ron Estes, KS | 4th District | 4th Term | 63% (+27)
2234 RHOB | 202-225-6216
estes.house.gov | X @repronestes
Bio—Wichita; Topeka, KS, 7/19/1956; MBA, Tennessee Technological Univ., 1983; businessman, farmer; KS treasurer, 2011-17; US House, 2017-present; m. Susan; Lutheran
Committees—Budget; Education & the Workforce; Ways and Means; Joint Economic
District Offices—Wichita, 316-262-8992

Republican

Dwight Evans, PA | 3rd District | 5th Term | 95% (+90)
1105 LHOB | 202-225-4001 | Fax: 225-5392
evans.house.gov | X @repdwightevans
Bio—Philadelphia; Philadelphia, PA, 5/16/1954; BA, La Salle Univ., 1975; teacher, employment counselor; PA House, 1980-2016; US House, 2016-present; single; Baptist
Committees—Ways and Means
District Offices—Philadelphia, 215-276-0340; Philadelphia, 215-254-3400

Democrat

Notes

United States House of Representatives

Mike Ezell, MS | 4th District | 1st Term | 73% (+49)
443 CHOB | 202-225-5772
ezell.house.gov | X @repezell
Bio—Pascagoula; Pascagoula, MS, 4/6/1959; BS, Univ. of Southern Mississippi, 1997; law enforcement officer; US House, 2023-present; m. Suzette; Baptist
Committees—Homeland Security; Transportation & Infrastructure
District Offices—Gulfport, 228-864-7670; Hattiesburg, 601-582-3246; Pascagoula, 228-202-5890; Laurel, 601-425-7247
Republican 

Pat Fallon, TX | 4th District | 2nd Term | 66% (+36)
2416 RHOB | 202-225-6673
fallon.house.gov | X @reppatfallon
Bio—Frisco; Pittsfield, MA, 12/19/1967; BA, Univ. of Notre Dame, 1990; USAF, 1990-94; entrepreneur, business executive; Frisco city council, 2009-12; TX House, 2013-19; TX Senate, 2019-21; US House, 2021-present; m. Susan; Catholic
Committees—Armed Services; Oversight & Accountability
District Offices—Sherman, 903-820-5170; New Boston, 903-716-7500; Rockwall, 972-771-0100
Republican 

Randy Feenstra, IA | 4th District | 2nd Term | 65% (+36)
1440 LHOB | 202-225-4426 | Fax: 225-3193
feenstra.house.gov | X @repfeenstra
Bio—Hull; Hull, IA, 1/14/1969; MPA, Iowa St. Univ.; bank insurance manager; IA Senate, 2009-20; US House, 2021-present; m. Lynette; Christian
Committees—Agriculture; Ways and Means
District Offices—Council Bluffs, 712-256-5653; Sioux City, 712-224-4692; Fort Dodge, 515-302-7060
Republican 

Drew Ferguson, GA | 3rd District | 4th Term | 68% (+38)
2239 RHOB | 202-225-5901
ferguson.house.gov | X @repdrewferguson
Bio—The Rock; Lansdale, AL, 11/15/1966; DMD, Medical Col. of Georgia, 1992; dentist; West Point aldermen, 1997-99; West Point mayor, 2008-16; US House, 2017-present; m. Julie; Christian
Committees—Budget; Ways and Means; Joint Economic
District Offices—Newnan, 770-683-2033
Republican 

Brad Finstad, MN | 1st District | 2nd Term | 53% (+12)
1605 LHOB | 202-225-2472
finstad.house.gov | X @bradfinstad
Bio—New Ulm; New Ulm, MN, 5/30/1976; BS, Univ. of Minnesota; farmer, public official; MN House, 2003-08; US House, 2022-present; m. Jackie; Catholic
Committees—Agriculture; Armed Services
District Offices—Rochester, 507-577-6140; New Ulm, 507-577-6151
Republican 

Michelle Fischbach, MN | 7th District | 2nd Term | 66% (+39)
1004 LHOB | 202-225-2165 | Fax: 225-1593
fischbach.house.gov | X @repfischbach
Bio—Regal; Woodbury, MN, 11/3/1965; JD, William Mitchell Col. of Law, 2011; public official; Paynesville city council, 1996; MN Senate, 1996-2018; MN lt. governor, 2018-19; US House, 2021-present; m. Scott; Catholic
Committees—Budget; Ethics; Rules; Ways and Means
District Offices—Moorhead, 218-422-2090; Willmar, 320-403-6100
Republican

United States House of Representatives

Scott Fitzgerald, WI | 5th District | 2nd Term | 64% (+29)
1507 LHOB | 202-225-5101
fitzgerald.house.gov | X @repfitzgerald
Bio—Clyman; Chicago, IL, 11/16/1963; BS, Univ. of Wisconsin, Oshkosh, 1985; USAR, 1981-2009; newspaper publisher; WI Senate, 1995-2020; US House, 2021-present; m. Lisa; Catholic
Committees—Financial Services; Judiciary
District Offices—Oconomowoc, 262-784-1111

Republican

Brian Fitzpatrick, PA | 1st District | 4th Term | 54% (+10)
271 CHOB | 202-225-4276 | Fax: 225-9511
fitzpatrick.house.gov | X @repbrianfitz
Bio—Levittown; Philadelphia, PA, 12/17/1973; JD, Dickinson School of Law, 2001; lawyer, accountant; US House, 2017-present; single; Catholic
Committees—Ways and Means; Intelligence
District Offices—Langhorne, 215-579-8102

Republican

Chuck Fleischmann, TN | 3rd District | 7th Term | 68% (+38)
2187 RHOB | 202-225-3271 | Fax: 225-3494
fleischmann.house.gov | X @repchuck
Bio—Chattanooga; Manhattan, NY, 10/11/1962; JD, Univ. of Tennessee, 1986; lawyer; US House, 2011-present; m. Brenda; Catholic
Committees—Appropriations; Science, Space, & Technology
District Offices—Athens, 423-745-4671; Chattanooga, 423-756-2342; Oak Ridge, 865-576-1976

Republican

Lizzie Fletcher, TX | 7th District | 3rd Term | 63% (+28)
346 CHOB | 202-225-2571 | Fax: 225-4381
fletcher.house.gov | X @repfletcher
Bio—Houston; Houston, TX, 2/13/1975; JD, Col. of William & Mary, 2006; lawyer; US House, 2019-present; m. Scott; Methodist
Committees—Energy & Commerce
District Offices—Houston, 713-353-8680; Sugar Land, 713-353-8680

Democrat

Mike Flood, NE | 1st District | 2nd Term | 57% (+16)
343 CHOB | 202-225-4806
flood.house.gov | X @usrepmikeflood
Bio—Norfolk; Omaha, NE, 2/23/1975; JD, Univ. of Nebraska, 2001; business owner, attorney; NE Legislature, 2005-13, 2021-22; US House, 2022-present; m. Mandi; Catholic
Committees—Financial Services
District Offices—Lincoln, 402-438-1598

Republican

Bill Foster, IL | 11th District | 8th Term | 56% (+13)
2366 RHOB | 202-225-3515
foster.house.gov | X @repbillfoster
Bio—Naperville; Madison, WI, 10/7/1955; PhD, Harvard Univ., 1984; physicist, entrepreneur; US House, 2008-11, 13-present; m. Aesook; not stated
Committees—Financial Services
District Offices—Aurora, 630-585-7672

Democrat

United States House of Representatives

Valerie Foushee, NC | 4th District | 1st Term | 66% (+34)
1716 LHOB | 202-225-1784
foushee.house.gov | X @valeriefoushee
Bio—Hillsborough; Chapel Hill, NC, 5/7/1956; BA, Univ. of North Carolina, 2008; law enforcement, public official; Orange Co. commissioners, 2004-12; NC House, 2013; NC Senate, 2013-22; US House, 2023-present; m. Stanley; Baptist
Committees—Science, Space, & Technology; Transportation & Infrastructure
District Offices—Durham, 919-967-7924
Democrat

Virginia Foxx, NC | 5th District | 10th Term | 63% (+26)
2462 RHOB | 202-225-2071 | Fax: 225-2995
foxx.house.gov | X @virginiafoxx
Bio—Banner Elk; New York, NY, 6/29/1943; EdD, Univ. of North Carolina, 1985; college instructor, landscape nursery owner; NC Senate, 1994-2004; US House, 2005-present; m. Tom; Catholic
Committees—Education & the Workforce (Chair); Oversight & Accountability
District Offices—Boone, 828-265-0240; Clemmons, 336-778-0211
Republican

Lois Frankel, FL | 22nd District | 6th Term | 55% (+10)
2305 RHOB | 202-225-9890
frankel.house.gov | X @reploisfrankel
Bio—West Palm Beach; New York, NY, 5/16/1948; JD, Georgetown Univ., 1973; lawyer; FL House, 1986-92, 1994-2002; West Palm Beach mayor, 2003-11; US House, 2013-present; single; Jewish
Committees—Appropriations
District Offices—Delray Beach, 561-998-9045
Democrat

Scott Franklin, FL | 18th District | 2nd Term | 74% (+49)
249 CHOB | 202-225-1252 | Fax: 226-0585
franklin.house.gov | X @repfranklin
Bio—Lakeland; Thomaston, GA, 8/23/1964; MBA, Embry-Riddle Aeronautical Univ., 1994; USN, 1986-2000; USNR, 2000-12; insurance agency owner; Lakeland commissioner, 2018-21; US House, 2021-present; m. Amy; Presbyterian
Committees—Appropriations; Science, Space, & Technology; Veterans' Affairs
District Offices—Lakeland, 863-644-8215; Lake Placid, 863-644-8215; Lake Wales, 863-644-8215
Republican

Maxwell Alejandro Frost, FL | 10th District | 1st Term | 59% (+20)
1224 LHOB | 202-225-2176
frost.house.gov | X @repmaxwellfrost
Bio—Orlando; Orlando, FL, 1/17/1997; attended Valencia Col.; campaign staffer, rideshare driver; US House, 2023-present; single; Baptist
Committees—Oversight & Accountability; Science, Space, & Technology
District Offices—Orlando, 321-388-9808
Democrat

Russell Fry, SC | 7th District | 1st Term | 64% (+30)
1626 LHOB | 202-225-9895
fry.house.gov | X @reprussellfry
Bio—Murrells Inlet; Surfside Beach, SC, 1/31/1985; JD, Charleston School of Law, 2011; lawyer; SC House, 2015-22; US House, 2023-present; m. Bronwen; Baptist
Committees—Judiciary; Oversight & Accountability
District Offices—Surfside Beach, 843-353-5377; Florence, 843-799-6880
Republican

United States House of Representatives

Russ Fulcher, ID | 1st District | 3rd Term | 71% (+45)
1514 LHOB | 202-225-6611
fulcher.house.gov | X @reprussfulcher
Bio—Meridian; Boise, ID, 3/9/1962; MBA, Boise St. Univ., 1988; businessman, realtor; ID Senate, 2005-14; US House, 2019-present; div.; Christian
Committees—Energy & Commerce; Natural Resources
District Offices—Meridian, 208-888-3188; Lewiston, 208-743-1388; Coeur d'Alene, 208-667-0127

Republican

Matt Gaetz, FL | 1st District | 4th Term | 67% (+36)
2021 RHOB | 202-225-4136
gaetz.house.gov | X @repmattgaetz
Bio—Niceville; Hollywood, FL, 5/7/1982; JD, Col. of William & Mary, 2007; lawyer; FL House, 2010-16; US House, 2017-present; m. Ginger; Baptist
Committees—Armed Services; Judiciary
District Offices—Crestview, 850-479-1183

Republican

Mike Gallagher, WI | 8th District | 4th Term | 72% (+56)
1211 LHOB | 202-225-5665
gallagher.house.gov | X @repgallagher
Bio—Green Bay; Green Bay, WI, 3/3/1984; PhD, Georgetown Univ., 2015; USMC, 2006-13; congressional staffer, businessman; US House, 2017-present; m. Anne; Catholic
Committees—Armed Services; Intelligence; Select CCP (Chair)
District Offices—De Pere, 920-301-4500

Republican

Ruben Gallego, AZ | 3rd District | 5th Term | 76% (+54)
1114 LHOB | 202-225-4065
rubengallego.house.gov | X @reprubengallego
Bio—Phoenix; Chicago, IL, 11/20/1979; AB, Harvard Univ., 2004; USMC, 2002-06; public affairs consultant; AZ House, 2010-14; US House, 2015-present; div.; Catholic
Committees—Armed Services; Natural Resources
District Offices—Phoenix, 602-256-0551

Democrat

John Garamendi, CA | 8th District | 8th Term | 75% (+51)
2004 RHOB | 202-225-1880 | Fax: 225-5914
garamendi.house.gov | X @repgaramendi
Bio—Walnut Grove; Camp Blanding, FL, 1/24/1945; MBA, Harvard Univ., 1970; businessman, rancher; CA Assembly 1974-76; CA Senate 1976-90; CA insurance commissioner, 1991-94, 2002-06; CA lt. governor, 2007-09; US House, 2009-present; m. Patti; Christian
Committees—Armed Services; Transportation & Infrastructure
District Offices—Richmond, 510-620-1001; Fairfield, 707-438-1822; Vallejo, 707-645-1888

Democrat

Andrew Garbarino, NY | 2nd District | 2nd Term | 59% (+21)
2344 RHOB | 202-225-7896 | Fax: 226-2279
garbarino.house.gov | X @repgarbarino
Bio—Bayport; Sayville, NY, 9/27/1984; JD, Hofstra Univ., 2009; lawyer, business owner; NY Assembly, 2013-20; US House, 2021-present; single; Catholic
Committees—Ethics; Financial Services; Homeland Security
District Offices—Patchogue, 631-541-4225

Republican

Notes

United States House of Representatives — Notes

Jesús G. "Chuy" García, IL | 4th District | 3rd Term | 68% (+40)
1519 LHOB | 202-225-8203
chuygarcia.house.gov | X @repchuygarcia
Bio—Chicago; Durango, Mexico, 4/12/1956; MA, Univ. of Illinois, 2002; public official; Chicago city council, 1986-93; IL Senate, 1993-98; Cook Co. commissioners, 2011-19; US House, 2019-present; m. Evelyn; Catholic
Committees—Transportation & Infrastructure
District Offices—Melrose Park, 773-342-0774; Chicago, 773-475-0833

Democrat

Mike Garcia, CA | 27th District | 3rd Term | 53% (+6)
144 CHOB | 202-225-1956
mikegarcia.house.gov | X @repmikegarcia
Bio—Santa Clarita; Granada Hills, CA, 4/24/1976; MA, Georgetown Univ., 1998; USN, 1999-2009; USNR, 2009-12; business executive, real estate developer; US House, 2020-present; m. Rebecca; Protestant
Committees—Appropriations; Science, Space, & Technology; Intelligence
District Offices—Palmdale, 661-839-0532; Santa Clarita, 661-568-4855

Republican

Robert Garcia, CA | 42nd District | 1st Term | 68% (+37)
1305 LHOB | 202-225-7924
robertgarcia.house.gov | X @reprobertgarcia
Bio—Long Beach; Lima, Peru, 12/2/1977; EdD, California St. Univ., 2010; communications director, newspaper publisher; Long Beach city council, 2009-14; Long Beach mayor, 2014-22; US House, 2023-present; single; Catholic
Committees—Homeland Security; Oversight & Accountability
District Offices—Long Beach, 562-512-8489

Democrat

Sylvia Garcia, TX | 29th District | 3rd Term | 71% (+43)
2419 RHOB | 202-225-1688
sylviagarcia.house.gov | X @repsylviagarcia
Bio—Houston; San Diego, TX, 9/6/1950; JD, Texas Southern Univ., 1978; lawyer, social worker; TX Senate, 2013-18; US House, 2019-present; single; Catholic
Committees—Financial Services
District Offices—Houston, 832-325-3150

Democrat

Carlos A. Gimenez, FL | 28th District | 2nd Term | 63% (+27)
448 CHOB | 202-225-2778
gimenez.house.gov | X @repcarlos
Bio—Miami; Havana, Cuba, 1/17/1954; BPA, Barry Univ., 1999; firefighter; Miami-Dade Co. commissioner, 2004-11; Miami-Dade Co. mayor, 2011-20; US House, 2021-present; m. Lourdes; Catholic
Committees—Armed Services; Homeland Security; Select CCP
District Offices—Miami, 305-222-0160; Florida City, 305-222-0160; Key West, 305-292-4485

Republican

Jared Golden, ME | 2nd District | 3rd Term | 53% (+6)
1710 LHOB | 202-225-6306 | Fax: 225-2943
golden.house.gov | X @repgolden
Bio—Lewiston; Lewiston, ME, 7/25/1982; BA, Bates Col., 2011; USMC, 2002-06; congressional staffer; ME House, 2014-19; US House, 2019-present; m. Isobel; not stated
Committees—Armed Services; Small Business
District Offices—Bangor, 207-249-7400; Caribou, 207-492-6009; Lewiston, 207-241-6767

Democrat

United States House of Representatives

Dan Goldman, NY | 10th District | 1st Term | 84% (+69)
245 CHOB | 202-225-7944
goldman.house.gov
Bio—New York; Washington, DC, 2/26/1976; JD, Stanford Univ., 2005; journalist, legal analyst, law clerk; US House, 2023-present; m. Corinne; Jewish
Committees—Homeland Security; Oversight & Accountability
District Offices—New York, 212-822-7878; Brooklyn, 718-312-7575

Democrat

Jimmy Gomez, CA | 34th District | 4th Term | 51% (+2)
506 CHOB | 202-225-6235
gomez.house.gov | X @repjimmygomez
Bio—Los Angeles; Fullerton, CA, 11/25/1974; MPP, Harvard Univ., 2003; congressional staffer, nonprofit executive; CA Assembly, 2012-17; US House, 2017-present; m. Mary; Catholic
Committees—Oversight & Accountability; Ways and Means; Intelligence
District Offices—Los Angeles, 213-481-1425

Democrat

Tony Gonzales, TX | 23rd District | 2nd Term | 55% (+17)
2244 RHOB | 202-225-4511 | Fax: 225-2237
gonzales.house.gov | X @reptonygonzales
Bio—San Antonio; San Antonio, TX, 10/10/1980; MA, American Public University, 2014; USN, 1999-2019; college faculty; US House, 2021-present; m. Angel; Catholic
Committees—Appropriations; Homeland Security
District Offices—Uvalde, 830-333-7410; Socorro, 915-990-1500; Fort Stockton, 432-299-6200; San Antonio, 210-806-9920; Del Rio, 830-308-6200

Republican

Vicente Gonzalez, TX | 34th District | 4th Term | 52% (+9)
154 CHOB | 202-225-2531
gonzalez.house.gov | X @repgonzalez
Bio—McAllen; Corpus Christi, TX, 9/4/1967; JD, Texas Wesleyan Univ., 1996; lawyer; US House, 2017-present; m. Lorena; Catholic
Committees—Financial Services
District Offices—Brownsville, 956-682-5545; Kingsville, 956-682-5545; Weslaco, 956-682-5545

Democrat

Jenniffer González-Colón, PR | 4th Term | 39% (+8)
2338 RHOB | 202-225-2615 | Fax: 225-2154
gonzalez-colon.house.gov | X @repjenniffer
Bio—Carolina; San Juan, PR, 8/5/1976; LLM, Inter-American Univ. of Puerto Rico, 2014; lawyer; PR House, 2002-16; US House, 2017-present; m. Jose; Catholic
Committees—Natural Resources; Transportation & Infrastructure
District Offices—San Juan, 787-723-6333

Republican

Bob Good, VA | 5th District | 2nd Term | 57% (+15)
461 CHOB | 202-225-4711 | Fax: 225-5681
good.house.gov | X @repbobgood
Bio—Lynchburg; Wilkes-Barre, PA, 9/11/1965; MBA, Liberty Univ., 2010; financial executive, college faculty; Campbell Co. supervisors, 2016-19; US House, 2021-present; m. Tracey; Christian
Committees—Budget; Education & the Workforce
District Offices—Lynchburg, 434-791-2596

Republican

United States House of Representatives | Notes

Lance Gooden, TX | 5th District | 3rd Term | 63% (+30)
2431 RHOB | 202-225-3484
gooden.house.gov | X @replancegooden
Bio—Terrell; Nashville, TN, 12/1/1982; BBA, Univ. of Texas, 2004; insurance broker; TX House, 2011-15, 2017-19; US House, 2019-present; m. Alexa; Church of Christ
Committees—Armed Services; Judiciary
District Offices—Canton, 903-502-5300

Republican

Paul A. Gosar, AZ | 9th District | 7th Term | Unc.
2057 RHOB | 202-225-2315
gosar.house.gov | X @repjoshg
Bio—Bullhead City; Rock Springs, WY, 11/27/1958; DDS, Creighton Univ., 1985; dentist; US House, 2011-present; m. Maude; Catholic
Committees—Natural Resources; Oversight & Accountability
District Offices—Goodyear, 623-707-0530

Republican

Josh Gottheimer, NJ | 5th District | 4th Term | 54% (+10)
203 CHOB | 202-225-4465
gottheimer.house.gov | X @repjoshg
Bio—Wyckoff; North Caldwell, NJ, 3/8/1975; JD, Harvard Univ., 2004; speechwriter, campaign staffer, business executive; US House, 2017-present; m. Marla; Jewish
Committees—Financial Services; Intelligence
District Offices—Fair Lawn, 201-389-1100; Newton, 973-940-1117; Fort Lee, 973-814-4076; Englewood, 973-814-4076

Democrat

Kay Granger, TX | 12th District | 14th Term | 64% (+29)
2308 RHOB | 202-225-5071 | Fax: 225-5683
granger.house.gov | X @repkaygranger
Bio—Fort Worth; Greenville, TX, 1/18/1943; BS, Texas Wesleyan Univ., 1965; teacher, business owner; Fort Worth city council, 1989-91; Fort Worth mayor, 1991-95; US House, 1997-present; div.; Methodist
Committees—Appropriations (Chair)
District Offices—Fort Worth, 817-338-0909

Republican

Garret Graves, LA | 6th District | 5th Term | 80% (+67)
2402 RHOB | 202-225-3901 | Fax: 225-7313
garretgraves.house.gov | X @repgarretgraves
Bio—Baton Rouge; Baton Rouge, LA, 1/31/1972; attended American Univ.; congressional staffer; US House, 2015-present; m. Carissa; Catholic
Committees—Natural Resources; Transportation & Infrastructure
District Offices—Gonzales, 225-450-1672; Baton Rouge, 225-442-1731; Livingston, 225-686-4413; Thibodaux, 985-448-4103

Republican

Sam Graves, MO | 6th District | 12th Term | 70% (+43)
1135 LHOB | 202-225-7041 | Fax: 225-8221
graves.house.gov | X @repsamgraves
Bio—Tarkio; Tarkio, MO, 11/7/1963; BS, Univ. of Missouri, 1986; public official; MO House, 1992-94; MO Senate, 1994-2000; US House, 2001-present; div.; Baptist
Committees—Armed Services; Transportation & Infrastructure (Chair)
District Offices—Hannibal, 573-221-3400; Kansas City, 816-792-3976; St. Joseph, 816-749-0800; Troy, 636-622-7106

Republican

United States House of Representatives

Notes

Al Green, TX | 9th District | 10th Term | 76% (+53)
2347 RHOB | 202-225-7508 | Fax: 225-2947
algreen.house.gov | X @repalgreen
Bio—Houston; New Orleans, LA, 9/1/1947; JD, Texas Southern Univ., 1974; lawyer; US House, 2005-present; div.; Baptist
Committees—Financial Services
District Offices—Houston, 713-383-9234; Missouri City, 713-383-9234

Democrat

Mark Green, TN | 7th District | 3rd Term | 59% (+22)
2446 RHOB | 202-225-2811
markgreen.house.gov | X @repmarkgreen
Bio—Clarksville; Jacksonville, FL, 11/8/1964; MD, Wright St. Univ., 1999; USA, 1986-2006; doctor, business executive; TN Senate, 2013-19; US House, 2019-present; m. Camilla; Christian
Committees—Foreign Affairs; Homeland Security (Chair)
District Offices—Clarksville, 931-266-4483; Franklin, 629-223-6050; Nashville, 629-999-4950

Republican

Marjorie Taylor Greene, GA | 14th District | 2nd Term | 65% (+32)
403 CHOB | 202-225-5211
greene.house.gov | X @repmtg
Bio—Rome; Milledgeville, GA, 5/27/1974; BBA, Univ. of Georgia, 1996; business owner; US House, 2021-present; div.; Christian
Committees—Homeland Security; Oversight & Accountability
District Offices—Dalton, 706-226-5320

Republican

Morgan Griffith, VA | 9th District | 7th Term | 73% (+47)
2202 RHOB | 202-225-3861 | Fax: 225-0076
morgangriffith.house.gov | X @repmgriffith
Bio—Salem; Philadelphia, PA, 3/15/1958; JD, Washington & Lee Univ., 1983; lawyer; VA House, 1994-2011; US House, 2011-present; m. Hilary; Protestant
Committees—Energy & Commerce; House Administration; Joint Printing
District Offices—Abingdon, 276-525-1405; Christiansburg, 540-381-5671

Republican

Raúl M. Grijalva, AZ | 7th District | 11th Term | 64% (+29)
1203 LHOB | 202-225-2435 | Fax: 225-1541
grijalva.house.gov | X @repraulgrijalva
Bio—Tucson; Tucson, AZ, 2/19/1948; BA, Univ. of Arizona, 1986; public official; Pima Co. supervisor, 1989-2002; US House, 2003-present; m. Ramona; Catholic
Committees—Education & the Workforce; Natural Resources (Rnk. Mem.)
District Offices—Tucson, 520-622-6788; Somerton, 928-343-7933; Tolleson, 623-536-3388

Democrat

Glenn Grothman, WI | 6th District | 5th Term | Unc.
1511 LHOB | 202-225-2476 | Fax: 225-2356
grothman.house.gov | X @repgrothman
Bio—Glenbeulah; Milwaukee, WI, 7/3/1955; JD, Univ. of Wisconsin, 1983; lawyer; WI Assembly, 1993-2004; WI Senate, 2004-14; US House, 2015-present; single; Lutheran
Committees—Budget; Education & the Workforce; Oversight & Accountability
District Offices—Fond du Lac, 920-907-0624

Republican

U.S. Congress Directory | 91

United States House of Representatives   Notes

Michael Guest, MS | 3rd District | 3rd Term | 70% (+41)
450 CHOB | 202-225-5031 | Fax: 225-5797
guest.house.gov | X @repmichaelguest
Bio—Brandon; Woodbury, NJ, 2/4/1970; JD, Univ. of Mississippi, 1995; lawyer; US House, 2019-present; m. Haley; Baptist
Committees—Appropriations; Ethics (Chair); Homeland Security
District Offices—Brandon, 769-241-6120; Starkville, 662-324-0007; Brookhaven, 601-823-3400; Meridian, 601-693-6681

Republican

Brett Guthrie, KY | 2nd District | 8th Term | 71% (+44)
2434 RHOB | 202-225-3501 | Fax: 226-2019
guthrie.house.gov | X @repguthrie
Bio—Bowling Green; Florence, AL, 2/18/1964; MPPM, Yale Univ., 1997; USA, 1987-90; USAR, 1990-2002; business executive; KY Senate, 1999-2008; US House, 2009-present; m. Beth; Church of Christ
Committees—Energy & Commerce
District Offices—Bowling Green, 270-842-9896

Republican

Harriet Hageman, WY | At Large | 1st Term | 66% (+43)
1531 LHOB | 202-225-2311
hageman.house.gov | X @rephageman
Bio—Cheyenne; Fort Laramie, WY, 10/18/1962; JD, Univ. of Wyoming, 1989; lawyer; US House, 2023-present; m. John Sundahl; Christian
Committees—Judiciary; Natural Resources
District Offices—Cheyenne, 307-829-3299; Casper, 307-261-6595

Republican

Josh Harder, CA | 9th District | 3rd Term | 54% (+10)
209 CHOB | 202-225-4540
harder.house.gov | X @repjoshharder
Bio—Tracy; Turlock, CA, 8/1/1986; MPP, Harvard Univ., 2014; entrepreneur, consultant; US House, 2019-present; m. Pam; Protestant
Committees—Appropriations
District Offices—Stockton, 209-579-5458

Democrat

Andy Harris, MD | 1st District | 7th Term | 54% (+11)
1536 LHOB | 202-225-5311
harris.house.gov | X @repandyharrismd
Bio—Cambridge; Brooklyn, NY, 1/25/1957; MD, Johns Hopkins Univ., 1980; USNR, 1988-2005; physician; MD Senate, 1999-2011; US House, 2011-present; m. Nicole; Catholic
Committees—Appropriations
District Offices—Bel Air, 410-588-5670; Chester, 410-643-5425; Salisbury, 443-944-8624

Republican

Diana Harshbarger, TN | 1st District | 2nd Term | 78% (+59)
167 CHOB | 202-225-6356
harshbarger.house.gov | X @repharshbarger
Bio—Kingsport; Kingsport, TN, 1/1/1960; PharmD, Mercer Univ., 1987; pharmacist, business owner; US House, 2021-present; m. Robert; Baptist
Committees—Energy & Commerce
District Offices—Morristown, 423-254-1400; Kingsport, 423-398-5186

Republican

United States House of Representatives

Jahana Hayes, CT | 5th District | 3rd Term | 50% (+.8)
2458 RHOB | 202-225-4476
hayes.house.gov | X @repjahanahayes
Bio—Wolcott; Waterbury, CT, 3/8/1973; MA, Univ. of Saint Joseph, 2012; teacher, school administrator; US House, 2019-present; m. Milford; Methodist
Committees—Agriculture; Education & the Workforce
District Offices—Waterbury, 860-223-8412

Democrat

Kevin Hern, OK | 1st District | 4th Term | 61% (+26)
1019 LHOB | 202-225-2211
hern.house.gov | X @repkevinhern
Bio—Tulsa; Belton, MO, 12/4/1961; MBA, Univ. of Arkansas, 1999; aerospace engineer, real estate broker, farmer, entrepreneur; US House, 2018-present; m. Tammy; Protestant
Committees—Ways and Means
District Offices—Tulsa, 918-935-3222

Republican

Clay Higgins, LA | 3rd District | 4th Term | 64% (+53)
572 CHOB | 202-225-2031
clayhiggins.house.gov | X @repclayhiggins
Bio—Lafayette; New Orleans, LA, 8/24/1961; attended Louisiana St. Univ., 1979-83, 1989-90; USA; LAARNG; law enforcement official; US House, 2017-present; m. Becca; Christian
Committees—Homeland Security; Oversight & Accountability
District Offices—Lafayette, 337-703-6105; Lake Charles, 337-656-2833

Republican

French Hill, AR | 2nd District | 5th Term | 60% (+25)
1533 LHOB | 202-225-2506 | Fax: 225-5903
hill.house.gov | X @repfrenchhill
Bio—Little Rock; Little Rock, AR, 12/5/1956; BS, Vanderbilt Univ., 1979; banker, businessman, public official; US House, 2015-present; m. Martha; Catholic
Committees—Financial Services; Foreign Affairs; Intelligence
District Offices—Little Rock, 501-324-5941; Conway, 501-902-5733

Republican

Jim Himes, CT | 4th District | 8th Term | 59% (+19)
2137 RHOB | 202-225-5541
himes.house.gov | X @jahimes
Bio—Cos Cob; Lima, Peru, 7/5/1966; MPhil, Oxford Univ., 1990; banking executive; US House, 2009-present; m. Mary; Presbyterian
Committees—Financial Services; Intelligence (Rnk. Mem.)
District Offices—Bridgeport, 203-333-6600; Stamford, 203-353-9400

Democrat

Ashley Hinson, IA | 2nd District | 2nd Term | 53% (+8)
1717 LHOB | 202-225-2911
hinson.house.gov | X @repashleyhinson
Bio—Marion; Des Moines, IA, 6/27/1983; BA, Univ. of Southern California, 2004; journalist; IA House, 2017-20; US House, 2021-present; m. Matt; Christian
Committees—Appropriations; Select CCP
District Offices—Cedar Rapids, 319-364-2288; Dubuque, 563-557-7789; Waterloo, 319-266-6925

Republican

Notes

United States House of Representatives

Steven Horsford, NV | 4th District | 4th Term | 52% (+5)
406 CHOB | 202-225-9894 | Fax: 225-9783
horsford.house.gov | X @rephorsford
Bio—Las Vegas; Las Vegas, NV, 4/29/1973; BA, Univ. of Nevada, 2014; business executive; NV Senate, 2004-12; US House, 2013-15, 2019-present; div.; Baptist
Committees—Armed Services; Financial Services
District Offices—North Las Vegas, 702-963-9360

Democrat

Erin Houchin, IN | 9th District | 1st Term | 63% (+30)
1632 LHOB | 202-225-5315
houchin.house.gov | X @rephouchin
Bio—Salem; Salem, IN, 9/24/1976; MA, George Washington Univ.; social worker, business owner, congressional staff; IN Senate, 2015-22; US House, 2021-present; m. Dustin; Protestant
Committees—Education & the Workforce; Financial Services; Rules
District Offices—Jeffersonville, 812-288-3999

Republican

Chrissy Houlahan, PA | 6th District | 3rd Term | 58% (+17)
1727 LHOB | 202-225-4315
houlahan.house.gov | X @rephoulahan
Bio—Devon; Naval Air Station Patuxent River, MD, 6/5/1967; MS, Massachusetts Institute of Technology, 1994; USAF, 1989-91; USAFR, 1991-2004; engineer, business executive; US House, 2019-present; m. Bart; not stated
Committees—Armed Services; Intelligence
District Offices—West Chester, 610-883-5050; Reading, 610-295-0815

Democrat

Steny Hoyer, MD | 5th District | 22nd Term | 65% (+32)
1705 LHOB | 202-225-4131 | Fax: 225-4300
hoyer.house.gov | X @repstenyhoyer
Bio—Mechanicsville; Manhattan, NY, 6/14/1939; JD, Georgetown Univ., 1966; lawyer; MD Senate, 1966-79; US House, 1981-present; wid.; Baptist
Committees—Appropriations
District Offices—Greenbelt, 301-474-0119; White Plains, 301-843-1577

Democrat

Val Hoyle, OR | 4th District | 1st Term | 50% (+7)
1620 LHOB | 202-225-6416
hoyle.house.gov | X @repvalhoyle
Bio—Springfield; Fairfield, CA, 2/14/1964; BA, Emmanuel College, 1992; consultant, nonprofit executive; OR House, 2009-17; US House, 2023-present; m. Stephen; Catholic
Committees—Natural Resources; Transportation & Infrastructure
District Offices—Eugene, 541-465-6732

Democrat

Richard Hudson, NC | 9th District | 6th Term | 56% (+13)
2112 RHOB | 202-225-3715 | Fax: 225-4036
hudson.house.gov | X @reprichhudson
Bio—Southern Pines; Franklin, VA, 11/4/1971; BA, Univ. of North Carolina, 1996; business owner, congressional staffer; US House, 2013-present; m. Renee; Christian
Committees—Energy & Commerce
District Offices—Southern Pines, 910-910-1924; Fayetteville, 910-997-2070

Republican

United States House of Representatives

Jared Huffman, CA | 2nd District | 6th Term | 74% (+49)
2445 RHOB | 202-225-5161 | Fax: 225-5163
huffman.house.gov | X @rephuffman
Bio—San Rafael; Independence, MO, 2/18/1964; JD, Boston Col., 1990; lawyer; CA Assembly, 2006-12; US House, 2013-present; m. Susan; Humanist
Committees—Natural Resources; Transportation & Infrastructure
District Offices—San Rafael, 415-258-9657; Fort Bragg, 707-962-0933; Eureka, 707-407-3585; Petaluma, 707-981-8967; Ukiah, 707-671-7449

Democrat

Bill Huizenga, MI | 4th District | 7th Term | 54% (+12)
2232 RHOB | 202-225-4401 | Fax: 226-0779
huizenga.house.gov | X @rephuizenga
Bio—Holland; Zeeland, MI, 1/31/1969; BA, Calvin Col., 1991; business owner, congressional staffer; MI House, 2003-08; US House, 2011-present; m. Natalie; Christian
Committees—Financial Services; Foreign Affairs
District Offices—Holland, 616-251-6741; Portage, 269-569-8595

Republican

Wesley Hunt, TX | 38th District | 1st Term | 62% (+27)
1520 LHOB | 202-225-5646
hunt.house.gov | X @repwph
Bio—Houston; Houston, TX, 11/13/1981; MILR, Cornell Univ., 2016; USA, 2004-12; loan officer, human resources professional; US House, 2023-present; m. Emily; Baptist
Committees—Judiciary; Natural Resources; Small Business
District Offices—Houston, 832-357-0555; Tomball, 346-246-7355

Republican

Darrell Issa, CA | 48th District | 11th Term | 60% (+21)
2108 RHOB | 202-225-5672
issa.house.gov | X @repdarrellissa
Bio—San Diego; Cleveland, OH, 11/1/1953; BA, Siena Heights Col., 1976; USA, 1970-80; business owner; US House, 2001-19, 2021-present; div.; Orthodox
Committees—Foreign Affairs; Judiciary; Science, Space, & Technology
District Offices—Escondido, 760-304-7575; Temecula, 760-304-7575

Republican

Glenn Ivey, MD | 4th District | 1st Term | 90% (+80)
1529 LHOB | 202-225-8699 | Fax: 225-2848
ivey.house.gov | X @repglennivey
Bio—Cheverly; Chelsea, MA, 2/27/1961; JD, Harvard Univ., 1986; lawyer, congressional staffer; US House, 2023-present; m. Jolene; Protestant
Committees—Ethics; Homeland Security; Judiciary
District Offices—Largo, 240-906-6262

Democrat

Jeff Jackson, NC | 14th District | 1st Term | 57% (+15)
1318 LHOB | 202-225-5634
jeffjackson.house.gov | X @repjeffjackson
Bio—Charlotte; Miami, FL, 9/12/1982; JD, Univ. of North Carolina, 2009; USA; USAR, 2002-03; NCARNG, 2003-present; lawyer; NC Senate, 2014-22; US House, 2023-present; m. Marisa; Presbyterian
Committees—Armed Services; Science, Space, & Technology
District Offices—Charlotte, 202-225-5634; Gastonia, 202-225-5634

Democrat

U.S. Congress Directory | 95

United States House of Representatives

Jonathan L. Jackson, IL | 1st District | 1st Term | 67% (+34)
1641 LHOB | 202-225-4372 | Fax: 226-0333
jonathanjackson.house.gov | X @rep_jackson
Bio—Chicago; Chicago, IL, 1/7/1966; MBA, Northwestern Univ., 1991; financial analyst, business owner, professor; US House, 2023-present; single; Baptist
Committees—Agriculture; Foreign Affairs
District Offices—Chicago, 773-779-2400

Democrat

Ronny Jackson, TX | 13th District | 2nd Term | 75% (+51)
446 CHOB | 202-225-3706 | Fax: 225-3486
jackson.house.gov | X @repronnyjackson
Bio—Amarillo; Levelland, TX, 5/4/1967; MD, Univ. of Texas, 1995; USNR, 1991-95; USN, 1995-2019; physician; US House, 2021-present; m. Jane; Church of Christ
Committees—Agriculture; Armed Services; Foreign Affairs
District Offices—Amarillo, 806-641-5600; Wichita Falls, 940-285-8000; Denton, 940-334-2030

Republican

Sheila Jackson Lee, TX | 18th District | 15th Term | 70% (+45)
2314 RHOB | 202-225-3816 | Fax: 225-3317
jacksonlee.house.gov | X @jacksonleetx18
Bio—Houston; Queens, NY, 1/12/1950; JD, Univ. of Virginia, 1975; lawyer; Houston city council, 1990-94; Houston municipal judge, 1987-90; US House, 1995-present; m. Elwyn Lee; Adventist
Committees—Budget; Homeland Security; Judiciary
District Offices—Houston, 713-691-4882; Houston, 713-227-7740; Houston, 713-861-4070; Houston, 713-655-0050

Democrat

Sara Jacobs, CA | 51st District | 2nd Term | 61% (+24)
1314 LHOB | 202-225-2040 | Fax: 225-2948
sarajacobs.house.gov | X @repsarajacobs
Bio—San Diego; San Diego, CA, 2/1/1989; MA, Columbia Univ., 2012; presidential campaign aide, nonprofit executive; US House, 2021-present; single; Jewish
Committees—Armed Services; Foreign Affairs
District Offices—San Diego, 619-280-5353

Democrat

John James, MI | 10th District | 1st Term | 48% (+.5)
1319 LHOB | 202-225-4961
james.house.gov | X @repjames
Bio—Farmington Hills; Southfield, MI, 6/8/1981; MBA, Univ. of Michigan, 2015; USA, 2004-12; business executive; US House, 2023-present; m. Elizabeth; Christian
Committees—Education & the Workforce; Foreign Affairs; Transportation & Infrastructure
District Offices—Warren, 586-498-7122

Republican

Pramila Jayapal, WA | 7th District | 4th Term | 85% (+71)
2346 RHOB | 202-225-3106 | Fax: 225-6197
jayapal.house.gov | X @repjayapal
Bio—Seattle; Chennai, India, 9/21/1965; MBA, Northwestern Univ., 1990; financial analyst, nonprofit executive; WA Senate, 2015-16; US House, 2017-present; m. Steve Williamson; not stated
Committees—Education & the Workforce; Judiciary
District Offices—Seattle, 206-674-0040

Democrat

Notes

United States House of Representatives

Hakeem Jeffries, NY | 8th District | 6th Term | 72% (+44)
2433 RHOB | 202-225-5936
jeffries.house.gov | X @repjeffries
Bio—Brooklyn; Brooklyn, NY, 8/4/1970; JD, New York Univ., 1997; lawyer; NY Assembly, 2007-12; US House, 2013-present; m. Kennisandra Arciniegas-Jeffries; Baptist
Committees—Minority Leader
District Offices—Brooklyn, 718-237-2211; Brooklyn, 718-373-0033

Democrat

Dusty Johnson, SD | At Large | 3rd Term | 77% (+55)
1714 LHOB | 202-225-2801
dustyjohnson.house.gov | X @repdustyjohnson
Bio—Mitchell; Pierre, SD, 9/30/1976; MPA, Univ. of Kansas, 2002; gubernatorial staff, business executive; SD public utilities commission, 2004-11; US House, 2019-present; m. Jacquelyn; Protestant
Committees—Agriculture; Transportation & Infrastructure; Select CCP
District Offices—Aberdeen, 605-622-1060; Rapid City, 605-646-6454; Sioux Falls, 605-275-2868

Republican

Henry C. "Hank" Johnson, Jr., GA | 4th District | 9th Term | 78% (+57)
2240 RHOB | 202-225-1605 | Fax: 226-0691
hankjohnson.house.gov | X @rephankjohnson
Bio—Lithonia; Washington, DC, 10/2/1954; JD, Texas Southern Univ., 1979; lawyer; DeKalb Co. commissioners, 2001-06; US House, 2007-present; m. Mereda; Buddhist
Committees—Judiciary; Transportation & Infrastructure
District Offices—Decatur, 770-987-2291

Democrat

Mike Johnson, LA | 4th District | 4th Term | Unc.
568 CHOB | 202-225-2777
mikejohnson.house.gov | X @speakerjohnson
Bio—Benton; Shreveport, LA, 1/30/1972; JD, Louisiana St. Univ., 1998; lawyer; LA House, 2015-17; US House, 2017-present; m. Kelly; Southern Baptist
Committees—Speaker
District Offices—Bossier City, 318-840-0309; Natchitoches, 318-951-4316; Leesville, 337-423-4232

Republican

Jim Jordan, OH | 4th District | 9th Term | 69% (+38)
2056 RHOB | 202-225-2676 | Fax: 226-0577
jordan.house.gov | X @jimjordan
Bio—Urbana; Troy, OH, 2/17/1964; JD, Capital Univ., 2001; lawyer; OH House, 1995-2000; OH Senate, 2001-06; US House, 2007-present; m. Polly; Protestant
Committees—Judiciary (Chair); Oversight & Accountability
District Offices—Lima, 419-999-6455; Mansfield, 419-982-8045

Republican

Dave Joyce, OH | 14th District | 6th Term | 61% (+23)
2065 RHOB | 202-225-5731
joyce.house.gov | X @repdavejoyce
Bio—South Russell Village; Cleveland, OH, 3/17/1957; JD, Univ. of Dayton, 1982; lawyer; US House, 2013-present; m. Kelly; Catholic
Committees—Appropriations; Ethics
District Offices—Mentor, 440-352-3939; Warren, 330-752-7673; Ravenna, 330-357-4139

Republican

Notes

U.S. Congress Directory | 97

United States House of Representatives

John Joyce, PA | 13th District | 3rd Term | Unc.
152 CHOB | 202-225-2431
johnjoyce.house.gov | X @repjohnjoyce
Bio—Hollidaysburg; Altoona, PA, 2/8/1957; MD, Temple Univ., 1983; internist, dermatologist; US House, 2019-present; m. Alice; Catholic
Committees—Energy & Commerce
District Offices—Johnstown, 814-485-6020; Lewistown, 717-357-6320; Abbottstown, 717-357-6320; Altoona, 814-656-6081; Chambersburg, 717-753-6344

Republican

Sydney Kamlager-Dove, CA | 37th District | 1st Term | 63% (+28)
1419 LHOB | 202-225-7084
kamlager-dove.house.gov | X @repkamlagerdove
Bio—Los Angeles; Chicago, IL, 7/20/1972; MA, Carnegie Mellon Univ., 1996; nonprofit executive, legislative staffer; CA Assembly, 2018-21; CA Senate, 2021-22; US House, 2023-present; m. Austin; Lutheran
Committees—Foreign Affairs; Natural Resources
District Offices—Los Angeles, 323-965-1422

Democrat

Marcy Kaptur, OH | 9th District | 21st Term | 56% (+13)
2186 RHOB | 202-225-4146
kaptur.house.gov | X @repmarcykaptur
Bio—Toledo; Toledo, OH, 6/17/1946; MA, Univ. of Michigan, 1974; urban planner; US House, 1983-present; single; Catholic
Committees—Appropriations
District Offices—Toledo, 419-259-7500

Democrat

Tom Kean, Jr., NJ | 7th District | 1st Term | 51% (+3)
251 CHOB | 202-225-5361
kean.house.gov | X @congressmankean
Bio—Westfield; Livingston, NJ, 9/5/1968; MALD, Tufts Univ., 1997; college instructor, consultant; NJ Assembly, 2001-03; NJ Senate, 2003-22; US House, 2023-present; m. Rhonda; Episcopalian
Committees—Foreign Affairs; Science, Space, & Technology; Transportation & Infrastructure
District Offices—Bernardsville, 908-547-3307

Republican

William R. Keating, MA | 9th District | 7th Term | 57% (+18)
2351 RHOB | 202-225-3111 | Fax: 225-5658
keating.house.gov | X @usrepkeating
Bio—Bourne; Norwood, MA, 9/6/1952; JD, Suffolk Univ., 1985; public official, lawyer; MA House, 1977-84; MA Senate, 1985-98; Norfolk Co. district attorney, 1998-2010; US House, 2011-present; m. Tevis; Catholic
Committees—Armed Services; Foreign Affairs
District Offices—Hyannis, 508-771-6868; New Bedford, 508-999-6462; Plymouth, 508-746-9000

Democrat

Mike Kelly, PA | 16th District | 7th Term | 59% (+19)
1707 LHOB | 202-225-5406 | Fax: 225-3103
kelly.house.gov | X @mikekellypa
Bio—Butler; Pittsburgh, PA, 5/10/1948; BA, Notre Dame Univ., 1970; business owner; Butler Co. council, 2006-09; US House, 2011-present; m. Victoria; Catholic
Committees—Ways and Means
District Offices—Erie, 814-454-8190; Sharon, 724-342-7170; Butler, 724-282-2557

Republican

United States House of Representatives

Robin Kelly, IL | 2nd District | 6th Term | 67% (+34)
2329 RHOB | 202-225-0773 | Fax: 225-4583
robinkelly.house.gov | X @reprobinkelly
Bio—Matteson; New York, NY, 4/30/1956; PhD, Northern Illinois Univ., 2004; counselor, public official; IL House, 2003-07; US House, 2013-present; wid.; Christian
Committees—Energy & Commerce
District Offices—Danville, 217-516-4556; Chicago, 773-321-2001; Matteson, 708-679-0078

Democrat

Trent Kelly, MS | 1st District | 5th Term | 72% (+46)
2243 RHOB | 202-225-4306 | Fax: 225-3549
trentkelly.house.gov | X @reptrentkelly
Bio—Saltillo; Union, MS, 3/1/1966; MA, U.S. Army War Col., 2010; MSARNG; lawyer; US House, 2015-present; m. Sheila; Methodist
Committees—Agriculture; Armed Services; Intelligence
District Offices—Tupelo, 662-841-8808; Columbus, 662-327-0748; Hernando, 662-687-0576; Eupora, 662-687-1545; Corinth, 662-687-1525; Oxford, 662-687-1540

Republican

Ro Khanna, CA | 17th District | 4th Term | 70% (+42)
306 CHOB | 202-225-2631
khanna.house.gov | X @reprokhanna
Bio—Fremont; Philadelphia, PA, 9/13/1976; JD, Yale Univ., 2001; lawyer, professor, author; US House, 2017-present; m. Ritu; Hindu
Committees—Armed Services; Oversight & Accountability; Select CCP
District Offices—Santa Clara, 408-436-2720

Democrat

Jen Kiggans, VA | 2nd District | 1st Term | 51% (+3)
1037 LHOB | 202-225-4215
kiggans.house.gov | X @repjenkiggans
Bio—Virginia Beach; Tampa, FL, 6/18/1971; MS Vanderbilt Univ., 2012; USN, 1993-2003; nurse practitioner; VA Senate, 2020-23; US House, 2023-present; m. Steve; Catholic
Committees—Armed Services; Natural Resources; Veterans' Affairs
District Offices—Virginia Beach, 757-364-7650; Onley, 757-666-6020; Suffolk, 757-942-6050

Republican

Dan Kildee, MI | 8th District | 6th Term | 53% (+10)
200 CHOB | 202-225-3611 | Fax: 225-6393
dankildee.house.gov | X @repdankildee
Bio—Flint Township; Flint, MI, 8/11/1958; BS, Central Michigan Univ., 2011; land bank founder, nonprofit executive; Genesee Co. commissioners, 1985-97; Genesee Co. treasurer, 1997-2009; US House, 2013-present; m. Jennifer; Catholic
Committees—Budget; Ways and Means
District Offices—Midland, 989-898-6060; Flint, 810-238-8627

Democrat

Kevin Kiley, CA | 3rd District | 1st Term | 53% (+7)
1032 LHOB | 202-225-2523
kiley.house.gov | X @repkiley
Bio—Rocklin; Rocklin, CA, 1/30/1985; JD, Yale Univ., 2012; lawyer, business owner; CA Assembly, 2016-22; US House, 2023-present; m. Chelsey; Christian
Committees—Education & the Workforce; Judiciary
District Offices—Rocklin, 916-724-2575

Republican

Notes

United States House of Representatives

Derek Kilmer, WA | 6th District | 6th Term | 60% (+20)
1226 LHOB | 202-225-5916
kilmer.house.gov | X @repderekkilmer
Bio—Gig Harbor; Port Angeles, WA, 1/1/1974; DPhil, Univ. of Oxford, 2003; businessman; WA House, 2005-07; WA Senate, 2007-12; US House, 2013-present; m. Jennifer; Methodist
Committees—Appropriations; House Administration; Joint Printing
District Offices—Bremerton, 360-373-9725; Port Angeles, 360-797-3623; Tacoma, 253-272-3515

Democrat

Andy Kim, NJ | 3rd District | 3rd Term | 55% (+12)
2444 RHOB | 202-225-4765 | Fax: 225-0778
kim.house.gov | X @repandykimnj
Bio—Moorestown; Boston, MA, 7/12/1982; PhD, Oxford Univ., 2010; government staffer; US House, 2019-present; m. Kammy Lai; Presbyterian
Committees—Armed Services; Foreign Affairs; Select CCP
District Offices—Freehold, 732-504-0490; Hamilton, 609-438-6290; Willingboro, 856-703-2700

Democrat

Young Kim, CA | 40th District | 2nd Term | 56% (+14)
1306 LHOB | 202-225-4111
youngkim.house.gov | X @repyoungkim
Bio—La Habra; Incheon, South Korea, 10/18/1962; BBA, Univ. of Southern California, 1985; business owner, congressional staffer; CA Assembly, 2014-16; US House, 2021-present; m. Charles; Christian
Committees—Financial Services; Foreign Affairs
District Offices—Mission Viejo, 949-268-6706; Anaheim, 714-984-2440

Republican

Raja Krishnamoorthi, IL | 8th District | 4th Term | 56% (+14)
2367 RHOB | 202-225-3711
krishnamoorthi.house.gov | X @congressmanraja
Bio—Schaumburg; New Delhi, India, 7/19/1973; JD, Harvard Univ., 2000; lawyer, business executive; US House, 2017-present; m. Priya; Hindu
Committees—Oversight & Accountability; Intelligence; Select CCP (Rnk. Mem.)
District Offices—Schaumburg, 847-413-1959

Democrat

Annie Kuster, NH | 2nd District | 6th Term | 55% (+12)
2201 RHOB | 202-225-5206 | Fax: 225-2946
kuster.house.gov | X @repanniekuster
Bio—Hopkinton; Concord, NH, 9/5/1956; JD, Georgetown Univ., 1984; author, lawyer, consultant; US House, 2013-present; m. Brad; Protestant
Committees—Energy & Commerce
District Offices—Concord, 603-226-1002; Nashua, 603-595-2006; Littleton, 603-444-7700

Democrat

David Kustoff, TN | 8th District | 4th Term | 73% (+50)
560 CHOB | 202-225-4714
kustoff.house.gov | X @repdavidkustoff
Bio—Germantown; Memphis, TN, 10/8/1966; JD, Univ. of Memphis, 1992; lawyer; US House, 2017-present; m. Roberta; Jewish
Committees—Ways and Means
District Offices—Dyersburg, 731-412-1037; Memphis, 901-682-4422; Jackson, 731-423-4848; Martin, 731-412-1043

Republican

Notes

United States House of Representatives

Darin LaHood, IL | 16th District | 5th Term | 66% (+33)
1424 LHOB | 202-225-6201 | Fax: 225-9249
lahood.house.gov | X @replahood
Bio—Peoria; Peoria, IL, 7/5/1968; JD, John Marshall Law School, 1997; lawyer, congressional staffer; IL Senate, 2011-15; US House, 2015-present; m. Kristen; Catholic
Committees—Ways and Means; Intelligence; Select CCP
District Offices—Peoria, 309-671-7027; Rockford, 779-238-4785; Normal, 309-445-8080
Republican

Nick LaLota, NY | 1st District | 1st Term | 55% (+11)
1530 LHOB | 202-225-3826
lalota.house.gov | X @replalota
Bio—Suffolk County; Bay Shore, NY, 6/23/1978; JD, Hofstra Univ., 2020; USN, 2000-07; stockbroker, legislative staffer; US House, 2023-present; m. Kaylie; Catholic
Committees—Armed Services; Homeland Security; Small Business
District Offices—Hauppauge, 631-289-1097; Rocky Point, 631-289-1097
Republican

Doug LaMalfa, CA | 1st District | 6th Term | 62% (+24)
408 CHOB | 202-225-3076
lamalfa.house.gov | X @replamalfa
Bio—Oroville; Oroville, CA, 7/2/1960; BS, California Polytechnic St. Univ., 1982; rice farmer; CA Assembly, 2002-08; CA Senate, 2010-12; US House, 2013-present; m. Jill; Christian
Committees—Agriculture; Natural Resources; Transportation & Infrastructure
District Offices—Chico, 530-343-1000; Redding, 530-223-5898; Yuba City, 530-645-6225
Republican

Doug Lamborn, CO | 5th District | 9th Term | 55% (+16)
2371 RHOB | 202-225-4422 | Fax: 226-2638
lamborn.house.gov | X @repdlamborn
Bio—Colorado Springs; Leavenworth, KS, 5/24/1954; JD, Univ. of Kansas, 1985; lawyer; CO House, 1995-98; CO Senate, 1998-2006; US House, 2007-present; m. Jeanie; Christian
Committees—Armed Services; Natural Resources
District Offices—Colorado Springs, 719-520-0055
Republican

Greg Landsman, OH | 1st District | 1st Term | 52% (+6)
1432 LHOB | 202-225-2216
landsman.house.gov | X @repgreglandsman
Bio—Cincinnati; Cincinnati, OH, 12/4/1976; MA, Harvard Univ., 2004; teacher, nonprofit executive; Cincinnati city council, 2018-2022; US House, 2023-present; m. Sarah; Jewish
Committees—Small Business; Veterans' Affairs
District Offices—Cincinnati, 513-810-7988; Lebanon, 513-409-6188
Democrat

Nick Langworthy, NY | 23rd District | 1st Term | 65% (+30)
1630 LHOB | 202-225-3161
langworthy.house.gov | X @replangworthy
Bio—Pendleton; Jamestown, NY, 2/27/1981; BA, Niagara Univ., 2003; political consultant, congressional staffer; US House, 2023-present; m. Erin; Protestant
Committees—Agriculture; Oversight & Accountability; Rules
District Offices—Jamestown, 716-488-8111; Olean, 585-543-5033; Corning, 607-377-3130; Williamsville, 716-547-6844
Republican

Notes

United States House of Representatives

Rick Larsen, WA | 2nd District | 12th Term | 60% (+20)
2163 RHOB | 202-225-2605 | Fax: 225-4420
larsen.house.gov | X @repricklarsen
Bio—Everett; Arlington, WA, 6/15/1965; MPA, Univ. of Minnesota, 1990; public official, lobbyist; Snohomish Co. council, 1998-2000; US House, 2001-present; m. Tiia Karlen; Methodist
Committees—Transportation & Infrastructure (Rnk. Mem.)
District Offices—Everett, 425-252-3188; Bellingham, 360-733-4500

Democrat

John B. Larson, CT | 1st District | 13th Term | 61% (+24)
1501 LHOB | 202-225-2265 | Fax: 225-1031
larson.house.gov | X @repjohnlarson
Bio—East Hartford; Hartford, CT, 7/22/1948; BA, Central Connecticut Univ., 1971; teacher, businessman; East Hartford town council, 1979-83; CT Senate, 1986-98; US House, 1999-present; m. Leslie; Catholic
Committees—Ways and Means
District Offices—East Hartford, 860-278-8888

Democrat

Bob Latta, OH | 5th District | 9th Term | 66% (+34)
2467 RHOB | 202-225-6405 | Fax: 225-1985
latta.house.gov | X @boblatta
Bio—Bowling Green; Bluffton, OH, 4/18/1956; JD, Univ. of Toledo, 1981; lawyer; Wood Co. commissioner, 1991-96; OH Senate, 1997-2000; OH House, 2001-07; US House, 2007-present; m. Marcia; Catholic
Committees—Energy & Commerce
District Offices—Bowling Green, 419-354-8700; Findlay, 419-422-7791; Elyria, 440-406-5010

Republican

Jake LaTurner, KS | 2nd District | 2nd Term | 57% (+15)
2441 RHOB | 202-225-6601
laturner.house.gov | X @replaturner
Bio—Topeka; Galena, KS, 2/17/1988; BA, Pittsburg St. Univ.; customer service representative, congressional staffer; KS Senate, 2013-17; KS treasurer, 2017-20; US House, 2021-present; m. Suzanne; Catholic
Committees—Appropriations; Oversight & Accountability
District Offices—Pittsburg, 620-308-7450; Topeka, 785-205-5253

Republican

Mike Lawler, NY | 17th District | 1st Term | 49% (+.6)
1013 LHOB | 202-225-6506
lawler.house.gov | X @repmikelawler
Bio—Pearl River; Suffern, NY, 9/9/1986; BA, Manhattan College, 2009; business owner; NY Assembly, 2020-23; US House, 2023-present; m. Doina; Catholic
Committees—Financial Services; Foreign Affairs
District Offices—Pearl River, 845-201-2060; Mahopac, 845-743-7130

Republican

Barbara Lee, CA | 12th District | 14th Term | 90% (+81)
2470 RHOB | 202-225-2661 | Fax: 225-9817
lee.house.gov | X @repbarbaralee
Bio—Oakland; El Paso, TX, 7/16/1946; MSW, Univ. of California, Berkeley, 1975; business owner, congressional staffer; CA Assembly, 1991-97; CA Senate, 1997-98; US House, 1998-present; single; Baptist
Committees—Appropriations; Budget
District Offices—Oakland, 510-763-0370

Democrat

United States House of Representatives

Laurel Lee, FL | 15th District | 1st Term | 58% (+17)
1118 LHOB | 202-225-5626
laurellee.house.gov | X @replaurellee
Bio—Tampa; 3/26/1974; JD, Univ. of Florida, 1999; lawyer; FL secretary of state, 2019-2022; US House, 2023-present; m. Tom; Protestant
Committees—Homeland Security; House Administration; Judiciary
District Offices—Tampa, 813-393-5077

Republican

Summer Lee, PA | 12th District | 1st Term | 56% (+12)
243 CHOB | 202-225-2135
summerlee.house.gov | X @repsummerlee
Bio—Swissvale; North Braddock, PA, 11/26/1987; JD, Howard Univ., 2015; community organizer; PA House, 2018-22; US House, 2023-present; single; Protestant
Committees—Oversight & Accountability; Science, Space, & Technology
District Offices—Pittsburgh, 412-214-5000; Clairton, 412-214-5000; Jeannette, 412-214-5000; Pittsburgh, 412-214-5000

Democrat

Susie Lee, NV | 3rd District | 3rd Term | 51% (+4)
365 CHOB | 202-225-3252
susielee.house.gov | X @repsusielee
Bio—Las Vegas; Canton, OH, 11/7/1966; MPM, Carnegie Mellon Univ., 1990; nonprofit executive; US House, 2019-present; div.; Catholic
Committees—Appropriations; Natural Resources
District Offices—Las Vegas, 702-963-9336

Democrat

Teresa Leger Fernandez, NM | 3rd District | 2nd Term | 58% (+16)
1510 LHOB | 202-225-6190
fernandez.house.gov | X @repteresalf
Bio—Santa Fe; Las Vegas, NM, 7/1/1959; JD, Stanford Univ., 1987; lawyer; US House, 2021-present; single; Catholic
Committees—Education & the Workforce; Natural Resources; Rules
District Offices—Santa Fe, 505-428-4680; Las Vegas, 505-570-7558

Democrat

Debbie Lesko, AZ | 8th District | 4th Term | Unc.
1214 LHOB | 202-225-4576
lesko.house.gov | X @repdlesko
Bio—Peoria; Sheboygan, WI, 11/14/1958; BBA, Univ. of Wisconsin, 1981; business owner; AZ House, 2008-14; AZ Senate, 2015-18; US House, 2018-present; m. Joe; Christian
Committees—Energy & Commerce
District Offices—Surprise, 623-776-7911

Republican

Julia Letlow, LA | 5th District | 2nd Term | 67% (+62)
142 CHOB | 202-225-8490
letlow.house.gov | X @repjulialetlow
Bio—Start; Monroe, LA, 3/16/1981; PhD, Univ. of South Florida, 2011; university administrator; US House, 2021-present; wid.; Presbyterian
Committees—Appropriations; Education & the Workforce
District Offices—Alexandria, 318-319-6465; Monroe, 318-570-6440; Amite, 985-284-5200

Republican

Notes

United States House of Representatives

Mike Levin, CA | 49th District | 3rd Term | 52% (+5)
2352 RHOB | 202-225-3906
mikelevin.house.gov | X @repmikelevin
Bio—San Juan Capistrano; Inglewood, CA, 10/20/1978; JD, Duke Univ., 2005; lawyer, business executive; US House, 2019-present; m. Chrissy; Catholic
Committees—Natural Resources; Veterans' Affairs
District Offices—Oceanside, 760-599-5000; Dana Point, 949-281-2449

Democrat

Ted W. Lieu, CA | 36th District | 5th Term | 69% (+40)
2454 RHOB | 202-225-3976
lieu.house.gov | X @reptedlieu
Bio—Torrance; Taipei, Taiwan, 3/29/1969; JD, Georgetown Univ., 1994; USAF, 1995-99; USAFR, 2000-21; lawyer; Torrance city council, 2002-05; CA Assembly, 2005-10; CA Senate, 2011-14; US House, 2015-present; m. Betty; Catholic
Committees—Foreign Affairs; Judiciary
District Offices—Los Angeles, 323-651-1040

Democrat

Zoe Lofgren, CA | 18th District | 15th Term | 65% (+32)
1401 LHOB | 202-225-3072
lofgren.house.gov | X @repzoelofgren
Bio—San Jose; San Mateo, CA, 12/21/1947; JD, Santa Clara Univ., 1975; lawyer, congressional staffer; Santa Clara Co. supervisors, 1980-94; US House, 1995-present; m. John Marshall Collins; Lutheran
Committees—Judiciary; Science, Space, & Technology (Rnk. Mem.)
District Offices—Salinas, 831-837-6000; San Jose, 408-271-8700

Democrat

Barry Loudermilk, GA | 11th District | 5th Term | 62% (+25)
2133 RHOB | 202-225-2931 | Fax: 225-2944
loudermilk.house.gov | X @reploudermilk
Bio—Cassville; Riverdale, GA, 12/22/1963; BS, Wayland Baptist Univ., 1992; USAF, 1984-92; business owner; GA House, 2005-10; GA Senate, 2011-13; US House, 2015-present; m. Desiree; Baptist
Committees—Financial Services; House Administration
District Offices—Woodstock, 770-429-1776; Cartersville, 770-429-1776

Republican

Frank Lucas, OK | 3rd District | 16th Term | 74% (+49)
2405 RHOB | 202-225-5565
lucas.house.gov | X @repfranklucas
Bio—Cheyenne; Cheyenne, OK, 1/6/1960; BS, Oklahoma St. Univ., 1982; public official; OK House, 1988-94; US House, 1994-present; m. Lynda; Baptist
Committees—Agriculture; Financial Services; Science, Space, & Technology (Chair)
District Offices—Yukon, 405-373-1958

Republican

Blaine Luetkemeyer, MO | 3rd District | 8th Term | 65% (+30)
2230 RHOB | 202-225-2956 | Fax: 225-5712
luetkemeyer.house.gov | X @repblaine
Bio—St. Elizabeth; Jefferson City, MO, 5/7/1952; BA, Lincoln Univ., 1974; business owner, banker, rancher; St. Elizabeth trustees, 1978-87; MO House, 1999-2005; US House, 2009-present; m. Jackie; Catholic
Committees—Financial Services; Small Business; Select CCP
District Offices—Jefferson City, 573-635-7232; Cottleville, 636-327-7055

Republican

United States House of Representatives

Anna Paulina Luna, FL | 13th District | 1st Term | 53% (+8)
1017 LHOB | 202-225-5961
luna.house.gov | X @repluna
Bio—St. Petersburg; Santa Ana, CA, 5/6/1989; BS, Univ. of West Florida, 2018; USAF, 2009-14; ORANG, 2017-18; non-profit executive, political commentator; US House, 2023-present; m. Andy; Christian
Committees—Natural Resources; Oversight & Accountability
District Offices—Seminole, 727-610-3980

Republican

Morgan Luttrell, TX | 8th District | 1st Term | 68% (+38)
1320 LHOB | 202-225-4901
luttrell.house.gov | X @repluttrell
Bio—Magnolia; Houston, TX, 11/7/1975; MS, Univ. of Texas, Dallas, 2016; USN, 2000-14; nonprofit executive, business owner, professor; US House, 2023-present; m. Leslie; Protestant
Committees—Armed Services; Homeland Security; Veterans' Affairs
District Offices—Magnolia, 281-305-7890

Republican

Stephen F. Lynch, MA | 8th District | 12th Term | 66% (+38)
2109 RHOB | 202-225-8273 | Fax: 225-3984
lynch.house.gov | X @repstephenlynch
Bio—South Boston; Boston, MA, 3/31/1955; MA, Harvard Univ., 1998; public official; MA House, 1995-96; MA Senate, 1997-2001; US House, 2001-present; m. Margaret; Catholic
Committees—Financial Services; Oversight & Accountability
District Offices—Boston, 617-428-2000; Brockton, 508-586-5555; Quincy, 617-657-6305

Democrat

Nancy Mace, SC | 1st District | 2nd Term | 56% (+14)
1728 LHOB | 202-225-3176
mace.house.gov | X @repnancymace
Bio—Charleston; Fayetteville, NC, 12/4/1977; MS, Univ. of Georgia, 2004; author, real estate broker, presidential campaign aide; SC House, 2018-20; US House, 2021-present; div.; Christian
Committees—Armed Services; Oversight & Accountability; Veterans' Affairs
District Offices—Mt. Pleasant, 843-352-7572; Beaufort, 843-521-2530

Republican

Seth Magaziner, RI | 2nd District | 1st Term | 50% (+4)
1218 LHOB | 202-225-2735
magaziner.house.gov | X @rep_magaziner
Bio—Cranston; Bristol, RI, 7/22/1983; MBA., Yale Univ., 2010; teacher, investment professional; RI treasurer, 2015-23; US House, 2023-present; m. Julia; not stated
Committees—Homeland Security; Natural Resources
District Offices—Warwick, 401-244-1201

Democrat

Nicole Malliotakis, NY | 11th District | 2nd Term | 62% (+24)
351 CHOB | 202-225-3371
malliotakis.house.gov | X @repmalliotakis
Bio—Staten Island; Manhattan, NY, 11/11/1980; MBA, Wagner Univ., 2010; gubernatorial staffer, campaign aide, public relations professional; NY Assembly, 2011-20; US House, 2021-present; div.; Greek Orthodox
Committees—Ways and Means; Joint Economic
District Offices—Staten Island, 718-568-2870; Brooklyn, 718-306-1620

Republican

United States House of Representatives

Celeste Maloy, UT | 2nd District | 1st Term | 56% (+23)
166 CHOB | 202-225-9730
maloy.house.gov | X @repmaloyutah
Bio—Cedar City; Cedar City, UT, 5/22/1981; JD, Brigham Young Univ., 2015; lawyer, soil conservationist, congressional staffer; US House, 2023-present; single; Mormon
Committees—Small Business; Transportation & Infrastructure
District Offices—Bountiful, 801-364-5550

Republican

Tracey Mann, KS | 1st District | 2nd Term | 67% (+35)
344 CHOB | 202-225-2715
mann.house.gov | X @repmann
Bio—Salina; Quinter, KS, 12/17/1976; BA, Kansas St. Univ., 2000; real estate broker; KS lt. governor, 2018-19; US House, 2021-present; m. Audrey; Christian
Committees—Agriculture; Small Business; Transportation & Infrastructure
District Offices—Manhattan, 785-370-7277; Dodge City, 620-682-7340

Republican

Kathy Manning, NC | 6th District | 2nd Term | 53% (+9)
307 CHOB | 202-225-3065 | Fax: 225-8611
manning.house.gov | X @repkmanning
Bio—Greensboro; Detroit, MI, 12/3/1956; JD, Univ. of Michigan, 1981; lawyer; US House, 2021-present; m. Randall Kaplan; Jewish
Committees—Education & the Workforce; Foreign Affairs
District Offices—Greensboro, 336-333-5005

Democrat

Thomas Massie, KY | 4th District | 7th Term | 65% (+34)
2453 RHOB | 202-225-3465
massie.house.gov | X @repthomasmassie
Bio—Garrison; Huntington, WV, 1/13/1971; MS, Massachusetts Institute of Technology, 1996; business owner, farmer; Lewis Co. judge executive, 2010-12; US House, 2012-present; m. Rhonda; Methodist
Committees—Judiciary; Rules; Transportation & Infrastructure
District Offices—Crescent Springs, 859-426-0080; LaGrange, 502-265-9119

Republican

Brian Mast, FL | 21st District | 4th Term | 63% (+27)
2182 RHOB | 202-225-3026 | Fax: 225-8398
mast.house.gov | X @repbrianmast
Bio—Fort Pierce; Grand Rapids, MI, 7/10/1980; ALB, Harvard Univ. Extension School, 2016; USA, 2000-12; ATF instructor, explosive specialist; US House, 2017-present; m. Brianna; Christian
Committees—Foreign Affairs; Transportation & Infrastructure
District Offices—Port St. Lucie, 772-336-2877; Stuart, 772-403-0900; Jupiter, 561-530-7778; Fort Pierce, 772-446-8855

Republican

Doris Matsui, CA | 7th District | 10th Term | 68% (+37)
2311 RHOB | 202-225-7163 | Fax: 225-0566
matsui.house.gov | X @dorismatsui
Bio—Sacramento; Poston, AZ, 9/25/1944; BA, Univ. of California, Berkeley, 1966; White House staffer; US House, 2005-present; m. Roger; Methodist
Committees—Energy & Commerce
District Offices—Sacramento, 916-498-5600

Democrat

Notes

United States House of Representatives

Lucy McBath, GA | 7th District | 3rd Term | 60% (+22)
2246 RHOB | 202-225-4501
mcbath.house.gov | X @replucymcbath
Bio—Marietta; Joliet, IL, 6/1/1960; BA, Virginia St. Univ., 1982; flight attendant; US House, 2019-present; m. Curtis; Protestant
Committees—Education & the Workforce; Judiciary
District Offices—Duluth, 470-773-6330

Democrat

Michael McCaul, TX | 10th District | 10th Term | 63% (+29)
2300 RHOB | 202-225-2401 | Fax: 225-5955
mccaul.house.gov | X @repmccaul
Bio—Austin; Dallas, TX, 1/14/1962; JD, St. Mary's Univ., 1987; lawyer; US House, 2005-present; m. Linda; Catholic
Committees—Foreign Affairs (Chair); Homeland Security
District Offices—Austin, 512-473-2357; College Station, 979-431-6480

Republican

Lisa McClain, MI | 9th District | 2nd Term | 63% (+31)
444 CHOB | 202-225-2106 | Fax: 226-1169
mcclain.house.gov | X @replisamcclain
Bio—Bruce; Stockbridge, MI, 4/7/1966; BBA, Northwood Univ., 1997; business executive, financial consultant; US House, 2021-present; m. Mike; Catholic
Committees—Armed Services; Budget; Education & the Workforce; Oversight & Accountability
District Offices—Lake Orion, 586-697-9300; Marlette, 586-697-9300

Republican

Jennifer McClellan, VA | 4th District | 1st Term | 74% (+49)
2417 RHOB | 202-225-6365
mcclellan.house.gov | X @repmcclellan
Bio—Richmond; Petersburg, VA, 12/28/1972; JD, Univ. of Virginia, 1997; lawyer; VA House, 2006-17; VA Senate, 2017-23; US House, 2023-present; m. David Mills; Presbyterian
Committees—Armed Services; Science, Space, & Technology
District Offices—Richmond, 804-486-1840; Lawrenceville, 804-690-5809

Democrat

Tom McClintock, CA | 5th District | 8th Term | 61% (+23)
2256 RHOB | 202-225-2511 | Fax: 225-5444
mcclintock.house.gov | X @repmcclintock
Bio—Elk Grove; Bronxville, NY, 7/10/1956; BA, Univ. of California, Los Angeles, 1978; journalist, public policy analyst; CA Assembly, 1982-92, 1996-2000; CA Senate, 2000-08; US House, 2009-present; wid.; Baptist
Committees—Budget; Judiciary; Natural Resources
District Offices—El Dorado Hills, 916-786-5560; Modesto, 209-550-6910

Republican

Betty McCollum, MN | 4th District | 12th Term | 67% (+35)
2426 RHOB | 202-225-6631 | Fax: 225-1968
mccollum.house.gov | X @bettymccollum04
Bio—St. Paul; Minneapolis, MN, 7/12/1954; BA, Col. of St. Catherine, 1987; public official; MN House, 1992-2001; US House, 2001-present; div.; Catholic
Committees—Appropriations
District Offices—St. Paul, 651-224-9191

Democrat

United States House of Representatives

Rich McCormick, GA | 6th District | 1st Term | 62% (+24)
1213 LHOB | 202-225-4272
mccormick.house.gov | X @repmccormick
Bio—Suwanee; Las Vegas, NV, 10/7/1968; MD, Morehouse School of Medicine, 2010; USMC, 1990-2006; USN, 2013-17; physician, college instructor; US House, 2023-present; m. Debra; Protestant
Committees—Armed Services; Foreign Affairs; Science, Space, & Technology
District Offices—Cumming, 770-232-3005

Republican

Morgan McGarvey, KY | 3rd District | 1st Term | 61% (+24)
1527 LHOB | 202-225-5401
mcgarvey.house.gov | X @repmcgarvey
Bio—Louisville; Louisville, KY, 12/23/1979; JD, Univ. of Kentucky, 2007; lawyer; KY Senate, 2013-23; US House, 2023-present; m. Chris; Presbyterian
Committees—Small Business; Veterans' Affairs
District Offices—Louisville, 502-582-5129

Democrat

Jim McGovern, MA | 2nd District | 14th Term | 64% (+32)
370 CHOB | 202-225-6101 | Fax: 225-5759
mcgovern.house.gov | X @repmcgovern
Bio—Worcester; Worcester, MA, 11/20/1959; MPA, American Univ., 1984; congressional staffer; US House, 1997-present; m. Lisa; Catholic
Committees—Agriculture; Rules (Rnk. Mem.)
District Offices—Northampton, 413-341-8700; Leominster, 978-466-3552; Worcester, 508-831-7356

Democrat

Patrick McHenry, NC | 10th District | 10th Term | 72% (+45)
2134 RHOB | 202-225-2576
mchenry.house.gov | X @patrickmchenry
Bio—Lake Norman; Charlotte, NC, 10/22/1975; BA, Belmont Abbey Col., 1999; realtor; NC House, 2002-04; US House, 2005-present; m. Giulia; Catholic
Committees—Financial Services (Chair)
District Offices—Hickory, 828-327-6100; Mooresville, 800-477-2576

Republican

Gregory W. Meeks, NY | 5th District | 14th Term | 75% (+50)
2310 RHOB | 202-225-3461 | Fax: 226-4169
meeks.house.gov | X @repgregorymeeks
Bio—Queens; East Harlem, NY, 9/25/1953; JD, Howard Univ., 1978; lawyer, public official; NY Assembly, 1992-98; US House, 1998-present; m. Simone-Marie; Methodist
Committees—Financial Services; Foreign Affairs (Rnk. Mem.)
District Offices—Arverne, 347-230-4032; Jamaica, 718-725-6000

Democrat

Rob Menendez, NJ | 8th District | 1st Term | 73% (+50)
1007 LHOB | 202-225-7919
menendez.house.gov | X @repmenendez
Bio—Jersey City; Hudson County, NJ, 7/12/1985; JD, Rutgers Law School, 2011; lawyer; US House, 2023-present; m. Alex; Catholic
Committees—Homeland Security; Transportation & Infrastructure
District Offices—Jersey City, 201-309-0301

Democrat

Notes

United States House of Representatives

Grace Meng, NY | 6th District | 6th Term | 64% (+28)
2209 RHOB | 202-225-2601 | Fax: 225-1589
meng.house.gov | X @repgracemeng
Bio—Queens; Queens, NY, 10/1/1975; JD, Yeshiva Univ., 2002; lawyer; NY Assembly, 2009-12; US House, 2013-present; m. Wayne; Christian
Committees—Appropriations
District Offices—Flushing, 718-358-6364

Democrat

Dan Meuser, PA | 9th District | 3rd Term | 69% (+39)
350 CHOB | 202-225-6511
meuser.house.gov | X @repmeuser
Bio—Dallas; Flushing, NY, 2/10/1964; BA, Cornell Univ., 1986; entrepreneur, business executive; PA revenue secretary, 2011-15; US House, 2019-present; m. Shelley; Catholic
Committees—Financial Services; Small Business
District Offices—Hamburg, 610-428-0869; Lebanon, 717-603-1459; Tunkhannock, 570-665-3083; Williamsport, 570-202-0658; Pottsville, 570-871-6370

Republican

Kweisi Mfume, MD | 7th District | 8th Term | 82% (+64)
2263 RHOB | 202-225-4741 | Fax: 225-3178
mfume.house.gov | X @repkweisimfume
Bio—Baltimore; Baltimore, MD, 10/24/1948; MA, Johns Hopkins Univ., 1984; professor, radio station program director, nonprofit executive; Baltimore city council, 1979-86; US House, 1987-96, 2020-present; m. Tiffany McMillian; Baptist
Committees—Oversight & Accountability; Small Business
District Offices—Baltimore, 410-685-9199; Catonsville, 410-818-2120

Democrat

Carol Miller, WV | 1st District | 3rd Term | 66% (+38)
465 CHOB | 202-225-3452
miller.house.gov | X @repcarolmiller
Bio—Huntington; Columbus, OH, 11/4/1950; BS, Columbia Col., 1972; bison farmer; WV House, 2007-19; US House, 2019-present; m. Matt; Baptist
Committees—Ways and Means
District Offices—Charleston, 681-945-6556; Beckley, 304-250-6177; Huntington, 304-522-2201

Republican

Mary Miller, IL | 15th District | 2nd Term | 71% (+42)
1740 LHOB | 202-225-5271 | Fax: 225-5880
marymiller.house.gov | X @repmarymiller
Bio—Oakland; Oak Park, IL, 8/7/1959; BS, Eastern Illinois Univ., 1981; farmer, teacher; US House, 2021-present; m. Chris; Protestant
Committees—Agriculture; Education & the Workforce
District Offices—Mahomet, 217-703-6100; Quincy, 217-640-6210

Republican

Max Miller, OH | 7th District | 1st Term | 55% (+11)
143 CHOB | 202-225-3876
maxmiller.house.gov | X @repmaxmiller
Bio—Rocky River; Shaker Heights, OH, 11/13/1988; BA, Cleveland St. Univ., 2013; USMCR, 2013-19; White House staffer; US House, 2023-present; m. Emily; Jewish
Committees—Agriculture; Science, Space, & Technology
District Offices—Parma, 440-692-6120; Medina, 330-661-6654

Republican

Notes

United States House of Representatives

Mariannette Miller-Meeks, IA | 1st District | 2nd Term | 52% (+7)
1034 LHOB | 202-225-6576
millermeeks.house.gov | X @repmmm
Bio—Le Claire; Herlong, CA, 9/6/1955; MD, Univ. of Texas, 1986; USA, 1976-82; USAR, 1983-2000; professor, ophthalmologist; IA Senate, 2019-20; US House, 2021-present; m. Curt; Catholic
Committees—Energy & Commerce; Veterans' Affairs
District Offices—Davenport, 563-232-0930; Indianola, 515-808-6040
Republican 

Cory Mills, FL | 7th District | 1st Term | 58% (+17)
1237 LHOB | 202-225-4035
mills.house.gov | X @repmillspress
Bio—New Smyrna Beach; Winter Haven, FL, 7/13/1980; BS, American Military Univ., 2010; USA; defense contractor, business owner; US House, 2023-present; m. Rana; Protestant
Committees—Armed Services; Foreign Affairs
District Offices—Lake Mary, 407-638-7900; Port Orange, 386-238-9711
Republican 

Marc Molinaro, NY | 19th District | 1st Term | 51% (+1.5)
1207 LHOB | 202-225-5441
molinaro.house.gov | X @repmolinarony19
Bio—Red Hook; Yonkers, NY, 10/8/1975; AA, Dutchess Comm. Col., 2001; public official; Tivoli trustees, 1994; Tivoli mayor, 1995-2007; Dutchess Co. legislature, 1999-2006; NY Assembly, 2007-11; Dutchess Co. executive, 2012-22; US House, 2023-present; m. Corinne; Christian
Committees—Agriculture; Small Business; Transportation & Infrastructure
District Offices—Binghamton, 607-242-0200; Leeds, 518-625-2100
Republican 

John Moolenaar, MI | 2nd District | 5th Term | 63% (+29)
246 CHOB | 202-225-3561 | Fax: 225-9679
moolenaar.house.gov | X @repmoolenaar
Bio—Caledonia; Midland, MI, 5/8/1961; MPA, Harvard Univ., 1989; chemist, businessman, school administrator; Midland city council, 1997-2000; MI House, 2003-08; MI Senate, 2011-14; US House, 2015-present; m. Amy; Protestant
Committees—Appropriations; Select CCP
District Offices—Caledonia, 616-528-7100; Clare, 989-802-6040
Republican 

Alex X. Mooney, WV | 2nd District | 5th Term | 65% (+31)
2228 RHOB | 202-225-2711 | Fax: 225-7856
mooney.house.gov | X @repalexmooney
Bio—Charles Town; Washington, DC, 6/7/1971; AB, Dartmouth Col., 1993; congressional staffer; MD Senate, 1999-2010; US House, 2015-present; m. Grace; Catholic
Committees—Financial Services
District Offices—Morgantown, 304-413-1995; Charles Town, 304-264-8810
Republican 

Barry Moore, AL | 2nd District | 2nd Term | 69% (+40)
1504 LHOB | 202-225-2901
barrymoore.house.gov | X @repbarrymoore
Bio—Enterprise; Coffee County, AL, 9/26/1966; BS, Auburn Univ., 1992; ALARNG; entrepreneur, business owner; AL House, 2010-18; US House, 2021-present; m. Heather; Baptist
Committees—Agriculture; Judiciary
District Offices—Andalusia, 334-428-1129; Dothan, 334-547-6630; Wetumpka, 334-478-6330; Troy, 334-465-7244
Republican

Notes

United States House of Representatives

Notes

Blake Moore, UT | 1st District | 2nd Term | 66% (+34)
1131 LHOB | 202-225-0453 | Fax: 225-5857
blakemoore.house.gov | X @repblakemoore
Bio—Salt Lake City; Ogden, UT, 6/22/1980; MPPA, Northwestern Univ., 2018; consultant, foreign service officer; US House, 2021-present; m. Jane; Mormon
Committees—Budget; Ways and Means
District Offices—Ogden, 801-625-0107

Republican

Gwen Moore, WI | 4th District | 10th Term | 75% (+53)
2252 RHOB | 202-225-4572
gwenmoore.house.gov | X @repgwenmoore
Bio—Milwaukee; Racine, WI, 4/18/1951; BA, Marquette Univ., 1978; public official; WI Assembly, 1989-92; WI Senate, 1993-2004; US House, 2005-present; single; Baptist
Committees—Ways and Means; Joint Economic
District Offices—Milwaukee, 414-297-1140

Democrat

Nathaniel Moran, TX | 1st District | 1st Term | 78% (+56)
1541 LHOB | 202-225-3035
moran.house.gov | X @repnatemoran
Bio—Whitehouse; AZ, 9/23/1974; JD, Texas Tech Univ., 2002; business owner, lawyer; Tyler city council, 2005-09; Smith Co. judge, 2016-22; US House, 2023-present; m. Kyna; Baptist
Committees—Education & the Workforce; Foreign Affairs; Judiciary
District Offices—Marshall, 903-561-6349; Texarkana, 903-561-6349; Longview, 903-561-6349; Tyler, 903-561-6349

Republican

Joe Morelle, NY | 25th District | 4th Term | 53% (+8)
570 CHOB | 202-225-3615
morelle.house.gov | X @repjoemorelle
Bio—Irondequoit; Utica, NY, 4/29/1957; BA, SUNY Geneseo, 1986; legislative staffer, businessman; Monroe Co. legislature, 1984-90; NY Assembly, 1990-2018; US House, 2018-present; m. Mary Beth; Catholic
Committees—Appropriations; House Administration (Rnk. Mem.); Joint Library; Joint Printing
District Offices—Rochester, 585-232-4850

Democrat

Jared Moskowitz, FL | 23rd District | 1st Term | 51% (+5)
1130 LHOB | 202-225-3001
moskowitz.house.gov | X @repmoskowitz
Bio—Parkland; Coral Springs, FL, 12/18/1980; JD, Nova Southeastern Univ., 2007; lawyer, business executive; Parkland commissioner, 2006-12; FL House, 2012-19; Broward Co. commissioner, 2022; US House, 2023-present; m. Leah; Jewish
Committees—Foreign Affairs; Oversight & Accountability
District Offices—Coral Springs, 754-240-6330; Fort Lauderdale, 754-240-6330; Boca Raton, 754-240-6330

Democrat

Seth Moulton, MA | 6th District | 5th Term | 61% (+27)
1126 LHOB | 202-225-8020 | Fax: 225-5915
moulton.house.gov | X @repmoulton
Bio—Salem; Salem, MA, 10/24/1978; MBA/MPP, Harvard Univ., 2011; USMC, 2002-08; business manager; US House, 2015-present; m. Liz; Protestant
Committees—Armed Services; Transportation & Infrastructure; Select CCP
District Offices—Salem, 978-531-1669

Democrat

U.S. Congress Directory | 111

United States House of Representatives

James Moylan, GU | 1st Term | 50% (+5)
1628 LHOB | 202-225-1188
moylan.house.gov | X @jmoylanforguam
Bio—Tumon; Tumon, GU, 7/18/1962; BS, Univ. of Guam; USA; parole officer, business owner; GU Senate, 2019-23; US House, 2023-present; single; not stated
Committees—Armed Services; Natural Resources
District Offices—Hagatna, 671-922-6673

Republican

Frank J. Mrvan, IN | 1st District | 2nd Term | 52% (+6)
1607 LHOB | 202-225-2461 | Fax: 225-2493
mrvan.house.gov | X @repmrvan
Bio—Highland; Hammond, IN, 4/16/1969; BA, Ball St. Univ., 1992; mortgage broker; North Township trustee, 2005-21; US House, 2021-present; m. Jane; Catholic
Committees—Education & the Workforce; Veterans' Affairs
District Offices—Merrillville, 219-795-1844

Democrat

Kevin Mullin, CA | 15th District | 1st Term | 55% (+11)
1404 LHOB | 202-225-3531
kevinmullin.house.gov | X @repkevinmullin
Bio—South San Francisco; San Mateo County, CA, 6/15/1970; MPA, San Francisco St. Univ., 1998; entrepreneur; South San Francisco city council, 2007-12; CA Assembly, 2012-22; US House, 2023-present; m. Jessica; Catholic
Committees—Natural Resources; Science, Space, & Technology
District Offices—San Mateo, 650-342-0300

Democrat

Greg Murphy, NC | 3rd District | 3rd Term | 66% (+34)
407 CHOB | 202-225-3415
gregmurphy.house.gov | X @repgregmurphy
Bio—Greenville; Raleigh, NC, 3/5/1963; MD, Univ. of North Carolina, 1989; urologic surgeon; NC House, 2015-19; US House, 2019-present; m. Wendy; Catholic
Committees—House Administration; Veterans' Affairs; Ways and Means; Joint Printing
District Offices—Greenville, 252-931-1003; Jacksonville, 910-937-6929; Manteo, 252-230-3549; New Bern, 252-636-6612

Republican

Jerrold Nadler, NY | 12th District | 17th Term | 82% (+62)
2132 RHOB | 202-225-5635
nadler.house.gov | X @repjerrynadler
Bio—New York; Brooklyn, NY, 6/13/1947; JD, Fordham Univ., 1978; legislative aide; NY Assembly, 1977-92; US House, 1992-present; m. Joyce Miller; Jewish
Committees—Judiciary (Rnk. Mem.)
District Offices—New York, 212-367-7350

Democrat

Grace F. Napolitano, CA | 31st District | 13th Term | 59% (+19)
1610 LHOB | 202-225-5256 | Fax: 225-0027
napolitano.house.gov | X @gracenapolitano
Bio—Norwalk; Brownsville, TX, 12/4/1936; attended Texas Southmost Col.; public official; Norwalk city council, 1986; Norwalk mayor, 1989-90; CA Assembly, 1992-98; US House, 1999-present; wid.; Catholic
Committees—Natural Resources; Transportation & Infrastructure
District Offices—El Monte, 626-350-0150

Democrat

United States House of Representatives

Notes

Richard Neal, MA | 1st District | 18th Term | 59% (+22)
372 CHOB | 202-225-5601 | Fax: 225-8112
neal.house.gov | X @represchardneal
Bio—Springfield; Springfield, MA, 2/14/1949; MA, Univ. of Hartford, 1976; public official; Springfield city council, 1978-84; Springfield mayor, 1984-88; US House, 1989-present; m. Maureen; Catholic
Committees—Ways and Means (Rnk. Mem.); Joint Taxation
District Offices—Springfield, 413-785-0325; Pittsfield, 413-442-0946
Democrat 

Joe Neguse, CO | 2nd District | 3rd Term | 69% (+42)
2400 RHOB | 202-225-2161
neguse.house.gov | X @repjoeneguse
Bio—Lafayette; Bakersfield, CA, 5/13/1984; JD, Univ. of Colorado, 2009; nonprofit executive; lawyer; US House, 2019-present; m. Andrea; Protestant
Committees—Judiciary; Natural Resources; Rules
District Offices—Fort Collins, 970-372-3971; Boulder, 303-335-1045; Frisco, 303-335-1045
Democrat

Troy Nehls, TX | 22nd District | 2nd Term | 62% (+27)
1104 LHOB | 202-225-5951
nehls.house.gov | X @reptroynehls
Bio—Richmond; Beaver Dam, WI, 4/7/1968; MS, Univ. of Houston; WIARNG; USAR; police officer; US House, 2021-present; m. Jill; Protestant
Committees—Judiciary; Transportation & Infrastructure
District Offices—Fulshear, 346-762-6600
Republican 

Dan Newhouse, WA | 4th District | 5th Term | 66% (+35)
504 CHOB | 202-225-5816 | Fax: 225-3251
newhouse.house.gov | X @repnewhouse
Bio—Sunnyside; Sunnyside, WA, 7/10/1955; BS, Washington St. Univ., 1977; farmer; WA House, 2003-09; US House, 2015-present; m. Joan; Presbyterian
Committees—Appropriations; Select CCP
District Offices—Richland, 509-713-7374; Grand Coulee, 509-433-7760; Yakima, 509-452-3243
Republican

Wiley Nickel, NC | 13th District | 1st Term | 51% (+3)
1133 LHOB | 202-225-4531
nickel.house.gov | X @repwileynickel
Bio—Cary; Fresno County, CA, 11/23/1975; JD, Pepperdine Univ., 2005; lawyer, White House staffer, business owner; NC Senate, 2019-22; US House, 2023-present; m. Caroline; Protestant
Committees—Financial Services
District Offices—Garner, 984-275-6150
Democrat 

Donald Norcross, NJ | 1st District | 6th Term | 62% (+27)
2427 RHOB | 202-225-6501
norcross.house.gov | X @donaldnorcross
Bio—Camden; Camden, NJ, 12/13/1958; AS, Camden County Col., 1979; electrician, union official; NJ Assembly, 2010; NJ Senate, 2010-14; US House, 2014-present; m. Andrea; Lutheran
Committees—Armed Services; Education & the Workforce
District Offices—Camden, 856-427-7000; Cherry Hill, 856-427-7000
Democrat

U.S. Congress Directory | 113

United States House of Representatives

Ralph Norman, SC | 5th District | 4th Term | 64% (+30)
569 CHOB | 202-225-5501 | Fax: 225-0464
norman.house.gov | X @repralphnorman
Bio—Rock Hill; Rock Hill, SC, 6/20/1953; BS, Presbyterian Col., 1975; real estate developer; SC House, 2005-06, 2009-17; US House, 2017-present; m. Elaine; Presbyterian
Committees—Budget; Financial Services; Rules
District Offices—Rock Hill, 803-327-1114

Republican

Eleanor Holmes Norton, DC | 17th Term | 84% (+79)
2136 RHOB | 202-225-8050 | Fax: 225-3002
norton.house.gov | X @eleanornorton
Bio—Washington, DC; Washington, DC, 6/13/1937; LLB, Yale Univ., 1964; lawyer, public official, professor; US House, 1991-present; single; Episcopalian
Committees—Oversight & Accountability; Transportation & Infrastructure
District Offices—Washington, 202-408-9041; Washington, 202-678-8900

Democrat

Zach Nunn, IA | 3rd District | 1st Term | 49% (+.7)
1232 LHOB | 202-225-5476
nunn.house.gov | X @zachnunn
Bio—Bondurant; Story City, IA, 5/4/1979; MSt, Cambridge Univ., 2007; USAF; IAANG; public official, cybersecurity consultant, professor; IA House, 2015-19; IA Senate, 2019-23; US House, 2023-present; m. Kelly; Catholic
Committees—Agriculture; Financial Services
District Offices—Des Moines, 515-400-8180; Ottumwa, 641-220-9641; Creston, 641-220-9093

Republican

Jay Obernolte, CA | 23rd District | 2nd Term | 61% (+22)
1029 LHOB | 202-225-5861
obernolte.house.gov | X @jayobernolte
Bio—Big Bear Lake; Chicago, IL, 8/18/1970; DPA, California Baptist Univ., 2020; entrepreneur, pilot; Big Bear city council, 2010-14; Big Bear mayor, 2012-14; CA Assembly, 2014-20; US House, 2021-present; m. Heather; Protestant
Committees—Energy & Commerce; Science, Space, & Technology
District Offices—Hesperia, 760-247-1815

Republican

Alexandria Ocasio-Cortez, NY | 14th District | 3rd Term | 71% (+44)
250 CHOB | 202-225-3965
ocasio-cortez.house.gov | X @repaoc
Bio—East Elmhurst; Manhattan, NY, 10/13/1989; BA, Boston Univ., 2011; community organizer; US House, 2019-present; single; Catholic
Committees—Natural Resources; Oversight & Accountability
District Offices—Bronx, 718-662-5970; Bronx, 718-662-5970

Democrat

Andy Ogles, TN | 5th District | 1st Term | 55% (+14)
151 CHOB | 202-225-4311
ogles.house.gov | X @repogles
Bio—Columbia; Nashville, TN, 6/18/1971; BS, Middle Tennessee St. Univ., 2007; business owner, nonprofit executive; Maury Co. mayor, 2018-22; US House, 2023-present; m. Monica; Protestant
Committees—Financial Services
District Offices—Columbia, 931-777-2140

Republican

United States House of Representatives

Ilhan Omar, MN | 5th District | 3rd Term | 74% (+50)
1730 LHOB | 202-225-4755
omar.house.gov | X @ilhan
Bio—Minneapolis; Mogadishu, Somalia, 10/4/1982; BS, North Dakota St. Univ., 2011; teacher, campaign staffer, non-profit executive; MN House, 2017-19; US House, 2019-present; m. Tim Mynett; Muslim
Committees—Budget; Education & the Workforce
District Offices—Minneapolis, 612-333-1272

Democrat

Burgess Owens, UT | 4th District | 2nd Term | 61% (+29)
309 CHOB | 202-225-3011
owens.house.gov | X @repburgessowens
Bio—Salt Lake County; Columbus, OH, 8/2/1951; BS, Univ. of Miami, Coral Gables, 1975; professional athlete, business executive; US House, 2021-present; div.; Mormon
Committees—Education & the Workforce; Transportation & Infrastructure
District Offices—West Jordan, 801-999-9801

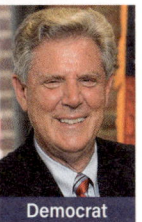

Republican

Frank Pallone, Jr., NJ | 6th District | 19th Term | 57% (+16)
2107 RHOB | 202-225-4671 | Fax: 225-9665
pallone.house.gov | X @frankpallone
Bio—Long Branch; Long Branch, NJ, 10/30/1951; JD, Rutgers Univ., 1978; lawyer; Long Branch city council, 1982-88; NJ Senate, 1983-88; US House, 1988-present; m. Sarah; Catholic
Committees—Energy & Commerce (Rnk. Mem.)
District Offices—Long Branch, 732-571-1140; New Brunswick, 732-249-8892

Democrat

Gary Palmer, AL | 6th District | 5th Term | 83% (+69)
170 CHOB | 202-225-4921 | Fax: 225-2082
palmer.house.gov | X @usrepgarypalmer
Bio—Hoover; Haleyville, AL, 5/14/1954; BS, Univ. of Alabama, 1977; cost engineer, nonprofit executive; US House, 2015-present; m. Ann; Christian
Committees—Energy & Commerce; Oversight & Accountability
District Offices—Birmingham, 205-968-1290

Republican

Jimmy Panetta, CA | 19th District | 4th Term | 68% (+37)
304 CHOB | 202-225-2861
panetta.house.gov | X @repjimmypanetta
Bio—Carmel Valley; Washington, DC, 10/1/1969; JD, Santa Clara Univ., 1996; USNR, 2003-11; lawyer; US House, 2017-present; m. Carrie; Catholic
Committees—Armed Services; Budget; Ways and Means
District Offices—Monterey, 831-424-2229; Santa Cruz, 831-429-1976; San Jose, 408-960-0333; Paso Robles, 805-400-6535

Democrat

Chris Pappas, NH | 1st District | 3rd Term | 54% (+8)
452 CHOB | 202-225-5456
pappas.house.gov | X @repchrispappas
Bio—Manchester; Manchester, NH, 6/4/1980; AB, Harvard Univ., 2002; restaurant manager; NH House, 2003-07; Hillsborough Co. treasurer, 2007-11; NH executive council, 2013-19; US House, 2019-present; m. Vann Bentley; Orthodox
Committees—Small Business; Transportation & Infrastructure; Veterans' Affairs
District Offices—Dover, 603-285-4300; Manchester, 603-935-6710

Democrat

Notes

United States House of Representatives

Bill Pascrell, Jr., NJ | 9th District | 14th Term | 54% (+11)
2409 RHOB | 202-225-5751 | Fax: 225-5782
pascrell.house.gov | X @billpascrell
Bio—Paterson; Paterson, NJ, 1/25/1937; MA, Fordham Univ., 1961; USA, 1961-62; USAR, 1962-67; teacher; NJ Assembly, 1988-96; Paterson mayor, 1990-96; US House, 1997-present; m. Elsie Marie; Catholic
Committees—Ways and Means
District Offices—Paterson, 973-523-5152

Democrat

Donald M. Payne, Jr., NJ | 10th District | 7th Term | 77% (+58)
106 CHOB | 202-225-3436 | Fax: 225-4160
payne.house.gov | X @repdonaldpayne
Bio—Newark; Newark, NJ, 12/17/1958; attended Kean Col.; public official; Essex Co. freeholders, 2005-12; Newark city council, 2006-12; US House, 2012-present; m. Beatrice; Baptist
Committees—Homeland Security; Transportation & Infrastructure
District Offices—Hillside, 862-229-2994; Newark, 973-645-3213; Jersey City, 201-369-0392

Democrat

Nancy Pelosi, CA | 11th District | 19th Term | 83% (+68)
1236 LHOB | 202-225-4965
pelosi.house.gov | X @speakerpelosi
Bio—San Francisco; Baltimore, MD, 3/26/1940; AB, Trinity Col., 1962; public official; US House, 1987-present; m. Paul; Catholic
Committees—none
District Offices—San Francisco, 415-556-4862

Democrat

Mary Sattler Peltola, AK | At Large | 2nd Term | 55% (+10)
153 CHOB | 202-225-5765
peltola.house.gov | X @reppeltola
Bio—Bethel; Anchorage, AK, 8/31/1973; attended the Univ. of Alaska, Anchorage, 1997-98; community development manager; AK House, 1999-2009; Bethel city council; US House, 2022-present; wid.; Orthodox
Committees—Natural Resources; Transportation & Infrastructure
District Offices—Anchorage, 907-921-6575

Democrat

Greg Pence, IN | 6th District | 3rd Term | 67% (+35)
404 CHOB | 202-225-3021
pence.house.gov | X @repgregpence
Bio—Columbus; Columbus, IN, 11/14/1956; MBA, Loyola Univ., 1985; USMC, 1979-83; small business owner, business executive; US House, 2019-present; m. Denise; Catholic
Committees—Energy & Commerce
District Offices—Columbus, 812-799-5230; Greenwood, 812-447-3647; Richmond, 765-660-1083

Republican

Marie Gluesenkamp Perez, WA | 3rd District | 1st Term | 50% (+.8)
1431 LHOB | 202-225-3536
gluesenkampperez.house.gov | X @repmgp
Bio—Skamania County; Harris County, TX, 6/4/1988; BA, Reed College, 2013; small business owner; US House, 2023-present; m. Dean; Christian
Committees—Agriculture; Small Business
District Offices—Vancouver, 360-695-6292

Democrat

United States House of Representatives

Scott Perry, PA | 10th District | 6th Term | 53% (+8)
2160 RHOB | 202-225-5836 | Fax: 226-1000
perry.house.gov | X @repscottperry
Bio—Dillsburg; San Diego, CA, 5/27/1962; BS, Pennsylvania St. Univ., 1991; PAARNG, 1980-2019; business owner; PA House, 2007-12; US House, 2013-present; m. Christy; Protestant
Committees—Foreign Affairs; Oversight & Accountability; Transportation & Infrastructure
District Offices—Mechanicsburg, 717-550-6565; Harrisburg, 717-603-4980; York, 717-893-7868

Republican

Scott Peters, CA | 50th District | 6th Term | 62% (+26)
1201 LHOB | 202-225-0508
scottpeters.house.gov | X @repscottpeters
Bio—San Diego; Springfield, OH, 6/17/1958; JD, New York Univ., 1984; lawyer, economist; San Diego city council, 2000-08; US House, 2013-present; m. Lynn; Lutheran
Committees—Budget; Energy & Commerce
District Offices—San Diego, 858-455-5550

Democrat

Brittany Pettersen, CO | 7th District | 1st Term | 56% (+15)
1230 LHOB | 202-225-2645
pettersen.house.gov | X @reppettersen
Bio—Lakewood; CO, 12/6/1981; BA, Metropolitan St. Univ. of Denver, 2006; nonprofit executive; CO House, 2013-18; CO Senate, 2019-22; US House, 2023-present; m. Ian; not stated
Committees—Financial Services
District Offices—Lakewood, 303-274-7944; Canon City, 719-458-6161

Democrat

August Pfluger, TX | 11th District | 2nd Term | Unc.
1124 LHOB | 202-225-3605
pfluger.house.gov | X @reppfluger
Bio—San Angelo; Harris County, TX, 12/28/1977; MA, Georgetown Univ., 2019; USAF; USAFR; fighter pilot; US House, 2021-present; m. Camille; Protestant
Committees—Energy & Commerce; Homeland Security
District Offices—Brownwood, 325-646-1950; Killeen, 254-669-6570; Llano, 325-247-2826; Midland, 432-687-2390; Odessa, 432-331-9667; San Angelo, 325-659-4010

Republican

Dean Phillips, MN | 3rd District | 3rd Term | 59% (+19)
2452 RHOB | 202-225-2871
phillips.house.gov | X @repdeanphillips
Bio—Plymouth; St. Paul, MN, 1/20/1969; MBA, Univ. of Minnesota, 2000; businessman; US House, 2019-present; m. Annalise Glick; Jewish
Committees—Foreign Affairs; Small Business
District Offices—Minnetonka, 952-656-5176

Democrat

Chellie Pingree, ME | 1st District | 8th Term | 61% (+25)
2354 RHOB | 202-225-6116
pingree.house.gov | X @chelliepingree
Bio—North Haven; Minneapolis, MN, 4/2/1955; BA, Col. of the Atlantic, 1979; farmer, businesswoman; ME Senate, 1992-2000; US House, 2009-present; div.; Lutheran
Committees—Agriculture; Appropriations
District Offices—Portland, 207-774-5019; Waterville, 207-873-5713

Democrat

United States House of Representatives

Stacey E. Plaskett, VI | 5th Term | Unc.
2059 RHOB | 202-225-1790 | Fax: 225-5517
plaskett.house.gov | X @staceyplaskett
Bio—St. Croix; New York, NY, 5/13/1966; JD, American Univ., 1994; lawyer; US House, 2015-present; m. Jonathan Buckney-Small; Lutheran
Committees—Intelligence
District Offices—Frederiksted, 340-778-5900; St. Thomas, 340-774-4408

Democrat

Mark Pocan, WI | 2nd District | 6th Term | 70% (+44)
1026 LHOB | 202-225-2906
pocan.house.gov | X @repmarkpocan
Bio—Vermont; Kenosha, WI, 8/14/1964; BA, Univ. of Wisconsin, 1986; businessman; Dane Co. supervisors, 1991-96; WI Assembly, 1999-2013; US House, 2013-present; m. Philip Frank; not stated
Committees—Appropriations
District Offices—Madison, 608-258-9800

Democrat

Katie Porter, CA | 47th District | 3rd Term | 51% (+3)
1233 LHOB | 202-225-5611
porter.house.gov | X @repkatieporter
Bio—Irvine; Fort Dodge, IA, 1/3/1974; JD, Harvard Univ., 2001; law professor; US House, 2019-present; single; Episcopalian
Committees—Natural Resources; Oversight & Accountability; Joint Economic
District Offices—Irvine, 949-668-6600

Democrat

Bill Posey, FL | 8th District | 8th Term | 64% (+30)
2150 RHOB | 202-225-3671 | Fax: 225-3516
posey.house.gov | X @congbillposey
Bio—Rockledge; Washington, DC, 12/18/1947; AA, Eastern Florida St. Col., 1969; realtor; Rockledge city council, 1976-86; FL House, 1992-2000; FL Senate, 2000-08; US House, 2009-present; m. Katie; Methodist
Committees—Financial Services; Science, Space, & Technology
District Offices—Melbourne, 321-632-1776; Vero Beach, 772-226-1701; Titusville, 321-383-6090

Republican

Ayanna Pressley, MA | 7th District | 3rd Term | 79% (+66)
402 CHOB | 202-225-5111 | Fax: 225-9322
pressley.house.gov | X @reppressley
Bio—Boston; Chicago, IL, 2/3/1974; attended Boston Univ, 1992-94; congressional staffer; Boston city council, 2010-19; US House, 2019-present; m. Conan Harris; Baptist
Committees—Financial Services
District Offices—Hyde Park, 617-850-0040

Democrat

Mike Quigley, IL | 5th District | 8th Term | 69% (+41)
2083 RHOB | 202-225-4061 | Fax: 225-5603
quigley.house.gov | X @repmikequigley
Bio—Chicago; Indianapolis, IN, 10/17/1958; JD, Loyola Univ., 1989; professor, lawyer, legislative aide; Cook Co. commissioners, 1998-09; US House, 2009-present; m. Barb; Protestant
Committees—Appropriations
District Offices—Chicago, 773-267-5926

Democrat

Notes

United States House of Representatives

Aumua Amata Coleman Radewagen, AS | 5th Term | Unc.
2001 RHOB | 202-225-8577 | Fax: 225-8757
radewagen.house.gov | X @repamata
Bio—Pago Pago; Washington, DC, 12/29/1947; BS, Univ. of Guam, 1975; journalist, congressional staffer; US House, 2015-present; m. Fred; Catholic
Committees—Foreign Affairs; Natural Resources; Veterans' Affairs
District Offices—Pagopago, 684-633-3601

Republican

Delia C. Ramirez, IL | 3rd District | 1st Term | 68% (+37)
1523 LHOB | 202-225-5701
ramirez.house.gov | X @repdeliaramirez
Bio—Chicago; Chicago, IL, 6/2/1983; BA, Northeastern Illinois Univ.; nonprofit executive; IL House, 2019-22; US House, 2023-present; m. Boris; Methodist
Committees—Homeland Security; Veterans' Affairs
District Offices—Chicago, 773-799-8219; West Chicago, 630-520-9494

Democrat

Jamie Raskin, MD | 8th District | 4th Term | 80% (+62)
2242 RHOB | 202-225-5341
raskin.house.gov | X @repraskin
Bio—Takoma Park; Washington, DC, 12/13/1962; JD, Harvard Univ., 1987; lawyer, professor; MD Senate, 2007-16; US House, 2017-present; m. Sarah Bloom Raskin; Jewish
Committees—Oversight & Accountability (Rnk. Mem.)
District Offices—Rockville, 301-354-1000

Democrat

Guy Reschenthaler, PA | 14th District | 3rd Term | Unc.
342 CHOB | 202-225-2065
reschenthaler.house.gov | X @greschenthaler
Bio—Peters Township; Pittsburgh, PA, 4/17/1983; JD, Duquesne Univ., 2007; USN, 2007-12; lawyer; PA magisterial district judge, 2013-15; PA Senate, 2015-18; US House, 2019-present; single; Protestant
Committees—Appropriations; Rules
District Offices—Washington, 724-206-4800; Latrobe, 724-219-4200

Republican

Cathy McMorris Rodgers, WA | 5th District | 10th Term | 59% (+19)
2188 RHOB | 202-225-2006
mcmorris.house.gov | X @cathymcmorris
Bio—Spokane; Salem, OR, 5/22/1969; MBA, Univ. of Washington, 2002; orchardist; WA House, 1994-2004; US House, 2005-present; m. Brian; Christian
Committees—Energy & Commerce (Chair)
District Offices—Spokane, 509-353-2374; Colville, 509-684-3481; Walla Walla, 509-529-9358

Republican

Hal Rogers, KY | 5th District | 22nd Term | 82% (+64)
2406 RHOB | 202-225-4601 | Fax: 225-0940
halrogers.house.gov | X @rephalrogers
Bio—Somerset; Barrier, KY, 12/31/1937; LLB, Univ. of Kentucky, 1964; KYNG, 1956-57, 1958-63; NCNG, 1957-58; lawyer; US House, 1981-present; m. Cynthia; Baptist
Committees—Appropriations
District Offices—Somerset, 606-679-8346; Prestonsburg, 606-886-0844; Hazard, 606-439-0794; Ashland, 606-467-6211

Republican

Notes

United States House of Representatives

Mike Rogers, AL | 3rd District | 11th Term | 71% (+46)
2469 RHOB | 202-225-3261 | Fax: 226-8485
mikerogers.house.gov | X @repmikerogersal
Bio—Weaver; Hammond, IN, 7/16/1958; JD, Birmingham School of Law, 1991; lawyer, public official; Calhoun Co. commission, 1987-90; AL House, 1994-2002; US House, 2003-present; m. Beth; Christian
Committees—Armed Services (Chair)
District Offices—Oxford, 256-236-5655; Opelika, 334-745-6221

Republican

John Rose, TN | 6th District | 3rd Term | 66% (+33)
2238 RHOB | 202-225-4231 | Fax: 225-6887
johnrose.house.gov | X @repjohnrose
Bio—Cookeville; Cookeville, TN, 2/23/1965; JD, Vanderbilt Univ., 1993; business executive, farmer; TN agriculture commissioner, 2002-03; US House, 2019-present; m. Chelsea; Protestant
Committees—Agriculture; Financial Services
District Offices—Gallatin, 615-206-8204; Cookeville, 931-854-9430

Republican

Matt Rosendale, MT | 2nd District | 2nd Term | 56% (+35)
1023 LHOB | 202-225-3211
rosendale.house.gov | X @reprosendale
Bio—Glendive; Baltimore, MD, 7/7/1960; attended Chesapeake Col.; rancher, real estate developer; MT House, 2011-13; MT Senate, 2013-17; MT auditor, 2017-20; US House, 2021-present; m. Jean; Catholic
Committees—Natural Resources; Veterans' Affairs
District Offices—Helena, 406-502-1435; Great Falls, 406-770-6260; Billings, 406-413-6720

Republican

Deborah Ross, NC | 2nd District | 2nd Term | 64% (+29)
1221 LHOB | 202-225-3032 | Fax: 225-0181
ross.house.gov | X @repdeborahross
Bio—Raleigh; Philadelphia, PA, 6/20/1963; JD, Univ. of North Carolina, 1990; lawyer; NC House, 2003-13; US House, 2021-present; m. Steve; Unitarian
Committees—Ethics; Judiciary; Science, Space, & Technology
District Offices—Raleigh, 919-334-0840

Democrat

David Rouzer, NC | 7th District | 5th Term | 57% (+15)
2333 RHOB | 202-225-2731 | Fax: 225-5773
rouzer.house.gov | X @repdavidrouzer
Bio—Wilmington; Landstuhl, Germany, 2/16/1972; BS, North Carolina St. Univ., 1994; businessman, congressional staffer; NC Senate, 2009-12; US House, 2015-present; single; Baptist
Committees—Agriculture; Transportation & Infrastructure
District Offices—Bolivia, 910-253-6111; Fayetteville, 910-500-4880; Wilmington, 910-395-0202; Lumberton, 910-702-6140

Republican

Chip Roy, TX | 21st District | 3rd Term | 62% (+26)
103 CHOB | 202-225-4236
roy.house.gov | X @repchiproy
Bio—Austin; Bethesda, MD, 8/7/1972; JD, Univ. of Texas, 2003; lawyer, banking executive, congressional staffer; US House, 2019-present; m. Carrah; Baptist
Committees—Budget; Judiciary; Rules
District Offices—Austin, 512-871-5959; Kerrville, 830-896-0154; San Antonio, 210-821-5024

Republican

Notes

United States House of Representatives

Notes

Raul Ruiz, CA | 25th District | 6th Term | 57% (+15)
2342 RHOB | 202-225-5330 | Fax: 225-1238
ruiz.house.gov | X @congressmanruiz
Bio—Indio; Zacatecas, Mexico, 8/25/1972; MPH, Harvard Univ., 2007; physician; US House, 2013-present; m. Monica; Adventist
Committees—Energy & Commerce
District Offices—Indio, 760-424-8888; Hemet, 951-765-2304; El Centro, 760-592-2646

Democrat

C.A. Dutch Ruppersberger, MD | 2nd District | 11th Term | 59% (+19)
2206 RHOB | 202-225-3061 | Fax: 225-3094
dutch.house.gov | X @callmedutch
Bio—Cockeysville; Baltimore, MD, 1/31/1946; JD, Univ. of Baltimore, 1970; lawyer; Baltimore Co. council, 1985-94; Baltimore Co. executive, 1994-2002; US House, 2003-present; m. Kay; Methodist
Committees—Appropriations
District Offices—Timonium, 410-628-2701

Democrat

John Rutherford, FL | 5th District | 4th Term | Unc.
1711 LHOB | 202-225-2501
rutherford.house.gov | X @reprutherfordfl
Bio—Jacksonville; Omaha, NE, 9/2/1952; BS, Florida St. Univ., 1974; police officer; Jacksonville sheriff, 2003-15; US House, 2017-present; m. Pat; Catholic
Committees—Appropriations; Ethics
District Offices—Jacksonville, 904-831-5205

Republican

Pat Ryan, NY | 18th District | 2nd Term | 51% (+2)
1030 LHOB | 202-225-5614
patryan.house.gov | X @reppatryanny
Bio—Gardiner; Kingston, NY, 3/28/1982; MA, Georgetown Univ., 2013; USA, 2004-09; business owner; Ulster Co. executive, 2019-22; US House, 2022-present; m. Rebecca; Catholic
Committees—Armed Services; Transportation & Infrastructure
District Offices—Poughkeepsie, 845-443-2930; Newburgh, 845-443-2930; Kingston, 845-443-2930

Democrat

Gregorio Kilili Camacho Sablan, MP | 8th Term | Unc.
2267 RHOB | 202-225-2646 | Fax: 226-4249
sablan.house.gov | X @kililisablan
Bio—Saipan; Saipan, MP, 1/19/1955; attended Univ. of Hawaii, 1989-90; USAR, 1981-86; public official, congressional staffer; MP House, 1982-86; US House, 2009-present; m. Andrea; Catholic
Committees—Education & the Workforce; Natural Resources
District Offices—Saipan, 670-323-2647; Rota, 670-532-2647; Tinian, 670-433-2647

Democrat

María Elvira Salazar, FL | 27th District | 2nd Term | 57% (+15)
2162 RHOB | 202-225-3931
salazar.house.gov | X @repmariasalazar
Bio—Miami; Miami, FL, 11/1/1961; MPA, Harvard Univ., 1995; journalist; US House, 2021-present; m. Lester Woerner; Protestant
Committees—Foreign Affairs; Small Business
District Offices—Miami, 305-668-2285; Palmetto Bay, 305-668-2285; Cutler Bay, 305-668-2285

Republican

United States House of Representatives

Andrea Salinas, OR | 6th District | 1st Term | 49% (+2)
109 CHOB | 202-225-5643
salinas.house.gov | X @repsalinas
Bio—Tigard; San Mateo County, CA, 12/6/1969; BA, Univ. of California, Berkeley, 1994; congressional staffer, lobbyist; OR House, 2017-23; US House, 2023-present; m. Chris; Catholic
Committees—Agriculture; Science, Space, & Technology
District Offices—Salem, 503-385-0906; Tualatin, 503-385-0906
Democrat

Linda T. Sánchez, CA | 38th District | 11th Term | 58% (+16)
2428 RHOB | 202-225-6676
lindasanchez.house.gov | X @replindasanchez
Bio—Whittier; Orange, CA, 1/28/1969; JD, Univ. of California, 1995; lawyer, union official; US House, 2003-present; m. James Sullivan; Catholic
Committees—Ways and Means
District Offices—Whittier, 562-860-5050
Democrat

John Sarbanes, MD | 3rd District | 9th Term | 60% (+20)
2370 RHOB | 202-225-4016 | Fax: 225-9219
sarbanes.house.gov | X @repsarbanes
Bio—Baltimore; Baltimore, MD, 5/22/1962; JD, Harvard Univ., 1988; lawyer; US House, 2007-present; m. Dina; Greek Orthodox
Committees—Energy & Commerce
District Offices—Annapolis, 410-295-1679; Columbia, 410-832-8890
Democrat

Steve Scalise, LA | 1st District | 9th Term | 72% (+48)
2049 RHOB | 202-225-3015
scalise.house.gov | X @stevescalise
Bio—Jefferson; New Orleans, LA, 10/6/1965; BS, Louisiana St. Univ., 1989; software engineer, business executive; LA House, 1996-2007; LA Senate, 2008; US House, 2008-present; m. Jennifer; Catholic
Committees—Majority Leader
District Offices—Metairie, 504-837-1259; Ponchatoula, 985-340-2185; Houma, 985-879-2300; Mandeville, 985-893-9064
Republican

Mary Gay Scanlon, PA | 5th District | 4th Term | 65% (+30)
1227 LHOB | 202-225-2011
scanlon.house.gov | X @repmgs
Bio—Swarthmore; Syracuse, NY, 8/30/1959; JD, Univ. of Pennsylvania, 1984; lawyer; US House, 2018-present; m. Mark; Catholic
Committees—Judiciary; Rules
District Offices—Chester, 610-626-2020
Democrat

Jan Schakowsky, IL | 9th District | 13th Term | 71% (+43)
2408 RHOB | 202-225-2111 | Fax: 226-6890
schakowsky.house.gov | X @janschakowsky
Bio—Evanston; Chicago, IL, 5/26/1944; BS, Univ. of Illinois, 1965; nonprofit director; IL House, 1990-98; US House, 1999-present; m. Robert Creamer; Jewish
Committees—Budget; Energy & Commerce
District Offices—Skokie, 773-506-7100
Democrat

United States House of Representatives

Notes

Adam Schiff, CA | 30th District | 12th Term | 71% (+42)
2309 RHOB | 202-225-4176 | Fax: 225-5828
schiff.house.gov | X @repadamschiff
Bio—Burbank; Framingham, MA, 6/22/1960; JD, Harvard Univ., 1985; lawyer; CA Senate, 1996-2001; US House, 2001-present; m. Eve; Jewish
Committees—Judiciary
District Offices—Burbank, 818-450-2900

Democrat

Brad Schneider, IL | 10th District | 5th Term | 63% (+26)
300 CHOB | 202-225-4835 | Fax: 225-0837
schneider.house.gov | X @repschneider
Bio—Highland Park; Denver, CO, 8/20/1961; MBA, Northwestern Univ., 1985; businessman; US House, 2013-15, 2017-present; m. Julie; Jewish
Committees—Foreign Affairs; Ways and Means
District Offices—Lincolnshire, 847-383-4870

Democrat

Hillary J. Scholten, MI | 3rd District | 1st Term | 54% (+13)
1317 LHOB | 202-225-3831
scholten.house.gov | X @repscholten
Bio—Grand Rapids; MI, 2/22/1982; JD, Univ. of Maryland, 2011; social worker, lawyer; US House, 2023-present; m. Jesse; Reformed
Committees—Small Business; Transportation & Infrastructure
District Offices—Grand Rapids, 616-451-8383

Democrat

Kim Schrier, WA | 8th District | 3rd Term | 53% (+7)
1110 LHOB | 202-225-7761
schrier.house.gov | X @repkimschrier
Bio—Sammamish; Los Angeles, CA, 8/23/1968; MD, Univ. of California, Davis, 1997; pediatrician; US House, 2019-present; m. David; Jewish
Committees—Energy & Commerce
District Offices—Wenatchee, 509-850-5340; Issaquah, 425-657-1001

Democrat

David Schweikert, AZ | 1st District | 7th Term | 50% (+.9)
460 CHOB | 202-225-2190
schweikert.house.gov | X @repdavid
Bio—Fountain Hills; Los Angeles, CA, 3/3/1962; MBA, Arizona St. Univ., 2005; business owner, realtor, financial consultant; AZ House, 1989-94; Maricopa Co. treasurer, 2004-06; US House, 2011-present; m. Joyce; Catholic
Committees—Ways and Means; Joint Economic (Vice Chair)
District Offices—Scottsdale, 480-946-2411

Republican

Austin Scott, GA | 8th District | 7th Term | 68% (+37)
2185 RHOB | 202-225-6531 | Fax: 225-3013
austinscott.house.gov | X @austinscottga08
Bio—Tifton; Augusta, GA, 12/10/1969; BBA, Univ. of Georgia, 1993; business owner; GA House, 1997-2010; US House, 2011-present; m. Vivien; Southern Baptist
Committees—Agriculture; Armed Services; Intelligence
District Offices—Tifton, 229-396-5175; Warner Robins, 478-971-1776

Republican

United States House of Representatives　　Notes

Bobby Scott, VA | 3rd District | 16th Term | 67% (+35)
2328 RHOB | 202-225-8351 | Fax: 225-8354
bobbyscott.house.gov | X @bobbyscott
Bio—Newport News; Washington, DC, 4/30/1947; JD, Boston Col., 1973; USAR, 1970-74; MAARNG, 1974-76; lawyer; VA House, 1978-83; VA Senate, 1983-93; US House, 1993-present; div.; Episcopalian
Committees—Budget; Education & the Workforce (Rnk. Mem.)
District Offices—Newport News, 757-380-1000
Democrat

David Scott, GA | 13th District | 11th Term | 81% (+64)
468 CHOB | 202-225-2939 | Fax: 225-4628
davidscott.house.gov | X @repdavidscott
Bio—Atlanta; Aynor, SC, 6/27/1945; MBA, Univ. of Pennsylvania, 1969; business owner; GA House, 1974-82; GA Senate, 1982-2002; US House, 2003-present; m. Alfredia; Baptist
Committees—Agriculture; Financial Services
District Offices—Riverdale, 770-210-5073
Democrat

Keith Self, TX | 3rd District | 1st Term | 60% (+24)
1113 LHOB | 202-225-4201
keithself.house.gov | X @repkeithself
Bio—McKinney; Philadelphia, PA, 3/20/1953; MA, Univ. of Southern California, Los Angeles, 1981; USA, 1975-99, 2002-03; career military, defense contractor; Collin Co. judge, 2007-18; US House, 2023-present; m. Tracy; Protestant
Committees—Foreign Affairs; Veterans' Affairs
District Offices—Mckinney, 972-202-4150; Greenville, 903-458-7037
Republican

Pete Sessions, TX | 17th District | 13th Term | 66% (+33)
2204 RHOB | 202-225-6105
sessions.house.gov | X @petesessions
Bio—Waco; Waco, TX, 3/22/1955; BS, Southwestern Univ., 1978; business executive; US House, 1997-2019, 2021-present; m. Karen; Methodist
Committees—Financial Services; Oversight & Accountability
District Offices—Waco, 254-633-4500
Republican

Terri Sewell, AL | 7th District | 7th Term | 63% (+29)
1035 LHOB | 202-225-2665 | Fax: 226-9567
sewell.house.gov | X @repterrisewell
Bio—Birmingham; Huntsville, AL, 1/1/1965; JD, Harvard Univ., 1992; lawyer; US House, 2011-present; single; African Methodist Episcopal
Committees—Armed Services; House Administration; Ways and Means; Joint Library
District Offices—Birmingham, 205-254-1960; Selma, 334-877-4414; Tuscaloosa, 205-752-5380; Montgomery, 334-262-1919
Democrat

Brad Sherman, CA | 32nd District | 14th Term | 69% (+38)
2365 RHOB | 202-225-5911 | Fax: 225-5879
sherman.house.gov | X @bradsherman
Bio—Sherman Oaks; Los Angeles, CA, 10/24/1954; JD, Harvard Univ., 1979; lawyer, accountant; CA Board of Equalization, 1990-95; US House, 1997-present; m. Lisa; Jewish
Committees—Financial Services; Foreign Affairs
District Offices—Sherman Oaks, 818-501-9200
Democrat

United States House of Representatives

Mikie Sherrill, NJ | 11th District | 3rd Term | 58% (+19)
1427 LHOB | 202-225-5034 | Fax: 225-3186
sherrill.house.gov | X @repsherrill
Bio—Montclair; Alexandria, VA, 1/19/1972; JD, Georgetown Univ., 2007; USN, 1994-2003; lawyer; US House, 2019-present; m. Jason Hedberg; Catholic
Committees—Armed Services; Select CCP
District Offices—Parsippany, 973-526-5668

Democrat

Mike Simpson, ID | 2nd District | 13th Term | 63% (+27)
2084 RHOB | 202-225-5531 | Fax: 225-8216
simpson.house.gov | X @congmikesimpson
Bio—Idaho Falls; Burley, ID, 9/8/1950; DMD, Washington Univ. School of Dental Medicine, 1978; dentist; ID House, 1984-98; US House, 1999-present; m. Kathy; Mormon
Committees—Appropriations
District Offices—Boise, 208-334-1953; Idaho Falls, 208-523-6701; Twin Falls, 208-734-7219

Republican

Elissa Slotkin, MI | 7th District | 3rd Term | 51% (+5)
2245 RHOB | 202-225-4872
slotkin.house.gov | X @repslotkin
Bio—Lansing; New York, NY, 7/10/1976; MA, Columbia Univ., 2003; government official; US House, 2019-present; div.; Jewish
Committees—Agriculture; Armed Services
District Offices—Lansing, 517-993-0510

Democrat

Adam Smith, WA | 9th District | 14th Term | 71% (+43)
2264 RHOB | 202-225-8901
adamsmith.house.gov | X @repadamsmith
Bio—Bellevue; Washington, DC, 6/15/1965; JD, Univ. of Washington, 1990; lawyer; WA Senate, 1991-96; US House, 1997-present; m. Sara; Episcopalian
Committees—Armed Services (Rnk. Mem.)
District Offices—Renton, 425-793-5180

Democrat

Adrian Smith, NE | 3rd District | 9th Term | 78% (+63)
502 CHOB | 202-225-6435 | Fax: 225-0207
adriansmith.house.gov | X @repadriansmith
Bio—Gering; Scottsbluff, NE, 12/19/1970; BS, Univ. of Nebraska, 1993; business owner, education coordinator; Gering city council, 1994-98; NE Legislature, 1999-2007; US House, 2007-present; m. Andrea; Christian
Committees—Ways and Means; Joint Taxation
District Offices—Nebraska City, 402-874-6050; Grand Island, 308-384-3900; Scottsbluff, 308-633-6333

Republican

Chris Smith, NJ | 4th District | 22nd Term | 66% (+36)
2373 RHOB | 202-225-3765 | Fax: 225-7768
chrissmith.house.gov
Bio—Manchester; Rahway, NJ, 3/4/1953; BA, Col. of New Jersey, 1975; businessman, nonprofit executive; US House, 1981-present; m. Marie; Catholic
Committees—Foreign Affairs
District Offices—Toms River, 732-504-0567; Middletown, 732-780-3035

Republican

Notes

United States House of Representatives

Jason Smith, MO | 8th District | 6th Term | 75% (+54)
1011 LHOB | 202-225-4404 | Fax: 226-0326
jasonsmith.house.gov | X @repjasonsmith
Bio—Salem; St. Louis, MO, 6/16/1980; JD, Oklahoma City Univ., 2004; farmer, lawyer; MO House, 2005-13; US House, 2013-present; single; Assemblies of God
Committees—Ways and Means (Chair); Joint Taxation (Vice Chair)
District Offices—Cape Girardeau, 573-335-0101; Farmington, 573-756-9755; Poplar Bluff, 573-609-2996; Rolla, 573-364-2455; West Plains, 417-255-1515

Republican

Lloyd Smucker, PA | 11th District | 4th Term | 61% (+23)
302 CHOB | 202-225-2411 | Fax: 225-2013
smucker.house.gov | X @repsmucker
Bio—Lancaster; Lancaster, PA, 1/23/1964; attended Franklin & Marshall Col., 1988-91; business owner; West Lampeter Township supervisors, 2005-09; PA Senate, 2009-16; US House, 2017-present; m. Cindy; Lutheran
Committees—Budget; Education & the Workforce; Ways and Means; Joint Economic
District Offices—Hanover, 717-969-6132; Lancaster, 717-393-0667; Red Lion, 717-969-6133

Republican

Eric Sorensen, IL | 17th District | 1st Term | 51% (+4)
1205 LHOB | 202-225-5905
sorensen.house.gov | X @repericsorensen
Bio—Moline; Rockford, IL, 3/18/1976; BS, Northern Illinois Univ., 1999; meteorologist; US House, 2023-present; single; Protestant
Committees—Agriculture; Science, Space, & Technology
District Offices—Rockford, 779-513-4960; Rock Island, 309-786-3406; Peoria, 309-621-7070

Democrat

Darren Soto, FL | 9th District | 4th Term | 53% (+7)
2353 RHOB | 202-225-9889
soto.house.gov | X @repdarrensoto
Bio—Kissimmee; Ringwood, NJ, 2/25/1978; JD, George Washington Univ., 2004; lawyer, financial analyst; FL House, 2007-12; FL Senate, 2012-16; US House, 2017-present; m. Amanda; Catholic
Committees—Agriculture; Energy & Commerce
District Offices—Orlando, 407-204-3370; Kissimmee, 407-452-1171

Democrat

Abigail Spanberger, VA | 7th District | 3rd Term | 52% (+5)
562 CHOB | 202-225-2815
spanberger.house.gov | X @repspanberger
Bio—Glen Allen; Red Bank, NJ, 8/7/1979; MBA, Purdue Univ., 2002; teacher, postal inspector, CIA officer; US House, 2019-present; m. Adam; Protestant
Committees—Agriculture; Intelligence
District Offices—Woodbridge, 703-987-2180; Fredericksburg, 540-321-6130

Democrat

Victoria Spartz, IN | 5th District | 2nd Term | 61% (+22)
1609 LHOB | 202-225-2276
spartz.house.gov | X @repspartz
Bio—Noblesville; Nosivka, Ukraine, 10/6/1978; MPA, Indiana Univ., 2006; financial executive, business owner, farmer, professor; IN Senate, 2017-20; US House, 2021-present; m. Jason; Orthodox
Committees—Judiciary
District Offices—Noblesville, 317-848-0201; Muncie, 765-639-0671

Republican

United States House of Representatives

Melanie Stansbury, NM | 1st District | 2nd Term | 55% (+12)
1421 LHOB | 202-225-6316
stansbury.house.gov | X @repstansbury
Bio—Albuquerque; Farmington, NM, 1/31/1979; MS, Cornell Univ., 2007; consultant, White House aide, congressional staffer; NM House, 2019-21; US House, 2021-present; single; not stated
Committees—Natural Resources; Oversight & Accountability
District Offices—Albuquerque, 505-346-6781

Democrat

Greg Stanton, AZ | 4th District | 3rd Term | 56% (+12)
207 CHOB | 202-225-9888
stanton.house.gov | X @repgregstanton
Bio—Phoenix; Long Island, NY, 3/8/1970; JD, Univ. of Michigan, 1995; lawyer; Phoenix city council, 2000-09; Phoenix mayor, 2012-18; US House, 2019-present; m. Nicole; Catholic
Committees—Foreign Affairs; Transportation & Infrastructure
District Offices—Mesa, 602-956-2463

Democrat

Pete Stauber, MN | 8th District | 3rd Term | 57% (+14)
145 CHOB | 202-225-6211
stauber.house.gov | X @reppetestauber
Bio—Hermantown; Duluth, MN, 5/10/1966; BS, Lake Superior St. Univ., 1990; professional athlete, police officer; Hermantown city council, 2001-05, 2011-13; St. Louis Co. commissioners, 2013-19; US House, 2019-present; m. Jodi; Catholic
Committees—Natural Resources; Small Business; Transportation & Infrastructure
District Offices—Hermantown, 218-481-6396

Republican

Michelle Steel, CA | 45th District | 2nd Term | 52% (+5)
1127 LHOB | 202-225-2415
steel.house.gov | X @repsteel
Bio—Orange County; Seoul, South Korea, 6/21/1955; MBA, Univ. of Southern California, 2010; businesswoman; CA Board of Equalization, 2007-15; Orange Co. supervisors, 2015-17; US House, 2021-present; m. Shawn; Protestant
Committees—Education & the Workforce; Ways and Means; Select CCP
District Offices—Cypress, 714-960-6483

Republican

Elise Stefanik, NY | 21st District | 5th Term | 59% (+18)
2211 RHOB | 202-225-4611
stefanik.house.gov | X @repstefanik
Bio—Schuylerville; Albany, NY, 7/2/1984; AB, Harvard Univ., 2006; White House staffer, businesswoman; US House, 2015-present; m. Matt; Catholic
Committees—Armed Services; Education & the Workforce; Intelligence
District Offices—Plattsburgh, 518-561-2324; Herkimer, 315-219-8005; East Greenbush, 518-242-4707; Ogdensburg, 315-541-2670

Republican

Bryan Steil, WI | 1st District | 3rd Term | 54% (+9)
1526 LHOB | 202-225-3031
steil.house.gov | X @repbryansteil
Bio—Janesville; Janesville, WI, 3/3/1981; JD, Univ. of Wisconsin, 2007; congressional staffer, lawyer; US House, 2019-present; single; Catholic
Committees—Financial Services; House Administration (Chair); Joint Library (Vice Chair); Joint Printing (Chair)
District Offices—Beloit, 608-752-4050; St Francis, 414-285-2120; Janesville, 608-752-4050; Bristol, 262-654-1901; Racine, 262-637-0510

Republican

Notes

United States House of Representatives

Greg Steube, FL | 17th District | 3rd Term | 63% (+28)
2457 RHOB | 202-225-5792 | Fax: 225-3132
steube.house.gov | X @repgregsteube
Bio—Sarasota; Bradenton, FL, 5/19/1978; JD, Univ. of Florida, 2003; USA, 2004-08; lawyer; FL House, 2010-16; FL Senate, 2016-18; US House, 2019-present; m. Jennifer; Christian
Committees—Ways and Means
District Offices—Sarasota, 941-499-3214; Venice, 941-499-3214; Punta Gorda, 941-499-3214

Republican

Haley Stevens, MI | 11th District | 3rd Term | 61% (+23)
2411 RHOB | 202-225-8171
stevens.house.gov | X @rephaleystevens
Bio—Birmingham; Rochester Hills, MI, 6/24/1983; MA, American Univ., 2007; campaign aide, business executive; US House, 2019-present; div.; Christian
Committees—Education & the Workforce; Science, Space, & Technology; Select CCP
District Offices—Farmington Hills, 734-853-3040

Democrat

Marilyn Strickland, WA | 10th District | 2nd Term | 56% (+14)
1708 LHOB | 202-225-9740
strickland.house.gov | X @repstricklandwa
Bio—Tacoma; Seoul, South Korea, 9/25/1962; MBA, Clark Atlanta Univ., 1992; marketing executive; Tacoma city council, 2008-09; Tacoma mayor, 2010-17; US House, 2021-present; m. Patrick Erwin; Protestant
Committees—Armed Services; Transportation & Infrastructure
District Offices—Lacey, 360-459-8514

Democrat

Dale W. Strong, AL | 5th District | 1st Term | 67% (+38)
1337 LHOB | 202-225-4801
strong.house.gov | X @repdalestrong
Bio—Huntsville; Huntsville, AL, 5/8/1970; BS, Athens St. Univ., 1992; public relations professional, emergency medical technician; Madison Co. commissioner, 1996-2022; US House, 2023-present; m. Laura; Baptist
Committees—Armed Services; Homeland Security; Science, Space, & Technology
District Offices—Huntsville, 256-551-0190; Decatur, 256-355-9400

Republican

Eric Swalwell, CA | 14th District | 6th Term | 69% (+39)
174 CHOB | 202-225-5065
swalwell.house.gov | X @repswalwell
Bio—Livermore; Sac City, IA, 11/16/1980; JD, Univ. of Maryland, 2006; lawyer; Dublin city council, 2010-12; US House, 2013-present; m. Brittany; Protestant
Committees—Homeland Security; Judiciary
District Offices—Castro Valley, 510-370-3322

Democrat

Emilia Strong Sykes, OH | 13th District | 1st Term | 52% (+5)
1217 LHOB | 202-225-6265
sykes.house.gov | X @repemiliasykes
Bio—Akron; Akron, OH, 1/4/1986; MPH, Univ. of Florida, 2011; lawyer, public official; OH House, 2015-23; US House, 2023-present; m. Kevin Boyce; Baptist
Committees—Science, Space, & Technology; Transportation & Infrastructure
District Offices—Akron, 330-400-5350

Democrat

United States House of Representatives

Mark Takano, CA | 39th District | 6th Term | 57% (+15)
2078 RHOB | 202-225-2305 | Fax: 225-7018
takano.house.gov | X @repmarktakano
Bio—Riverside; Riverside, CA, 12/10/1960; MFA, Univ. of California, Riverside, 2010; teacher, college administrator; US House, 2013-present; single; Methodist
Committees—Education & the Workforce; Veterans' Affairs (Rnk. Mem.)
District Offices—Riverside, 951-222-0203

Democrat

Claudia Tenney, NY | 24th District | 3rd Term | 66% (+32)
2349 RHOB | 202-225-3665
tenney.house.gov | X @reptenney
Bio—Canandaigua; New Hartford, NY, 2/4/1961; JD, Cincinnati Univ., 1987; media owner, lawyer; NY Assembly, 2011-16; US House, 2017-19, 2021-present; div.; Presbyterian
Committees—Science, Space, & Technology; Ways and Means
District Offices—Lockport, 716-514-5130; Victor, 585-869-2060; Oswego, 315-236-7088

Republican

Shri Thanedar, MI | 13th District | 1st Term | 71% (+47)
1039 LHOB | 202-225-5802 | Fax: 226-2356
thanedar.house.gov | X @repshrithanedar
Bio—Detroit; Chikodi, India, 2/22/1955; PhD, Univ. of Akron, 1982; chemist, business owner; MI House, 2021-23; US House, 2023-present; m. Shashi; Protestant
Committees—Homeland Security; Small Business
District Offices—Detroit, 313-880-2400

Democrat

Bennie G. Thompson, MS | 2nd District | 16th Term | 60% (+20)
2466 RHOB | 202-225-5876 | Fax: 225-5898
benniethompson.house.gov | X @benniegthompson
Bio—Bolton; Bolton, MS, 1/28/1948; MS, Jackson St. Univ., 1972; teacher; Bolton alderman, 1969-73; Bolton mayor, 1973-79; Hinds Co. supervisors, 1980-93; US House, 1993-present; m. London; Methodist
Committees—Homeland Security (Rnk. Mem.)
District Offices—Natchez, 601-492-9003; Mound Bayou, 662-741-9003; Marks, 662-326-9003; Bolton, 601-866-9003; Greenville, 662-335-9003; Greenwood, 662-455-9003; Jackson, 601-946-9003

Democrat

Glenn "GT" Thompson, PA | 15th District | 8th Term | 69% (+40)
400 CHOB | 202-225-5121 | Fax: 225-5796
thompson.house.gov | X @congressmangt
Bio—Howard; Howard, PA, 7/27/1959; MEd, Temple Univ., 1988; rehabilitation therapist manager; US House, 2009-present; m. Penny Ammerman-Thompson; Protestant
Committees—Agriculture (Chair); Education & the Workforce
District Offices—Bellefonte, 814-353-0215; Oil City, 814-670-0432

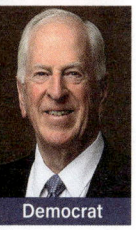

Republican

Mike Thompson, CA | 4th District | 13th Term | 67% (+36)
268 CHOB | 202-225-3311 | Fax: 225-4335
mikethompson.house.gov | X @repthompson
Bio—St. Helena; St. Helena, CA, 1/24/1951; MA, California St. Univ., 1996; USA, 1969-72; public official; CA Senate, 1990-98; US House, 1999-present; m. Janet; Catholic
Committees—Ways and Means
District Offices—Napa, 707-226-9898; Woodland, 530-753-5301; Santa Rosa, 707-542-7182

Democrat

United States House of Representatives

Tom Tiffany, WI | 7th District | 3rd Term | 61% (+24)
451 CHOB | 202-225-3365
tiffany.house.gov | X @reptiffany
Bio—Minocqua; Wabasha, MN, 12/30/1957; BS, Univ. of Wisconsin, River Falls, 1980; business owner; Little Rice supervisors, 2009-13; WI Assembly, 2011-13; WI Senate, 2013-20; US House, 2020-present; m. Chris; Protestant
Committees—Judiciary; Natural Resources
District Offices—Wausau, 715-298-9344

Republican

William Timmons, SC | 4th District | 3rd Term | Unc.
267 CHOB | 202-225-6030
timmons.house.gov | X @reptimmons
Bio—Greenville; Greenville, SC, 4/30/1984; MS, New York University, 2021; SCANG, 2018-present; lawyer, businessman, congressional staffer; SC Senate, 2016-19; US House, 2019-present; sep.; Christian
Committees—Financial Services; Oversight & Accountability
District Offices—Greer, 864-241-0175

Republican

Dina Titus, NV | 1st District | 7th Term | 51% (+6)
2464 RHOB | 202-225-5965 | Fax: 225-3119
titus.house.gov | X @repdinatitus
Bio—Las Vegas; Thomasville, GA, 5/23/1950; PhD, Florida St. Univ., 1976; professor; NV Senate, 1989-2008; US House, 2009-11, 2013-present; m. Thomas Wright; Greek Orthodox
Committees—Foreign Affairs; Homeland Security; Transportation & Infrastructure
District Offices—Las Vegas, 702-220-9823

Democrat

Rashida Tlaib, MI | 12th District | 3rd Term | 70% (+45)
2438 RHOB | 202-225-5126
tlaib.house.gov | X @reprashida
Bio—Detroit; Detroit, MI, 7/24/1976; JD, Western Michigan Univ., 2004; lawyer; MI House, 2009-14; US House, 2019-present; div.; Muslim
Committees—Financial Services; Oversight & Accountability
District Offices—Detroit, 313-463-6220; Southfield, 313-203-7540; Inkster, 313-463-6220

Democrat

Jill Tokuda, HI | 2nd District | 1st Term | 59% (+26)
1005 LHOB | 202-225-4906
tokuda.house.gov | X @repjilltokuda
Bio—Kaneohe; Honolulu County, HI, 3/3/1976; BA, George Washington Univ., 1997; nonprofit executive, business owner; HI Senate, 2007-18; US House, 2023-present; m. Kyle Michibata; Protestant
Committees—Agriculture; Armed Services
District Offices—Honolulu, 808-746-6220

Democrat

Paul Tonko, NY | 20th District | 8th Term | 55% (+10)
2369 RHOB | 202-225-5076 | Fax: 225-5077
tonko.house.gov | X @reppaultonko
Bio—Amsterdam; Amsterdam, NY, 6/18/1949; BS, Clarkson Univ., 1971; public works engineer; Montgomery Co. supervisors, 1976-83; NY Assembly, 1983-2007; US House, 2009-present; single; Catholic
Committees—Energy & Commerce; Science, Space, & Technology
District Offices—Albany, 518-465-0700; Saratoga Springs, 518-374-4547

Democrat

Notes

United States House of Representatives

Norma J. Torres, CA | 35th District | 5th Term | 57% (+15)
2227 RHOB | 202-225-6161 | Fax: 225-8671
torres.house.gov | X @normajtorres
Bio—Pomona; Escuintla, Guatemala, 4/4/1965; BA, National Labor Col., 2012; emergency dispatcher, sales representative; Pomona city council, 2000-06; Pomona mayor, 2006-08; CA Assembly, 2008-13; CA Senate, 2013-14; US House, 2015-present; m. Louis; Catholic
Committees—Appropriations; House Administration
District Offices—Ontario, 909-481-6474

Democrat

Ritchie Torres, NY | 15th District | 2nd Term | 83% (+66)
1414 LHOB | 202-225-4361
ritchietorres.house.gov | X @repritchie
Bio—Bronx; New York, NY, 3/12/1988; attended New York Univ., 2006-07; civil servant, community organizer; New York city council, 2014-20; US House, 2021-present; single; Christian
Committees—Financial Services; Select CCP
District Offices—Bronx, 718-503-9610

Democrat

Lori Trahan, MA | 3rd District | 3rd Term | 61% (+26)
2439 RHOB | 202-225-3411
trahan.house.gov | X @reploritrahan
Bio—Westford; Lowell, MA, 10/27/1973; BS, Georgetown Univ., 1995; businesswoman, congressional staffer; US House, 2019-present; m. Dave; Catholic
Committees—Energy & Commerce
District Offices—Lowell, 978-459-0101

Democrat

David Trone, MD | 6th District | 3rd Term | 54% (+10)
2404 RHOB | 202-225-2721
trone.house.gov | X @repdavidtrone
Bio—Potomac; Cheverly, MD, 9/21/1955; MBA, Univ. of Pennsylvania, 1985; entrepreneur, business owner; US House, 2019-present; m. June; Lutheran
Committees—Appropriations; Budget; Joint Economic
District Offices—Frederick, 301-926-0300; Hagerstown, 240-382-6464; Germantown, 240-803-6119

Democrat

Mike Turner, OH | 10th District | 11th Term | 61% (+23)
2183 RHOB | 202-225-6465 | Fax: 225-6754
turner.house.gov | X @repmiketurner
Bio—Dayton; Dayton, OH, 1/11/1960; PhD, Georgetown Univ., 2022; lawyer; Dayton mayor, 1994-2002; US House, 2003-present; div.; Protestant
Committees—Armed Services; Oversight & Accountability; Intelligence (Chair)
District Offices—Dayton, 937-225-2843

Republican

Lauren Underwood, IL | 14th District | 3rd Term | 54% (+8)
1410 LHOB | 202-225-2976
underwood.house.gov | X @repunderwood
Bio—Naperville; Mayfield Heights, OH, 10/4/1986; MSN/MPH, Johns Hopkins Univ., 2009; nurse, professor; US House, 2019-present; single; Protestant
Committees—Appropriations
District Offices—Joliet, 630-549-2190; Sandwich, 630-549-2190

Democrat

Notes

U.S. Congress Directory | 131

United States House of Representatives

David G. Valadao, CA | 22nd District | 5th Term | 51% (+3)
2465 RHOB | 202-225-4695
valadao.house.gov | X @repdavidvaladao
Bio—Hanford; Hanford, CA, 4/14/1977; attended Col. of the Sequoias, 1996-98; farmer, business owner; CA Assembly, 2010-12; US House, 2013-19, 2021-present; m. Terra; Catholic
Committees—Appropriations; Budget
District Offices—Bakersfield, 661-864-7736; Hanford, 559-460-6070
Republican

Jeff Van Drew, NJ | 2nd District | 3rd Term | 58% (+19)
2447 RHOB | 202-225-6572
vandrew.house.gov | X @congressmanjvd
Bio—Dennis Township; Manhattan, NY, 2/23/1953; DDS, Fairleigh Dickinson Univ., 1979; dentist; Dennis Township mayor, 1994-95, 1997-2003; Cape May Co. Freeholder, 1994-97; NJ Assembly, 2001-07; NJ Senate, 2008-19; US House, 2019-present; m. Ricarda; Catholic
Committees—Judiciary; Transportation & Infrastructure
District Offices—Northfield, 609-625-5008
Republican

Beth Van Duyne, TX | 24th District | 2nd Term | 59% (+20)
1725 LHOB | 202-225-6605 | Fax: 225-0074
vanduyne.house.gov | X @repbethvanduyne
Bio—Irving; Ithaca, NY, 11/16/1970; BA, Cornell Univ., 1995; consultant, business executive; Irving city council, 2004-10; Irving mayor, 2011-17; US House, 2021-present; div.; Episcopalian
Committees—Small Business; Ways and Means
District Offices—Dallas, 972-966-5500; Keller, 972-966-5500
Republican

Derrick Van Orden, WI | 3rd District | 1st Term | 51% (+4)
1513 LHOB | 202-225-5506
vanorden.house.gov | X @repvanorden
Bio—Prairie du Chien; Hennepin County, MN, 9/15/1969; BS, Excelsior Univ.; USN, 1988-2014; actor, business owner; US House, 2023-present; m. Sara Jane; Protestant
Committees—Agriculture; Transportation & Infrastructure; Veterans' Affairs
District Offices—La Crosse, 608-782-2558; Eau Claire, 715-831-9214
Republican

Juan Vargas, CA | 52nd District | 6th Term | 66% (+33)
2334 RHOB | 202-225-8045 | Fax: 225-2772
vargas.house.gov | X @repjuanvargas
Bio—San Diego; National City, CA, 3/7/1961; JD, Harvard Univ., 1991; lawyer, business executive; San Diego city council, 1993-2000; CA Assembly, 2000-06; CA Senate, 2010-12; US House, 2013-present; m. Adrienne; Catholic
Committees—Financial Services
District Offices—Chula Vista, 619-422-5963
Democrat

Gabe Vasquez, NM | 2nd District | 1st Term | 50% (+.7)
1517 LHOB | 202-225-2365
vasquez.house.gov | X @repgabevasquez
Bio—Las Cruces; El Paso, TX, 8/3/1984; BA, New Mexico St. Univ., 2008; newspaper editor, nonprofit executive, congressional staffer; Las Cruces city council, 2017-21; US House, 2023-present; single; Catholic
Committees—Agriculture; Armed Services
District Offices—Albuquerque, 505-208-4777; Las Cruces, 575-323-6390
Democrat

United States House of Representatives

Marc Veasey, TX | 33rd District | 6th Term | 71% (+46)
2348 RHOB | 202-225-9897 | Fax: 225-9702
veasey.house.gov | X @repveasey
Bio—Fort Worth; Fort Worth, TX, 1/3/1971; BS, Texas Wesleyan Univ., 1995; journalist, congressional staffer, realtor; TX House, 2004-12; US House, 2013-present; m. Tonya; Christian
Committees—Armed Services; Energy & Commerce
District Offices—Dallas, 214-741-1387; Fort Worth, 817-920-9086

Democrat

Nydia M. Velázquez, NY | 7th District | 16th Term | 81% (+62)
2302 RHOB | 202-225-2361
velazquez.house.gov | X @nydiavelazquez
Bio—Brooklyn; Yabucoa, PR, 3/28/1953; MA, New York Univ., 1976; college faculty, public official; New York city council, 1984; US House, 1993-present; div.; Catholic
Committees—Financial Services; Natural Resources; Small Business (Rnk. Mem.)
District Offices—Sunnyside, 718-340-6244; Brooklyn, 718-599-3658

Democrat

Ann Wagner, MO | 2nd District | 6th Term | 54% (+12)
2350 RHOB | 202-225-1621
wagner.house.gov | X @repannwagner
Bio—Ballwin; St. Louis, MO, 9/13/1962; BSBA, Univ. of Missouri, 1984; businesswoman; US ambassador to Luxembourg, 2005-09; US House, 2013-present; m. Ray; Catholic
Committees—Financial Services; Foreign Affairs
District Offices—Washington, 636-231-1001; Ballwin, 636-779-5449

Republican

Tim Walberg, MI | 5th District | 8th Term | 62% (+27)
2266 RHOB | 202-225-6276 | Fax: 225-6281
walberg.house.gov | X @repwalberg
Bio—Tipton; Chicago, IL, 4/12/1951; MA, Wheaton Col., 1978; minister; MI House, 1983-98; US House, 2007-09, 2011-present; m. Sue; Christian
Committees—Education & the Workforce; Energy & Commerce
District Offices—Niles, 269-479-3115; Jackson, 517-780-9075

Republican

Mike Waltz, FL | 6th District | 3rd Term | 75% (+51)
244 CHOB | 202-225-2706
waltz.house.gov | X @repmichaelwaltz
Bio—St. Augustine; Boynton Beach, FL, 1/31/1974; BA, Virginia Military Institute, 1996; USA, 1996-2000; USAR, 2000-present; government official, business owner, author; US House, 2019-present; m. Julia Nesheiwat; Protestant
Committees—Armed Services; Foreign Affairs; Oversight & Accountability; Intelligence
District Offices—Palm Coast, 386-302-0442; Ormond Beach, 386-281-4949; DeLand, 386-279-0707

Republican

Debbie Wasserman Schultz, FL | 25th District | 10th Term | 55% (+10)
270 CHOB | 202-225-7931 | Fax: 226-2052
wassermanschultz.house.gov | X @repdwstweets
Bio—Weston; Forest Hills, NY, 9/27/1966; MA, Univ. of Florida, 1990; congressional staffer, public official; FL House, 1992-2000; FL Senate, 2000-04; US House, 2005-present; m. Steve; Jewish
Committees—Appropriations
District Offices—Sunrise, 954-845-1179

Democrat

Notes

United States House of Representatives

Maxine Waters, CA | 43rd District | 17th Term | 77% (+55)
2221 RHOB | 202-225-2201 | Fax: 225-7854
waters.house.gov | X @repmaxinewaters
Bio—Los Angeles; St. Louis, MO, 8/15/1938; BA, California St. Univ., Los Angeles, 1970; teacher; CA Assembly, 1977-91; US House, 1991-present; m. Sidney Williams; Christian
Committees—Financial Services (Rnk. Mem.)
District Offices—Hawthorne, 323-757-8900

Democrat

Bonnie Watson Coleman, NJ | 12th District | 5th Term | 63% (+27)
168 CHOB | 202-225-5801 | Fax: 225-6025
watsoncoleman.house.gov | X @repbonnie
Bio—Ewing Township; Camden, NJ, 2/6/1945; BA, Thomas Edison St. Col., 1985; public official; NJ Assembly, 1998-2014; US House, 2015-present; m. William; Baptist
Committees—Appropriations
District Offices—Ewing, 609-883-0026

Democrat

Randy Weber, TX | 14th District | 6th Term | 70% (+40)
107 CHOB | 202-225-2831 | Fax: 225-0271
weber.house.gov | X @txrandy14
Bio—Friendswood; Pearland, TX, 7/2/1953; BS, Univ. of Houston, Clear Lake, 1977; business owner; Pearland city council, 1990-96; TX House, 2008-12; US House, 2013-present; m. Brenda; Baptist
Committees—Energy & Commerce; Science, Space, & Technology
District Offices—Beaumont, 409-835-0108; Lake Jackson, 979-285-0231; League City, 281-316-0231

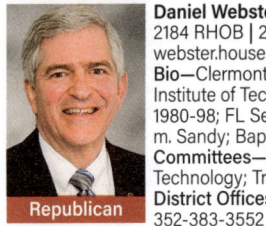

Republican

Daniel Webster, FL | 11th District | 7th Term | 63% (+28)
2184 RHOB | 202-225-1002
webster.house.gov | X @repwebster
Bio—Clermont; Charleston, WV, 4/27/1949; BEE, Georgia Institute of Technology, 1971; business owner; FL House, 1980-98; FL Senate, 1998-2008; US House, 2011-present; m. Sandy; Baptist
Committees—Natural Resources; Science, Space, & Technology; Transportation & Infrastructure
District Offices—Clermont, 352-241-9220; The Villages, 352-383-3552

Republican

Brad Wenstrup, OH | 2nd District | 6th Term | 74% (+49)
2335 RHOB | 202-225-3164 | Fax: 225-1992
wenstrup.house.gov | X @repbradwenstrup
Bio—Hillsboro; Cincinnati, OH, 6/17/1958; BS/DPM, William M. Scholl Col. of Podiatric Medicine, 1985; USAR, 1998-2022; physician; US House, 2013-present; m. Monica; Catholic
Committees—Ways and Means; Intelligence
District Offices—Cincinnati, 513-474-7777; Chillicothe, 740-672-7040; Peebles, 513-605-1380

Republican

Bruce Westerman, AR | 4th District | 5th Term | 71% (+45)
202 CHOB | 202-225-3772
westerman.house.gov | X @repwesterman
Bio—Hot Springs; Hot Springs, AR, 11/18/1967; MF, Yale Univ., 2001; engineer; AR House, 2010-14; US House, 2015-present; m. Sharon; Baptist
Committees—Natural Resources (Chair); Transportation & Infrastructure
District Offices—Hot Springs, 501-609-9796; Pine Bluff, 870-536-8178; Ozark, 501-609-9796; El Dorado, 870-864-8946

Republican

Notes

United States House of Representatives

Jennifer Wexton, VA | 10th District | 3rd Term | 53% (+7)
1210 LHOB | 202-225-5136 | Fax: 225-0437
wexton.house.gov | X @repwexton
Bio—Leesburg; Washington, DC, 5/27/1968; JD, Col. of William & Mary, 1995; lawyer; VA Senate, 2014-18; US House, 2019-present; m. Andrew; not stated
Committees—Appropriations; Budget
District Offices—Leesburg, 703-236-1300; Manassas, 703-234-3800

Democrat

Susan Wild, PA | 7th District | 4th Term | 51% (+2)
1027 LHOB | 202-225-6411
wild.house.gov | X @repsusanwild
Bio—Allentown; Wiesbaden, Germany, 6/7/1957; JD, George Washington Univ., 1982; lawyer; US House, 2018-present; single; Jewish
Committees—Education & the Workforce; Ethics (Rnk. Mem.); Foreign Affairs
District Offices—Allentown, 484-781-6000; Easton, 610-333-1170; Lehighton, 570-807-0333

Democrat

Brandon Williams, NY | 22nd District | 1st Term | 51% (+1)
1022 LHOB | 202-225-3701
brandonwilliams.house.gov | X @repwilliams
Bio—Syracuse; Dallas, TX, 5/22/1967; MBA, Univ. of Pennsylvania, 1998; USN, 1991-96; investment banker, business owner; US House, 2023-present; m. Stephanie; Protestant
Committees—Education & the Workforce; Science, Space, & Technology; Transportation & Infrastructure
District Offices—Syracuse, 315-233-4333; Utica, 315-732-0713

Republican

Nikema Williams, GA | 5th District | 2nd Term | 82% (+65)
1406 LHOB | 202-225-3801
nikemawilliams.house.gov | X @repnikema
Bio—Atlanta; Columbus, GA, 7/30/1978; BA, Talladega Col., 2000; nonprofit executive; GA Senate, 2017-21; US House, 2021-present; m. Leslie Small; Methodist
Committees—Financial Services
District Offices—Atlanta, 404-659-0116

Democrat

Roger Williams, TX | 25th District | 6th Term | Unc.
2336 RHOB | 202-225-9896 | Fax: 225-9692
williams.house.gov | X @reprwilliams
Bio—Weatherford; Evanston, IL, 9/13/1949; BA, Texas Christian Univ., 1972; professional athlete, baseball coach, small business owner; TX secretary of state, 2005-07; US House, 2013-present; m. Patty; Christian
Committees—Financial Services; Small Business (Chair)
District Offices—Arlington, 682-218-5965; Cleburne, 682-218-5965

Republican

Frederica S. Wilson, FL | 24th District | 7th Term | 71% (+44)
2080 RHOB | 202-225-4506 | Fax: 226-0777
wilson.house.gov | X @repwilson
Bio—Miami Gardens; Miami, FL, 11/5/1942; MS, Univ. of Miami, 1972; elementary school principal; FL House, 1998-2002; FL Senate, 2002-10; US House, 2011-present; wid.; Episcopalian
Committees—Education & the Workforce; Transportation & Infrastructure
District Offices—Miami Gardens, 305-690-5905; West Park, 954-989-2688

Democrat

Notes

United States House of Representatives

Joe Wilson, SC | 2nd District | 12th Term | 60% (+20)
1436 LHOB | 202-225-2452
joewilson.house.gov | X @repjoewilson
Bio—Springdale; Charleston, SC, 7/31/1947; JD, Univ. of South Carolina, 1972; USAR, 1972-75; SCARNG, 1975-2003; lawyer, congressional staffer; SC Senate, 1984-2001; US House, 2001-present; m. Roxanne; Presbyterian
Committees—Armed Services; Education & the Workforce; Foreign Affairs
District Offices—Aiken, 803-642-6416; West Columbia, 803-939-0041
Republican

Rob Wittman, VA | 1st District | 9th Term | 55% (+13)
2055 RHOB | 202-225-4261 | Fax: 225-4382
wittman.house.gov | X @robwittman
Bio—Montross; Washington, DC, 2/3/1959; PhD, Virginia Commonwealth Univ., 2002; public health official; Montross town council, 1986-96; Westmoreland Co. board of supervisors, 1996-2005; VA House, 2006-07; US House, 2007-present; m. Kathryn; Episcopalian
Committees—Armed Services; Natural Resources; Select CCP
District Offices—Yorktown, 757-527-6270; Tappahannock, 804-443-0668; Glen Allen, 804-401-4120
Republican

Steve Womack, AR | 3rd District | 7th Term | 63% (+31)
2412 RHOB | 202-225-4301 | Fax: 225-5713
womack.house.gov | X @repstevewomack
Bio—Rogers; Russellville, AR, 2/18/1957; BA, Arkansas Tech Univ., 1979; ARARNG, 1979-2009; radio station manager, consultant; Rogers city council, 1983-84, 1997-98; Rogers mayor, 1999-2010; US House, 2011-present; m. Terri; Southern Baptist
Committees—Appropriations
District Offices—Rogers, 479-464-0446; Fort Smith, 479-424-1146
Republican

Rudy Yakym III, IN | 2nd District | 2nd Term | 64% (+32)
349 CHOB | 202-225-3915
yakym.house.gov | X @reprudyyakym
Bio—Granger; South Bend, IN, 2/24/1984; MBA, Univ. of Notre Dame, 2019; congressional staffer, business executive; US House, 2022-present; m. Sallyann; Protestant
Committees—Budget; Transportation & Infrastructure
District Offices—Mishawaka, 574-204-2645; Rochester, 574-223-4373
Republican

Ryan Zinke, MT | 1st District | 3rd Term | 49% (+3)
512 CHOB | 202-225-5628
zinke.house.gov | X @repryanzinke
Bio—Whitefish; Bozeman, MT, 11/1/1961; MS, Univ. of San Diego, 2003; USN, 1985-2008; business executive; MT Senate, 2009-12; US interior secretary, 2017-18; US House, 2015-17, 2023-present; m. Lolita; Lutheran
Committees—Appropriations; Science, Space, & Technology
District Offices—Missoula, 406-317-0276; Kalispell, 406-317-0277
Republican

House Vacancies

(as of February 11, 2024)

Offices remain open under the supervision of the Clerk of the House for constituent services. Staff may not take positions on public policy.

CALIFORNIA 20TH

Rep. Kevin McCarthy (R) resigned on December 31, 2023. A special election is scheduled for March 19, 2024. If necessary, a special general election is scheduled for May 21, 2024.

Washington, DC | 2468 RHOB | 202-225-2915

Clovis, CA | 559-701-2530

Bakersfield, CA | 661-327-3611

NEW YORK 3RD

Rep. George Santos (R) was expelled on December 1, 2023. A special election is scheduled for February 13, 2024.

Washington, DC | 1117 LHOB | 202-225-3335

Douglaston, NY | 718-631-0400

Jericho, NY | 516-861-1070

> **SPECIAL ELECTION UPDATE**
> Tom Suozzi (D) defeated Mazi Pilip (R), 54 percent to 46 percent. Upon his swearing in, the party ratio in the House will be 219 Republicans, 213 Democrats, and 3 vacancies.
>
> *Results were not official at the time this directory was printed.*

NEW YORK 26TH

Rep. Brian Higgins (D) resigned on February 2, 2024. A special election will be held April 30, 2024.

Washington, DC | 2269 RHOB | 202-225-3306

Buffalo, NY | 716-852-3501

Niagara Falls, NY | 716-282-1274

OHIO 6TH

Rep. Bill Johnson (R) resigned on January 21, 2014. A special primary is scheduled for March 19, 2024. A special general election is scheduled for June 11, 2024.

Washington, DC | 2082 RHOB | 202-225-5705

Marietta, OH | 740-376-0868

Canfield, OH | 330-967-7312

Notes

House Standing Committees

AGRICULTURE
1301 LHOB | 202-225-2171 | agriculture.house.gov

REPUBLICANS (29)
Glenn Thompson, PA, Chair | Frank Lucas, OK | Austin Scott, GA | Rick Crawford, AR | Scott DesJarlais, TN | Doug LaMalfa, CA | David Rouzer, NC | Trent Kelly, MS | Don Bacon, NE | Mike Bost, IL | Dusty Johnson, SD | Jim Baird, IN | Tracey Mann, KS | Randy Feenstra, IA | Mary Miller, IL | Barry Moore, AL | Kat Cammack, FL | Brad Finstad, MN | John Rose, TN | Ronny Jackson, TX | Marc Molinaro, NY | Monica De La Cruz, TX | Nick Langworthy, NY | John Duarte, CA | Zach Nunn, IA | Mark Alford, MO | Derrick Van Orden, WI | Lori Chavez-DeRemer, OR | Max Miller, OH

DEMOCRATS (25)
David Scott, GA, Rnk. Mem. | Jim Costa, CA | Jim McGovern, MA | Alma S. Adams, NC | Abigail Spanberger, VA | Jahana Hayes, CT | Shontel Brown, OH | Sharice Davids, KS | Elissa Slotkin, MI | Yadira Caraveo, CO | Andrea Salinas, OR | Marie Gluesenkamp Perez, WA | Don Davis, NC | Jill Tokuda, HI | Nikki Budzinski, IL | Eric Sorensen, IL | Gabe Vasquez, NM | Jasmine Crockett, TX | Jonathan L. Jackson, IL | Greg Casar, TX | Chellie Pingree, ME | Salud Carbajal, CA | Angie Craig, MN | Darren Soto, FL | Sanford D. Bishop, GA

Rep. Staff Dir.: Parish Braden | Dem. Staff Dir.: Anne Simmons

SUBCOMMITTEES
The chair and ranking member are ex officio members of all subcommittees.

Commodity Markets, Digital Assets, and Rural Development
Rep: Johnson, Chair | Lucas | Scott | Rouzer | Bacon | Mann | Rose | Molinaro | Langworthy | Nunn | Chavez-DeRemer | Max Miller
Dem: Caraveo, Rnk. Mem. | Davis | Costa | Salinas | Perez | Budzinski | Jackson | Casar | Craig | Crockett | Vacancy

Conservation, Research, and Biotechnology
Rep: Baird, Chair | Lucas | Bost | Mary Miller | Cammack | Finstad | Duarte | Alford
Dem: Spanberger, Rnk. Mem. | Davids | Slotkin | Budzinski | Sorensen | Tokuda | Vasquez

Forestry
Rep: LaMalfa, Chair | Kelly | Moore | Duarte | Chavez-DeRemer
Dem: Salinas, Rnk. Mem. | Perez | Vasquez | Pingree

General Farm Commodities, Risk Management, and Credit
Rep: Scott, Chair | Crawford | LaMalfa | Rouzer | Johnson | Mary Miller | Moore | Finstad | Rose | Jackson | De La Cruz | Duarte | Nunn | Alford
Dem: Brown, Rnk. Mem. | Davids | Davis | Sorensen | Crockett | Budzinski | Carbajal | Craig | Adams | Bishop | Vacancy

Livestock, Dairy, and Poultry
Rep: Mann, Chair | DesJarlais | Kelly | Bacon | Baird | Feenstra | Moore | Jackson | Molinaro | Alford | Van Orden
Dem: Costa, Rnk. Mem. | Spanberger | Hayes | Caraveo | Tokuda | Pingree | Soto | Davis | Vacancy | Vacancy

Nutrition, Foreign Agriculture, and Horticulture
Rep: Finstad, Chair | Scott | DesJarlais | Baird | Mann | Rose | Molinaro | De La Cruz | Langworthy | Van Orden | Max Miller
Dem: Hayes, Rnk. Mem. | McGovern | Adams | Tokuda | Crockett | Jackson | Casar | Brown | Salinas | Caraveo

House Standing Committees

APPROPRIATIONS
H-307 Capitol | 202-225-2771 | appropriations.house.gov

REPUBLICANS (34)
Kay Granger, TX, Chair | Hal Rogers, KY | Robert Aderholt, AL | Mike Simpson, ID | John Carter, TX | Ken Calvert, CA | Tom Cole, OK | Mario Diaz-Balart, FL | Steve Womack, AR | Chuck Fleischmann, TN | Dave Joyce, OH | Andy Harris, MD | Mark Amodei, NV | David G. Valadao, CA | Dan Newhouse, WA | John Moolenaar, MI | John Rutherford, FL | Ben Cline, VA | Guy Reschenthaler, PA | Mike Garcia, CA | Ashley Hinson, IA | Tony Gonzales, TX | Julia Letlow, LA | Michael Cloud, TX | Michael Guest, MS | Ryan Zinke, MT | Andrew Clyde, GA | Jake LaTurner, KS | Jerry Carl, AL | Stephanie Bice, OK | Scott Franklin, FL | Jake Ellzey, TX | Juan Ciscomani, AZ | Chuck Edwards, NC

DEMOCRATS (27)
Rosa DeLauro, CT, Rnk. Mem. | Steny Hoyer, MD | Marcy Kaptur, OH | Sanford D. Bishop, GA | Barbara Lee, CA | Betty McCollum, MN | C.A. Dutch Ruppersberger, MD | Debbie Wasserman Schultz, FL | Henry Cuellar, TX | Chellie Pingree, ME | Mike Quigley, IL | Derek Kilmer, WA | Matt Cartwright, PA | Grace Meng, NY | Mark Pocan, WI | Pete Aguilar, CA | Lois Frankel, FL | Bonnie Watson Coleman, NJ | Norma J. Torres, CA | Ed Case, HI | Adriano Espaillat, NY | Josh Harder, CA | Jennifer Wexton, VA | David Trone, MD | Lauren Underwood, IL | Susie Lee, NV | Joe Morelle, NY

Rep. Staff Dir.: Anne Marie Chotvacs | Dem. Staff Dir.: Chris Bigelow

SUBCOMMITTEES
The chair and ranking member are ex officio members of subcommittees on which they do not serve as regular members.

Agriculture, Rural Development, Food and Drug Administration, and Related Agencies
Rep: Harris, Chair | Valadao | Moolenaar | Newhouse | Letlow | Cline | Hinson | Carl | Franklin
Dem: Bishop, Rnk. Mem. | Pingree | Underwood | Kaptur | Barbara Lee | Wasserman Schultz

Commerce, Justice, Science, and Related Agencies
Rep: Rogers, Chair | Aderholt | Carter | Cline | Garcia | Gonzales | Clyde | Ellzey
Dem: Cartwright, Rnk. Mem. | Meng | Ruppersberger | Trone | Morelle

Defense
Rep: Calvert, Chair | Rogers | Cole | Womack | Aderholt | Carter | Diaz-Balart | Joyce | Garcia | Vacancy
Dem: McCollum, Rnk. Mem. | Ruppersberger | Kaptur | Cuellar | Kilmer | Aguilar | Case

Energy and Water Development and Related Agencies
Rep: Fleischmann, Chair | Simpson | Calvert | Newhouse | Reschenthaler | Garcia | Letlow | Guest | Bice
Dem: Kaptur, Rnk. Mem. | Wasserman Schultz | Susie Lee | Quigley | Morelle | Kilmer

Financial Services and General Government
Rep: Womack, Chair | Amodei | Joyce | Moolenaar | Hinson | Cloud | Carl | Ciscomani
Dem: Hoyer, Rnk. Mem. | Cartwright | Pocan | Bishop | Torres

Homeland Security
Rep: Joyce, Chair | Rutherford | Harris | Newhouse | Hinson | Cloud | Guest
Dem: Cuellar, Rnk. Mem. | Underwood | Case | Trone

Interior, Environment, and Related Agencies
Rep: Simpson, Chair | Amodei | Reschenthaler | Cloud | Zinke | Ellzey | Vacancy
Dem: Pingree, Rnk. Mem. | McCollum | Kilmer | Harder

Labor, Health and Human Services, Education, and Related Agencies
Rep: Aderholt, Chair | Simpson | Harris | Fleischmann | Moolenaar | Letlow | Clyde | LaTurner | Ellzey | Ciscomani
Dem: DeLauro, Rnk. Mem. | Hoyer | Barbara Lee | Pocan | Frankel | Watson Coleman | Harder

House Standing Committees

SUBCOMMITTEES (Appropriations)

Legislative Branch
Rep: Amodei, Chair | Clyde | LaTurner | Bice | Franklin
Dem: Espaillat, Rnk. Mem. | Wexton | Quigley

Military Construction, Veterans Affairs, and Related Agencies
Rep: Carter, Chair | Valadao | Rutherford | Gonzales | Guest | Zinke | Bice | Franklin
Dem: Wasserman Schultz, Rnk. Mem. | Bishop | Susie Lee | Cuellar | Pingree

State, Foreign Operations, and Related Programs
Rep: Diaz-Balart, Chair | Rogers | Reschenthaler | Fleischmann | LaTurner | Carl | Vacancy
Dem: Lee, Rnk. Mem. | Meng | Frankel | Torres

Transportation, Housing and Urban Development, and Related Agencies
Rep: Cole, Chair | Diaz-Balart | Womack | Rutherford | Gonzales | Valadao | Cline | Zinke | Ciscomani
Dem: Quigley, Rnk. Mem. | Watson Coleman | Torres | Aguilar | Espaillat | Wexton

ARMED SERVICES

2216 RHOB | 202-225-4151 | Fax: 225-9077 | armedservices.house.gov

REPUBLICANS (31)
Mike Rogers, AL, Chair | Joe Wilson, SC | Mike Turner, OH | Doug Lamborn, CO | Rob Wittman, VA | Austin Scott, GA | Sam Graves, MO | Elise Stefanik, NY | Scott DesJarlais, TN | Trent Kelly, MS | Mike Gallagher, WI | Matt Gaetz, FL | Don Bacon, NE | Jim Banks, IN | Jack Bergman, MI | Mike Waltz, FL | Lisa McClain, MI | Ronny Jackson, TX | Pat Fallon, TX | Carlos A. Gimenez, FL | Nancy Mace, SC | Brad Finstad, MN | Dale W. Strong, AL | Morgan Luttrell, TX | Jen Kiggans, VA | Nick LaLota, NY | James Moylan, GU | Mark Alford, MO | Cory Mills, FL | Rich McCormick, GA | Lance Gooden, TX

DEMOCRATS (28)
Adam Smith, WA, Rnk. Mem. | Joe Courtney, CT | John Garamendi, CA | Donald Norcross, NJ | Ruben Gallego, AZ | Seth Moulton, MA | Salud Carbajal, CA | Ro Khanna, CA | William R. Keating, MA | Andy Kim, NJ | Chrissy Houlahan, PA | Elissa Slotkin, MI | Mikie Sherrill, NJ | Veronica Escobar, TX | Jared Golden, ME | Sara Jacobs, CA | Marilyn Strickland, WA | Pat Ryan, NY | Jeff Jackson, NC | Gabe Vasquez, NM | Chris Deluzio, PA | Jill Tokuda, HI | Don Davis, NC | Jennifer McClellan, VA | Terri Sewell, AL | Steven Horsford, NV | Jimmy Panetta, CA | Marc Veasey, TX

Rep. Staff Dir.: Christopher Vieson | Dem. Staff Dir.: Brian Garrett

SUBCOMMITTEES
The chair and ranking member are ex officio members of all subcommittees.

Cyber, Information Technologies, and Innovation
Rep: Gallagher, Chair | Gaetz | McClain | Fallon | Strong | Luttrell | Kiggans | LaLota | McCormick
Dem: Khanna, Rnk. Mem. | Moulton | Keating | Kim | Slotkin | Golden | Ryan | Deluzio

Intelligence and Special Operations
Rep: Bergman, Chair | Scott | Stefanik | Kelly | Jackson | Mace | Luttrell | Mills
Dem: Gallego, Rnk. Mem. | Keating | Slotkin | Jacobs | Jackson | McClellan | Panetta

Military Personnel
Rep: Banks, Chair | Stefanik | Gaetz | Bergman | Waltz | Finstad | Moylan | Alford | Mills
Dem: Kim, Rnk. Mem. | Houlahan | Escobar | Strickland | Tokuda | Davis | Sewell | Horsford

Readiness
Rep: Waltz, Chair | Wilson | Scott | Gimenez | Finstad | Strong | Kiggans | Moylan | Vacancy
Dem: Garamendi, Rnk. Mem. | Sherrill | Escobar | Strickland | Vasquez | Tokuda | Davis | Veasey

Seapower and Projection Forces
Rep: Kelly, Chair | Wittman | DesJarlais | Gallagher | Bergman | Jackson | Mace | Kiggans | Alford | Vacancy
Dem: Courtney, Rnk. Mem. | Garamendi | Norcross | Golden | Jacobs | Deluzio | McClellan | Panetta

House Standing Committees

SUBCOMMITTEES (Armed Services)

Strategic Forces
Rep: Lamborn, Chair | Wilson | Turner | Stefanik | DesJarlais | Bacon | Banks | Waltz | Strong
Dem: Moulton, Rnk. Mem. | Garamendi | Norcross | Carbajal | Khanna | Houlahan | Vasquez | Veasey

Tactical Air and Land Forces
Rep: Wittman, Chair | Turner | Lamborn | Graves | Bacon | McClain | Fallon | Gimenez | LaLota | McCormick
Dem: Norcross, Rnk. Mem. | Courtney | Gallego | Carbajal | Sherrill | Ryan | Jackson | Horsford

BUDGET
204 CHOB | 202-226-7270 | budget.house.gov

REPUBLICANS (21)
Jodey Arrington, TX, Chair | Ralph Norman, SC | Tom McClintock, CA | Glenn Grothman, WI | Lloyd Smucker, PA | Michael C. Burgess, TX | Earl L. Carter, GA | Ben Cline, VA | Bob Good, VA | Jack Bergman, MI | Drew Ferguson, GA | Chip Roy, TX | Blake Moore, UT | David G. Valadao, CA | Ron Estes, KS | Lisa McClain, MI | Michelle Fischbach, MN | Rudy Yakym, IN | Josh Brecheen, OK | Vacancy | Vacancy

DEMOCRATS (16)
Brendan F. Boyle, PA, Rnk. Mem. | Jan Schakowsky, IL | Earl Blumenauer, OR | Dan Kildee, MI | Scott Peters, CA | Barbara Lee, CA | Lloyd Doggett, TX | Jimmy Panetta, CA | Jennifer Wexton, VA | Sheila Jackson Lee, TX | Ilhan Omar, MN | David Trone, MD | Becca Balint, VT | Bobby Scott, VA | Adriano Espaillat, NY | Vacancy

Rep. Staff Dir.: Gary Andres | Dem. Staff Dir.: Greg Waring

NO SUBCOMMITTEES

EDUCATION AND THE WORKFORCE
2176 RHOB | 202-225-4527 | edworkforce.house.gov

REPUBLICANS (25)
Virginia Foxx, NC, Chair | Joe Wilson, SC | Glenn Thompson, PA | Tim Walberg, MI | Glenn Grothman, WI | Elise Stefanik, NY | Rick W. Allen, GA | Jim Banks, IN | James Comer, KY | Lloyd Smucker, PA | Burgess Owens, UT | Bob Good, VA | Lisa McClain, MI | Mary Miller, IL | Michelle Steel, CA | Ron Estes, KS | Julia Letlow, LA | Kevin Kiley, CA | Aaron Bean, FL | Eric Burlison, MO | Nathaniel Moran, TX | John James, MI | Lori Chavez-DeRemer, OR | Brandon Williams, NY | Erin Houchin, IN

DEMOCRATS (20)
Bobby Scott, VA, Rnk. Mem. | Raúl M. Grijalva, AZ | Joe Courtney, CT | Gregorio Kilili Camacho Sablan, MP | Frederica S. Wilson, FL | Suzanne Bonamici, OR | Mark Takano, CA | Alma S. Adams, NC | Mark DeSaulnier, CA | Donald Norcross, NJ | Pramila Jayapal, WA | Susan Wild, PA | Lucy McBath, GA | Jahana Hayes, CT | Ilhan Omar, MN | Haley Stevens, MI | Teresa Leger Fernandez, NM | Kathy Manning, NC | Frank J. Mrvan, IN | Jamaal Bowman, NY

Rep. Staff Dir.: Cyrus Artz | Dem. Staff Dir.: Veronique Pluviose

SUBCOMMITTEES
The chair and ranking member are ex officio members of subcommittees on which they do not serve as regular members.

Early Childhood, Elementary, and Secondary Education
Rep: Bean, Chair | Thompson | Owens | McClain | Miller | Steel | Kiley | Moran | Williams | Foxx
Dem: Bonamici, Rnk. Mem. | Grijalva | Sablan | Hayes | Bowman | Wilson | DeSaulnier | Norcross

House Standing Committees

SUBCOMMITTEES (Education)

Health, Employment, Labor, and Pensions
Rep: Good, Chair | Wilson | Walberg | Allen | Banks | Comer | Smucker | Steel | Bean | Burlison | Chavez-DeRemer | Houchin
Dem: DeSaulnier, Rnk. Mem. | Courtney | Norcross | Wild | Mrvan | Jayapal | McBath | Hayes | Omar | Manning

Higher Education and Workforce Development
Rep: Owens, Chair | Thompson | Grothman | Stefanik | Banks | Smucker | Good | Moran | James | Chavez-DeRemer | Williams | Houchin | Foxx
Dem: Wilson, Rnk. Mem. | Takano | Jayapal | Leger Fernandez | Manning | McBath | Grijalva | Courtney | Sablan | Bonamici | Adams

Workforce Protections
Rep: Kiley, Chair | Grothman | Stefanik | Comer | Miller | Burlison
Dem: Adams, Rnk. Mem. | Omar | Stevens | Takano

ENERGY AND COMMERCE
2125 RHOB | 202-225-3641 | energycommerce.house.gov

REPUBLICANS (29)
Cathy McMorris Rodgers, WA, Chair | Michael C. Burgess, TX | Bob Latta, OH | Brett Guthrie, KY | Morgan Griffith, VA | Gus M. Bilirakis, FL | Larry Bucshon, IN | Richard Hudson, NC | Tim Walberg, MI | Earl L. Carter, GA | Jeff Duncan, SC | Gary Palmer, AL | Neal Dunn, FL | John Curtis, UT | Debbie Lesko, AZ | Greg Pence, IN | Dan Crenshaw, TX | John Joyce, PA | Kelly Armstrong, ND | Randy Weber, TX | Rick W. Allen, GA | Troy Balderson, OH | Russ Fulcher, ID | August Pfluger, TX | Diana Harshbarger, TN | Mariannette Miller-Meeks, IA | Kat Cammack, FL | Jay Obernolte, CA | Vacancy

DEMOCRATS (23)
Frank Pallone, NJ, Rnk. Mem. | Anna G. Eshoo, CA | Diana DeGette, CO | Jan Schakowsky, IL | Doris Matsui, CA | Kathy Castor, FL | John Sarbanes, MD | Paul Tonko, NY | Yvette Clarke, NY | Tony Cárdenas, CA | Raul Ruiz, CA | Scott Peters, CA | Debbie Dingell, MI | Marc Veasey, TX | Annie Kuster, NH | Robin Kelly, IL | Nanette Diaz Barragán, CA | Lisa Blunt Rochester, DE | Darren Soto, FL | Angie Craig, MN | Kim Schrier, WA | Lori Trahan, MA | Lizzie Fletcher, TX

Rep. Staff Dir.: Nate Hodson | Dem. Staff Dir.: Tiffany Guarascio

SUBCOMMITTEES
The chair and ranking member are ex officio members of all subcommittees.

Communications & Technology
Rep: Latta, Chair | Bilirakis | Walberg | Carter | Dunn | Curtis | Joyce | Weber | Allen | Balderson | Fulcher | Pfluger | Harshbarger | Cammack | Obernolte
Dem: Matsui, Rnk. Mem. | Clarke | Veasey | Soto | Eshoo | Cárdenas | Craig | Fletcher | Dingell | Kuster | Kelly

Energy, Climate, & Grid Security
Rep: Duncan, Chair | Burgess | Latta | Guthrie | Griffith | Bucshon | Walberg | Palmer | Curtis | Lesko | Pence | Armstrong | Weber | Balderson | Pfluger | Vacancy
Dem: DeGette, Rnk. Mem. | Peters | Fletcher | Matsui | Tonko | Veasey | Kuster | Schrier | Castor | Sarbanes | Cárdenas | Blunt Rochester

Environment, Manufacturing, & Critical Materials
Rep: Carter | Palmer | Crenshaw | Joyce | Weber | Allen | Balderson | Fulcher | Pfluger | Miller-Meeks | Obernolte | Vacancy
Dem: Tonko, Rnk. Mem. | DeGette | Schakowsky | Sarbanes | Clarke | Ruiz | Peters | Barragán

House Standing Committees

SUBCOMMITTEES (Energy)

Health
Rep: Guthrie, Chair | Burgess | Latta | Griffith | Bilirakis | Bucshon | Hudson | Carter | Dunn | Pence | Crenshaw | Joyce | Harshbarger | Miller-Meeks | Obernolte | Vacancy
Dem: Eshoo, Rnk. Mem. | Sarbanes | Cárdenas | Ruiz | Dingell | Kuster | Kelly | Barragán | Blunt Rochester | Craig | Schrier | Trahan

Innovation, Data, and Commerce
Rep: Bilirakis, Chair | Bucshon | Walberg | Duncan | Dunn | Lesko | Pence | Armstrong | Allen | Fulcher | Harshbarger | Cammack
Dem: Schakowsky, Rnk. Mem. | Castor | Dingell | Kelly | Blunt Rochester | Soto | Trahan | Clarke

Oversight & Investigations
Rep: Griffith, Chair | Burgess | Guthrie | Duncan | Palmer | Lesko | Crenshaw | Armstrong | Cammack
Dem: Castor, Rnk. Mem. | DeGette | Schakowsky | Tonko | Ruiz | Peters

ETHICS
1015 LHOB | 202-225-7103 | Fax: 225-7392 | ethics.house.gov

REPUBLICANS (5)
Michael Guest, MS, Chair | Dave Joyce, OH | John Rutherford, FL | Andrew Garbarino, NY | Michelle Fischbach, MN

DEMOCRATS (5)
Susan Wild, PA, Rnk. Mem. | Veronica Escobar, TX | Mark DeSaulnier, CA | Deborah Ross, NC | Glenn Ivey, MD

Staff Dir.: Tom Rust

NO SUBCOMMITTEES

FINANCIAL SERVICES
2129 RHOB | 202-225-7502 | financialservices.house.gov

REPUBLICANS (29)
Patrick McHenry, NC, Chair | Frank Lucas, OK | Pete Sessions, TX | Bill Posey, FL | Blaine Luetkemeyer, MO | Bill Huizenga, MI | Ann Wagner, MO | Andy Barr, KY | Roger Williams, TX | French Hill, AR | Tom Emmer, MN | Barry Loudermilk, GA | Alex X. Mooney, WV | Warren Davidson, OH | John Rose, TN | Bryan Steil, WI | William Timmons, SC | Ralph Norman, SC | Dan Meuser, PA | Young Kim, CA | Byron Donalds, FL | Andrew Garbarino, NY | Scott Fitzgerald, WI | Mike Flood, NE | Mike Lawler, NY | Monica De La Cruz, TX | Andy Ogles, TN | Erin Houchin, IN | Zach Nunn, IA

DEMOCRATS (23)
Maxine Waters, CA, Rnk. Mem. | Nydia M. Velázquez, NY | Brad Sherman, CA | Gregory W. Meeks, NY | David Scott, GA | Stephen F. Lynch, MA | Al Green, TX | Emanuel Cleaver, MO | Jim Himes, CT | Bill Foster, IL | Joyce Beatty, OH | Juan Vargas, CA | Josh Gottheimer, NJ | Vicente Gonzalez, TX | Sean Casten, IL | Ayanna Pressley, MA | Steven Horsford, NV | Rashida Tlaib, MI | Ritchie Torres, NY | Sylvia Garcia, TX | Nikema Williams, GA | Wiley Nickel, NC | Brittany Pettersen, CO

Rep. Staff Dir.: Matt Hoffmann | Dem. Staff Dir.: Charla Ouertatani

House Standing Committees

SUBCOMMITTEES (Financial Services)
The chair and ranking member are ex officio members of all subcommittees.

Capital Markets
Rep: Wagner, Chair | Lucas | Sessions | Huizenga | Hill | Emmer | Mooney | Steil | Meuser | Garbarino | Lawler | Nunn | Houchin
Dem: Sherman, Rnk. Mem. | Meeks | Scott | Vargas | Gottheimer | Gonzalez | Casten | Nickel | Lynch | Cleaver

Digital Assets, Financial Technology and Inclusion
Rep: Hill, Chair | Lucas | Emmer | Davidson | Rose | Steil | Timmons | Donalds | Flood | Houchin
Dem: Lynch, Rnk. Mem. | Foster | Gottheimer | Torres | Sherman | Green | Casten | Nickel

Financial Institutions and Monetary Policy
Rep: Barr, Chair | Posey | Luetkemeyer | Williams | Loudermilk | Rose | Timmons | Norman | Fitzgerald | Kim | Donalds | De La Cruz | Ogles
Dem: Foster, Rnk. Mem. | Velázquez | Sherman | Meeks | Scott | Green | Beatty | Vargas | Casten | Pressley

Housing and Insurance
Rep: Davidson, Chair | Posey | Luetkemeyer | Norman | Fitzgerald | Garbarino | Flood | Lawler | De La Cruz | Houchin
Dem: Cleaver, Rnk. Mem. | Velázquez | Tlaib | Torres | Pressley | Garcia | Williams | Horsford | Pettersen

National Security, Illicit Finance, and International Financial Institutions
Rep: Luetkemeyer, Chair | Barr | Williams | Loudermilk | Meuser | Kim | Nunn | De La Cruz | Ogles
Dem: Beatty, Rnk. Mem. | Gonzalez | Nickel | Pettersen | Foster | Vargas | Gottheimer

Oversight and Investigations
Rep: Huizenga, Chair | Sessions | Wagner | Mooney | Rose | Meuser | Ogles
Dem: Green | Horsford | Tlaib | Garcia | Williams

FOREIGN AFFAIRS
2170 RHOB | 202-226-8467 | foreignaffairs.house.gov

REPUBLICANS (27)
Michael McCaul, TX, Chair | Chris Smith, NJ | Joe Wilson, SC | Scott Perry, PA | Darrell Issa, CA | Ann Wagner, MO | Brian Mast, FL | Ken Buck, CO | Tim Burchett, TN | Mark Green, TN | Andy Barr, KY | Ronny Jackson, TX | Young Kim, CA | María Elvira Salazar, FL | Bill Huizenga, MI | Aumua Amata Coleman Radewagen, AS | French Hill, AR | Warren Davidson, OH | Jim Baird, IN | Mike Waltz, FL | Tom Kean, NJ | Mike Lawler, NY | Cory Mills, FL | Rich McCormick, GA | Nathaniel Moran, TX | John James, MI | Keith Self, TX

DEMOCRATS (24)
Gregory W. Meeks, NY, Rnk. Mem. | Brad Sherman, CA | Gerry Connolly, VA | William R. Keating, MA | Ami Bera, CA | Joaquin Castro, TX | Dina Titus, NV | Ted W. Lieu, CA | Susan Wild, PA | Dean Phillips, MN | Colin Allred, TX | Andy Kim, NJ | Sara Jacobs, CA | Kathy Manning, NC | Sheila Cherfilus-McCormick, FL | Greg Stanton, AZ | Madeleine Dean, PA | Jared Moskowitz, FL | Jonathan L. Jackson, IL | Sydney Kamlager-Dove, CA | Jim Costa, CA | Jason Crow, CO | Gabe Amo, RI | Brad Schneider, IL

Rep. Staff Dir.: Brendan Shields | Dem. Staff Dir.: Sophia Lafargue

SUBCOMMITTEES
The chair and ranking member are ex officio members of all subcommittees.

Africa
Rep: James, Chair | Smith | Kim | Baird | Kean | Mills
Dem: Jacobs, Rnk. Mem. | Cherfilus-McCormick | Allred | Jackson

House Standing Committees

SUBCOMMITTEES (Foreign Affairs)

Europe
Rep: Kean, Chair | Wilson | Issa | Wagner | Huizenga | Lawler | Moran | Self
Dem: Keating, Rnk. Mem. | Titus | Dean | Costa | Wild | Amo

Global Health, Global Human Rights and International Organizations
Rep: Smith, Chair | Salazar | Radewagen | Hill | McCormick | James
Dem: Wild, Rnk. Mem. | Bera | Jacobs | Manning

Indo-Pacific
Rep: Kim, Chair | Wagner | Buck | Green | Barr | Radewagen | Davidson | Waltz
Dem: Bera, Rnk. Mem. | Kim | Sherman | Connolly | Keating | Castro

Middle East, North Africa, and Central Asia
Rep: Wilson, Chair | Mast | Burchett | Jackson | Baird | Lawler | McCormick
Dem: Phillips, Rnk. Mem. | Sherman | Connolly | Manning | Amo

Oversight & Accountability
Rep: Mast, Chair | Perry | Issa | Burchett | Hill | Waltz | Mills | Moran
Dem: Crow, Rnk. Mem. | Titus | Allred | Kim | Cherfilus-McCormick | Dean

Western Hemisphere
Rep: Salazar, Chair | Green | Huizenga | Davidson | Self | James
Dem: Castro, Rnk. Mem. | Stanton | Moskowitz | Kamlager-Dove

HOMELAND SECURITY
176 FHOB | 202-226-8417 | homeland.house.gov

REPUBLICANS (18)
Mark Green, TN, Chair | Michael McCaul, TX | Clay Higgins, LA | Michael Guest, MS | Dan Bishop, NC | Carlos A. Gimenez, FL | August Pfluger, TX | Andrew Garbarino, NY | Marjorie Taylor Greene, GA | Tony Gonzales, TX | Nick LaLota, NY | Mike Ezell, MS | Anthony D'Esposito, NY | Laurel Lee, FL | Morgan Luttrell, TX | Dale W. Strong, AL | Josh Brecheen, OK | Eli Crane, AZ

DEMOCRATS (15)
Bennie G. Thompson, MS, Rnk. Mem. | Sheila Jackson Lee, TX | Donald M. Payne, NJ | Eric Swalwell, CA | Lou Correa, CA | Troy A. Carter, LA | Shri Thanedar, MI | Seth Magaziner, RI | Glenn Ivey, MD | Dan Goldman, NY | Robert Garcia, CA | Delia C. Ramirez, IL | Rob Menendez, NJ | Yvette Clarke, NY | Dina Titus, NV

Rep. Staff Dir.: Stephen Siao | Dem. Staff Dir.: Hope Goins

SUBCOMMITTEES
The chair and ranking member are ex officio members of all subcommittees.

Border Security and Enforcement
Rep: Higgins, Chair | Guest | Greene | Gonzales | Luttrell | Brecheen
Dem: Correa, Rnk. Mem. | Jackson Lee | Thanedar | Garcia | Ramirez

Counterterrorism, Law Enforcement, and Intelligence
Rep: Pfluger, Chair | Bishop | Gonzales | D'Esposito | Crane
Dem: Magaziner, Rnk. Mem. | Correa | Goldman | Titus

Cybersecurity and Infrastructure Protection
Rep: Garbarino, Chair | Gimenez | Ezell | Lee | Luttrell
Dem: Swalwell, Rnk. Mem. | Jackson Lee | Carter | Menendez

Emergency Management and Technology
Rep: D'Esposito, Chair | LaLota | Strong | Brecheen
Dem: Carter, Rnk. Mem. | Payne | Goldman

House Standing Committees

SUBCOMMITTEES (Homeland Security)

Oversight, Investigations, and Accountability
Rep: Bishop, Chair | Greene | Ezell | Strong | Crane
Dem: Ivey, Rnk. Mem. | Thanedar | Ramirez | Clarke

Transportation and Maritime Security
Rep: Gimenez, Chair | Higgins | LaLota | Lee
Dem: Thanedar, Rnk. Mem. | Payne | Garcia

HOUSE ADMINISTRATION
1309 LHOB | 202-225-8281 | cha.house.gov

REPUBLICANS (8)
Bryan Steil, WI, Chair | Barry Loudermilk, GA | Morgan Griffith, VA | Greg Murphy, NC | Stephanie Bice, OK | Mike Carey, OH | Laurel Lee, FL | Anthony D'Esposito, NY

DEMOCRATS (4)
Joe Morelle, NY, Rnk. Mem. | Terri Sewell, AL | Derek Kilmer, WA | Norma J. Torres, CA

Rep. Staff Dir.: Mike Platt | Dem. Staff Dir.: Jamie Fleet

SUBCOMMITTEES
The chair and ranking member are ex officio members of subcommittees on which they do not serve as regular members.

Elections
Rep: Lee, Chair | Loudermilk | Bice | D'Esposito
Dem: Sewell, Rnk. Mem. | Torres

Modernization
Rep: Bice, Chair | Carey
Dem: Kilmer, Rnk. Mem. | Morelle

Oversight
Rep: Loudermilk, Chair | Griffith | Murphy | D'Esposito
Dem: Torres, Rnk. Mem. | Kilmer

JUDICIARY
2138 RHOB | 202-225-6906 | judiciary.house.gov

REPUBLICANS (25)
Jim Jordan, OH, Chair | Darrell Issa, CA | Ken Buck, CO | Matt Gaetz, FL | Andy Biggs, AZ | Tom McClintock, CA | Tom Tiffany, WI | Thomas Massie, KY | Chip Roy, TX | Dan Bishop, NC | Victoria Spartz, IN | Scott Fitzgerald, WI | Cliff Bentz, OR | Ben Cline, VA | Lance Gooden, TX | Jeff Van Drew, NJ | Troy Nehls, TX | Barry Moore, AL | Kevin Kiley, CA | Harriet Hageman, WY | Nathaniel Moran, TX | Laurel Lee, FL | Wesley Hunt, TX | Russell Fry, SC | Kelly Armstrong, ND

DEMOCRATS (19)
Jerrold Nadler, NY, Rnk. Mem. | Zoe Lofgren, CA | Sheila Jackson Lee, TX | Steve Cohen, TN | Henry C. Johnson, GA | Adam Schiff, CA | Eric Swalwell, CA | Ted W. Lieu, CA | Pramila Jayapal, WA | Lou Correa, CA | Mary Gay Scanlon, PA | Joe Neguse, CO | Lucy McBath, GA | Madeleine Dean, PA | Veronica Escobar, TX | Deborah Ross, NC | Cori Bush, MO | Glenn Ivey, MD | Becca Balint, VT

Rep. Staff Dir.: Chris Hixon | Dem. Staff Dir.: Aaron Hiller

House Standing Committees

SUBCOMMITTEES (Judiciary)
The chair and ranking member are ex officio members of subcommittees on which they do not serve as regular members.

Administrative State, Regulatory Reform, and Antitrust
Rep: Massie, Chair | Issa | Buck | Gaetz | Bishop | Spartz | Fitzgerald | Bentz | Cline | Gooden | Van Drew | Hageman | Moran | Vacancy
Dem: Correa, Rnk. Mem. | Johnson | Swalwell | Lieu | Jayapal | Scanlon | Neguse | McBath | Lofgren | Cohen | Ivey | Balint

Constitution and Limited Government
Rep: McClintock | Roy | Bishop | Kiley | Hageman | Hunt | Fry | Vacancy
Dem: Scanlon, Rnk. Mem. | Cohen | Escobar | Bush | Jackson Lee | Balint

Courts, Intellectual Property, and the Internet
Rep: Issa, Chair | Massie | Fitzgerald | Bentz | Cline | Gooden | Kiley | Moran | Lee | Fry
Dem: Johnson, Rnk. Mem. | Lieu | Neguse | Ross | Schiff | Lofgren | Dean | Ivey

Crime and Federal Government Surveillance
Rep: Biggs, Chair | Gaetz | Tiffany | Nehls | Moore | Kiley | Lee | Fry
Dem: Jackson Lee, Rnk. Mem. | McBath | Dean | Bush | Cohen | Johnson

Immigration Integrity, Security, and Enforcement
Rep: McClintock, Chair | Buck | Biggs | Tiffany | Roy | Spartz | Van Drew | Nehls | Moore | Hunt
Dem: Jayapal, Rnk. Mem. | Lofgren | Correa | Escobar | Jackson Lee | Ross | Swalwell | Vacancy

Responsiveness and Accountability To Oversight
Rep: Cline, Chair | Van Drew | Moran | Lee
Dem: Swalwell, Rnk. Mem. | Ivey

Select Subcommittee on the Weaponization of the Federal Government
Rep: Jordan, Chair | Issa | Massie | Elise Stefanik | Gaetz | Greg Steube | Bishop | Kat Cammack | Hageman | Warren Davidson | Fry
Dem: Stacey Plaskett, Rnk. Mem. | Stephen F. Lynch | Linda T. Sánchez | Debbie Wasserman Schultz | Gerry Connolly | John Garamendi | Collin Allred | Sylvia Garcia | Dan Goldman

NATURAL RESOURCES
1324 LHOB | 202-225-2761 | Fax: 225-0534 | naturalresources.house.gov

REPUBLICANS (25)
Bruce Westerman, AR, Chair | Doug Lamborn, CO | Rob Wittman, VA | Tom McClintock, CA | Paul A. Gosar, AZ | Garret Graves, LA | Aumua Amata Coleman Radewagen, AS | Doug LaMalfa, CA | Daniel Webster, FL | Jenniffer González-Colón, PR | Russ Fulcher, ID | Pete Stauber, MN | John Curtis, UT | Tom Tiffany, WI | Jerry Carl, AL | Matt Rosendale, MT | Lauren Boebert, CO | Cliff Bentz, OR | Jen Kiggans, VA | James Moylan, GU | Wesley Hunt, TX | Mike Collins, GA | Anna Paulina Luna, FL | John Duarte, CA | Harriet Hageman, WY

DEMOCRATS (20)
Raúl M. Grijalva, AZ, Rnk. Mem. | Grace F. Napolitano, CA | Gregorio Kilili Camacho Sablan, MP | Jared Huffman, CA | Ruben Gallego, AZ | Joe Neguse, CO | Mike Levin, CA | Katie Porter, CA | Teresa Leger Fernandez, NM | Melanie Stansbury, NM | Mary Sattler Peltola, AK | Alexandria Ocasio-Cortez, NY | Kevin Mullin, CA | Val Hoyle, OR | Sydney Kamlager-Dove, CA | Seth Magaziner, RI | Nydia M. Velázquez, NY | Ed Case, HI | Debbie Dingell, MI | Susie Lee, NV

Rep. Staff Dir.: Vivian Moeglein | Dem. Staff Dir.: Lora Snyder

House Standing Committees

SUBCOMMITTEES (Natural Resources)
The chair and ranking member are ex officio members of subcommittees on which they do not serve as regular members.

Energy and Mineral Resources
Rep: Stauber, Chair | Lamborn | Wittman | Gosar | Graves | Webster | Fulcher | Curtis | Tiffany | Rosendale | Boebert | Hunt | Collins | Duarte
Dem: Ocasio-Cortez, Rnk. Mem. | Huffman | Mullin | Kamlager-Dove | Magaziner | Velázquez | Dingell | Grijalva | Napolitano | Lee | Vacancy | Vacancy

Federal Lands
Rep: Tiffany, Chair | Lamborn | McClintock | Fulcher | Stauber | Curtis | Bentz | Kiggans | Moylan
Dem: Neguse, Rnk. Mem. | Porter | Kamlager-Dove | Sablan | Levin | Leger Fernandez | Peltola

Indian and Insular Affairs
Rep: Hageman, Chair | Radewagen | LaMalfa | González-Colón | Carl | Moylan
Dem: Leger Fernandez, Rnk. Mem. | Sablan | Gallego | Velázquez | Case

Oversight and Investigations
Rep: Gosar, Chair | Rosendale | Hunt | Collins | Luna
Dem: Stansbury | Case | Gallego | Lee

Water, Wildlife and Fisheries
Rep: Bentz, Chair | Wittman | McClintock | Graves | Radewagen | LaMalfa | Webster | González-Colón | Carl | Boebert | Kiggans | Luna | Duarte | Hageman
Dem: Huffman, Rnk. Mem. | Napolitano | Levin | Peltola | Mullin | Hoyle | Magaziner | Dingell | Gallego | Neguse | Porter | Case

OVERSIGHT AND ACCOUNTABILITY
2157 RHOB | 202-225-5074 | Fax: 225-3974 | oversight.house.gov

REPUBLICANS (26)
James Comer, KY, Chair | Jim Jordan, OH | Mike Turner, OH | Paul A. Gosar, AZ | Virginia Foxx, NC | Glenn Grothman, WI | Michael Cloud, TX | Gary Palmer, AL | Clay Higgins, LA | Pete Sessions, TX | Andy Biggs, AZ | Nancy Mace, SC | Jake LaTurner, KS | Pat Fallon, TX | Byron Donalds, FL | Scott Perry, PA | William Timmons, SC | Tim Burchett, TN | Marjorie Taylor Greene, GA | Lisa McClain, MI | Lauren Boebert, CO | Russell Fry, SC | Anna Paulina Luna, FL | Nick Langworthy, NY | Eric Burlison, MO | Mike Waltz, FL

DEMOCRATS (21)
Jamie Raskin, MD, Rnk. Mem. | Eleanor Holmes Norton, DC | Stephen F. Lynch, MA | Gerry Connolly, VA | Raja Krishnamoorthi, IL | Ro Khanna, CA | Kweisi Mfume, MD | Alexandria Ocasio-Cortez, NY | Katie Porter, CA | Cori Bush, MO | Jimmy Gomez, CA | Shontel Brown, OH | Melanie Stansbury, NM | Robert Garcia, CA | Maxwell Alejandro Frost, FL | Summer Lee, PA | Greg Casar, TX | Jasmine Crockett, TX | Dan Goldman, NY | Jared Moskowitz, FL | Rashida Tlaib, MI

Rep. Staff Dir.: Mark Marin | Dem. Staff Dir.: Julie Tagen

SUBCOMMITTEES
The chair and ranking member are ex officio members of all subcommittees.

Cybersecurity, Information Technology, and Government Innovation
Rep: Mace, Chair | Timmons | Burchett | Greene | Luna | Langworthy | Burlison | Vacancy | Vacancy
Dem: Connolly, Rnk. Mem. | Khanna | Lynch | Mfume | Gomez | Moskowitz | Vacancy

Economic Growth, Energy Policy, and Regulatory Affairs
Rep: Fallon, Chair | Donalds | Perry | McClain | Boebert | Fry | Luna | Langworthy | Vacancy
Dem: Bush, Rnk. Mem. | Brown | Stansbury | Norton | Krishnamoorthi | Khanna | Vacancy

Government Operations and the Federal Workforce
Rep: Sessions, Chair | Palmer | Higgins | Biggs | Donalds | Timmons | Burchett | Greene | Boebert | Fry | Burlison | Vacancy
Dem: Mfume, Rnk. Mem. | Norton | Frost | Casar | Connolly | Stansbury | Garcia | Lee | Crockett | Tlaib

House Standing Committees

SUBCOMMITTEES (Oversight)

Health Care and Financial Services
Rep: McClain, Chair | Gosar | Foxx | Grothman | Fry | Luna | Langworthy | Burlison | Vacancy
Dem: Porter, Rnk. Mem. | Ocasio-Cortez | Gomez | Casar | Lee | Crockett | Vacancy

National Security, the Border, and Foreign Affairs
Rep: Grothman, Chair | Gosar | Foxx | Higgins | Sessions | Biggs | Mace | LaTurner | Fallon | Perry | Vacancy
Dem: Garcia, Rnk. Mem. | Lynch | Goldman | Moskowitz | Porter | Bush | Frost | Vacancy | Vacancy

Select Subcommittee on the Coronavirus Pandemic
Rep: Wenstrup, Chair | Malliotakis | Miller-Meeks | Lesko | Cloud | Joyce | Greene | Jackson | McCormick
Dem: Ruiz, Rnk. Mem. | Dingell | Mfume | Ross | Garcia | Bera | Tokuda

RULES

H312 Capitol | 202-225-9191 | Fax: 226-1508 | rules.house.gov

REPUBLICANS (9)
Tom Cole, OK, Chair | Michael C. Burgess, TX | Guy Reschenthaler, PA | Michelle Fischbach, MN | Thomas Massie, KY | Ralph Norman, SC | Chip Roy, TX | Erin Houchin, IN | Nick Langworthy, NY

DEMOCRATS (4)
Jim McGovern, MA, Rnk. Mem. | Mary Gay Scanlon, PA | Joe Neguse, CO | Teresa Leger Fernandez, NM

Rep. Staff Dir.: Kelly Dixon Chambers | Dem. Staff Dir.: Don Sisson

SUBCOMMITTEES

Legislative and Budget Process
Rep: Fischbach, Chair | Cole | Norman | Roy | Langworthy
Dem: Leger Fernandez, Rnk. Mem. | Neguse

Rules and Organization of the House
Rep: Burgess, Chair | Cole | Reschenthaler | Massie | Houchin
Dem: Scanlon, Rnk. Mem. | McGovern

SCIENCE, SPACE, AND TECHNOLOGY

2321 RHOB | 202-225-6371 | Fax: 226-0113 | science.house.gov

REPUBLICANS (22)
Frank Lucas, OK, Chair | Bill Posey, FL | Randy Weber, TX | Brian Babin, TX | Jim Baird, IN | Daniel Webster, FL | Mike Garcia, CA | Stephanie Bice, OK | Jay Obernolte, CA | Chuck Fleischmann, TN | Darrell Issa, CA | Rick Crawford, AR | Claudia Tenney, NY | Ryan Zinke, MT | Scott Franklin, FL | Dale W. Strong, AL | Max Miller, OH | Rich McCormick, GA | Mike Collins, GA | Brandon Williams, NY | Tom Kean, NJ | Vacancy

DEMOCRATS (18)
Zoe Lofgren, CA, Rnk. Mem. | Suzanne Bonamici, OR | Haley Stevens, MI | Jamaal Bowman, NY | Deborah Ross, NC | Eric Sorensen, IL | Andrea Salinas, OR | Valerie Foushee, NC | Kevin Mullin, CA | Jeff Jackson, NC | Emilia Strong Sykes, OH | Maxwell Alejandro Frost, FL | Yadira Caraveo, CO | Summer Lee, PA | Jennifer McClellan, VA | Gabe Amo, RI | Sean Casten, IL | Paul Tonko, NY

Rep. Staff Dir.: Josh Mathis | Dem. Chief of Staff: John Piazza

House Standing Committees

SUBCOMMITTEES (Science)
The chair and ranking member are ex officio members of all subcommittees.

Energy
Rep: Williams, Chair | Weber | Baird | Bice | Fleischmann | Tenney | Miller | Kean
Dem: Bowman, Rnk. Mem. | Lee | Ross | Sorensen | Salinas | Foushee

Environment
Rep: Miller, Chair | Posey | Crawford | Zinke | Collins
Dem: Ross, Rnk. Mem. | Bonamici | Frost

Investigations and Oversight
Rep: Obernolte, Chair | Babin | Miller | McCormick | Vacancy
Dem: Foushee, Rnk. Mem. | Mullin | Jackson

Research and Technology
Rep: Collins, Chair | Baird | Issa | Crawford | Franklin | Williams | Kean
Dem: Stevens, Rnk. Mem. | Salinas | Mullin | Sykes | Bonamici

Space and Aeronautics
Rep: Babin, Chair | Posey | Webster | Garcia | Issa | Strong | McCormick
Dem: Sorensen, Rnk. Mem. | Jackson | Caraveo | Bowman | McClellan

SMALL BUSINESS
2361 RHOB | 202-225-5821 | smallbusiness.house.gov

REPUBLICANS (15)
Roger Williams, TX, Chair | Blaine Luetkemeyer, MO | Pete Stauber, MN | Dan Meuser, PA | Beth Van Duyne, TX | María Elvira Salazar, FL | Tracey Mann, KS | Jake Ellzey, TX | Marc Molinaro, NY | Mark Alford, MO | Eli Crane, AZ | Aaron Bean, FL | Wesley Hunt, TX | Nick LaLota, NY | Celeste Maloy, UT

DEMOCRATS (12)
Nydia M. Velázquez, NY, Rnk. Mem. | Jared Golden, ME | Kweisi Mfume, MD | Dean Phillips, MN | Greg Landsman, OH | Marie Gluesenkamp Perez, WA | Shri Thanedar, MI | Morgan McGarvey, KY | Hillary J. Scholten, MI | Judy Chu, CA | Sharice Davids, KS | Chris Pappas, NH

Rep. Staff Dir.: Ben Johnson | Dem. Staff Dir.: Melissa Jung

SUBCOMMITTEES
The chair and ranking member are ex officio members of all subcommittees.

Contracting and Infrastructure
Rep: LaLota, Chair | Salazar | Ellzey | Molinaro | Bean | Maloy
Dem: Scholten, Rnk. Mem. | Mfume | McGarvey | Chu | Thanedar

Economic Growth, Tax, and Capital Access
Rep: Meuser, Chair | Luetkemeyer | Van Duyne | Alford | LaLota
Dem: Landsman, Rnk. Mem. | Phillips | Chu | Davids | Golden

Innovation, Entrepreneurship, and Workforce Development
Rep: Molinaro, Chair | Mann | Salazar | Ellzey | Crane
Dem: McGarvey, Rnk. Mem. | Thanedar | Pappas | Phillips | Chu

Oversight, Investigations, and Regulations
Rep: Van Duyne, Chair | Alford | Crane | Bean | Hunt
Dem: Mfume, Rnk. Mem. | Perez | Golden | Vacancy | Vacancy

Rural Development, Energy, and Supply Chains
Rep: Hunt, Chair | Luetkemeyer | Stauber | Meuser | Mann | Maloy
Dem: Perez, Rnk. Mem. | Golden | Scholten | Landsman | Vacancy

House Standing Committees

TRANSPORTATION AND INFRASTRUCTURE
2165 RHOB | 202-225-9446 | transportation.house.gov

REPUBLICANS (35)
Sam Graves, MO, Chair | Rick Crawford, AR | Daniel Webster, FL | Thomas Massie, KY | Scott Perry, PA | Brian Babin, TX | Garret Graves, LA | David Rouzer, NC | Mike Bost, IL | Doug LaMalfa, CA | Bruce Westerman, AR | Brian Mast, FL | Jenniffer González-Colón, PR | Pete Stauber, MN | Tim Burchett, TN | Dusty Johnson, SD | Jeff Van Drew, NJ | Troy Nehls, TX | Tracey Mann, KS | Burgess Owens, UT | Rudy Yakym, IN | Lori Chavez-DeRemer, OR | Tom Kean, NJ | Anthony D'Esposito, NY | Eric Burlison, MO | John James, MI | Derrick Van Orden, WI | Brandon Williams, NY | Marc Molinaro, NY | Mike Collins, GA | Mike Ezell, MS | John Duarte, CA | Aaron Bean, FL | Celeste Maloy, UT | Vacancy

DEMOCRATS (30)
Rick Larsen, WA, Rnk. Mem. | Eleanor Holmes Norton, DC | Grace F. Napolitano, CA | Steve Cohen, TN | John Garamendi, CA | Henry C. Johnson, GA | André D. Carson, IN | Dina Titus, NV | Jared Huffman, CA | Julia Brownley, CA | Frederica S. Wilson, FL | Donald M. Payne, NJ | Mark DeSaulnier, CA | Salud Carbajal, CA | Greg Stanton, AZ | Colin Allred, TX | Sharice Davids, KS | Jesús G. García, IL | Chris Pappas, NH | Seth Moulton, MA | Jake Auchincloss, MA | Marilyn Strickland, WA | Troy A. Carter, LA | Pat Ryan, NY | Mary Sattler Peltola, AK | Rob Menendez, NJ | Val Hoyle, OR | Emilia Strong Sykes, OH | Hillary J. Scholten, MI | Valerie Foushee, NC

Rep. Staff Dir.: Jack Ruddy | Dem. Staff Dir.: Katherine Dedrick

SUBCOMMITTEES
The chair and ranking member are ex officio members of all subcommittees.

Aviation
Rep: Garret Graves, Chair | Crawford | Massie | Perry | Westerman | Mast | Stauber | Burchett | Johnson | Van Drew | Mann | Owens | Yakym | Chavez-DeRemer | Kean | D'Esposito | James | Molinaro | Collins | Bean | Vacancy
Dem: Cohen, Rnk. Mem. | Johnson | Carson | Brownley | DeSaulnier | Stanton | Allred | Davids | Garcia | Auchincloss | Peltola | Scholten | Titus | Payne | Carbajal | Menendez | Norton | Wilson

Coast Guard and Maritime Transportation
Rep: Webster, Chair | Babin | Mast | González-Colón | Van Drew | Ezell | Bean
Dem: Carbajal, Rnk. Mem. | Garamendi | Pappas | Auchincloss | Peltola | Scholten

Economic Development, Public Buildings and Emergency Management
Rep: Perry, Chair | Garret Graves | González-Colón | Chavez-DeRemer | D'Esposito | Van Orden | Ezell | Vacancy
Dem: Titus, Rnk. Mem. | Norton | Davids | Carter | Napolitano | Garamendi | Huffman

Highways and Transit
Rep: Crawford, Chair | Webster | Massie | Bost | LaMalfa | Stauber | Burchett | Johnson | Van Drew | Nehls | Mann | Owens | Yakym | Chavez-DeRemer | Kean | D'Esposito | Burlison | Van Orden | Williams | Molinaro | Collins | Duarte | Bean | Vacancy | Vacancy
Dem: Norton, Rnk. Mem. | Huffman | Pappas | Strickland | Ryan | Menendez | Hoyle | Foushee | Napolitano | Cohen | Johnson | Brownley | Stanton | Allred | Garcia | Moulton | Sykes | Garamendi | Titus | Carbajal | Auchincloss | DeSaulnier

Railroads, Pipelines, and Hazardous Materials
Rep: Nehls, Chair | Babin | Rouzer | Bost | LaMalfa | Westerman | Stauber | Burchett | Johnson | Mann | Yakym | Kean | Burlison | Williams | Molinaro | Duarte | Vacancy
Dem: Payne, Rnk. Mem. | Wilson | Moulton | Carter | Carson | DeSaulnier | Strickland | Foushee | Napolitano | Cohen | Johnson | Huffman | Garcia | Menendez

Water Resources and Environment
Rep: Rouzer, Chair | Webster | Massie | Babin | Bost | LaMalfa | Westerman | Mast | González-Colón | Owens | Burlison | James | Van Orden | Williams | Collins | Ezell | Duarte | Vacancy
Dem: Napolitano, Rnk. Mem. | Garamendi | Sykes | Huffman | Wilson | Ryan | Hoyle | Scholten | Brownley | DeSaulnier | Stanton | Pappas | Moulton | Carter | Norton

House Standing Committees

VETERANS' AFFAIRS
364 CHOB | 202-225-3527 | veterans.house.gov

REPUBLICANS (14)
Mike Bost, IL, Chair | Aumua Amata Coleman Radewagen, AS | Jack Bergman, MI | Nancy Mace, SC | Matt Rosendale, MT | Marianette Miller-Meeks, IA | Greg Murphy, NC | Scott Franklin, FL | Derrick Van Orden, WI | Morgan Luttrell, TX | Juan Ciscomani, AZ | Eli Crane, AZ | Keith Self, TX | Jen Kiggans, VA

DEMOCRATS (11)
Mark Takano, CA, Rnk. Mem. | Julia Brownley, CA | Mike Levin, CA | Chris Pappas, NH | Frank J. Mrvan, IN | Sheila Cherfilus-McCormick, FL | Chris Deluzio, PA | Morgan McGarvey, KY | Delia C. Ramirez, IL | Greg Landsman, OH | Nikki Budzinski, IL

Rep. Staff Dir.: Jon Clark | Dem. Staff Dir.: Matt Reel

SUBCOMMITTEES
The chair and ranking member are ex officio members of all subcommittees.

Disability Assistance and Memorial Affairs
Rep: Luttrell, Chair | Franklin | Ciscomani | Crane | Self
Dem: Pappas, Rnk. Mem. | Deluzio | McGarvey | Ramirez

Economic Opportunity
Rep: Van Orden, Chair | Mace | Franklin | Ciscomani | Crane
Dem: Levin, Rnk. Mem. | Mrvan | McGarvey | Ramirez

Health
Rep: Miller-Meeks, Chair | Radewagen | Bergman | Murphy | Van Orden | Luttrell | Kiggans
Dem: Brownley, Rnk. Mem. | Levin | Deluzio | Landsman | Budzinski

Oversight and Investigations
Rep: Kiggans, Chair | Radewagen | Bergman | Rosendale
Dem: Mrvan, Rnk. Mem. | Pappas | Cherfilus-McCormick

Technology Modernization
Rep: Rosendale, Chair | Mace | Self
Dem: Cherfilus-McCormick, Rnk. Mem. | Landsman

WAYS AND MEANS
1139 LHOB | 202-225-3625 | waysandmeans.house.gov

REPUBLICANS (25)
Jason Smith, MO, Chair | Vern Buchanan, FL | Adrian Smith, NE | Mike Kelly, PA | David Schweikert, AZ | Darin LaHood, IL | Brad Wenstrup, OH | Jodey Arrington, TX | Drew Ferguson, GA | Ron Estes, KS | Lloyd Smucker, PA | Kevin Hern, OK | Carol Miller, WV | Greg Murphy, NC | David Kustoff, TN | Brian Fitzpatrick, PA | Greg Steube, FL | Claudia Tenney, NY | Michelle Fischbach, MN | Blake Moore, UT | Michelle Steel, CA | Beth Van Duyne, TX | Randy Feenstra, IA | Nicole Malliotakis, NY | Mike Carey, OH

DEMOCRATS (18)
Richard Neal, MA, Rnk. Mem. | Lloyd Doggett, TX | Mike Thompson, CA | John B. Larson, CT | Earl Blumenauer, OR | Bill Pascrell, NJ | Danny K. Davis, IL | Linda T. Sánchez, CA | Terri Sewell, AL | Suzan DelBene, WA | Judy Chu, CA | Gwen Moore, WI | Dan Kildee, MI | Don Beyer, VA | Dwight Evans, PA | Brad Schneider, IL | Jimmy Panetta, CA | Jimmy Gomez, CA

Rep. Staff Dir.: Mark Roman | Dem. Staff Dir.: Brandon Casey

House Standing Committees

SUBCOMMITTEES (Ways and Means)
The chair and ranking member are ex officio members of all subcommittees.

Health
Rep: Buchanan, Chair | Adrian Smith | Kelly | Wenstrup | Murphy | Hern | Miller | Fitzpatrick | Tenney | Moore | Steel
Dem: Doggett, Rnk. Mem. | Thompson | Blumenauer | Sewell | Chu | Evans | Davis | Beyer

Oversight
Rep: Schweikert, Chair | Fitzpatrick | Steube | Tenney | Fischbach | Van Duyne | Feenstra | Malliotakis
Dem: Pascrell, Rnk. Mem. | Chu | DelBene | Beyer | Gomez

Social Security
Rep: Ferguson, Chair | Carey | Schweikert | Estes | Moore | Feenstra | Steube | Kustoff
Dem: Larson, Rnk. Mem. | Pascrell | Sánchez | Kildee | Moore

Tax
Rep: Kelly, Chair | Schweikert | Arrington | Ferguson | Hern | Estes | Smucker | Kustoff | Van Duyne | Feenstra | Malliotakis
Dem: Thompson, Rnk. Mem. | Doggett | Larson | Sánchez | DelBene | Moore | Schneider | Gomez

Trade
Rep: Adrian Smith, Chair | Buchanan | LaHood | Arrington | Estes | Miller | Smucker | Murphy | Steube | Fischbach | Kustoff
Dem: Blumenauer, Rnk. Mem. | Kildee | Panetta | DelBene | Beyer | Sánchez | Sewell | Schneider

Work and Welfare
Rep: LaHood, Chair | Wenstrup | Carey | Moore | Steel | Smucker | Adrian Smith | Tenney
Dem: Davis, Rnk. Mem. | Chu | Moore | Evans | Gomez

House Select Committees

PERMANENT SELECT COMMITTEE ON INTELLIGENCE
HVC-304 Capitol | 202-225-4121 | Fax: 225-1991 | intelligence.house.gov

REPUBLICANS (14)
Mike Turner, OH, Chair | Brad Wenstrup, OH | Rick Crawford, AR | Elise Stefanik, NY | Trent Kelly, MS | Darin LaHood, IL | Brian Fitzpatrick, PA | Mike Gallagher, WI | Austin Scott, GA | French Hill, AR | Dan Crenshaw, TX | Mike Waltz, FL | Mike Garcia, CA | Vacancy

DEMOCRATS (11)
Jim Himes, CT, Rnk. Mem. | André D. Carson, IN | Joaquin Castro, TX | Raja Krishnamoorthi, IL | Jason Crow, CO | Ami Bera, CA | Stacey E. Plaskett, VI | Josh Gottheimer, NJ | Jimmy Gomez, CA | Chrissy Houlahan, PA | Abigail Spanberger, VA

Rep. Staff Dir.: Adam Howard | Dem. Staff Dir.: Jeff Lowenstein

SUBCOMMITTEES
The chair and ranking member are ex officio members of all subcommittees.

Central Intelligence Agency
Rep: Crawford, Chair | Stefanik | Gallagher | Scott | Crenshaw | Waltz
Dem: Carson, Rnk. Mem. | Castro | Krishnamoorthi | Crow

Defense Intelligence & Overhead Architecture
Rep: Kelly, Chair | Wenstrup | Crawford | Fitzpatrick | Garcia | Vacancy
Dem: Houlahan, Rnk. Mem. | Crow | Plaskett | Spanberger

National Intelligence Enterprise
Rep: Fitzpatrick, Chair | Wenstrup | Kelly | LaHood | Hill | Crenshaw
Dem: Plaskett, Rnk. Mem. | Bera | Gottheimer | Spanberger

National Security Agency & Cyber
Rep: LaHood, Chair | Gallagher | Scott | Hill | Waltz | Garcia
Dem: Gottheimer, Rnk. Mem. | Castro | Bera | Gomez

Oversight & Investigations
Rep: Wenstrup, Chair
Dem: Gomez, Rnk. Mem.

SELECT COMMITTEE ON THE STRATEGIC COMPETITION BETWEEN THE UNITED STATES AND THE CHINESE COMMUNIST PARTY
548 CHOB | 202-226-9678 | selectcommitteeontheccp.house.gov

REPUBLICANS (13)
Mike Gallagher, WI, Chair | Rob Wittman, VA | Blaine Luetkemeyer, MO | Andy Barr, KY | Dan Newhouse, WA | John Moolenaar, MI | Darin LaHood, IL | Neal Dunn, FL | Jim Banks, IN | Dusty Johnson, SD | Michelle Steel, CA | Ashley Hinson, IA | Carlos A. Gimenez, FL

DEMOCRATS (11)
Raja Krishnamoorthi, IL, Rnk. Mem. | Kathy Castor, FL | André D. Carson, IN | Seth Moulton, MA | Ro Khanna, CA | Andy Kim, NJ | Mikie Sherrill, NJ | Haley Stevens, MI | Jake Auchincloss, MA | Ritchie Torres, NY | Shontel Brown, OH

Rep. Staff Dir.: Dave Hanke | Dem. Staff Dir.: Jonathan Stivers

Joint Committees

ECONOMIC

SD-G01 | 202-224-5171 | jec.senate.gov

DEMOCRATS (10)

Senate
Martin Heinrich, NM, Chair | Amy Klobuchar, MN | Maggie Hassan, NH | Mark Kelly, AZ | Peter Welch, VT | John Fetterman, PA

House
Don Beyer, VA | David Trone, MD | Gwen Moore, WI | Katie Porter, CA

REPUBLICANS (10)

Senate
Mike Lee, UT | Tom Cotton, AR | Eric Schmitt, MO | J.D. Vance, OH

House
David Schweikert, AZ, Vice Chair | Jodey Arrington, TX | Ron Estes, KS | Drew Ferguson, GA | Lloyd Smucker, PA | Nicole Malliotakis, NY

Exec. Dir.: Jessica Martinez | Rep. Staff Dir.: Ron Donado

LIBRARY

1309 LHOB | 202-225-8281 | cha.house.gov/joint-committee-on-library

DEMOCRATS (5)

Senate
Amy Klobuchar, MN, Chair | Mark R. Warner, VA | Jon Ossoff, GA

House
Joe Morelle, NY | Terri Sewell, AL

REPUBLICANS (5)

Senate
Deb Fischer, NE | Cindy Hyde-Smith, MS

House
Bryan Steil, WI, Vice Chair | Mark Amodei, NV | Mike Carey, OH

Joint Committees

PRINTING

1309 LHOB | 202-225-8281 | cha.house.gov/joint-committee-on-printing

DEMOCRATS (5)
Senate
Amy Klobuchar, MN, Vice Chair | Jeff Merkley, OR | Alex Padilla, CA

House
Joe Morelle, NY | Derek Kilmer, WA

REPUBLICANS (5)
Senate
Deb Fischer, NE | Bill Hagerty, TN

House
Bryan Steil, WI, Chair | Morgan Griffith, VA | Greg Murphy, NC

TAXATION

502 FHOB | 202-225-3621 | www.jct.gov

DEMOCRATS (5)
Senate
Ron Wyden, OR, Chair | Debbie Stabenow, MI | Maria Cantwell, WA

House
Richard Neal, MA | Lloyd Doggett, TX

REPUBLICANS (5)
Senate
Mike Crapo, ID | Chuck Grassley, IA

House
Jason Smith, MO, Vice Chair | Vern Buchanan, FL | Adrian Smith, NE

Chief of Staff: Thomas A. Barthold

2024 Election Schedule

Dates subject to change | General Election—Tuesday, November 5, 2024

State	Presidential Primary	Presidential Caucus	Senate Election	Congressional Primary	Congressional Runoff (if necessary)
Alabama	3/5			3/5	4/16
Alaska	4/6 (D)	3/5 (R)		8/20	
Arizona	3/19		x	8/6	
Arkansas	3/5			3/5	4/2
California	3/5		x	3/5	
Colorado	3/5			6/25	
Connecticut	4/2		x	8/13	
Delaware	4/2		x	9/10	
Florida	3/19		x	8/20	
Georgia	3/12			5/21	6/18
Hawaii	4/6 (D)	3/12 (R)	x	8/10	
Idaho		3/2 (R) | 5/23 (D)		5/21	
Illinois	3/19			3/19	
Indiana	5/7		x	5/7	
Iowa		1/15 (R) | 3/5 (D)		6/4	
Kansas	3/19			8/6	
Kentucky	5/21			5/21	
Louisiana	3/23			11/5	12/7
Maine	3/5		x	6/11	
Maryland	5/14		x	5/14	
Massachusetts	3/5		x	9/3	
Michigan	2/27		x	8/6	
Minnesota	3/5		x	8/13	
Mississippi	3/12		x	3/12	4/2
Missouri	3/23 (D)	3/2 (R)	x	8/6	
Montana	6/4		x	6/4	
Nebraska	5/14		x	5/14	
Nevada	2/6	2/8 (R)	x	6/11	
New Hampshire	1/23			9/10	
New Jersey	6/4		x	6/4	
New Mexico	6/4		x	6/4	
New York	4/2		x	6/25	
North Carolina	3/5			3/5	5/14
North Dakota	4/6 (D)	3/4 (R)	x	6/11	
Ohio	3/19		x	3/19	
Oklahoma	3/5			6/18	8/27
Oregon	5/21			5/21	
Pennsylvania	4/23		x	4/23	
Rhode Island	4/2		x	9/10	
South Carolina	2/3 (D) | 2/24 (R)			6/11	6/25
South Dakota	6/4			6/4	7/30
Tennessee	3/5		x	8/1	
Texas	3/5		x	3/5	5/28
Utah	3/5 (D)	3/5 (R)	x	6/25	
Vermont	3/5		x	8/13	
Virginia	3/5		x	6/18	
Washington	3/12		x	8/6	
West Virginia	5/14		x	5/14	
Wisconsin	4/2		x	8/13	
Wyoming		4/13 (D) | TBD (R)	x	8/20	
American Samoa		3/5 (D) | TBD (R)		n/a	
DC	6/4			6/4	
Guam		6/8 (D) | TBD (R)		8/3	
Northern Mariana Islands	3/12 (D)	TBD (R)		n/a	
Puerto Rico	3/17 (D) | TBD (R)			6/2	
Virgin Islands		2/8 (R) | TBD (D)		8/3	

State Maps, Stats, and Governors

ALABAMA

(This is the new map that will be used in the November election.)

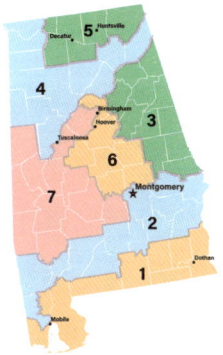

Senators
Tommy Tuberville (R)
Katie Britt (R)

Representatives (6 R/1 D)
1st - Jerry Carl (R)
2nd - Barry Moore (R)
3rd - Mike Rogers (R)
4th - Robert Aderholt (R)
5th - Dale Strong (R)
6th - Gary Palmer (R)
7th - Terri Sewell (D)

www.alabama.gov

Pop. 5,074,296 | **Rank** 24th | **Trend** 1% | **Male %** 48.50% | **Female %** 51.50%
Caucasian 69.80% | **Black/AfrAm** 27.30% | **NatAm/AN** 1.90% | **Asian** 2.20% | **NH/PI** 0.30% | **Other** 4.10% | **Hisp/Lat** 4.90%
Land Area 50,633 sq. mi. | **Water Area** 1,773 sq. mi. | **Area Rank** 28th

Registered Voters 3,466,701 | *No party registration.*

STATE LEGISLATURE | www.legislature.state.al.us
Senate Total 35 (27 R/8 D) | **House Total** 105 (76 R/27 D/2 Vac) | **2024 Session** Feb 6 to May 20

Governor Kay Ivey | Next Election 2026 | 3rd Term | 67% (+38)
State Capitol, 600 Dexter Avenue, Montgomery AL 36130
334-242-7100 | Fax: 334-353-0004 | governor.alabama.gov | X governorkayivey
Bio—Montgomery; Camden, AL, 10/15/1944; BA, Auburn Univ., 1967; teacher, bank officer, public official; AL treasurer, 2003-11; AL lt. governor, 2011-17; AL governor, 2017-present; div.; Baptist

Republican

ALASKA

Senators
Lisa Murkowski (R)
Dan Sullivan (R)

Representative (1 D)
AL - Mary Sattler Peltola (D)

alaska.gov

Pop. 733,583 | **Rank** 48th | **Trend** 0% | **Male %** 52.60% | **Female %** 47.40%
Caucasian 72.60% | **Black/AfrAm** 5.30% | **NatAm/AN** 20.20% | **Asian** 9.10% | **NH/PI** 2.90% | **Other** 5.70% | **Hisp/Lat** 7.70%
Land Area 570,866 sq. mi. | **Water Area** 94,722 sq. mi. | **Area Rank** 1st

Registered Voters 601,850 | **Dem.** 12% | **Rep.** 24% | **Other** 64%

STATE LEGISLATURE | akleg.gov
Senate Total 20 (11 R/9 D) | **House Total** 40 (22 R/13 D/4 UNA/1 Ind) | **2024 Session** Jan 16 to May 15

Governor Mike Dunleavy | Next Election 2026 | 2nd Term | 50% (+26)
State Capitol, P.O. Box 110001, Juneau AK 99811
907-465-3500 | gov.alaska.gov | X govdunleavy
Bio—Wasilla; Scranton, PA, 5/5/1961; MEd, Univ. of AK, Fairbanks, 1992; logger, educator; AK Senate, 2013-18; AK governor, 2018-present; m. Rose; Catholic

Republican

U.S. Congress Directory | 159

State Maps, Stats, and Governors

ARIZONA

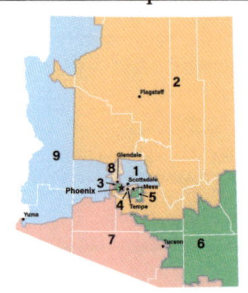

az.gov

Senators
Kyrsten Sinema (I)
Mark Kelly (D)

Representatives (6 R/3 D)
1 - David Schweikert (R)
2 - Eli Crane (R)
3 - Ruben Gallego (D)
4 - Greg Stanton (D)
5 - Andy Biggs (R)
6 - Juan Ciscomani (R)
7 - Raúl M. Grijalva (D)
8 - Debbie Lesko (R)
9 - Paul A. Gosar (R)

Pop. 7,359,197 | Rank 14th | Trend 3% | Male % 50.00% | Female % 50.00%
Caucasian 76.50% | Black/AfrAm 6.40% | NatAm/AN 6.00% | Asian 5.00% | NH/PI 0.50% | Other 25.90% | Hisp/Lat 32.50%
Land Area 113,623 sq. mi. | Water Area 332 sq. mi. | Area Rank 6th

Registered Voters 4,209,527 | Dem. 30% | Rep. 34% | Other 36%

STATE LEGISLATURE | www.azleg.gov
Senate Total 30 (16 R/14 D) | House Total 60 (31 R/29 D) | 2024 Session Jan 8 to Apr 20

Governor Katie Hobbs | Next Election 2026 | 1st Term | 50% (+1)
State Capitol, 1700 West Washington St., Phoenix AZ 85007
602-542-4331 | azgovernor.gov | X governorhobbs
Bio—Phoenix; Phoenix, AZ, 12/28/1969; MSW, AZ St. Univ., 1995; social worker; AZ House; 2011-12; AZ Senate, 2012-19; AZ secretary of state, 2019-23; AZ governor, 2023-present; m. Patrick Goodman

Democrat

ARKANSAS

portal.arkansas.gov

Senators
John Boozman (R)
Tom Cotton (R)

Representatives (4 R)
1 - Rick Crawford (R)
2 - French Hill (R)
3 - Steve Womack (R)
4 - Bruce Westerman (R)

Pop. 3,045,637 | Rank 33rd | Trend 1% | Male % 49.40% | Female % 50.60%
Caucasian 79.30% | Black/AfrAm 16.30% | NatAm/AN 3.00% | Asian 2.20% | NH/PI 0.80% | Other 9.80% | Hisp/Lat 8.40%
Land Area 52,024 sq. mi. | Water Area 1,141 sq. mi. | Area Rank 27th

Registered Voters 1,765,681 | Dem. 5% | Rep. 7% | Other 88%

GENERAL ASSEMBLY | www.arkleg.state.ar.us
Senate Total 35 (29 R/6 D) | House Total 100 (82 R/18 D) | 2024 Session Apr 10 to May 9

Governor Sarah Huckabee Sanders | Next Election 2026 | 1st Term | 63% (+28)
State Capitol, 500 Woodlane Street, Room 250, Little Rock AR 72201
501-682-2345 | governor.arkansas.gov | X sarahhuckabee
Bio—Little Rock; Hope, AR, 8/13/1982; BA, Ouachita Baptist Univ., 2004; press secretary, political advisor; AR governor, 2023-present; m. Bryan; Christian

Republican

State Maps, Stats, and Governors

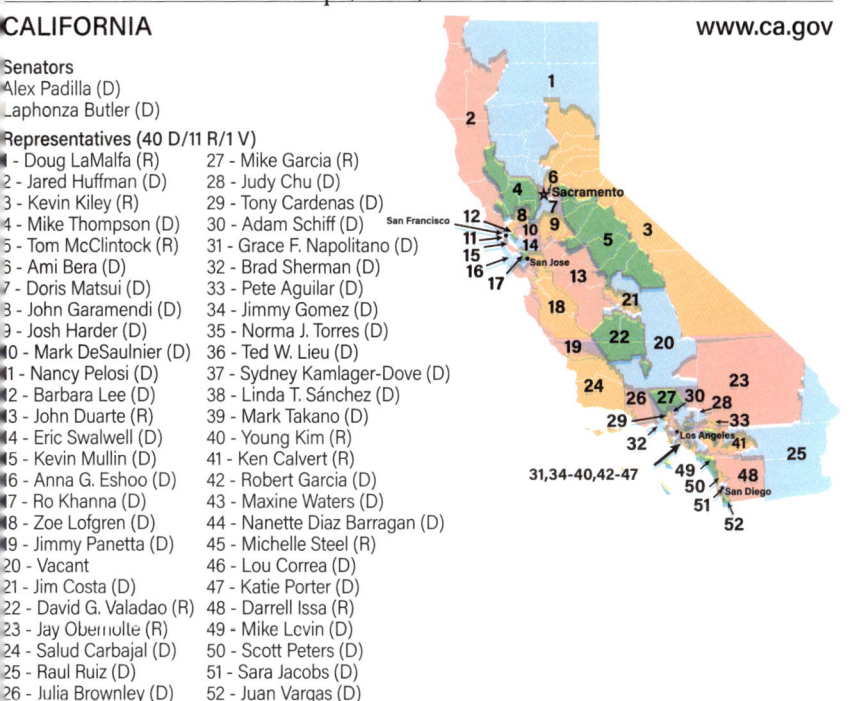

CALIFORNIA

www.ca.gov

Senators
Alex Padilla (D)
Laphonza Butler (D)

Representatives (40 D/11 R/1 V)
- 1 - Doug LaMalfa (R)
- 2 - Jared Huffman (D)
- 3 - Kevin Kiley (R)
- 4 - Mike Thompson (D)
- 5 - Tom McClintock (R)
- 6 - Ami Bera (D)
- 7 - Doris Matsui (D)
- 8 - John Garamendi (D)
- 9 - Josh Harder (D)
- 10 - Mark DeSaulnier (D)
- 11 - Nancy Pelosi (D)
- 12 - Barbara Lee (D)
- 13 - John Duarte (R)
- 14 - Eric Swalwell (D)
- 15 - Kevin Mullin (D)
- 16 - Anna G. Eshoo (D)
- 17 - Ro Khanna (D)
- 18 - Zoe Lofgren (D)
- 19 - Jimmy Panetta (D)
- 20 - Vacant
- 21 - Jim Costa (D)
- 22 - David G. Valadao (R)
- 23 - Jay Obernolte (R)
- 24 - Salud Carbajal (D)
- 25 - Raul Ruiz (D)
- 26 - Julia Brownley (D)
- 27 - Mike Garcia (R)
- 28 - Judy Chu (D)
- 29 - Tony Cardenas (D)
- 30 - Adam Schiff (D)
- 31 - Grace F. Napolitano (D)
- 32 - Brad Sherman (D)
- 33 - Pete Aguilar (D)
- 34 - Jimmy Gomez (D)
- 35 - Norma J. Torres (D)
- 36 - Ted W. Lieu (D)
- 37 - Sydney Kamlager-Dove (D)
- 38 - Linda T. Sánchez (D)
- 39 - Mark Takano (D)
- 40 - Young Kim (R)
- 41 - Ken Calvert (R)
- 42 - Robert Garcia (D)
- 43 - Maxine Waters (D)
- 44 - Nanette Diaz Barragan (D)
- 45 - Michelle Steel (R)
- 46 - Lou Correa (D)
- 47 - Katie Porter (D)
- 48 - Darrell Issa (R)
- 49 - Mike Levin (D)
- 50 - Scott Peters (D)
- 51 - Sara Jacobs (D)
- 52 - Juan Vargas (D)

Pop. 39,029,342 | **Rank** 1st | **Trend** -1% | **Male %** 50.10% | **Female %** 49.90%
Caucasian 56.60% | **Black/AfrAm** 7.30% | **NatAm/AN** 3.20% | **Asian** 18.10% | **NH/PI** 0.90% | **Other** 34.30% | **Hisp/Lat** 40.30%
Land Area 155,813 sq. mi. | **Water Area** 7,838 sq. mi. | **Area Rank** 3rd

Registered Voters 21,980,768 | **Dem.** 47% | **Rep.** 24% | **Other** 29%

STATE LEGISLATURE | leginfo.legislature.ca.gov
Senate Total 40 (32 D/8 R) | **House Total** 80 (62 D/18 R) | **2024 Session** Jan 3 to Aug 30

Governor Gavin Newsom | Next Election 2026 | 2nd Term | 59% (+18)
State Capitol, Suite 1173, Sacramento CA 95814
916-445-2841 | Fax: 916-558-3160 | www.gov.ca.gov | X cagovernor
Bio—Fair Oaks; San Francisco, CA, 10/10/1967; BS, Santa Clara Univ., 1989; businessman, public official; San Francisco mayor, 2004-11; CA lt. governor, 2011-19; CA governor, 2019-present; m. Jennifer; Catholic
Democrat

State Maps, Stats, and Governors

COLORADO

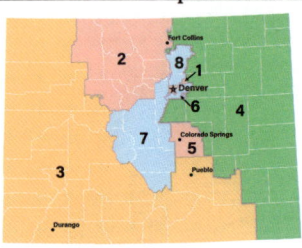

Senators — www.colorado.gov
Michael Bennet (D)
John Hickenlooper (D)

Representatives (5 D/3 R)
1 - Diana DeGette (D)
2 - Joe Neguse (D)
3 - Lauren Boebert (R)
4 - Ken Buck (R)
5 - Doug Lamborn (R)
6 - Jason Crow (D)
7 - Brittany Pettersen (D)
8 - Yadira Caraveo (D)

Pop. 5,839,926 | **Rank** 21st | **Trend** 1% | **Male %** 50.70% | **Female %** 49.30%
Caucasian 84.30% | **Black/AfrAm** 5.70% | **NatAm/AN** 3.20% | **Asian** 5.00% | **NH/PI** 0.40% |
Other 17.00% | **Hisp/Lat** 22.50%
Land Area 103,610 sq. mi. | **Water Area** 457 sq. mi. | **Area Rank** 8th

Registered Voters 3,810,616 | **Dem.** 27% | **Rep.** 24% | **Other** 50%

GENERAL ASSEMBLY | leg.colorado.gov
Senate Total 35 (23 D/12 R) | **House Total** 65 (46 D/19 R) | **2024 Session** Jan 10 to May 8

Governor Jared Polis | Next Election 2026 | 2nd Term | 59% (+19)
136 State Capitol, Denver CO 80203
303-866-2471 | Fax: 303-866-2003 | www.colorado.gov/governor | X govofco
Bio—Boulder; Boulder, CO, 5/12/1975; AB, Princeton Univ., 1996; business owner; US House, 2009-19; CO governor, 2019-present; m. Marlon Reis; Jewish

Democrat

CONNECTICUT

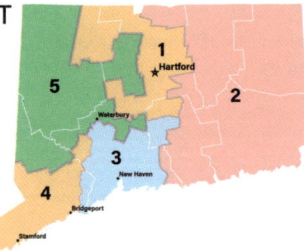

Senators — portal.ct.gov
Richard Blumenthal (D)
Chris Murphy (D)

Representatives (5 D)
1 - John B. Larson (D)
2 - Joe Courtney (D)
3 - Rosa DeLauro (D)
4 - Jim Himes (D)
5 - Jahana Hayes (D)

Pop. 3,626,205 | **Rank** 29th | **Trend** 0% | **Male %** 49.00% | **Female %** 51.00%
Caucasian 75.20% | **Black/AfrAm** 13.80% | **NatAm/AN** 1.50% | **Asian** 5.90% | **NH/PI** 0.20% |
Other 16.00% | **Hisp/Lat** 18.20%
Land Area 4,841 sq. mi. | **Water Area** 701 sq. mi. | **Area Rank** 48th

Registered Voters 2,217,227 | **Dem.** 36% | **Rep.** 21% | **Other** 43%

GENERAL ASSEMBLY | www.cga.ct.gov
Senate Total 36 (24 D/12 R) | **House Total** 151 (98 D/53 R) | **2024 Session** Feb 7 to May 8

Governor Ned Lamont | Next Election 2026 | 2nd Term | 56% (+13)
210 Capitol Avenue, Hartford CT 06106
800-406-1527 | portal.ct.gov/governor | X govnedlamont
Bio—Greenwich; Washington, DC, 1/3/1954; MBA, Yale Univ., 1980; businessman; Greenwich selectman, 1987-89; CT governor, 2019-present; m. Annie

Democrat

State Maps, Stats, and Governors

DELAWARE

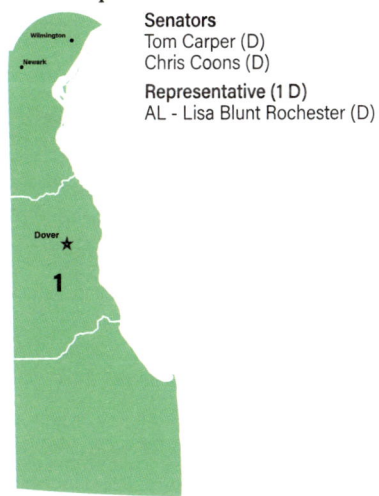

delaware.gov

Senators
Tom Carper (D)
Chris Coons (D)

Representative (1 D)
AL - Lisa Blunt Rochester (D)

Pop. 1,018,396 | **Rank** 45th | **Trend** 3% | **Male %** 48.60% | **Female %** 51.40%
Caucasian 68.20% | **Black/AfrAm** 25.30% | **NatAm/AN** 1.60% | **Asian** 5.20% | **NH/PI** 0.10% |
Other 9.90% | **Hisp/Lat** 10.30%
Land Area 1,948 sq. mi. | **Water Area** 540 sq. mi. | **Area Rank** 49th
Registered Voters 768,978 | **Dem.** 46% | **Rep.** 27% | **Other** 27%

GENERAL ASSEMBLY | legis.delaware.gov
Senate Total 21 (15 D/6 R) | **House Total** 41 (26 D/14 R/1 Vac) | **2024 Session** Jan 9 to June 30

Governor John Carney | Next Election 2024 | 2nd Term | 59% (+21)
Legislative Hall, Dover DE 19901
302-744-4101 | Fax: 302-739-2775 | governor.delaware.gov | X johncarneyde
Bio—Wilmington; Wilmington, DE, 5/20/1956; MPA, Univ. of DE, 1987; energy executive, public official; DE lt. governor, 2001-09; US House, 2011-17; DE governor, 2017-present; m. Tracey; Catholic

Democrat

State Maps, Stats, and Governors

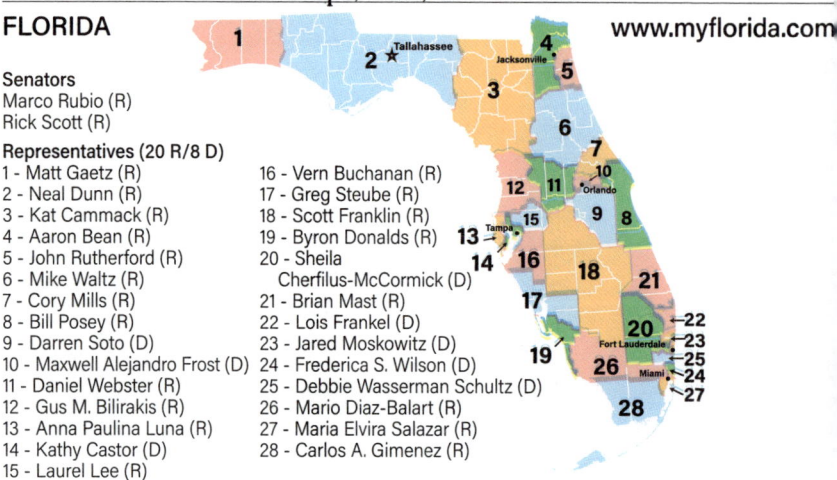

FLORIDA

www.myflorida.com

Senators
Marco Rubio (R)
Rick Scott (R)

Representatives (20 R/8 D)
1 - Matt Gaetz (R)
2 - Neal Dunn (R)
3 - Kat Cammack (R)
4 - Aaron Bean (R)
5 - John Rutherford (R)
6 - Mike Waltz (R)
7 - Cory Mills (R)
8 - Bill Posey (R)
9 - Darren Soto (D)
10 - Maxwell Alejandro Frost (D)
11 - Daniel Webster (R)
12 - Gus M. Bilirakis (R)
13 - Anna Paulina Luna (R)
14 - Kathy Castor (D)
15 - Laurel Lee (R)
16 - Vern Buchanan (R)
17 - Greg Steube (R)
18 - Scott Franklin (R)
19 - Byron Donalds (R)
20 - Sheila Cherfilus-McCormick (D)
21 - Brian Mast (R)
22 - Lois Frankel (D)
23 - Jared Moskowitz (D)
24 - Frederica S. Wilson (D)
25 - Debbie Wasserman Schultz (D)
26 - Mario Diaz-Balart (R)
27 - Maria Elvira Salazar (R)
28 - Carlos A. Gimenez (R)

Pop. 22,244,823 | **Rank** 3rd | **Trend** 3% | **Male %** 49.20% | **Female %** 50.80%
Caucasian 73.90% | **Black/AfrAm** 17.70% | **NatAm/AN** 1.40% | **Asian** 3.90% | **NH/PI** 0.20% | **Other** 22.80% | **Hisp/Lat** 27.10%
Land Area 53,634 sq. mi. | **Water Area** 12,106 sq. mi. | **Area Rank** 26th

Registered Voters 13,540,135 | **Dem.** 33% | **Rep.** 38% | **Other** 29%

STATE LEGISLATURE | www.leg.state.fl.us
Senate Total 40 (28 R/12 D) | **House Total** 120 (83 R/35 D/2 Vac) | **2024 Session** Jan 9 to Mar 8

Governor Ron DeSantis | Next Election 2026 | 2nd Term | 59% (+19)
The Capitol, 400 South Monroe Street, Tallahassee FL 32399
850-488-7146 | Fax: 850-487-0801 | www.flgov.com | **X** govrondesantis
Bio—Jacksonville, FL, 9/14/1978; JD, Harvard Univ., 2005; USN, 2004-10; USNR, 2010-19; lawyer; US House, 2013-18; FL governor, 2019-present; m. Casey; Catholic

Republican

State Maps, Stats, and Governors

GEORGIA
georgia.gov

(A new map is expected to be used in the November election.)

Senators
Jon Ossoff (D)
Raphael Warnock (D)

Representatives (9 R/5 D)
1 - Earl L. "Buddy" Carter (R)
2 - Sanford D. Bishop, Jr. (D)
3 - Drew Ferguson (R)
4 - Henry C. "Hank" Johnson, Jr. (D)
5 - Nikema Williams (D)
6 - Rich McCormick (R)
7 - Lucy McBath (D)
8 - Austin Scott (R)
9 - Andrew Clyde (R)
10 - Mike Collins (R)
11 - Barry Loudermilk (R)
12 - Rick W. Allen (R)
13 - David Scott (D)
14 - Marjorie Taylor Greene (R)

Pop. 10,912,876 | **Rank** 8th | **Trend** 2% | **Male %** 48.80% | **Female %** 51.20%
Caucasian 58.70% | **Black/AfrAm** 33.60% | **NatAm/AN** 2.10% | **Asian** 5.40% | **NH/PI** 0.20% | **Other** 9.00% | **Hisp/Lat** 10.40%
Land Area 57,701 sq. mi. | **Water Area** 1,706 sq. mi. | **Area Rank** 21st

Registered Voters 6,877,701 | *No party registration.*

GENERAL ASSEMBLY | www.legis.ga.gov
Senate Total 56 (33 R/23 D) | **House Total** 180 (102 R/78 D) | **2024 Session** Jan 8 to Mar 28

Governor Brian Kemp | Next Election 2026 | 2nd Term | 53% (+8)
203 State Capitol, Atlanta GA 30334
404-656-1776 | Fax: 404-657-7332 | gov.georgia.gov | X govkemp
Bio—Athens; Athens, GA, 11/2/1963; BS, Univ. of GA; small business owner; GA Senate, 2003-07; GA secretary of state, 2010-18; GA governor, 2019-present; m. Marty; Episcopal

Republican

HAWAII
www.hawaii.gov

Senators
Brian Schatz (D)
Mazie K. Hirono (D)

Representatives (2 D)
1 - Ed Case (D)
2 - Jill Tokuda (D)

Pop. 1,440,196 | **Rank** 40th | **Trend** -1% | **Male %** 50.40% | **Female %** 49.60%
Caucasian 43.80% | **Black/AfrAm** 4.00% | **NatAm/AN** 3.20% | **Asian** 56.40% | **NH/PI** 28.10% | **Other** 5.80% | **Hisp/Lat** 11.10%
Land Area 6,421 sq. mi. | **Water Area** 4,546 sq. mi. | **Area Rank** 47th

Registered Voters 767,559 | *No party registration.*

STATE LEGISLATURE | www.capitol.hawaii.gov
Senate Total 25 (23 D/2 R) | **House Total** 51 (45 D/6 R) | **2024 Session** Jan 17 to May 2

Governor Josh Green | Next Election 2026 | 1st Term | 63% (+26)
Executive Chambers, State Capitol, Honolulu HI 96813
808-586-0034 | governor.hawaii.gov | X govjoshgreenmd
Bio—Kingston, NY, 2/11/1970; MD, PA St. Univ., 1997; physician; HI House, 2004-08; HI Senate, 2008-18; HI lt. governor, 2018-22; HI governor, 2022-present; m. Jaime; Jewish

Democrat

State Maps, Stats, and Governors

IDAHO

www.state.id.us

Senators
Mike Crapo (R)
Jim Risch (R)

Representatives (2 R)
1 - Russ Fulcher (R)
2 - Mike Simpson (R)

Pop. 1,939,033 | **Rank** 38th | **Trend** 5% | **Male %** 50.40% | **Female %** 49.60%
Caucasian 91.40% | **Black/AfrAm** 1.50% | **NatAm/AN** 3.20% | **Asian** 2.60% | **NH/PI** 0.40% |
Other 11.50% | **Hisp/Lat** 13.50%
Land Area 82,623 sq. mi. | **Water Area** 923 sq. mi. | **Area Rank** 11th

Registered Voters 996,731 | **Dem.** 13% | **Rep.** 58% | **Other** 29%

STATE LEGISLATURE | legislature.idaho.gov
Senate Total 35 (28 R/7 D) | **House Total** 70 (59 R/11 D) | **2024 Session** Jan 8 to Mar 29

Governor Brad Little | Next Election 2026 | 2nd Term | 61% (+40)
700 West Jefferson Street, 2nd Floor, Boise ID 83702
208-334-2100 | Fax: 208-334-2175 | gov.idaho.gov | X governorlittle

Bio—Emmett; Emmett, ID, 2/15/1954; BS, Univ. of ID, 1977; rancher, public official; ID Senate, 2001-09; ID lt. governor, 2009-19; ID governor, 2019-present; m. Teresa; Episcopal

Republican

ILLINOIS

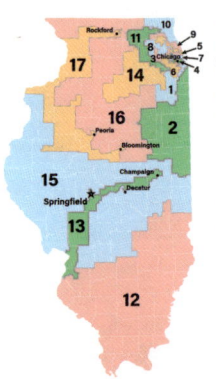

www.illinois.gov

Senators
Dick Durbin (D)
Tammy Duckworth (D)

Representatives (14 D/3 R)
1 - Jonathan L. Jackson (D)
2 - Robin Kelly (D)
3 - Delia C. Ramirez (D)
4 - Jesús G. "Chuy" García (D)
5 - Mike Quigley (D)
6 - Sean Casten (D)
7 - Danny K. Davis (D)
8 - Raja Krishnamoorthi (D)
9 - Jan Schakowsky (D)
10 - Brad Schneider (D)
11 - Bill Foster (D)
12 - Mike Bost (R)
13 - Nikki Budzinski (D)
14 - Lauren Underwood (D)
15 - Mary Miller (R)
16 - Darin LaHood (R)
17 - Eric Sorensen (D)

Pop. 12,582,032 | **Rank** 6th | **Trend** -2% | **Male %** 49.50% | **Female %** 50.50%
Caucasian 71.30% | **Black/AfrAm** 15.30% | **NatAm/AN** 2.00% | **Asian** 7.00% | **NH/PI** 0.20% |
Other 15.70% | **Hisp/Lat** 18.30%
Land Area 55,499 sq. mi. | **Water Area** 2,399 sq. mi. | **Area Rank** 24th

Registered Voters 8,224,350 | *No party registration.*

GENERAL ASSEMBLY | www.ilga.gov/
Senate Total 59 (40 D/19 R) | **House Total** 118 (78 D/40 R) | **2024 Session** Jan 10

Governor JB Pritzker | Next Election 2026 | 2nd Term | 55% (+12)
207 Statehouse, Springfield IL 62706
217-782-6830 | Fax: 217-524-4049 | gov.illinois.gov | X govpritzker

Bio—Chicago; Palo Alto, CA, 1/19/1965; JD, Northwestern Univ., 1993; lawyer, venture capitalist; IL governor, 2019-present; m. MK; Jewish

Democrat

State Maps, Stats, and Governors

INDIANA

www.in.gov

Senators
Todd Young (R)
Mike Braun (R)

Representatives (7 R/2 D)
1 - Frank J. Mrvan (D)
2 - Rudy Yakym III (R)
3 - Jim Banks (R)
4 - Jim Baird (R)
5 - Victoria Spartz (R)
6 - Greg Pence (R)
7 - André D. Carson (D)
8 - Larry Bucshon (R)
9 - Erin Houchin (R)

Pop. 6,833,037 | **Rank** 17th | **Trend** 1% | **Male %** 49.70% | **Female %** 50.30%
Caucasian 84.10% | **Black/AfrAm** 11.30% | **NatAm/AN** 1.80% | **Asian** 3.20% | **NH/PI** 0.10% | **Other** 7.00% | **Hisp/Lat** 7.80%
Land Area 35,817 sq. mi. | **Water Area** 593 sq. mi. | **Area Rank** 38th

Registered Voters 4,305,933 | *No party registration.*

GENERAL ASSEMBLY | iga.in.gov
Senate Total 50 (40 R/10 D) | **House Total** 100 (70 R/30 D) | **2024 Session** Jan 8 to Mar 14

Governor Eric Holcomb | Next Election 2024 | 2nd Term | 57% (+24)
State House, Room 206, Indianapolis IN 46204
317-232-4567 | Fax: 317-232-3343 | www.in.gov/gov | X govholcomb
Bio—Indianapolis; Indianapolis, IN, 5/2/1968; BA, Hanover Col., 1990; USN, 1990-96; political advisor, public official; IN lt. governor, 2016-17; IN governor, 2017-present; m. Janet
Republican

IOWA

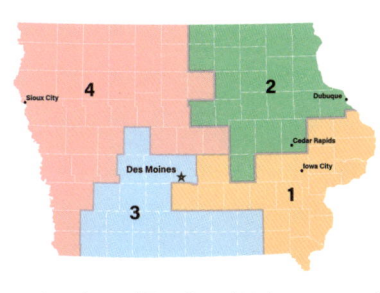

www.iowa.gov

Senators
Chuck Grassley (R)
Joni Ernst (R)

Representatives (4 R)
1 - Marianette Miller-Meeks (R)
2 - Ashley Hinson (R)
3 - Zach Nunn (R)
4 - Randy Feenstra (R)

Pop. 3,200,517 | **Rank** 31st | **Trend** 0% | **Male %** 50.20% | **Female %** 49.80%
Caucasian 90.70% | **Black/AfrAm** 5.30% | **NatAm/AN** 1.70% | **Asian** 3.10% | **NH/PI** 0.40% | **Other** 5.80% | **Hisp/Lat** 6.80%
Land Area 55,839 sq. mi. | **Water Area** 419 sq. mi. | **Area Rank** 23rd

Registered Voters 1,518,210 | **Dem.** 31% | **Rep.** 39% | **Other** 30%

GENERAL ASSEMBLY | www.legis.iowa.gov
Senate Total 50 (34 R/16 D) | **House Total** 100 (64 R/36 D) | **2024 Session** Jan 8 to Apr 16

Governor Kim Reynolds | Next Election 2026 | 3rd Term | 58% (+19)
State Capitol, Des Moines IA 50319
515-281-5211 | Fax: 515-281-6611 | governor.iowa.gov | X iagovernor
Bio—St. Charles, IA, 8/4/1959; BLS, IA St. Univ., 2016 ; public official; Clarke County Treasurer; IA Senate, 2009-10; IA lt. governor, 2011-17; IA governor, 2017-present; m. Kevin; Lutheran
Republican

U.S. Congress Directory | 167

State Maps, Stats, and Governors

KANSAS

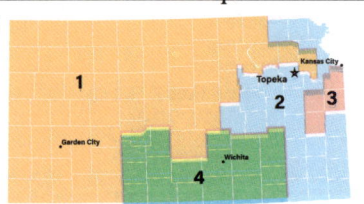

portal.kansas.gov

Senators
Jerry Moran (R)
Roger Marshall (R)

Representatives (3 R/1 D)
1 - Tracey Mann (R)
2 - Jake LaTurner (R)
3 - Sharice Davids (D)
4 - Ron Estes (R)

Pop. 2,937,150 | **Rank** 35th | **Trend** 0% | **Male %** 50.20% | **Female %** 49.80%
Caucasian 85.80% | **Black/AfrAm** 7.60% | **NatAm/AN** 3.30% | **Asian** 3.80% | **NH/PI** 0.30% | **Other** 10.00% | **Hisp/Lat** 13.00%
Land Area 81,737 sq. mi. | **Water Area** 520 sq. mi. | **Area Rank** 13th

Registered Voters 1,954,355 | **Dem.** 26% | **Rep.** 44% | **Other** 30%

STATE LEGISLATURE | www.kslegislature.org
Senate Total 40 (28 R/11 D/1 Ind) | **House Total** 125 (85 R/40 D) | **2024 Session** Jan 8 to May 17

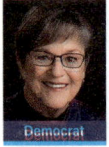

Governor Laura Kelly | Next Election 2026 | 2nd Term | 49% (+2)
Capitol, 300 SW 10th Avenue, Suite 212S, Topeka KS 66612
785-296-3232 | Fax: 785-296-7973 | governor.kansas.gov | X govlaurakelly
Bio—Topeka; New York, NY, 1/24/1950; MS, IN Univ.; recreation therapist; KS Senate, 2005-19; KS governor, 2019-present; m. Ted Daughety; Catholic

Democrat

KENTUCKY

kentucky.gov

Senators
Mitch McConnell (R)
Rand Paul (R)

Representatives (5 R/1 D)
1 - James Comer (R)
2 - Brett Guthrie (R)
3 - Morgan McGarvey (D)
4 - Thomas Massie (R)
5 - Hal Rogers (R)
6 - Andy Barr (R)

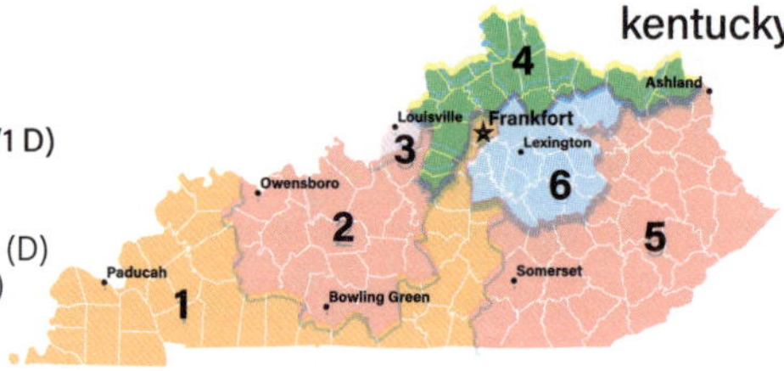

Pop. 4,512,310 | **Rank** 26th | **Trend** 0% | **Male %** 49.50% | **Female %** 50.50%
Caucasian 88.80% | **Black/AfrAm** 9.60% | **NatAm/AN** 1.70% | **Asian** 2.00% | **NH/PI** 0.20% | **Other** 4.20% | **Hisp/Lat** 4.20%
Land Area 39,481 sq. mi. | **Water Area** 916 sq. mi. | **Area Rank** 36th

Registered Voters 3,491,259 | **Dem.** 44% | **Rep.** 46% | **Other** 10%

GENERAL ASSEMBLY | legislature.ky.gov
Senate Total 38 (31 R / 7 D) | **House Total** 100 (80 R / 20 D) | **2024 Session** Jan 2 to Apr 15

Governor Andy Beshear | Next Election 2027 | 2nd Term | 53% (+5)
700 Capitol Avenue, Suite 100, Frankfort KY 40601
502-564-2611 | Fax: 502-564-0437 | governor.ky.gov | X govandybeshear
Bio—Louisville, KY, 11/29/1977; JD, Univ. of VA, 2003; lawyer; KY attorney general, 2016-19; KY governor, 2019-present; m. Britainy; Christian

Democrat

State Maps, Stats, and Governors

LOUISIANA

(A new map will be used in the November election.)

Senators
Bill Cassidy (R)
John Kennedy (R)

Representatives (5 R/1 D)
1 - Steve Scalise (R)
2 - Troy A. Carter, Sr. (D)
3 - Clay Higgins (R)
4 - Mike Johnson (R)
5 - Julia Letlow (R)
6 - Garret Graves (R)

www.louisiana.gov

Pop. 4,590,241 | **Rank** 25th | **Trend** -2% | **Male %** 49.00% | **Female %** 51.00%
Caucasian 63.90% | **Black/AfrAm** 33.30% | **NatAm/AN** 2.30% | **Asian** 2.30% | **NH/PI** 0.10% | **Other** 5.60% | **Hisp/Lat** 5.70%
Land Area 43,193 sq. mi. | **Water Area** 9,168 sq. mi. | **Area Rank** 33rd

Registered Voters 2,976,948 | **Dem.** 38% | **Rep.** 34% | **Other** 28%

STATE LEGISLATURE | legis.la.gov
Senate Total 39 (28 R/11 D) | **House Total** 105 (73 R/32 D) | **2024 Session** Mar 11 to June 3

Governor Jeff Landry | Next Election 2027 | 1st Term | 52% (+26)
P.O. Box 94004, Baton Rouge LA 70804
225-342-7015 | gov.louisiana.gov | **X** lagovjefflandry
Bio—Broussard; Saint Martinville, LA, 12/23/1970; JD, Loyola Univ., New Orleans, 2004; LAARNG, 1987-98; lawyer, business owner; US House, 2011-13; LA attorney general, 2016-24; LA governor, 2024-present; m. Sharon; Catholic
Republican

MAINE

Senators
Susan Collins (R)
Angus King (I)

Representatives (2 D)
1 - Chellie Pingree (D)
2 - Jared Golden (D)

www.maine.gov

Pop. 1,385,340 | **Rank** 42nd | **Trend** 2% | **Male %** 49.40% | **Female %** 50.60%
Caucasian 96.00% | **Black/AfrAm** 2.60% | **NatAm/AN** 1.80% | **Asian** 1.80% | **NH/PI** 0.10% | **Other** 3.30% | **Hisp/Lat** 2.10%
Land Area 30,837 sq. mi. | **Water Area** 4,534 sq. mi. | **Area Rank** 39th

Registered Voters 929,017 | **Dem.** 37% | **Rep.** 30% | **Other** 33%

STATE LEGISLATURE | legislature.maine.gov
Senate Total 35 (22 D/13 R) | **House Total** 151 (81 D/68 R/2 Ind) | **2024 Session** Jan 3 to Apr 17

Governor Janet Mills | Next Election 2026 | 2nd Term | 55% (+13)
1 State House Station, Augusta ME 4333
207-287-3531 | Fax: 207-287-1034 | www.maine.gov/governor/mills | **X** govjanetmills
Bio—Farmington; Farmington, ME, 12/30/1947; JD, Univ. of ME; lawyer, public official; ME House, 2003-09; ME attorney general, 2009-11, 2013-19; ME governor, 2019-present; wid.
Democrat

U.S. Congress Directory | 169

State Maps, Stats, and Governors

MARYLAND

www.maryland.gov

Senators
Ben Cardin (D)
Chris Van Hollen (D)

Representatives (7 D/1 R)
1 - Andy Harris (R)
2 - C.A. Dutch Ruppersberger (D)
3 - John Sarbanes (D)
4 - Glenn Ivey (D)
5 - Steny Hoyer (D)
6 - David Trone (D)
7 - Kweisi Mfume (D)
8 - Jamie Raskin (D)

Pop. 6,164,660 | **Rank** 19th | **Trend** 0% | **Male %** 48.70% | **Female %** 51.30%
Caucasian 55.40% | **Black/AfrAm** 32.60% | **NatAm/AN** 1.70% | **Asian** 8.10% | **NH/PI** 0.30% |
Other 11.00% | **Hisp/Lat** 11.40%
Land Area 9,709 sq. mi. | **Water Area** 2,694 sq. mi. | **Area Rank** 42nd

Registered Voters 4,170,689 | **Dem.** 53% | **Rep.** 24% | **Other** 23%

GENERAL ASSEMBLY | mgaleg.maryland.gov
Senate Total 47 (33 D/13 R/1 Vac) | **House Total** 141 (102 D/39 R) | **2024 Session** Jan 10 to Apr 8

Governor Wes Moore | **Next Election** 2026 | 1st Term | 65% (+33)
State House, 100 State Circle, Annapolis MD 21401
410-974-3901 | governor.maryland.gov | X govwesmoore
Bio—Baltimore; Takoma Park, MD, 10/15/1978; MA, Univ. of Oxford, 2004; USA, 1998-2004; investment banker, nonprofit executive; MD governor, 2023-present; m. Dawn

Democrat

MASSACHUSETTS

www.mass.gov

Senators
Elizabeth Warren (D)
Edward J. Markey (D)

Representatives (9 D)
1 - Richard Neal (D)
2 - Jim McGovern (D)
3 - Lori Trahan (D)
4 - Jake Auchincloss (D)
5 - Katherine Clark (D)
6 - Seth Moulton (D)
7 - Ayanna Pressley (D)
8 - Stephen F. Lynch (D)
9 - William R. Keating (D)

Pop. 6,981,974 | **Rank** 16th | **Trend** -1% | **Male %** 49.00% | **Female %** 51.00%
Caucasian 77.80% | **Black/AfrAm** 10.20% | **NatAm/AN** 1.10% | **Asian** 8.40% | **NH/PI** 0.10% |
Other 14.00% | **Hisp/Lat** 13.00%
Land Area 7,799 sq. mi. | **Water Area** 2,752 sq. mi. | **Area Rank** 45th

Registered Voters 4,781,556 | **Dem.** 29% | **Rep.** 9% | **Other** 62%

GENERAL COURT | malegislature.gov
Senate Total 40 (36 D/4 R) | **House Total** 160 (134 D/24 R/1 UNE/1 Vac) | **2024 Session** Jan 3

Governor Maura Healey | **Next Election** 2026 | 1st Term | 64% (+29)
State House, Room 360, Boston MA 02133
617-725-4005 | mass.gov/governor | X massgovernor
Bio—Cambridge; Bethesda, MD, 2/8/1971; JD, Northeastern Univ., 1998; MA attorney general, 2015-23; MA governor, 2023-present; single

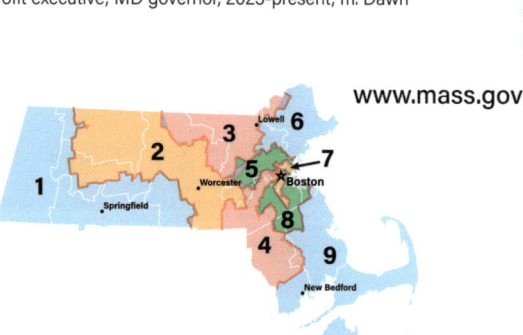

Democrat

NLPC | 170

State Maps, Stats, and Governors

MICHIGAN

www.michigan.gov

Senators
Debbie Stabenow (D)
Gary Peters (D)

Representatives (7 D/6 R)
1 - Jack Bergman (R)
2 - John Moolenaar (R)
3 - Hillary J. Scholten (D)
4 - Bill Huizenga (R)
5 - Tim Walberg (R)
6 - Debbie Dingell (D)
7 - Elissa Slotkin (D)
8 - Dan Kildee (D)
9 - Lisa McClain (R)
10 - John James (R)
11 - Haley Stevens (D)
12 - Rashida Tlaib (D)
13 - Shri Thanedar (D)

Pop. 10,034,118 | **Rank** 10th | **Trend** 0% | **Male %** 49.60% | **Female %** 50.40%
Caucasian 80.70% | **Black/AfrAm** 15.30% | **NatAm/AN** 1.90% | **Asian** 4.20% | **NH/PI** 0.10% | **Other** 5.40% | **Hisp/Lat** 5.70%
Land Area 56,591 sq. mi. | **Water Area** 40,097 sq. mi. | **Area Rank** 22nd

Registered Voters 7,721,482 | *No party registration.*

STATE LEGISLATURE | www.legislature.mi.gov
Senate Total 38 (20 D/18 R) | **House Total** 110 (54 D/54 R/2 Vac) | **2024 Session** Jan 10

Governor Gretchen Whitmer | Next Election 2026 | 2nd Term | 54% (+11)
P.O. Box 30013, Lansing MI 48909
517-373-3400 | www.michigan.gov/whitmer | X govwhitmer
Bio—Lansing; East Lansing, MI, 8/23/1971; lawyer, public official; MI House, 2000-06; MI Senate, 2006-15; MI governor, 2019-present ; m. Marc Mallory; Christian

Democrat

MINNESOTA

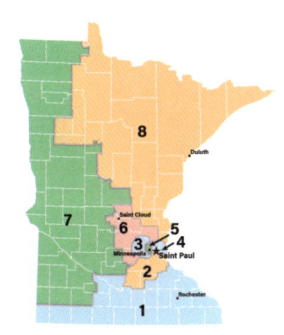

mn.gov

Senators
Amy Klobuchar (D)
Tina Smith (D)

Representatives (4 D/4 R)
1 - Brad Finstad (R)
2 - Angie Craig (D)
3 - Dean Phillips (D)
4 - Betty McCollum (D)
5 - Ilhan Omar (D)
6 - Tom Emmer (R)
7 - Michelle Fischbach (R)
8 - Pete Stauber (R)

Pop. 5,717,184 | **Rank** 22nd | **Trend** 0% | **Male %** 50.20% | **Female %** 49.80%
Caucasian 83.50% | **Black/AfrAm** 8.80% | **NatAm/AN** 2.40% | **Asian** 6.30% | **NH/PI** 0.20% | **Other** 6.00% | **Hisp/Lat** 5.80%
Land Area 79,605 sq. mi. | **Water Area** 7,312 sq. mi. | **Area Rank** 14th

Registered Voters 3,514,355 | *No party registration.*

STATE LEGISLATURE | www.leg.state.mn.us
Senate Total 67 (34 D/33 R) | **House Total** 134 (70 D/64 R) | **2024 Session** Feb 12 to May 20

Governor Tim Walz | Next Election 2026 | 2nd Term | 52% (+8)
130 State Capitol, 75 Rev. Dr. Martin Luther King Jr. Blvd., St. Paul MN 55155
651-201-3400 | Fax: 651-797-1850 | mn.gov/governor | X govtimwalz
Bio—West Point, NE, 4/6/1964; MS, MN St. Univ., 2001; NENG, 1981-96; MNNG, 1996-2005; teacher; US House, 2007-19; MN governor, 2019-present; m. Gwen; Lutheran

Democrat

State Maps, Stats, and Governors

MISSISSIPPI

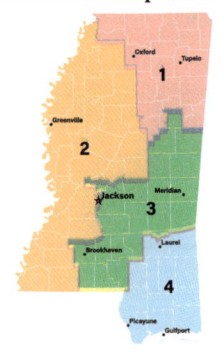

Senators
Roger F. Wicker (R)
Cindy Hyde-Smith (R)

Representatives (3 R/1 D)
1 - Trent Kelly (R)
2 - Bennie G. Thompson (D)
3 - Michael Guest (R)
4 - Mike Ezell (R)

www.ms.gov

Pop. 2,940,057 | **Rank** 34th | **Trend** -1% | **Male %** 48.50% | **Female %** 51.50%
Caucasian 59.80% | **Black/AfrAm** 38.20% | **NatAm/AN** 1.70% | **Asian** 1.40% | **NH/PI** 0.10% | **Other** 3.70% | **Hisp/Lat** 3.30%
Land Area 46,913 sq. mi. | **Water Area** 1,515 sq. mi. | **Area Rank** 31st

Registered Voters 1,932,172 | *No party registration.*

STATE LEGISLATURE | www.legislature.ms.gov
Senate Total 52 (36 R/16 D) | **House Total** 122 (79 R/41 D/2 Ind) | **2024 Session** Jan 2 to May 5

Governor Tate Reeves | Next Election 2027 | 2nd Term | 51% (+3)
P.O. Box 139, Jackson MS 39205
601-359-3150 | Fax: 601-359-3741 | governorreeves.ms.gov | X tatereeves
Bio—Florence, MS, 6/5/1974; BS, Millsaps Col.; financial analyst, public official; MS treasurer, 2004-12; MS lt. governor, 2012-20; MS governor, 2020-present; m. Elee; Christian

Republican

MISSOURI

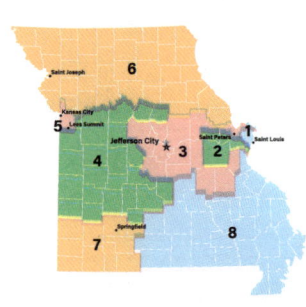

Senators
Josh Hawley (R)
Eric Schmitt (R)

Representatives (6 R/2 D)
1 - Cori Bush (D)
2 - Ann Wagner (R)
3 - Blaine Luetkemeyer (R)
4 - Mark Alford (R)
5 - Emanuel Cleaver (D)
6 - Sam Graves (R)
7 - Eric Burlison (R)
8 - Jason Smith (R)

www.mo.gov

Pop. 6,177,957 | **Rank** 18th | **Trend** 0% | **Male %** 49.30% | **Female %** 50.70%
Caucasian 84.60% | **Black/AfrAm** 12.50% | **NatAm/AN** 2.20% | **Asian** 2.90% | **NH/PI** 0.30% | **Other** 5.30% | **Hisp/Lat** 4.70%
Land Area 68,727 sq. mi. | **Water Area** 961 sq. mi. | **Area Rank** 18th

Registered Voters 4,047,817 | *No party registration.*

GENERAL ASSEMBLY | www.mo.gov/government/legislative-branch
Senate Total 34 (24 R/10 D) | **House Total** 163 (111 R/51 D/1 Vac) | **2024 Session** Jan 3 to May 10

Governor Mike Parson | Next Election 2024 | 2nd Term | 57% (+16)
Capitol Building, Room 216, P.O. Box 720, Jefferson City MO 65102
573-751-3222 | Fax: 573-526-3291 | governor.mo.gov | X govparsonmo
Bio—Bolivar; Wheatland, MO, 9/17/1955; HS diploma; USA, 1975-81; law enforcement officer, business owner, public official; Polk Co. sheriff, 1993-2004; MO House, 2005-11; MO Senate, 2011-17; MO lt. governor, 2017-18; MO governor, 2018-present; m. Teresa; Baptist

Republican

NLPC | 172

State Maps, Stats, and Governors

MONTANA
mt.gov

Senators
Jon Tester (D)
Steve Daines (R)

Representatives (2 R)
1 - Ryan Zinke (R)
2 - Matt Rosendale (R)

Pop. 1,122,867 | Rank 43rd | Trend 3% | Male % 50.50% | Female % 49.50%
Caucasian 91.70% | Black/AfrAm 0.90% | NatAm/AN 8.30% | Asian 1.70% | NH/PI 0.40% | Other 4.40% | Hisp/Lat 4.40%
Land Area 145,509 sq. mi. | Water Area 1,493 sq. mi. | Area Rank 4th

Registered Voters 677,865 | *No party registration.*

STATE LEGISLATURE | leg.mt.gov
Senate Total 50 (34 R/16 D) | House Total 100 (68 R/32 D) | No regular session in 2024

Governor Greg Gianforte | Next Election 2024 | 1st Term | 54% (+13)
State Capitol, Helena MT 59620
406-444-3111 | Fax: 406-444-5529 | governor.mt.gov | X govgianforte
Bio—Bozeman; San Diego, CA, 4/17/1961; MS, Stevens Institute of Technology, 1983; entrepreneur, engineer; US House, 2017-21; MT governor, 2021-present; m. Susan; Christian
Republican

NEBRASKA
www.nebraska.gov

Senators
Deb Fischer (R)
Pete Ricketts (R)

Representatives (3 R)
1 - Mike Flood (R)
2 - Don Bacon (R)
3 - Adrian Smith (R)

Pop. 1,967,923 | Rank 37th | Trend 0% | Male % 50.20% | Female % 49.80%
Caucasian 86.80% | Black/AfrAm 6.50% | NatAm/AN 2.80% | Asian 3.40% | NH/PI 0.20% | Other 9.80% | Hisp/Lat 12.30%
Land Area 76,796 sq. mi. | Water Area 531 sq. mi. | Area Rank 15th

Registered Voters 1,226,425 | Dem. 27% | Rep. 49% | Other 24%

STATE LEGISLATURE | nebraskalegislature.gov
Senate Total 49 (non-partisan) | 2024 Session Jan 3 to Apr 18

Governor Jim Pillen | Next Election 2026 | 1st Term | 60% (+24)
P.O. Box 94848, Lincoln NE 68509
402-471-2244 | governor.nebraska.gov | X teampillen
Bio—Columbus; Columbus, NE, 12/31/1955; DVM, KS St. Univ., 1983; veterinarian, hog farmer; NE governor, 2023-present; m. Suzanne ; Catholic
Republican

State Maps, Stats, and Governors

NEVADA

nv.gov

Senators
Catherine Cortez Masto (D)
Jacky Rosen (D)

Representatives (3 D/1 R)
1 - Dina Titus (D)
2 - Mark Amodei (R)
3 - Susie Lee (D)
4 - Steven Horsford (D)

Pop. 3,177,772 | **Rank** 32nd | **Trend** 2% | **Male %** 50.30% | **Female %** 49.70%
Caucasian 65.20% | **Black/AfrAm** 12.20% | **NatAm/AN** 3.50% | **Asian** 11.90% | **NH/PI** 1.60% | **Other** 25.00% | **Hisp/Lat** 30.30%
Land Area 109,831 sq. mi. | **Water Area** 710 sq. mi. | **Area Rank** 7th

Registered Voters 2,284,681 | **Dem.** 31% | **Rep.** 28% | **Other** 41%

STATE LEGISLATURE | www.leg.state.nv.us
Senate Total 21 (13 D/7 R/1 Vac) | **House Total** 42 (26 D/14 R/2 Vac) | No regular session in 2024

Governor Joe Lombardo | Next Election 2026 | 1st Term | 49% (+1)
Capitol Building, 101 North Carson Street, Carson City NV 89701
775-684-5670 | gov.nv.gov | X josephmlombardo

Bio—Las Vegas; Sapporo, Japan, 11/8/1962; MS, Univ. of NV, Las Vegas, 2006; USAR; ARNG; law enforcement officer; Clark Co. sheriff, 2015-2023; NV governor, 2023-present; m. Donna; Catholic

Republican

NEW HAMPSHIRE

www.nh.gov

Senators
Jeanne Shaheen (D)
Maggie Hassan (D)

Representatives (2 D)
1 - Chris Pappas (D)
2 - Annie Kuster (D)

Pop. 1,395,231 | **Rank** 41st | **Trend** 1% | **Male %** 49.90% | **Female %** 50.10%
Caucasian 93.90% | **Black/AfrAm** 2.40% | **NatAm/AN** 1.30% | **Asian** 3.70% | **NH/PI** 0.10% | **Other** 5.50% | **Hisp/Lat** 4.50%
Land Area 8,951 sq. mi. | **Water Area** 396 sq. mi. | **Area Rank** 44th

Registered Voters 873,359 | **Dem.** 30% | **Rep.** 31% | **Other** 39%

GENERAL COURT | www.gencourt.state.nh.us
Senate Total 24 (14 R/10 D) | **House Total** 400 (198 R/197 D/2 Ind/3 Vac) | **2024 Session** Jan 3 to June 28

Governor Chris Sununu | Next Election 2024 | 4th Term | 57% (+15)
107 North Main Street, Concord NH 3301
603-271-2121 | Fax: 603-271-7640 | www.governor.nh.gov | X govchrissununu

Bio—Newfields; Salem, NH, 11/5/1974; BS, MA Institute of Technology, 1988; environmental engineer; NH executive council, 2011-17; NH governor, 2017-present; m. Valerie

Republican

State Maps, Stats, and Governors

NEW JERSEY

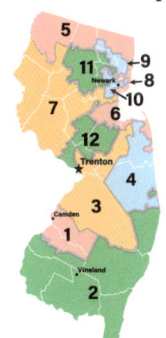

Senators
Bob Menendez (D)
Cory A. Booker (D)

Representatives (9 D/3 R)
1 - Donald Norcross (D)
2 - Jeff Van Drew (R)
3 - Andy Kim (D)
4 - Chris Smith (R)
5 - Josh Gottheimer (D)
6 - Frank Pallone, Jr. (D)
7 - Tom Kean, Jr. (R)
8 - Rob Menendez (D)
9 - Bill Pascrell, Jr. (D)
10 - Donald M. Payne, Jr. (D)
11 - Mikie Sherrill (D)
12 - Bonnie Watson Coleman (D)

www.nj.gov

Pop. 9,261,699 | **Rank** 11th | **Trend** 0% | **Male %** 49.30% | **Female %** 50.70%
Caucasian 64.80% | **Black/AfrAm** 15.20% | **NatAm/AN** 1.50% | **Asian** 11.30% | **NH/PI** 0.20% | **Other** 19.90% | **Hisp/Lat** 21.90%
Land Area 7,353 sq. mi. | **Water Area** 1,368 sq. mi. | **Area Rank** 46th

Registered Voters 6,511,169 | **Dem.** 38% | **Rep.** 24% | **Other** 38%

STATE LEGISLATURE | www.njleg.state.nj.us
Senate Total 40 (25 D/15 R) | **House Total** 80 (51 D/29 R) | **2024 Session** Jan 9

Governor Phil Murphy | Next Election 2025 | 2nd Term | 51% (+3)
The State House, P.O. Box 001, Trenton NJ 08625
609-292-6000 | Fax: 609-777-2922 | www.state.nj.us/governor | X govmurphy
Bio—Middletown; Boston, MA, 8/16/1957; MBA, Univ. of PA, 1983; investment banker; US ambassador to Germany, 2009-13; NJ governor, 2018-present; m. Tammy; Catholic

Democrat

NEW MEXICO

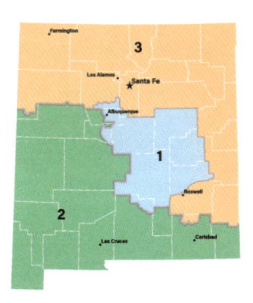

Senators
Martin Heinrich (D)
Ben Ray Luján (D)

Representatives (3 D)
1 - Melanie Stansbury (D)
2 - Gabe Vasquez (D)
3 - Teresa Leger Fernandez (D)

www.nm.gov

Pop. 2,113,344 | **Rank** 36th | **Trend** 0% | **Male %** 49.60% | **Female %** 50.40%
Caucasian 70.80% | **Black/AfrAm** 3.40% | **NatAm/AN** 11.80% | **Asian** 2.80% | **NH/PI** 0.30% | **Other** 37.40% | **Hisp/Lat** 50.20%
Land Area 121,280 sq. mi. | **Water Area** 281 sq. mi. | **Area Rank** 5th

Registered Voters 1,326,033 | **Dem.** 44% | **Rep.** 31% | **Other** 25%

STATE LEGISLATURE | www.nmlegis.gov/
Senate Total 42 (27 D/14 R/1 Vac) | **House Total** 70 (45 D/25 R) | **2024 Session** Jan 16 to Feb 15

Governor Michelle Lujan Grisham | Next Election 2026 | 2nd Term | 52% (+6)
State Capitol, Fourth Floor, Santa Fe NM 87501
505-476-2200 | Fax: 505-476-2226 | www.governor.state.nm.us | X govmlg
Bio—Albuquerque; Los Alamos, NM, 10/24/1959; JD, Univ. of NM, 1987; lawyer, public official; NM secretary of aging and long-term services, 2002-04; NM secretary of health, 2004-07; Bernalillo Co board of commissioners, 2010-12; US House, 2013-18; NM governor, 2019-present; m. Manuel Cordova; Catholic

Democrat

State Maps, Stats, and Governors

NEW YORK
www.ny.gov

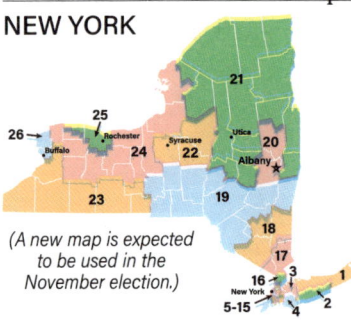

(A new map is expected to be used in the November election.)

Senators
Chuck Schumer (D)
Kirsten Gillibrand (D)

Representatives (14 D/10 R/2 V)
1 - Nick LaLota (R)
2 - Andrew Garbarino (R)
3 - Vacant
4 - Anthony D'Esposito (R)
5 - Gregory W. Meeks (D)
6 - Grace Meng (D)
7 - Nydia M. Velázquez (D)
8 - Hakeem Jeffries (D)
9 - Yvette Clarke (D)
10 - Dan Goldman (D)
11 - Nicole Malliotakis (R)
12 - Jerrold Nadler (D)
13 - Adriano Espaillat (D)
14 - Alexandria Ocasio-Cortez (D)
15 - Ritchie Torres (D)
16 - Jamaal Bowman (D)
17 - Mike Lawler (R)
18 - Pat Ryan (D)
19 - Marc Molinaro (R)
20 - Paul Tonko (D)
21 - Elise Stefanik (R)
22 - Brandon Williams (R)
23 - Nick Langworthy (R)
24 - Claudia Tenney (R)
25 - Joe Morelle (D)
26 - Vacant

Pop. 19,677,151 | **Rank** 4th | **Trend** -3% | **Male %** 48.90% | **Female %** 51.10%
Caucasian 63.40% | **Black/AfrAm** 17.60% | **NatAm/AN** 1.70% | **Asian** 10.30% | **NH/PI** 0.20% | **Other** 17.90% | **Hisp/Lat** 19.70%
Land Area 47,111 sq. mi. | **Water Area** 7,429 sq. mi. | **Area Rank** 30th

Registered Voters 12,040,156 | **Dem.** 49% | **Rep.** 22% | **Other** 29%

STATE LEGISLATURE | nyassembly.gov
Senate Total 63 (42 D/21 R) | **House Total** 150 (102 D/48 R) | **2024 Session** Jan 3

Governor Kathy Hochul | Next Election 2026 | 2nd Term | 53% (+6)
State Capitol, Albany NY 12224
518-474-8390 | www.governor.ny.gov | X govkathyhochul
Bio—Buffalo; Buffalo, NY, 8/27/1958; JD, Catholic Univ., 1983; lawyer, public official; US House, 2011-13; NY lt. governor, 2015-21; NY governor, 2021-present ; m. Bill; Catholic
Democrat

NORTH CAROLINA
www.nc.gov

(A new map is expected to be used in the November election.)

Senators
Thom Tillis (R)
Ted Budd (R)

Representatives (7 D/7 R)
1 - Don Davis (D)
2 - Deborah Ross (D)
3 - Greg Murphy (R)
4 - Valerie Foushee (D)
5 - Virginia Foxx (R)
6 - Kathy Manning (D)
7 - David Rouzer (R)
8 - Dan Bishop (R)
9 - Richard Hudson (R)
10 - Patrick McHenry (R)
11 - Chuck Edwards (R)
12 - Alma S. Adams (D)
13 - Wiley Nickel (D)
14 - Jeff Jackson (D)

Pop. 10,698,973 | **Rank** 9th | **Trend** 2% | **Male %** 48.90% | **Female %** 51.10%
Caucasian 69.40% | **Black/AfrAm** 22.80% | **NatAm/AN** 2.60% | **Asian** 4.10% | **NH/PI** 0.20% | **Other** 9.40% | **Hisp/Lat** 10.40%
Land Area 48,607 sq. mi. | **Water Area** 5,197 sq. mi. | **Area Rank** 29th

Registered Voters 7,423,773 | **Dem.** 33% | **Rep.** 30% | **Other** 37%

GENERAL ASSEMBLY | www.ncleg.gov
Senate Total 50 (30 R/20 D) | **House Total** 120 (72 R/48 D) | **2024 Session** Apr 24 to July 31

Governor Roy Cooper | Next Election 2024 | 2nd Term | 52% (+5)
20301 Mail Service Center, Raleigh NC 27699
919-814-2000 | Fax: 919-733-2120 | governor.nc.gov | X nc_governor
Bio—Rocky Mount; Nash Co., NC, 6/13/1957; JD, Univ. of NC, 1982; lawyer, public official; NC House, 1987-91; NC Senate, 1991-2001; NC attorney general, 2001-17; NC governor, 2017-present; m. Kristen; Presbyterian
Democrat

State Maps, Stats, and Governors

NORTH DAKOTA

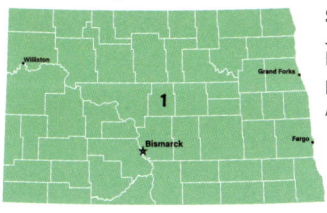

www.nd.gov

Senators
John Hoeven (R)
Kevin Cramer (R)

Representative (1 R)
AL - Kelly Armstrong (R)

Pop. 779,261 | **Rank** 47th | **Trend** 0% | **Male %** 51.20% | **Female %** 48.80%
Caucasian 88.20% | **Black/AfrAm** 4.20% | **NatAm/AN** 6.20% | **Asian** 2.20% | **NH/PI** 0.60% | **Other** 4.00% | **Hisp/Lat** 4.40%
Land Area 68,977 sq. mi. | **Water Area** 1,703 sq. mi. | **Area Rank** 17th

Registered Voters 422,819 | *No party registration.*

STATE LEGISLATURE | www.legis.nd.gov
Senate Total 47 (43 R/4 D) | **House Total** 94 (82 R/12 D) | No regular session in 2024

Governor Doug Burgum | Next Election 2024 | 2nd Term | 66% (+41)
State Capitol, 600 East Boulevard Ave., Dept. 101, Bismarck ND 58505
701-328-2200 | www.governor.nd.gov | X dougburgum
Bio—Arthur, ND, 8/1/1956; MBA, Stanford Univ., 1980; tech executive, real estate developer, venture capitalist; ND governor, 2016-present; m. Kathryn

Republican

OHIO

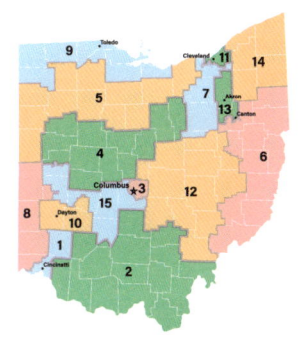

ohio.gov

Senators
Sherrod Brown (D)
J.D. Vance (R)

Representatives (9 R/5 D/1 V)
1 - Greg Landsman (D)
2 - Brad Wenstrup (R)
3 - Joyce Beatty (D)
4 - Jim Jordan (R)
5 - Bob Latta (R)
6 - Vacant
7 - Max Miller (R)
8 - Warren Davidson (R)
9 - Marcy Kaptur (D)
10 - Mike Turner (R)
11 - Shontel Brown (D)
12 - Troy Balderson (R)
13 - Emilia Strong Sykes (D)
14 - Dave Joyce (R)
15 - Mike Carey (R)

Pop. 11,756,058 | **Rank** 7th | **Trend** 0% | **Male %** 49.40% | **Female %** 50.60%
Caucasian 83.10% | **Black/AfrAm** 14.50% | **NatAm/AN** 1.60% | **Asian** 3.20% | **NH/PI** 0.10% | **Other** 4.40% | **Hisp/Lat** 4.40%
Land Area 40,848 sq. mi. | **Water Area** 3,966 sq. mi. | **Area Rank** 35th

Registered Voters 7,519,199 | *No party registration.*

GENERAL ASSEMBLY | www.legislature.ohio.gov
Senate Total 33 (26 R/7 D) | **House Total** 99 (66 R/32 D/1 Vac) | **2024 Session** Jan 2

Governor Mike DeWine | Next Election 2026 | 2nd Term | 63% (+26)
77 South High Street, 30th Floor, Columbus OH 43215
614-466-3555 | Fax: 614-466-9354 | governor.ohio.gov | X govmikedewine
Bio—Cedarville; Springfield, OH, 1/5/1947; JD, OH Northern Univ., 1972; lawyer, public official; OH Senate, 1981-82; US House, 1983-91; OH lt. governor, 1991-95; US Senate, 1995-2007; OH attorney general, 2011-19; OH governor, 2019-present; m. Frances; Catholic

Republican

U.S. Congress Directory | 177

State Maps, Stats, and Governors

OKLAHOMA
oklahoma.gov

Senators
James Lankford (R)
Markwayne Mullin (R)

Representatives (5 R)
1 - Kevin Hern (R)
2 - Josh Brecheen (R)
3 - Frank Lucas (R)
4 - Tom Cole (R)
5 - Stephanie Bice (R)

Pop. 4,019,800 | **Rank** 28th | **Trend** 1% | **Male %** 49.90% | **Female %** 50.10%
Caucasian 78.60% | **Black/AfrAm** 9.80% | **NatAm/AN** 14.30% | **Asian** 3.20% | **NH/PI** 0.40% | **Other** 9.20% | **Hisp/Lat** 12.10%
Land Area 68,578 sq. mi. | **Water Area** 1,303 sq. mi. | **Area Rank** 19th

Registered Voters 2,299,289 | **Dem.** 28% | **Rep.** 52% | **Other** 20%

STATE LEGISLATURE | www.oklegislature.gov
Senate Total 48 (39 R/8 D/1 Vac) | **House Total** 101 (80 R/20 D/1 Vac) | **2024 Session** Feb 5 to May 31

Governor Kevin Stitt | **Next Election** 2026 | 2nd Term | 55% (+14)
State Capitol Building, 2300 Lincoln Blvd., Room 212, Oklahoma City OK 73105
405-521-2342 | Fax: 405-521-3353 | oklahoma.gov/governor | X govstitt
Bio—Tulsa; Milton, FL, 12/28/1972; BS OK St. Univ.; entrepreneur, businessman; OK governor, 2019-present; m. Sarah; Christian

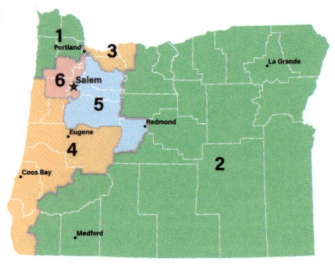

Republican

OREGON
www.oregon.gov

Senators
Ron Wyden (D)
Jeff Merkley (D)

Representatives (4 D/2 R)
1 - Suzanne Bonamici (D)
2 - Cliff Bentz (R)
3 - Earl Blumenauer (D)
4 - Val Hoyle (D)
5 - Lori Chavez-DeRemer (R)
6 - Andrea Salinas (D)

Pop. 4,240,137 | **Rank** 27th | **Trend** 0% | **Male %** 50.00% | **Female %** 50.00%
Caucasian 85.80% | **Black/AfrAm** 3.30% | **NatAm/AN** 3.80% | **Asian** 6.80% | **NH/PI** 0.90% | **Other** 12.30% | **Hisp/Lat** 14.40%
Land Area 95,963 sq. mi. | **Water Area** 2,390 sq. mi. | **Area Rank** 10th

Registered Voters 3,003,968 | **Dem.** 33% | **Rep.** 24% | **Other** 43%

STATE LEGISLATURE | www.oregonlegislature.gov
Senate Total 30 (17 D/12 R/1 Ind) | **House Total** 60 (35 D/25 R) | **2024 Session** Feb 5 to Mar 10

Governor Tina Kotek | **Next Election** 2026 | 1st Term | 47% (+3)
State Capitol Building, 900 Court Street NE, Suite 254, Salem OR 97301
503-378-4582 | www.oregon.gov/gov | X govtinakotek
Bio—Portland; York, PA, 9/30/1966; MA, Univ. of WA; public policy advocate, public official; OR House, 2007-22; OR governor, 2023-present; m. Aimee Wilson; Episcopal

Democrat

State Maps, Stats, and Governors

PENNSYLVANIA

www.pa.gov

Senators
Bob Casey (D)
John Fetterman (D)

Representatives (9 D/8 R)
1 - Brian Fitzpatrick (R)
2 - Brendan F. Boyle (D)
3 - Dwight Evans (D)
4 - Madeleine Dean (D)
5 - Mary Gay Scanlon (D)
6 - Chrissy Houlahan (D)
7 - Susan Wild (D)
8 - Matt Cartwright (D)
9 - Dan Meuser (R)
10 - Scott Perry (R)
11 - Lloyd Smucker (R)
12 - Summer Lee (D)
13 - John Joyce (R)
14 - Guy Reschenthaler (R)
15 - Glenn "GT" Thompson (R)
16 - Mike Kelly (R)
17 - Chris Deluzio (D)

Pop. 12,972,008 | **Rank** 5th | **Trend** 0% | **Male %** 49.30% | **Female %** 50.70%
Caucasian 80.90% | **Black/AfrAm** 12.90% | **NatAm/AN** 1.40% | **Asian** 4.60% | **NH/PI** 0.20% |
Other 8.00% | **Hisp/Lat** 8.60%
Land Area 44,730 sq. mi. | **Water Area** 1,312 sq. mi. | **Area Rank** 32nd
Registered Voters 8,663,982 | **Dem.** 45% | **Rep.** 40% | **Other** 15%
GENERAL ASSEMBLY | www.legis.state.pa.us
Senate Total 50 (28 R/22 D) | **House Total** 203 (102 D/101 R) | **2024 Session** Jan 2 to Nov 30

Governor Josh Shapiro | **Next Election** 2026 | **1st Term** | **56% (+15)**
Main Capitol Building, Room 225, Harrisburg PA 17120
717-787-2500 | www.governor.pa.gov | **X** governorshapiro
Bio—Abington; Kansas City, MO, 6/20/1973; JD, Georgetown Univ., 2002; political advisor, public official; PA House, 2005-12; Montgomery Co. commissioner, 2012-17; PA attorney general, 2017-23; PA governor, 2023-present; m. Lori; Jewish
Democrat

RHODE ISLAND

www.ri.gov

Senators
Jack Reed (D)
Sheldon Whitehouse (D)

Representatives (2 D)
1 - Gabe Amo (D)
2 - Seth Magaziner (D)

Pop. 1,093,734 | **Rank** 44th | **Trend** 0% | **Male %** 49.00% | **Female %** 51.00%
Caucasian 80.10% | **Black/AfrAm** 10.20% | **NatAm/AN** 1.80% | **Asian** 4.60% | **NH/PI** 0.10% |
Other 16.90% | **Hisp/Lat** 17.60%
Land Area 1,034 sq. mi. | **Water Area** 511 sq. mi. | **Area Rank** 50th
Registered Voters 723,881 | **Dem.** 40% | **Rep.** 14% | **Other** 47%
GENERAL ASSEMBLY | www.rilin.state.ri.us
Senate Total 38 (33 D/5 R) | **House Total** 75 (65 D/9 R/1 Ind) | **2024 Session** Jan 2 to June 30

Governor Dan McKee | **Next Election** 2026 | **2nd Term** | **58% (+19)**
State House, 82 Smith Street, Providence RI 02903
401-222-2080 | governor.ri.gov | **X** govdanmckee
Bio—Cumberland; Cumberland, RI, 6/16/1951; MPA, Harvard Univ.; public official, businessman; Cumberland town council, 1992-98; Cumberland mayor, 2000-04, 2006-14; RI lt. governor, 2015-21; RI governor, 2021-present; m. Susan
Democrat

State Maps, Stats, and Governors

SOUTH CAROLINA   www.sc.gov

Senators
Lindsey Graham (R)
Tim Scott (R)

Representatives (6 R/1 D)
1 - Nancy Mace (R)
2 - Joe Wilson (R)
3 - Jeff Duncan (R)
4 - William Timmons (R)
5 - Ralph Norman (R)
6 - James E. Clyburn (D)
7 - Russell Fry (R)

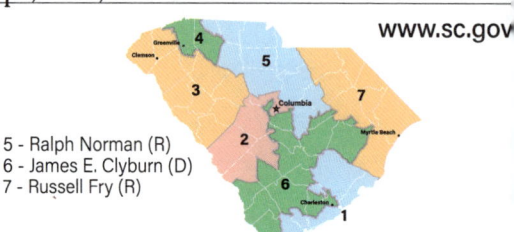

Pop. 5,282,634 | **Rank** 23rd | **Trend** 3% | **Male %** 48.60% | **Female %** 51.40%
Caucasian 69.50% | **Black/AfrAm** 26.90% | **NatAm/AN** 1.80% | **Asian** 2.40% | **NH/PI** 0.10% |
Other 6.10% | **Hisp/Lat** 6.50%
Land Area 30,056 sq. mi. | **Water Area** 1,959 sq. mi. | **Area Rank** 40th

Registered Voters 3,403,082 | *No party registration.*

GENERAL ASSEMBLY | www.scstatehouse.gov
Senate Total 46 (30 R/15 D/1 Ind) | **House Total** 124 (88 R/36 D) | **2024 Session** Jan 9 to May 9

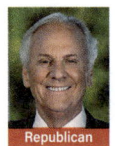

Governor Henry McMaster | **Next Election** 2026 | **3rd Term** | **58%** (+17)
1205 Pendleton Street, Columbia SC 29201
803-734-2100 | Fax: 803-734-5167 | governor.sc.gov | **X** henrymcmaster
Bio—Columbia; Columbia, SC, 5/27/1947; JD, Univ. of SC, 1973; USAR; lawyer; SC attorney general, 2003-11; SC lt. governor, 2015-17; SC governor, 2017-present ; m. Peggy; Presbyterian

Republican

SOUTH DAKOTA   www.sd.gov

Senators
John Thune (R)
Mike Rounds (R)

Representative (1 R)
AL - Dusty Johnson (R)

Pop. 909,824 | **Rank** 46th | **Trend** 2% | **Male %** 50.80% | **Female %** 49.20%
Caucasian 86.70% | **Black/AfrAm** 3.50% | **NatAm/AN** 10.40% | **Asian** 2.30% | **NH/PI** 0.20% |
Other 3.80% | **Hisp/Lat** 4.70%
Land Area 75,790 sq. mi. | **Water Area** 1,306 sq. mi. | **Area Rank** 16th

Registered Voters 597,842 | **Dem.** 24% | **Rep.** 50% | **Other** 25%

STATE LEGISLATURE | sdlegislature.gov
Senate Total 35 (31 R/4 D) | **House Total** 70 (63 R/7 D) | **2024 Session** Jan 9 to Mar 25

Governor Kristi Noem | **Next Election** 2026 | **2nd Term** | **62%** (+27)
500 East Capitol Avenue, Pierre SD 57501
605-773-3212 | Fax: 605-773-4711 | sd.gov/governor | **X** govkristinoem
Bio—Castlewood; Watertown, SD, 11/30/1971; BA, SD St. Univ., 2011; farmer, rancher; SD House, 2007-10; US House, 2011-19; SD governor, 2019-present; m. Bryon; Protestant

Republican

State Maps, Stats, and Governors

TENNESSEE

Senators
Marsha Blackburn (R)
Bill Hagerty (R)

www.tn.gov

Representatives (8 R/1 D)
1 - Diana Harshbarger (R)
2 - Tim Burchett (R)
3 - Chuck Fleischmann (R)
4 - Scott DesJarlais (R)
5 - Andy Ogles (R)
6 - John Rose (R)
7 - Mark Green (R)
8 - David Kustoff (R)
9 - Steve Cohen (D)

Pop. 7,051,339 | **Rank** 15th | **Trend** 2% | **Male %** 49.10% | **Female %** 50.90%
Caucasian 79.50% | **Black/AfrAm** 17.30% | **NatAm/AN** 1.80% | **Asian** 2.60% | **NH/PI** 0.20% | **Other** 5.80% | **Hisp/Lat** 6.30%
Land Area 41,227 sq. mi. | **Water Area** 906 sq. mi. | **Area Rank** 34th

Registered Voters 4,166,638 | *No party registration.*

GENERAL ASSEMBLY | www.legislature.state.tn.us
Senate Total 33 (27 R/6 D) | **House Total** 99 (75 R/24 D) | **2024 Session** Jan 9 to Apr 25

Governor Bill Lee | Next Election 2026 | 2nd Term | 65% (+32)
State Capitol, Nashville TN 37243
615-741-2001 | www.tn.gov/governor | X govbilllee
Bio—Franklin; Franklin, TN, 10/9/1959; BS, Auburn Univ., 1981; businessman; TN governor, 2019-present; m. Maria; Christian

Republican

TEXAS

www.texas.gov

Representatives (25 R/13 D)
1 - Nathaniel Moran (R)
2 - Dan Crenshaw (R)
3 - Keith Self (R)
4 - Pat Fallon (R)
5 - Lance Gooden (R)
6 - Jake Ellzey (R)
7 - Lizzie Fletcher (D)
8 - Morgan Luttrell (R)
9 - Al Green (D)
10 - Michael McCaul (R)
11 - August Pfluger (R)
12 - Kay Granger (R)
13 - Ronny Jackson (R)
14 - Randy Weber (R)
15 - Monica De La Cruz (R)
16 - Veronica Escobar (D)
17 - Pete Sessions (R)
18 - Sheila Jackson Lee (D)
19 - Jodey Arrington (R)
20 - Joaquin Castro (D)
21 - Chip Roy (R)
22 - Troy Nehls (R)
23 - Tony Gonzales (R)
24 - Beth Van Duyne (R)
25 - Roger Williams (R)
26 - Michael C. Burgess (R)
27 - Michael Cloud (R)
28 - Henry Cuellar (D)
29 - Sylvia Garcia (D)
30 - Jasmine Crockett (D)
31 - John Carter (R)
32 - Colin Allred (D)
33 - Marc Veasey (D)
34 - Vicente Gonzalez (D)
35 - Greg Casar (D)
36 - Brian Babin (R)
37 - Lloyd Doggett (D)
38 - Wesley Hunt (R)

Senators
John Cornyn (R)
Ted Cruz (R)

Pop. 30,029,572 | **Rank** 2nd | **Trend** 3% | **Male %** 50.00% | **Female %** 50.00%
Caucasian 70.60% | **Black/AfrAm** 13.90% | **NatAm/AN** 2.50% | **Asian** 6.50% | **NH/PI** 0.30% | **Other** 31.00% | **Hisp/Lat** 40.20%
Land Area 261,194 sq. mi. | **Water Area** 7,331 sq. mi. | **Area Rank** 2nd

Registered Voters 16,625,506 | *No party registration.*

STATE LEGISLATURE | capitol.texas.gov
Senate Total 31 (19 R/12 D) | **House Total** 150 (86 R/64 D) | No regular session in 2024

Governor Greg Abbott | Next Election 2026 | 3rd Term | 55% (+11)
P.O. Box 12428, Austin TX 78711
512-463-2000 | Fax: 512-463-5571 | gov.texas.gov | X govabbott
Bio—Houston; Wichita Falls, TX, 11/13/1957; JD, Vanderbilt Univ., 1984; lawyer, public official; TX supreme court, 1995-2001; TX attorney general, 2002-15; TX governor, 2015-present; m. Cecilia; Catholic

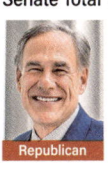

Republican

U.S. Congress Directory | 181

State Maps, Stats, and Governors

UTAH

www.utah.gov

Senators
Mike Lee (R)
Mitt Romney (R)

Representatives (4 R)
1 - Blake Moore (R)
2 - Celeste Maloy (R)
3 - John Curtis (R)
4 - Burgess Owens (R)

Pop. 3,380,800 | **Rank** 30th | **Trend** 3% | **Male %** 50.80% | **Female %** 49.20%
Caucasian 87.70% | **Black/AfrAm** 2.20% | **NatAm/AN** 2.40% | **Asian** 3.90% | **NH/PI** 1.70% | **Other** 11.80% | **Hisp/Lat** 15.10%
Land Area 82,355 sq. mi. | **Water Area** 2,521 sq. mi. | **Area Rank** 12th

Registered Voters 1,687,567 | **Dem.** 14% | **Rep.** 52% | **Other** 34%

STATE LEGISLATURE | le.utah.gov
Senate Total 29 (23 R/6 D) | **House Total** 75 (61 R/14 D) | **2024 Session** Jan 16 to Mar 1

Governor Spencer Cox | Next Election 2024 | 1st Term | 63% (+33)
State Capitol, Suite 200, Salt Lake City UT 84114
801-538-1000 | governor.utah.gov | X govcox
Bio—Fairview; Fairview, UT, 7/11/1975; JD, Washington & Lee Univ., 2001; lawyer; Sanpete Co. commission, 2008-12; UT House, 2013; UT lt. governor, 2013-21; UT governor, 2021-present; m. Abby; Mormon
Republican

VERMONT

www.vermont.gov

Senators
Bernie Sanders (I)
Peter Welch (D)

Representatives (1 D)
AL - Becca Balint (D)

Pop. 647,064 | **Rank** 49th | **Trend** 1% | **Male %** 49.60% | **Female %** 50.40%
Caucasian 96.20% | **Black/AfrAm** 2.10% | **NatAm/AN** 1.80% | **Asian** 2.60% | **NH/PI** 0.00% | **Other** 3.30% | **Hisp/Lat** 2.30%
Land Area 9,215 sq. mi. | **Water Area** 398 sq. mi. | **Area Rank** 43rd

Registered Voters 462,397 | *No party registration.*

GENERAL ASSEMBLY | legislature.vermont.gov
Senate Total 30 (23 D/7 R) | **House Total** 150 (104 D/37 R/5 Pro/3 Ind/1 Lib) | **2024 Session** Jan 3 to May 9

Governor Phil Scott | Next Election 2024 | 4th Term | 71% (+47)
109 State Street, Pavilion Office Building, Montpelier VT 05609
802-828-3333 | Fax: 802-828-3339 | governor.vermont.gov | X govphilscott
Bio—Berlin; Barre, VT, 8/4/1958; BS, Univ. of VT, 1980; businessman, public official; VT Senate, 2001-11; VT lt. governor, 2011-17; VT governor, 2017-present; m. Diana
Republican

NLPC | 182

State Maps, Stats, and Governors

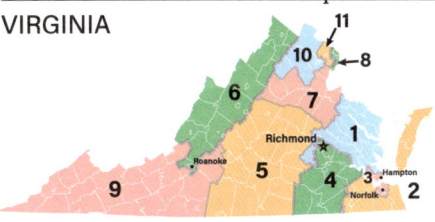

VIRGINIA

www.virginia.gov

Senators
Mark R. Warner (D)
Tim Kaine (D)

Representatives (6 D/5 R)
1 - Rob Wittman (R)
2 - Jen Kiggans (R)
3 - Bobby Scott (D)
4 - Jennifer McClellan (D)
5 - Bob Good (R)
6 - Ben Cline (R)
7 - Abigail Spanberger (D)
8 - Don Beyer (D)
9 - Morgan Griffith (R)
10 - Jennifer Wexton (D)
11 - Gerry Connolly (D)

Pop. 8,683,619 | **Rank** 12th | **Trend** 0% | **Male %** 49.50% | **Female %** 50.50%
Caucasian 68.60% | **Black/AfrAm** 21.30% | **NatAm/AN** 1.60% | **Asian** 8.70% | **NH/PI** 0.30% |
Other 9.60% | **Hisp/Lat** 10.40%
Land Area 39,472 sq. mi. | **Water Area** 3,292 sq. mi. | **Area Rank** 37th

Registered Voters 5,743,089 | *No party registration.*

GENERAL ASSEMBLY | virginiageneralassembly.gov
Senate Total 40 (21 D/19 R) | **House Total** 100 (51 D/49 R) | **2024 Session** Jan 10 to Mar 9

Governor Glenn Youngkin | Next Election 2025 | 1st Term | 51% (+2)
State Capitol, 3rd Floor, Richmond VA 23219
804-786-2211 | www.governor.virginia.gov | X governorva
Bio—Great Falls; Richmond, VA, 12/9/1966; MBA, Harvard Univ., 1994; financial executive;
VA governor, 2022-present; m. Suzanne ; Christian
Republican

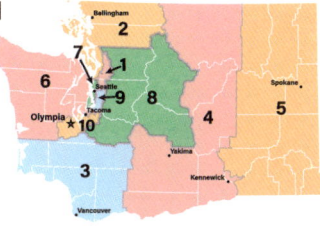

WASHINGTON

wa.gov

Senators
Patty Murray (D)
Maria Cantwell (D)

Representatives (8 D/2 R)
1 - Suzan DelBene (D)
2 - Rick Larsen (D)
3 - Marie Gluesenkamp Perez (D)
4 - Dan Newhouse (R)
5 - Cathy McMorris Rodgers (R)
6 - Derek Kilmer (D)
7 - Pramila Jayapal (D)
8 - Kim Schrier (D)
9 - Adam Smith (D)
10 - Marilyn Strickland (D)

Pop. 7,785,786 | **Rank** 13th | **Trend** 1% | **Male %** 50.50% | **Female %** 49.50%
Caucasian 77.70% | **Black/AfrAm** 6.10% | **NatAm/AN** 3.50% | **Asian** 12.70% | **NH/PI** 1.40% |
Other 12.40% | **Hisp/Lat** 14.00%
Land Area 66,438 sq. mi. | **Water Area** 4,844 sq. mi. | **Area Rank** 20th

Registered Voters 4,970,937 | *No party registration.*

STATE LEGISLATURE | leg.wa.gov
Senate Total 49 (29 D/20 R) | **House Total** 98 (58 D/40 R) | **2024 Session** Jan 8 to Mar 7

Governor Jay Inslee | Next Election 2024 | 3rd Term | 57% (+13)
P.O. Box 40002, Olympia WA 98504
360-902-4111 | Fax: 360-753-4110 | governor.wa.gov | X govinslee
Bio—Bainbridge Island; Seattle, WA, 2/9/1951; JD, Willamette Univ., 1976; lawyer; WA House,
1988-92; US House, 1999-2012; WA governor, 2013-present; m. Trudi
Democrat

State Maps, Stats, and Governors

WEST VIRGINIA

www.wv.gov

Senators
Joe Manchin (D)
Shelley Moore Capito (R)

Representatives (2 R)
1 - Carol Miller (R)
2 - Alex X. Mooney (R)

Pop. 1,775,156 | **Rank** 39th | **Trend** -1% | **Male %** 49.70% | **Female %** 50.30%
Caucasian 94.90% | **Black/AfrAm** 4.70% | **NatAm/AN** 1.50% | **Asian** 1.30% | **NH/PI** 0.00% | **Other** 2.50% | **Hisp/Lat** 1.90%
Land Area 24,035 sq. mi. | **Water Area** 189 sq. mi. | **Area Rank** 41st

Registered Voters 1,174,769 | **Dem.** 31% | **Rep.** 40% | **Other** 29%

STATE LEGISLATURE | www.wvlegislature.gov
Senate Total 34 (31 R/3 D) | **House Total** 100 (89 R/11 D) | **2024 Session** Jan 10 to Mar 9

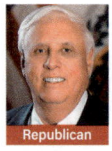

Governor Jim Justice | Next Election 2024 | 2nd Term | 65% (+34)
1900 Kanawha St., Charleston WV 25305
304-558-2000 | Fax: 304-342-7025 | governor.wv.gov | X wvgovernor
Bio—Lewisburg; Charleston, WV, 4/27/1951; MBA, Marshall Univ.; farmer, coal executive, businessman; WV governor, 2017-present; m. Cathy; Baptist

Republican

WISCONSIN

www.wisconsin.gov

Senators
Ron Johnson (R)
Tammy Baldwin (D)

Representatives (6 R/2 D)
1 - Bryan Steil (R)
2 - Mark Pocan (D)
3 - Derrick Van Orden (R)
4 - Gwen Moore (D)
5 - Scott Fitzgerald (R)
6 - Glenn Grothman (R)
7 - Tom Tiffany (R)
8 - Mike Gallagher (R)

Pop. 5,892,539 | **Rank** 20th | **Trend** 0% | **Male %** 50.20% | **Female %** 49.80%
Caucasian 88.00% | **Black/AfrAm** 7.60% | **NatAm/AN** 2.00% | **Asian** 3.70% | **NH/PI** 0.10% | **Other** 6.90% | **Hisp/Lat** 7.60%
Land Area 54,153 sq. mi. | **Water Area** 11,327 sq. mi. | **Area Rank** 25th

Registered Voters 4,772,962 | *No party registration.*

STATE LEGISLATURE | legis.wisconsin.gov
Senate Total 33 (22 R/11 D) | **House Total** 99 (64 R/35 D) | **2024 Session** Jan 16

Governor Tony Evers | Next Election 2026 | 2nd Term | 51% (+3)
115 East State Capitol, Madison WI 53707
608-266-1212 | evers.wi.gov | X govevers
Bio—Plymouth, WI, 11/5/1951; PhD, Univ. of WI, 1986; educator, public official; WI superintendent of public instruction, 2009-19; WI governor, 2019-present; m. Kathy

Democrat

NLPC | 184

State Maps, Stats, and Governors

WYOMING

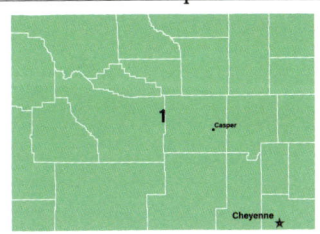

Senators
John Barrasso (R)
Cynthia Lummis (R)

Representative (1 R)
AL - Harriet Hageman (R)

www.wyo.gov

Pop. 581,381 | **Rank** 50th | **Trend** 1% | **Male %** 51.20% | **Female %** 48.80%
Caucasian 92.60% | **Black/AfrAm** 1.40% | **NatAm/AN** 4.10% | **Asian** 1.50% | **NH/PI** 0.50% | **Other** 8.80% | **Hisp/Lat** 10.80%
Land Area 97,063 sq. mi. | **Water Area** 721 sq. mi. | **Area Rank** 9th

Registered Voters 217,353 | **Dem.** 11% | **Rep.** 82% | **Other** 8%

STATE LEGISLATURE | www.wyoleg.gov
Senate Total 31 (29 R/2 D) | **House Total** 62 (57 R/5 D) | **2024 Session** Feb 12 to Mar 8

Governor Mark Gordon | Next Election 2026 | 2nd Term | 79% (+62)
State Capitol Building, Room 124, Cheyenne WY 82002
307-777-7434 | governor.wyo.gov | X governorgordon
Bio—Buffalo; New York, NY, 3/14/1957; BA, Middlebury Col., 1979; rancher; WY treasurer, 2012-19; WY governor, 2019-present; m. Jennie

Republican

AMERICAN SAMOA

www.americansamoa.gov

Delegate
Aumua Amata Coleman Radewagen (R)

Pop. 49,710 | **Male %** 50.80% | **Female %** 49.20%
Asian 7.80% | **NH/PI** 93.00% | **Other** 3.90% | **Hisp/Lat** 0.80%

Registered Voters 12,780 | *No party registration.*

LEGISLATURE | www.americansamoa.gov/fono
Senate Total 18 (non-partisan) | **2024 Session** TBD

Governor Lemanu P.S. Mauga | Next Election 2024 | 1st Term | 60% (+38)
Executive Office Building, Third Floor, Pago Pago AS 96799
684-633-4116 | www.americansamoa.gov
Bio—Nu'uuli, AS, 1/3/1960; MPA, San Diego St. Univ.; USMC; USA; career military, public official; AS Senate; AS lt. governor, 2013-21; AS governor, 2021-present; m. Ella; Congregational

Democrat

State Maps, Stats, and Governors

DISTRICT OF COLUMBIA

Delegate
Eleanor Holmes Norton (D)

dc.gov

Pop. 671,803 | **Male %** 47.60% | **Female %** 52.40%
Caucasian 47.20% | Black/AfrAm 46.00% | NatAm/AN 1.70% |
Asian 5.90% | NH/PI 0.30% |
Other 10.50% | Hisp/Lat 11.70%
Land Area 61 sq. mi. | Water Area 7 sq. mi. | **Area Rank** 51st

Registered Voters 545,762 | **Dem.** 76% | **Rep.** 5% | **Other** 19%

CITY COUNCIL | dccouncil.gov
Senate Total 13 (11 D/0 R/2 Ind) | **2024 Session** Jan 2

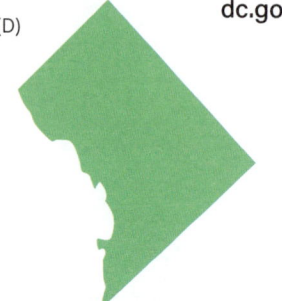

Mayor Muriel Bowser | Next Election 2026 | 3rd Term | 75% (+60)
John A. Wilson Building, 1350 Pennsylvania Avenue, NW, Washington DC 20004
202-727-2643 | mayor.dc.gov | **X** mayorbowser
Bio—Washington, DC; Washington, DC, 8/2/1972; MPA, American Univ.; public official; DC city council, 2007-15; DC mayor, 2015-present; single

Democrat

GUAM

www.guam.gov

Pop. 153,836 | **Male %** 50.90% | **Female %** 49.10%
Asian 43.00% | NH/PI 54.20% | Other 13.00% | Hisp/Lat 2.90%

Registered Voters 54,250 | *No party registration.*

LEGISLATURE | guamlegislature.com/index
Senate Total 15 (9 D/6 R) | **2024 Session** Jan 8

★Hagatna

Delegate
James Moylan (R)

Governor Lou Leon Guerrero | Next Election 2026 | 2nd Term | 55% (+11)
Ricardo J Bordallo Governor's Complex, 513 West Marine Corps Drive, Hagatna Guam 96910
671-472-8931 | Fax: 671-477-4826 | governor.guam.gov | **X** louleonguerrero
Bio—Guam, 11/8/1950; MPH Univ. of CA, Los Angeles, 1979; nurse, businesswoman; GU legislature, 1995-99, 2001-07; GU governor, 2019-present; m. Jeff Cook

Democrat

State Maps, Stats, and Governors

NORTHERN MARIANA ISLANDS

governor.gov.mp

Delegate
Gregorio Kilili Camacho Sablan (D)

Pop. 47,329 | **Male %** 52.60% | **Female %** 47.40%
Asian 52.80% | **NH/PI** 50.30% | **Other** 4.30% | **Hisp/Lat** 1.20%

Registered Voters 17,728 | *No party registration.*

LEGISLATURE | www.cnmileg.gov.mp
Senate Total 9 (2 D/4 R/3 Ind) | **House Total** 20 (4 D/3 R/13 Ind) | **2024 Session** TBD

Governor Arnold Placios | Next Election 2026 | 1st Term | 54% (+8)
Caller Box 10007, Saipan MP 96950
670-237-2200 | governor.gov.mp
Bio—Saipan, MP, 8/22/1955; BA, Portland St. Univ.; MP House; MP Senate, 2015-19; MP lt. governor, 2019-23; MP governor, 2023-present; m. Wella

Independent

PUERTO RICO

www.pr.gov

Resident Commissioner
Jenniffer González-Colón (R)

Pop. 3,221,789 | **Male %** 47.50% | **Female %** 52.50%
Caucasian 60.70% | **Black/AfrAm** 13.10% | **NatAm/AN** 2.20% | **Asian** 0.30% | **NH/PI** 0.00% |
Other 66.50% | **Hisp/Lat** 99.00%
Land Area 3,423 sq. mi. | **Water Area** 1,900 sq. mi.

Registered Voters 2,355,894 | *No party registration.*

LEGISLATURE | www.oslpr.org
Senate Total 27 (12 DPP/10 NPP/1 PR Ind/1 Ind/1 PD/2 MVC) |
House Total 51 (26 DPP/21 NPP/2 MVC/1 PIP/1 PD) | **2024 Session** Jan 9

Governor Pedro Pierluisi | Next Election 2024 | 1st Term | 33% (+1)
La Fortaleza, P.O. Box 9020082, San Juan PR 00902
787-721-2400 | www.fortaleza.pr.gov | X govpierluisi
Bio—San Juan, PR, 4/26/1959; JD, George Washington Univ., 1984; lawyer; US House, 2009-17; PR governor, 2021-present; div.; Catholic

Democrat

VIRGIN ISLANDS

WWW.VI.GOV

Delegate
Stacey E. Plaskett (D)

Pop. 87,146 | **Male %** 48.60% | **Female %** 51.40%
Caucasian 15.10% | **Black/AfrAm** 77.80% | **Other** 14.60% | **Hisp/Lat** 18.40%

Registered Voters 29,553 | **Dem.** 68% | **Rep.** 3% | **Other** 29%

LEGISLATURE | www.legvi.org
Senate Total 15 (11 D/4 Ind) | **2024 Session** Jan 9

Governor Albert Bryan | Next Election 2026 | 2nd Term | 56% (+18)
Government House, 21-22 Kongens Gad, Charlotte Amalie, St. Thomas VI 00802
340-774-0001 | Fax: 340-693-4374 | www.vi.gov | X govhouseusvi
Bio—St. Thomas, VI, 2/21/1968; MBA, Univ. of the Virgin Islands, 2003; entrepreneur, non-profit executive; VI labor commissioner; VI governor, 2019-present; sep.

Governor Re-election Years

UP FOR RE-ELECTION IN 2024

Democrat
Lemanu P.S. Mauga (AS) | John Carney (DE)* | Roy Cooper (NC)* | Pedro Pierluisi (PR) | Jay Inslee (WA)*

Republican
Eric Holcomb (IN)* | Mike Parson (MO)* | Greg Gianforte (MT) | Chris Sununu (NH)*# | Doug Burgum (ND)* | Spencer Cox (UT) | Phil Scott (VT)# | Jim Justice (WV)*

UP FOR RE-ELECTION IN 2025

Democrat
Phil Murphy (NJ)*

Republican
Glenn Youngkin (VA)*

UP FOR RE-ELECTION IN 2026

Democrat
Katie Hobbs (AZ) | Gavin Newsom (CA)* | Jared Polis (CO)* | Ned Lamont (CT) | Muriel Bowser (DC)^ | Lou Leon Guerrero (Guam)* | Josh Green (HI) | JB Pritzker (IL) | Laura Kelly (KS)* | Janet Mills (ME)* | Wes Moore (MD) | Maura Healey (MA) | Gretchen Whitmer (MI)* | Tim Walz (MN) | Michelle Lujan Grisham (NM)* | Kathy Hochul (NY) | Tina Kotek (OR) | Josh Shapiro (PA) | Dan McKee (RI) | Albert Bryan (VI)* | Tony Evers (WI)

Independent
Arnold Placios (MP)

Republican
Kay Ivey (AL)* | Mike Dunleavy (AK)* | Sarah Huckabee Sanders (AR) | Ron DeSantis (FL)* | Brian Kemp (GA)* | Brad Little (ID) | Kim Reynolds (IA) | Jim Pillen (NE) | Joe Lombardo (NV) | Mike DeWine (OH)* | Kevin Stitt (OK)* | Henry McMaster (SC)* | Kristi Noem (SD)* | Bill Lee (TN)* | Greg Abbott (TX) | Mark Gordon (WY)*

UP FOR RE-ELECTION IN 2027

Democrat
Andy Beshear (KY)*

Republican
Jeff Landry (LA) | Tate Reeves (MS)*

= 2-year term
* = term limited/not running
^ = mayoral election

Engaging with Congress

ADDRESSING CORRESPONDENCE

If you choose to send a letter, the accepted form of address is as follows:

To a Senator
The Honorable John H. Doe
United States Senate
Washington, DC 20510

Salutation
Dear Senator Doe:

Close
Sincerely,

To a Representative
The Honorable Jane H. Doe
House of Representatives
Washington, DC 20515

Salutation
Dear Mrs. (or Miss, Ms., Mr.) Doe:

Close
Sincerely,

If you are writing to a committee chairperson in that capacity:

To a Senate Chair
The Honorable John H. Doe
Chairman/woman, Committee on (name)
United States Senate
Washington, DC 20510

To a House Chair
The Honorable Jane H. Doe
Chairman/woman, Committee on (name)
House of Representatives
Washington, DC 20515

Dear Mr. Chairman, or Dear Madam Chairwoman

If you are writing to the Speaker of the House:

The Honorable Jane H. Doe
Speaker of the House of Representatives
Washington, DC 20515

Dear Mr./Madame Speaker:

Note: The Majority and Minority leaders in both chambers are addressed in the same manner as a Senator or Representative.

Engaging with Congress

IN CONVERSATION

When meeting with a Senator in person, refer to him or her as:
Senator Doe, or Senator

When meeting with a Representative in person, refer to him or her as:
Mr. Doe, Mrs. Doe, or Miss Doe

TIPS FOR YOUR E-MAIL OR LETTER

Whichever method you choose, some good rules of thumb are:

- Be succinct. A large Senate office can receive up to 25,000 emails a week.
- State your purpose in the opening sentence. If you are writing about a specific piece of legislation, refer to the bill by the bill number.
- Personalize, personalize, personalize. Messages with a personal touch are more likely to receive a response than a form letter. You can do this any number of ways, such as stating who you are, including your credentials, explaining how the issue affects you personally, or why the issue interests you. Just remember #1 and be brief.
- If you have a specific "ask" or require a response, make sure that is clearly communicated.
- Stick to one issue per message.
- Include your contact information in your letter or e-mail. True, you are already entering your address if you send a message through the website, but anything that helps an office quickly identify the sender is helpful.

Notes